BARCODE ON
NEXT PAGE

**W9-BTP-070**

# THE MERTON ANNUAL

Studies in Culture, Spirituality, and Social Concerns

| Volume 29 | 2016 |
|---|---|

Editcd by

## Deborah Pope Kehoe    Joseph Quinn Raab

*Merton*
*271.2*
*M575m*
*V.29*

WITHDRAWN

Kenrick Glennon
Seminary Library

Charles L. Souvay Memorial

## THE MERTON ANNUAL
### Studies in Culture, Spirituality, and Social Concerns

*THE MERTON ANNUAL* publishes articles about Thomas Merton and about related matters of major concern to his life and work. Its purpose is to enhance Merton's reputation as a writer and monk, to continue to develop his message for our times, and to provide a regular outlet for substantial Merton-related scholarship. *THE MERTON ANNUAL* includes as regular features reviews, review-essays, a bibliographic survey, interviews, and first appearances of unpublished or obscurely published Merton materials, photographs, and art. Essays about related literary and spiritual matters will also be considered. Manuscripts and books for review may be sent to the editors.

### EDITORS

Deborah Pope Kehoe
Division of Humanities and Languages
Northeast Mississippi Community College
Booneville, MS 38829
mertonannual@gmail.com

Joseph Quinn Raab
Religious Studies Department
Siena Heights University
Adrian, MI 49221
mertonannual@gmail.com

### EDITORIAL COMMITTEE

William Apel (McMinnville, OR), Victor Kramer (Decatur, GA), Roger Lipsey (Garrison, NY), Gray Matthews (Memphis, TN), Patrick F. O'Connell (Copy Editor) (Erie, PA), Paul M. Pearson (Louisville, KY), Malgorzata Poks (Koszecin, Poland), Lynn Szabo (Vancouver, BC), Bonnie B. Thurston (Wheeling, WV), Monica Weis (Rochester, NY).

Grateful acknowledgement is expressed to The Merton Legacy Trust and the Thomas Merton Center at Bellarmine University for permission to reproduce the calligraphy by Thomas Merton for the cover artwork. Letters: "To Sister Prisca, O.S.B." (February 10, 1964); "To Mother Benedict Duss, O.S.B." (March 26, 1964); "To Sister Miriam Benedict, O.S.B." (September 16, 1967) from *The School of Charity: The Letters of Thomas Merton on Religious Renewal and Spiritual Direction*, edited by Brother Patrick Hart, Copyright © 1990 by the Merton Legacy Trust: reprinted by permission of Farrar, Straus and Giroux. "A Letter to My Friends" by Thomas Merton, from THE COLLECTED POEMS OF THOMAS MERTON, copyright ©1946 by New Directions Publishing Corporation, 1977 by The Trustees of the Merton Legacy Trust: reprinted by permission of New Directions Publishing Corp; "Advent" by Thomas Merton, from THE COLLECTED POEMS OF THOMAS MERTON, copyright ©1946 by New Directions Publishing Corporation: reprinted by permission of New Directions Publishing Corp.; "Carol" by Thomas Merton, from THE COLLECTED POEMS OF THOMAS MERTON, copyright ©1946, 1947 by New Directions Publishing Corp.: reprinted by permission of New Directions Publishing Corp.; "Trappists Working" by Thomas Merton, from THE COLLECTED POEMS OF THOMAS MERTON, copyright ©1946 by New Directions Publishing Corporation: reprinted by permission of New Directions Publishing Corp.; "Candlemas Procession" by Thomas Merton, from THE COLLECTED POEMS OF THOMAS MERTON, copyright ©1948 by New Directions Publishing Corporation, 1977 by The Trustees of the Merton Legacy Trust: reprinted by permission of New Directions Publishing Corp.

PUBLISHED BY:
Fons Vitae
49 Mockingbird Valley Drive
Louisville, KY 40207
502.897.3641
Fonsvitaeky@aol.com
http://www.fonsvitae.com

SPONSORED BY:
International Thomas Merton Society
Thomas Merton Center
Bellarmine University
2001 Newburg Road
Louisville, KY 40205
502.272.8187 or 8177
merton@bellarmine.edu
http://www.merton.org/ITMS/

Further details about membership and subscribing to *The Merton Seasonal* and *The Merton Annual* are available at http://www.merton.org/ITMS/membership.aspx or by contacting the Thomas Merton Center at the above address.

For members of the International Thomas Merton Society, available for $15.00, plus shipping and handling. Individual copies are available through bookstores and directly from the publisher for $19.95. Institutions $39.95. *Copyright:* All rights reserved.

ISBN 978-1891785-955    ISSN 0894-4857

Printed in Canada

# The Merton Annual

| Volume 29 | 2016 |
|---|---|

## Reviews

# Introduction: Thin Places and Thick Descriptions

*Joseph Quinn Raab*

Hawk. First the shadow flying downward along the wall of sunlit foliage. Then the bird itself, trim, compact substance, in the sky overhead, quite distinct from woods and trees, flying in freedom. Barred tail, speckled wings, with sunlight shining through them. He cut a half circle in emptiness over the elm. Then he seemed to put his hands in his pockets and sped, without a wing beat, like a bullet, to plunge into the grove across the open field.

Thomas Merton[1]

Where there is a lot of fuss about "spirituality," "enlightenment" or just "turning on" it is often because there are buzzards hovering around a corpse. . . . Zen enriches no one. There is no body to be found. The birds may come and circle for a while in the place where it is thought to be. But they soon go elsewhere. When they are gone, the "nothing," the "no-body" that was there, suddenly appears. . . . It was there all the time but the scavengers missed it, because it was not their kind of prey.

Thomas Merton[2]

## Introduction

A few years ago, Eric Weiner published a travel piece in *The New York Times* about "thin places" – where the usually thick distance between heaven and earth, the particular and the universal, thins out or even dissolves.[3] He was using an old Celtic concept of thin places to write about potential pilgrimage destinations – some expected, like St. Peter's Basilica and the Blue Mosque, but others not so, like an obscure bar in Tokyo and a trendy bookstore in Portland. He ended with an answer to his own provocative question:

> If God is everywhere and "everywhen," as the Australian aboriginals put it so wonderfully, then why are some places thin and others not?

---

1. Thomas Merton, *Conjectures of a Guilty Bystander* (Garden City, NY: Doubleday, 1966) 224.

2. Thomas Merton, *Zen and the Birds of Appetite* (New York: New Directions, 1968) ix.

3. Eric Weiner, "Thin Places, Where We Are Jolted Out of Old Ways of Seeing the World," *The New York Times* (11 March 2012); available online at: http://www.nytimes.com/2012/03/11/travel/thin-places-where-we-are-jolted-out-of-old-ways-of-seeing-the-world.html.

Why isn't the whole world thin? Maybe it is, but we are too thick to recognize it. Maybe thin places offer glimpses not of heaven but of earth as it really is, unencumbered. Unmasked.

Thomas Merton mindfully inhabited an exceptionally thin world. He seemed especially attuned to the omnipresence of the normally imperceptible. However common this aesthetic sensibility may in fact be in the general population, the gift for communicating it is rare. Merton unquestionably had that gift. He wrote with what Flannery O'Connor would likely describe as the "Hebrew genius for making the absolute concrete."⁴ His thick descriptions of particular places and moments narrow the distance between heaven and earth, or perhaps simply unmask a once hidden but always present wholeness.

Clifford Geertz, an iconic American intellectual, popularized the term "thick description" in reference to an anthropologist's aim. Geertz described the science of anthropology not as an experimental one in search of a law, but as an interpretive one in search of meaning.⁵ He argued that thick descriptions, rich in meaning, do not come from the disconnected, aloof and disinterested observer. They require participation and getting dirty. One who is attentively embedded and involved in a context can mediate a meaningful interpretation, or render the thick description. In a similar way, Merton had seen his own task as a contemplative in search of meaning not merely as an experiential one, but also as an interpretive one. Through his interpretations of his own experiences, he enabled many of his readers to "co-experience God," as Dermot Lane says, "not so much as something seen in the world but as the basis of all seeing . . . not as a being before us but as the source of all beings, not as a particular meaning but as the ultimate context in which all meanings subsist."⁶ In this way, "thick descriptions" of the spiritual awakenings that can be occasioned by attentiveness to the most common things serve to penetrate our ordinarily thick skulls and unmask for us what Merton calls "the hidden ground of Love." ⁷

---

4. Flannery O'Connor, *Mystery and Manners: Occasional Prose*, ed. Sally and Robert Fitzgerald (New York: Farrar, Straus & Giroux, 1969) 202.

5. Clifford Geertz, "Thick Description: Toward an Interpretive Theory of Culture" in Clifford Geertz, *The Interpretation of Cultures: Selected Essays* (New York: Basic Books, 1973) 3-30.

6. Dermot A. Lane, *The Experience of God: An Invitation to Do Theology* (Mahwah, NJ: Paulist Press, 1981) 19.

7. Thomas Merton, *The Hidden Ground of Love: Letters on Religious Experience and Social Concerns*, ed. William H. Shannon (New York: Farrar, Straus, Giroux, 1985) 115.

## Volume 29

Thanks to the intentional vision of David Belcastro,[8] many of the featured essays that comprise volume 29 of *The Merton Annual* are intensely concerned with physical places and spaces, domestic and wild. For example, **Paul M. Pearson**'s "From Clairvaux to Mount Olivet: Thomas Merton's Geography of Place" reveals how Merton's understanding of the relationship between physical landscapes and personal identities, which he inherited from his parents, stayed with him and deepened over the years. Even though Merton briefly but mistakenly thought of his arrival at the monastery as a kind of end to his geographical journey, Pearson shows how Merton reawakened to the importance of such when he was writing *The Sign of Jonas* and how geography and place continued from then on to shape his self-understanding.

The piece that follows Pearson's, "'This Terrific Sense of Geography': Spatial Thinking in Merton's Journals" by **Kathleen M. Baker**, provides a second example. Baker, herself a poet and professor of geography, draws on some recent research in cognitive science and renders a concise and thought-provoking exploration of how Merton thought in spatial modes and how that kind of thinking contributed to his tremendous capacity for insight and his remarkable memory evinced in his journal writings.

Following Baker, **Jason M. Brown** continues the geographical theme in his piece "Thomas Merton, Wildness and the Sacramental Power of Place." By relying on Merton, but also on the work of Monica Weis, John Muir and William Cronon, Brown encourages a shift away from our current paradigm that bifurcates the world into "wild places" and domesticated ones – the former cordoned off while the latter get developed and exploited – toward a more sustainable and integrated view that does not oppose culture to nature. Brown finds in Merton's writings a model for how we might be able to appreciate not only the sacramental power of wild places but also "the wildness in the places we call home."

One of the more significant places in Merton's life, and one he nearly made a home, is a northern neighborhood of Manhattan known for its music and literature and its degrading poverty. Merton first loved Har-

8. David Belcastro retired from his post as co-editor of *The Merton Annual* after the publication of volume 28 but he played a significant role in setting the articles for volume 29. I am grateful to David for his many years of service to this publication and for his mentoring of me. I look forward to working with Deborah Kehoe, the newly appointed co-editor of *The Merton Annual*, on future volumes. As always, I am grateful to Patrick F. O'Connell and to Paul M. Pearson for their invaluable help in preparing this publication.

lem for its romantic allure, but then for all its wounds and ugliness. In "The Persistence of Harlem in the Life and Legacy of Thomas Merton," **Michael N. McGregor** shows how impactful "a handful of nights" in Harlem would be for a rich white kid in shaping his sense of the gospel call to the works of mercy and voluntary poverty. Regarding Merton's volunteer work in Harlem, and with his own gift for "thick description," McGregor writes that "it wasn't until Merton touched those dresses, felt the dirt from those shoes, and saw the people his sorting efforts were helping, that he understood at a deeper level – the level of empathy and compassion – what actual poverty and degradation were like; the unsentimental conditions of daily life in Harlem."

Harlem had its attractions for the young Merton, but so did Gethsemani. He was torn a bit between his call to cloistered living, where vowed poverty would mean little more than that his preference for Christ would not be challenged by the presence of too much wine and too many flesh-and-blood women, and his desire to live the gospel in the messiness of actual poverty, where hungry and needy people might draw more on his *caritas* but also on his *cupiditas*. Gethsemani of course won the struggle and turned out to be Merton's most enduring earthly home. The next piece in this volume focuses on Merton's arrival and his most immediate response to the place itself through the lens of some early poems. In "Trappists, Working – Trappists, Praying: The Earliest Monastic Poetry of Thomas Merton," **Patrick F. O'Connell** explores poems that give some sense of "the disjunctions and continuities between the life within and beyond the monastery walls, between the world he had left behind and the world he had chosen, or for which he had been mysteriously chosen."

Keeping with a focus on poetry, we move from Merton's early compositions dating from the time of his entrance into the monastery, to his own later interest in the poetry of early Irish hermits. **Monica Weis, SSJ** recently released a book exploring Thomas Merton's interest in Celtic spirituality more broadly, in which she also touches on the concept of "thin places."[9] Her article here, entitled "Was Thomas Merton Merely Dabbling in Early Irish Poetry?" is a condensed and significantly reworked chapter from that new book.[10] Through an examination of a mimeographed anthology of Merton's favorite early Irish poetry, Weis explores various dimensions of the Celtic world view, including the view that "kinship with

---

9. Monica Weis, *Thomas Merton and the Celts: A New World Opening Up* (Eugene, OR: Pickwick, 2016) 70-71.

10. This is a reworking of chapter five, "Contemporary Welsh Poetry and Early Irish Hermit Poetry" (83-107).

nature is an act of praise." Her work reveals the vivid parallels between Merton's mysticism and that of the early Irish hermit poets. She finds in the Irish poetry, and in Merton's own, an attentiveness to and validation of nature as such, as unmasked.

Perhaps nowhere is Merton's attentiveness to the holiness of ordinary things more pronounced than in his essay *Day of a Stranger*, which is the focus of the next article. **Michael Plekon**'s "'What I Wear Is Pants. What I Do Is Live. How I Pray Is Breathe' – Merton and the Spiritual Life in the Twenty-First Century" is an insightful exploration of Merton's "daily liturgy of living" with all of his mundane chores – like scrubbing the coffee pot and spraying for insects – that somehow rise to the level of religious ritual simply by his living mindfully. Through the prism of the thickly descriptive *Day of a Stranger* Plekon focuses on the hermitage as a place so thin that the category of "spiritual life" as a separate kind of thing becomes almost silly. Since Merton was mindful of the holy even as race riots raged and metallic birds with explosive eggs flew overhead, Plekon shows him to be a fit exemplar for seekers in our present century which is turning out to be no less fraught.

The article that follows Plekon's is connected to those explosive eggs that hid in the breasts of those giant metallic birds. In his essay "Public Intellectual, Democratic Dissenter: Thomas Merton on Nuclear Weapons," **Donald Grayston** considers important dimensions of Merton's social critique. In his piece, Grayston partially reconstructs the context of American Catholicism in the nineteen sixties, when the election of John F. Kennedy spawned a kind of flowering of Catholic culture in America, but not a monolithic one. Grayston describes Merton's position in that emerging landscape as one of a prophetic intellectual disturbing the general public and nationalistic Catholics, be they ecclesiastical authorities or run-of-the-mill parishioners. Grayston's recalling of Merton's social analysis is eerily timely given the precarious nature of the Iran nuclear deal and the president-elect's belief that nuclear proliferation is both inevitable and good.[11]

Grayston's article is followed by one that recalls some familiarly thin places in Merton's life as well as some of those in the life of his friend and correspondent Henry Miller. In his piece "Thomas Merton and Henry Miller: A Correspondence in Vision," **Angus F. Stuart** describes

---

11. See Gene Gerzhoy and Nick Miller, "Donald Trump thinks more countries should have nuclear weapons. Here's what the research says," *The Washington Post* (6 April 2016); available online at: https://www.washingtonpost.com/news/monkey-cage/wp/2016/04/06/should-more-countries-have-nuclear-weapons-donald-trump-thinks-so/?utm_term=.23ccf25a9cc6.

the similarities between these two literary giants of the twentieth century from their physical reciprocal resemblance to their spiritual awakenings. Stuart's piece provides glimpses into Merton's epiphany on the streets of Louisville as it compares with Miller's awakening through the streets of Maroussi in Greece. The corner of Fourth and Walnut helped reveal to Merton the illusory nature of his "supposed holiness" while Greece opened Miller's eyes to his own pride and arrogance – the pride of "a city man" living a "false and restricted life." Whether he is describing Merton resembling an ex-con hiding in the woods of Kentucky, or Miller as a secular monk tucked into the coastal mountains of Big Sur, California, Stuart cleverly conveys numerous points of convergence between these friends whose lives on the surface can appear worlds apart.

Reconciling what is apparently disparate is a theme that carries into the next piece by **Anthony E. Clark**. "Finding Our Way: Thomas Merton, John Wu and the Christian Dialogue with Early China" is a fascinating exploration of Merton's and Wu's shared interest in Daoism and Zen Buddhism. In this article Clark skillfully elucidates how both Merton and Wu delighted in the profound consonance each discovered in the voices of the Christian desert fathers and mothers and those of the early Daoist masters. That consonance – the voice of Wisdom – called Merton and Wu out of the dusty haze of worldly snares into the clarity and freedom of solitude and peace.

However, the wisdom in those voices is not merely preserved on printed pages or in digital files but lives in contemplative communities and speaks through wise teachers. **Padraic O'Hare**'s article "Young Adult Spiritual Lives: Merton, Moran and Monastic Resources" explores the importance of "contemplation education" which is a kind of pedagogy that goes well beyond the dissemination of information and imparts or engenders genuine meaning and purpose. O'Hare elucidates a contemplative vision of education by drawing on teachers such as Raimundo Panikkar, Gabriel Moran, Michael Casey, Joan Chittister, Rowan Williams and Thomas Merton and examines the effect of such an education on a group of young adults who experience it through participation in a particular Benedictine community.

*The Merton Annual* normally includes interviews and previously unpublished original material from Thomas Merton, as well as a bibliographic review essay, and volume 29 is no exception. The articles discussed above are preceded in this volume by a couple of introductory pieces and concluded with a bibliographic review of 2015. The first piece that appears in the present volume then is "'A Quite Exceptional Convent': The Regina Laudis Correspondence," introduced and edited by **Patrick**

**F. O'Connell**. With the permission of the abbess and the surviving nuns of Regina Laudis Abbey who had exchanged letters with Thomas Merton, all the extant correspondence between Merton and the Regina Laudis sisters is now made available, testifying to the mutual regard of Merton and members of this community, and to a love for the Shakers which he shared with these remarkable Benedictine nuns. The following piece is an interview with hermit and ecologist **Charles Brandt** entitled "A Single Sacred Community," which was co-conducted by **Donald Grayston** and **David Chang**. Brandt named his hermitage, located in Black Creek on Vancouver Island in British Columbia, "Merton House"; it is a place the Celts would surely consider exceptionally thin. This fascinating three-way conversation reveals some kindred spirits whose experiences and interests intersect in a variety of ways.

The final piece that follows the scholarly articles and introduces the review section of this volume is **Joseph Raab**'s "Relevance and Ambivalence: A Bibliographic Review of Thomas Merton's Centenary (2015)." This survey highlights a wide variety of publications that appeared in the centenary of Merton's birth in the world of Merton studies and in the increasing number of fields that are finding him relevant in the twenty-first century. Merton's status as a classic, it is suggested, is secure, but that only means that he will continue to delight and disturb, prompting an ambivalent response – one of gratitude for Merton as a spiritual guide, yet one of frustration that the ills and injustices that evoke Merton's prophetic voice stubbornly persist.

## Conclusion

Merton can be described as a master of thick description and one adept at recognizing thin places; but what about the rest of us for whom, of late, places have seemed thick and descriptions very thin? In Merton's rural Kentucky the barren farmlands have become fields of slogans. Scraped earth has sprouted a bumper crop of bold Trump banners, petitioning to "Make America Great Again" and to "Lock Her Up!" It's a new kind of angry monoculture with the occasional rare exception of a "Stronger Together" sign standing out like a defiant weed. Political doublespeak, tawdry tweets and conspiracy theories hardly veil our basest fears and desires. The thinnest descriptions of life's meaning and the crudest assessments of its purpose and value populate the Instagram, Twitter and Facebook feeds, and even the old-fashioned airwaves. Language is ever in crisis. The insubstantial rhetoric and the thin slogans make it harder for us to remove, let alone see through, our thickly biased lenses to the hidden ground of love. But herein lies some consolation. Faith assures that whatever cruelties we foist upon one another, Sophia will not be made a prisoner. She continues to play in creation. Let us hope that the essays that follow help to unmask for us the world's thinness and reveal that eternal dance, the hidden wholeness that cannot be directly seen, or touched, or put in a genus, or distinguished by a difference, yet is present.[12]

---

12. I'm paraphrasing Bernard Lonergan, who in his book *Topics in Education* (Toronto: University of Toronto Press, 1993) described the world as "a cipher, a revelation, an unveiling the presence of one who is not seen, touched, grasped, put in a genus, distinguished by a difference, yet is present" (222).

# "A Quite Exceptional Convent":
# The Regina Laudis Correspondence

*Edited with an Introduction by Patrick F. O'Connell*

## Introduction

The Abbey of Regina Laudis ("Queen of Praise") in Bethlehem, Connecticut, the first fully enclosed Benedictine monastery of women in the United States, was founded in 1948 by Mother Benedict Duss, OSB (1910-2005), a nun from the Abbey of Jouarre in France.[1] Vera Duss was born in Pittsburgh but spent much of her early life in France, where her mother had moved in 1913 to be near her French father, after separating from her husband. Vera was baptized as a Catholic in Paris in January 1916. After attending Catholic elementary and secondary schools there she began medical studies and received her MD from the Sorbonne in June 1936. Almost immediately afterward she entered the convent of Jouarre and was given the name Soeur (after final vows Mère) Benoît; she served as physician for the abbey as well as for neighbors in the surrounding community. After the start of the Second World War in 1939 and the Fall of France the following year, as an "enemy alien" Mère Benoît was forced to go into hiding. Following the liberation of France in 1944 she began to think of bringing enclosed Benedictine life to America, receiving permission but little encouragement from her abbess at Jouarre. In the complicated process of obtaining authorization for the foundation from the Vatican she met and was supported by Jacques Maritain, post-war French Ambassador to the Vatican, Archbishop Angelo Giuseppe Roncalli (the future Pope John XXIII), Papal Nuncio to France, and Monsignor Giovanni Battista Montini (the future Pope Paul VI), Vatican Undersecretary of State.[2] Having secured permission from the Vatican to attempt an American foundation, Mother Benedict and her companion Mother Mary Aline left for the United States in August 1946, and by August 1947 had a signed order from Rome authorizing her to proceed with the foundation, to be located at Bethlehem in western Connecticut, where she and her co-

---

1. For a thorough presentation of the life of Mother Benedict and the history of the abbey she founded, see Antoinette Bosco, *Mother Benedict, Foundress of the Abbey of Regina Laudis: A Memoir*, Foreword by Mother Dolores Hart (San Francisco: Ignatius Press, 2007) (subsequent references will be cited as "Bosco" parenthetically in the text).

2. See Bosco 145-46, 164, 173-74 (Maritain); 149-53, 165-66, 175, 180-81 (Roncalli); 169-73, 210-11, 250, 254, 257-58, 269 (Montini).

foundress would soon be joined by six more volunteers from Jouarre. The foundation was officially begun with the consecration of the enclosure by Bishop Henry O'Brien of Hartford on September 2, 1948, with Mother Benedict as prioress. The young community overcame various hardships over the next two decades, in the process attracting vocations of numerous women distinguished in the professions, academia and the arts,[3] the best known being actress Dolores Hart, who entered Regina Laudis in June 1963 at the age of 25, abandoning a career that had already included twelve films and an appearance on Broadway.[4] On February 10, 1976 the monastery was raised to the rank of an abbey with Mother Benedict as its first abbess, a position she retained until 1997, when she became abbess emerita, dying at the age of 94 on October 2, 2005. Mother David Serna became Administratrix of the community when Mother Benedict retired and was elected second abbess early in 2001, with Mother Dolores Hart as her prioress, after the final revisions of the monastery's Constitutions were approved.[5] She served as abbess until May 2015, when she was succeeded by Mother Lucia Kuppens.[6]

In a January 29, 1964 letter to Edward Deming Andrews (1894-1964), a prominent scholar of the Shaker movement, Thomas Merton wrote:

> Did I tell you I got a very interesting set of notes from a Benedictine nun at Regina Laudis, Bethlehem, Conn., about a visit she and another nun paid to the Shakers at Sabbathday Lake? I am sure you would be very interested. If you do not know Regina Laudis you ought to get to know it. A quite exceptional convent. You should perhaps try to have a conversation with this Sister Prisca, and the Prioress, Mother Benedict, is also a very fine person and would be most interested, I think, in speaking to you about the Shakers.[7]

Merton refers here to the first extant piece of the rich correspondence between himself and various members of the Regina Laudis community,

---

3. See Bosco 20 for a partial list.

4. In addition to information in Bosco (279-82, 386-88 n. 10), see her autobiography: Mother Dolores Hart, OSB and Richard DeNeut, *The Ear of the Heart: An Actress' Journey from Hollywood to Holy Vows* (San Francisco: Ignatius Press, 2013) (subsequent references will be cited as "Hart" parenthetically in the text).

5. See Bosco 358-59, 392-93 n. 4.

6. Further information on Regina Laudis can be found on the monastery website: http://abbeyofreginalaudis.org.

7. Thomas Merton, *The Hidden Ground of Love: Letters on Religious Experience and Social Concerns*, ed. William H. Shannon (New York: Farrar, Straus, Giroux, 1985) 39; subsequent references will be cited as "*HGL*" parenthetically in the text.

that would continue until the year before his death in 1968.[8] There had actually been some contact between Merton and the nuns of Regina Laudis at least shortly before the letter from Sr. Prisca. In a January 9, 1964 letter to Jacques Maritain, Merton refers to the gift of a book of poetry by Maritain's wife Raïssa that had been printed years earlier at Regina Laudis: "the nuns at Bethlehem (Regina Laudis) sent me a copy of *Portes de l'horizon*. That is a completely lovely book, which in any case I had known long since, for you and Raïssa sent me a copy from Princeton when it came out. But I am happy to have another copy."[9] Largely in response to various articles and books by Merton, some of them read to the community during meals, at least five of the Regina Laudis nuns wrote to Merton between 1964 and 1967.[10] While his own three extant responses have been previously published, their full significance and the warmth of his relationship with the community are much more apparent when read in conjunction with the letters of the sisters, none of which has previously appeared in print. This correspondence provides further evidence of his deep concern for the renewal of women's religious communities, especially contemplative communities, in the aftermath of the Second Vatican Council, as witnessed by the tapes he made for various houses of nuns during his years (1965-68) in the hermitage[11] and by the two retreats he coordinated for contemplative prioresses in December 1967 and May 1968.[12] In fact in letters to two of those who would attend

---

8. This correspondence is found in the archives of the Thomas Merton Center [TMC] at Bellarmine University, Louisville, KY, the official and most extensive repository of Merton's papers.

9. Thomas Merton, *The Courage for Truth: Letters to Writers*, ed. Christine M. Bochen (New York: Farrar, Straus, Giroux, 1993) 44. One of the earliest books the nuns produced on their small hand-printing press was this selection of sixteen poems by Raïssa Maritain, published in 1952 in a bilingual edition (see Bosco 233, 245-46). The reason a copy was sent more than a decade later to Merton may well have been the inclusion of his own translations of some of her poetry in his recent volume of verse: Thomas Merton, *Emblems of a Season of Fury* (New York: New Directions, 1963) 104-13.

10. Merton had also been an important early influence on Dolores Hart, who became a Catholic convert as an elementary school student, though in entering Regina Laudis she found his attraction to solitude less relevant to her own spiritual journey. She writes in her autobiography: "Merton's *No Man Is an Island* had been tightly woven into my life. When I was younger I found him very appealing. But he found his way to God in isolation, and although I still appreciated his writing, ever since I visited Regina Laudis I realized that his search for God did not coincide with the way I needed to find him" (Hart 124).

11. For details, see Patrick F. O'Connell, review of 2013 CD sets, *The Merton Annual* 27 (2014) 226-31.

12. Thomas Merton, *The Springs of Contemplation: A Retreat at the Abbey of Gethsemani*, ed. Jane Marie Richardson, SL (New York: Farrar, Straus, Giroux, 1992); the

the second of these retreats Merton mentioned Mother Benedict's name as a possible participant,[13] though in the event, for whatever unknown reason, she was not present.[14] But while there were no actual meetings between Merton and any Regina Laudis sisters, the friendship by letter that developed with representatives of the community provides striking testimony to the ongoing mutual respect and affection between Thomas Merton and this "exceptional convent."[15]

### TALS[16] from Prisca Dougherty, OSB to Merton[17]

Pax!                                                    January 20, 1964

Dear Father Merton:

I read with rather sensitive interest your article on the Shakers in

---

recordings of this material are now available commercially: Thomas Merton, *Solitude and Togetherness* [11CDs] and Thomas Merton, *The Prophet's Freedom* [8CDs] (Rockville, MD: Now You Know Media, 2013); for a comparison of the audio versions and the edited text see the review of this material by Patrick F. O'Connell, *The Merton Annual* 26 (2013) 230-32.

13. December 26, 1967 letter to Mother Angela Collins: "What I have been thinking of planning is a small meeting with three or four Carmelites (you pick them) and a couple of Benedictines like Mother Benedicta [*sic*] of Regina Laudis and maybe one of her nuns"; February 16, 1968 letter to Sr. Elaine M. Bane: "would you like to come down here for a small meeting toward the end of May, in the week before Pentecost? Like May 27th to 30th? I am only inviting a few, the Carmelite Prioress of Savannah who couldn't come in December and who will pick a couple of Carmelites. Then you and maybe the Benedictine Prioress of Regina Laudis" (Thomas Merton, *The School of Charity: Letters on Religious Renewal and Spiritual Direction*, ed. Patrick Hart [New York: Farrar, Straus, Giroux, 1990] 358, 366; subsequent references will be cited as "*SC*" parenthetically in the text).

14. See Merton's journal entry for May 28, 1968 for the names of the participants in this small retreat: Mother Angela and two other Carmelites, Sr. Elaine, and the prioress of the Poor Clare convent of New Orleans (Thomas Merton, *The Other Side of the Mountain: The End of the Journey. Journals, vol. 7: 1967-1968*, ed. Patrick Hart [San Francisco: HarperCollins, 1998] 123; subsequent references will be cited as "*OSM*" parenthetically in the text).

15. The editors of *The Merton Annual* are deeply grateful to Mother Abbess Lucia Kuppens, OSB, for her permission and encouragement to publish the following material, and to Mother David Serna, OSB and Mother Miriam Benedict, OSB, the two surviving Regina Laudis correspondents of Thomas Merton, for graciously allowing their letters to appear here.

16. The following abbreviations are used for the letters: HCS: handwritten card signed; HLS: handwritten letter signed; TALS: typed annotated letter signed; TL[c]: typed letter [carbon]; TLS: typed letter signed.

17. Mary Agnes Dougherty, who had been a member of the Catholic Worker community in Rochester, NY, was clothed as a member of the Regina Laudis community in the spring of 1952 and given the name Prisca (see Bosco 246); she later became one of the original members of the Regina Laudis foundation of Our Lady of the Rock on Shaw Island, WA in 1977 (see Bosco 328).

Jubilee.[18] The enclosed is an informal impression of a visit to the Shakers filed in our Library for reference.[19] Sr. Jerome[20] and myself who are not bound to the enclosure[21] made this visit after hearing of the Shakers thru Fr. R. Whitson of Fordham.[22] We stayed at a Catholic College nearby[23] and went each morning to the Village. Our purpose was not clearly defined* – the Holy Spirit inspired Reverend Mother, I believe, to send us;

18. Thomas Merton, "The Shakers: American Celibates and Craftsmen Who Danced in the Glory of God," *Jubilee* 11 (January 1964) 36-41; reprinted in slightly revised form as "Pleasant Hill: A Shaker Village in Kentucky" in Thomas Merton, *Mystics and Zen Masters* (New York: Farrar, Straus and Giroux, 1967) 193-202 (subsequent references will be cited as "*MZM*" parenthetically in the text). It is also found, with numerous illustrations, in the most extensive presentation of Merton's interest in the Shakers: Thomas Merton, *Seeking Paradise: The Spirit of the Shakers*, ed. Paul M. Pearson (Maryknoll, NY: Orbis, 2003) 54-71 (subsequent references will be cited as "*SP*" parenthetically in the text).

19. Sent with the letter were two enclosures. One was a four-page typescript created from a single folded 8.5" x 11" page, headed "SHAKER TRIP TO SABBATHDAY LAKE COMMUNITY / Poland Springs, Maine (Sept. 15-20, 1962)," written by Sr. Prisca, listing the names of the thirteen community members, all women, some with short descriptions, followed by a description of the physical setting of the buildings, time of shared prayer (combining Shaker and Benedictine elements), preparation and sharing of meals, and a brief note about a visit made by a friend to the Canterbury, NH community; Sr. Prisca called the group "a most tolerant, flexible, absolutely honest, humorous, natural, religious people with a true sense of joy and happiness, and an amazing trust in God's will and providence." The other was a three-page typescript, similarly folded, by Sr. Jerome, headed "Impressions of our visit to the Shaker Village, Sabbathday Lake, Maine, with regard to similarities between the Holy Rule of St. Benedict and the rule of life of the Shakers," with sections on "Cenobitic Life," "Ora et Labora" (focusing on the Shaker motto "Hands to Work and Hearts to God") and "General Remarks" (vows, bells, hospitality, intellectual pursuits).

20. A widow and convert brought up in Italy and Bavaria, Melanie von Nagel Mussayassul was clothed as a member of the community in March 1958 at the age of 48 and given the name Jerome (see Bosco 261-62).

21. Originally the members of the community included two classes, choir nuns, bound to enclosure, and oblate sisters, who were not cloistered; after Vatican II, the Regina Laudis Constitution specified that there was a single class of nuns "with two accents of call" living in a complementary relationship – those who remained within the enclosure and the "*missae*" ("those sent") whose vocation included time outside the cloister. Originally the choir nuns were called "Mother" and the oblate members "Sister" but after the revision all fully professed members of the community were given the title "Mother" (see Bosco 310, 377-78 n. 1; 383-84 n. 1).

22. In the summer of 1962 Fr. Whitson, chair of the Theology Department at Fordham, gave a series of fourteen conferences on American Protestant history to the Regina Laudis community, the last four of which focused on the Shakers (Bosco 277); Fr. Whitson would later edit the volume *The Shakers: Two Centuries of Spiritual Reflection* in the Classics of Western Spirituality series (New York: Paulist Press, 1983).

23. St. Joseph's College in N. Windham, ME ("SHAKER TRIP" typescript 1).

Sr. Jerome was interested in furniture and dyes and I in herbs and then we vaguely saw similarities in our way of life. You will note that you left out our beloved Community of Sabbathday Lake[24] in your article. Anyhow we thought you would be interested to learn of our first-hand experience. I have asked Philadelphia Museum to send you a copy of their spring 1962 bulletin given over entirely to the Shakers with an illustrated article on the "inspirational writings".[25] We saw some at Sabbathday Lake. However they achieved the minuteness of writing and paintings (they made their own paints) with dim light is almost incomprehensible. Our friendship has continued through correspondence; they sent one of their devoted male helpers to see us and we suspect that he may possibly become a "brethren". After our return our économe[26] made use of the Shaker Cookbook and presented us one Sunday with a Shaker dinner. At Christmas time they send us a Shaker recipe fruitcake. At the time of Pope John's death[27] they wrote a letter of condolence to us saying how close they felt to him.

Our next venture – after we visit the Anglican Sisters in Newburgh N.Y.[28] (the whole community in separate groups, has visited us) – I hope

---

24. Established in 1783, the Sabbathday Lake Shaker Village in New Gloucester, ME is currently the only active Shaker community in the world: see http://maineshakers. com. The community was extensively featured in the Ken Burns film *The Shakers: Hands to Work, Hearts to God* (Florentine Films, 1984).

25. *The Shakers: Their Arts and Crafts*, ed. Margaret Frost, Philadelphia Museum Bulletin 57, n. 273 (Spring 1962).

26. I.e. the community steward, in charge of the kitchen.

27. Pope John died on June 3, 1963.

28. The Order of St. Helena was founded in 1945 in Versailles, KY by nine former members of the Order of St. Anne, as an Anglican (Episcopal) monastic order for women; its convent in Newburgh (Vail's Gate), NY, founded in 1954, closed in 2008; the order's remaining convent is located in North Augusta, SC. In a journal entry for November 30, 1963 Merton refers to a visit of some of the sisters from Versailles (Thomas Merton, *Dancing in the Water of Life: Seeking Peace in the Hermitage. Journals, vol. 5: 1963-1965*, ed. Robert E. Daggy [San Francisco: HarperCollins, 1997] 40; subsequent references will be cited as "*DWL*" parenthetically in the text). On February 8, 1964 Merton received a letter from Sr. Grace of the Versailles community thanking him for sending various writings to the group (TMC archives); nine letters were exchanged between Merton and Sr. Bridget of the same convent between March 1964 and June 1965 (TMC archives).

may be to the Society of Brothers[29] in Norfold [i.e. Norfolk], Conn.[30] We have one of their publications "Children in Community", a masterpiece of commonsense, psychology and Christianity-lived.[31] Maybe you would be interested in this recent publication, the notice of which is enclosed.

I forgot to say that we have some excellent pictures of our visit to Sabbathday Lake, one especially of all of us in front of the Meeting-house. And as a little addendum – I was connected with the C.W. for sometime in my home town before entering R.L. and had as my god-mothers at Clothing Dorothy Day and a negress active in the apostolate at home.[32] Reverend Mother agreeably "suffers" with me and my radical ideas. We pray for you and all your work toward a Radical Christianity. It is not easy, though, to be consistent in living our ideals, we are ever confronted with our own poor humanity helpless except thru the strength of the Spirit.

Sincerely in Christ
Sister Prisca O.S.B.

*I really meant our Sisters to meet the Shaker Community in the spirit of Christ + St Benedict that they might also study their approach to Community life. S$^r$ – B. D.[33]

---

29. I.e. the Bruderhof, a community founded by Eberhard Arnold (1883-1935) in Germany in 1920, rooted in the Anabaptist tradition, committed to pacifism, community of goods and practice of the beatitudes. Persecuted by the Nazis, the group fled to England and Paraguay in the mid-1930s and in the early 1950s most of the Bruderhof relocated to the United States and attracted a significant number of American members, settling in communities at Rifton, NY and elsewhere. Two of Merton's talks in Alaska, "Building Community on God's Love" and "Community, Politics, and Contemplation" (*Thomas Merton in Alaska: The Alaskan Conferences, Journals, and Letters*, ed. Robert E. Daggy [New York: New Directions, 1989] 93-105, 107-14) drew extensively on Arnold's work; they were later republished in Eberhard Arnold, *Why We Live in Community* (Farmington, PA: Plough Publishing, 1995) 31-66.

30. The Deer Spring Bruderhof in Norfolk, founded in 1958, closed in 1998.

31. *Children in Community* (New York: Plough Publishing, 1963); in a July 4, 1964 letter to Hector Black, a member of the Bruderhof, Merton expresses his thanks for the gift of books, including a life of Eberhard Arnold and *Children in Community*, which he calls "a very special success," adding: "The texts are marvelous and the pictures a real joy. I shall never get tired of this book, and the other monks and I will continue to enjoy it as long as we live, I hope. It will remain a deep bond with you" (*SC* 220).

32. Catholic Worker founder Dorothy Day and Harriet Schuyler, a leader in interracial activities in Rochester and founder of the Mother Cabrini Circle, were present as attendants at the investiture of Sr. Prisca as a member of the Regina Laudis community (see Bosco 246).

33. A handwritten note by Mother Benedict, the prioress, in the margins of Sr. Prisca's letter, a practice also seen in the August 21, 1967 and September 24, 1967 letters from Sr. Miriam Benedict.

## HCS from Benedict Duss, OSB to Merton[34]

Sainte Agnes[35]
1964

Mon Père, mon très cher Père,

Always happy to be able to share some little thing with you who share so much with you.

I rejoice that Pax + fortitudo + gratia + gaudium seem increasingly to be yours in Passione Domini.

## TL[c] from Merton to Prisca Dougherty, OSB[36]

jhs

Feb 10, 1964

Dear Sister Prisca:

Thank you very much for sending your notes on the Sabbathday Lake Shaker Community. I found them very moving indeed. Certainly your visit there was peculiarly blessed. As a matter of fact I was confused, thinking that the only community left was the Canterbury NH one and that there were only half a dozen old ladies there.[37] Your notes suggest that some of the sisters are relatively young.[38] That is hopeful. What a pity that they should die out altogether. I have always been very impressed by their eschatalogical [*sic*] spirit, their sense of themselves as a sign of the last days and the new creation.

---

34. This brief handwritten note is probably a response to a letter from Merton (not extant) expressing gratitude for the gift of the volume of Raïssa Maritain's poetry printed at the monastery. It was written on the back of an illustrated note card with a drawing of a house surrounded by the legend: "BURNET FOR A MERRY HEART / THYME FOR COURAGE / SOUTHERNWOOD FOR CONSTANCY / MINT FOR WISDOM" and the reference "*Design and Fragrance by CLAIRE BURKE, Charlottesville, Virginia*" (the company still exists today). Sr. Prisca's letter was typed on the inside of this card.

35. The feast of St. Agnes is celebrated on January 21.

36. A slightly abridged version of this letter is found in *SC* 197-98. See also the journal entry for the following day, February 11: "The other day I got a fine letter from Sister Prisca at Regina Laudis [Abbey [*sic*], Bethlehem, Connecticut] about a visit she and another Sister had made to the Shaker Community at Sabbathday Lake in Maine. It was a very touching and beautiful meeting, full of authentic religious meaning and deep charity" (*DWL* 74).

37. The Canterbury Shaker Village, founded in 1792, continued to be a residence for a few remaining Shaker eldresses until 1990; it was incorporated as a non-profit museum and historic site in 1969 and became a national historical landmark in 1993.

38. "Sisters Frances [Carr] and Marie [Burgess] are the youngest, around the middle thirties" ("SHAKER TRIP" typescript 1). (Sister Frances Carr died on January 2, 2017 at the age of 89.)

I have been doing a book on art[39] and want to use some of the Shaker prints in it, or at least one. I am in contact with E. D. Andrews[40] who has access to everything and can provide what I need, I hope. He is doing a new edition of his book on Shaker furniture and it sounds fine.[41]

Are the Anglican sisters in Newburgh the St Helena Order? They have a house in Versailles Ky near here and a few of the nuns have been over. I am also in contact with the novice master at the Holy Cross Fathers on the Hudson.[42]

The Bulletin from the Phila. Museum apparently did not come. I am sure they must have sent it but maybe I just did not get it. I will try to find out. I would like to have whatever I can on the Shakers. There is an immense amount of unpublished material. I am afraid I will never be able to get in deep enough to do a book on them but I want to build up my article into a more meaty one on the Pleasant Hill community in particular, with some history.[43]

Bro Thomas at South Union[44] has sent me some records from the

---

39. This is reference to the never-published book *Art and Worship*; for a discussion of this work and its travails, see Donna Kristoff, OSU, "'Light That Is Not Light': A Consideration of Thomas Merton and the Icon," *The Merton Annual* 2 (1989) 85-117.

40. See Merton's letters to Andrews in *HGL* 31-39, and the more complete version, including both sides of the correspondence between Merton and Andrews, as well as his wife, in *A Meeting of Angels: The Correspondence of Thomas Merton with Edward Deming & Faith Andrews*, ed. Paul M. Pearson (Frankfort, KY: Broadstone Books, 2008).

41. Merton wrote the Introduction to this work, which did not appear until after the death of both Andrews and Merton: Edward Deming Andrews and Faith Andrews, *Religion in Wood: A Book of Shaker Furniture* (Bloomington: Indiana University Press, 1973) vii-xv; *SP* 72-89.

42. The Order of the Holy Cross is an Anglican/Episcopal Benedictine community founded in 1884 by James Huntington; its New York monastery is located in West Park, north of Poughkeepsie; it was closely associated with the women's Order of St. Helena. On January 18, 1964, Fr. Kenneth Terry, the master of postulants at West Park, wrote to Merton after Sr. Bridget of the St. Helena Convent in Versailles, KY had sent him some of Merton's mimeographed conference notes (TMC archives).

43. The Pleasant Hill Shaker Village, which Merton visited at least six times between 1959 and 1968 (see *SP* 16), was founded in 1806 and officially dissolved in 1910 (see *SP* 69-70); in 1961, a non-profit corporation was established to restore the site and in 1968 it was first opened to the public.

44. Br. Thomas Whitaker, OSB was a monk of St. Maur's Priory, South Union, KY, founded in 1947 on the grounds of a former Shaker village; Merton's extant correspondence with Br. Thomas, including discussion of the Shakers, consists in four unpublished letters, three to Merton and one from him (TMC archives). It was at Br. Thomas' instigation that Srs. Prisca and Jerome wrote up their notes on their visit to Sabbathday Lake ("Impressions" typescript 3).

Western Reserve collection[45] I think (I will have to get at them again, I have only heard a side or two and could not get too excited about them at the time).

Best wishes and blessings to your Mother Prioress and all the community We feel very close to you. Fr Gregory from Mount Saviour[46] was down for a few days. A very pleasant visit. Let us be united in prayer through Lent in the light of Christ and the peace of the desert, though the peace of the desert is always a bit militant. There is no Christian peace that is not militant, but precisely it is militant, not violent. May we grow in understanding and in joy.

Again, my very best wishes and blessings to all of you.

Cordially in Christ,

## TL[c] from Merton to Benedict Duss, OSB[47]

March 26, 1964

Dear Mother Benedict:

It seems that I still owe some response to notes from several members of the Regina Laudis community, and I take this opportunity to write you all an Easter Greeting, to ask your prayers, to share with you the joy of the Feast.

First of all I was most interested in Sister Prisca's account of the visit to the Shakers. Such contacts are deeply significant and there is no question that the Shakers were deeply imbued with a spirit like that of St Benedict. It showed in the work of their hands, which was worship in spirit and in truth.[48]

---

45. The Western Reserve Historical Society, located in Cleveland, OH, has the largest extant collection of Shaker artifacts, as well as extensive documentary materials and Shaker artwork.

46. Fr. Gregory Borgstedt, OSB (1908-75), the novice master at the "primitive Benedictine" monastery of Mount Saviour in Elmira, NY, had come to Gethsemani in early February, 1964 (see the journal entry for February 11, 1964 [*DWL* 75]); a recording of his conference to the Gethsemani novices on February 3, 1964 is in the TMC archives. Damasus Winzen, OSB (1901-71), the founding superior of Mount Saviour, had been the original chaplain at Regina Laudis (see Bosco 191, 198, 208-209, 219-22, 236-37). There are nine unpublished letters exchanged between Fr. Gregory and Merton between 1964 and 1968 (TMC archives), as well as sixteen items of correspondence between 1950 and 1968 with Dom Damasus (three published: *SC* 18-19 [Holy Week 1950]; 90-91 [August 22, 1955]; 232-33 [September 8, 1964]); see also Joel Rippinger, OSB, "Damasus Winzen and Thomas Merton: Pathfinders, Companions, and Prophets in American Monasticism," *Cistercian Studies Quarterly* 51.3 (2016) 373-83.

47. This letter is published in *SC* 211-12 (the headnote refers to her as abbess rather than prioress; Regina Laudis would not be raised to an abbey until 1976).

48. A reference to John 4:24.

I am grateful that someone there responded to the article on the "Monk in the Diaspora"[49] which has been rather attacked by a Benedictine of one of the big monasteries.[50] It is strange to be up against the confused ideas of Christian optimism that struggle with one another in the Church today. To be an optimist in the eyes of some people, one has to believe in the ever greater and greater success of those institutional aspects of the Church, those rather secular glories and achievements, which seem precisely to be stifling her true life and progress in some ways. But one must expect conflict, confusion, and inertia even when the inertia thinks itself to be progress. And after all, how do we know and how can we judge? Anyway, please pray for me.

There is certainly life and hope in the monastic movement, but not always where the biggest buildings and the greatest activities flourish. I always think of Regina Laudis as a place where there is genuine life, and a human dimension. Here too, in spite of our confusions and difficulties, the Lord has been good to us, and there is a living spirit and a genuine progress, especially since our numbers have grown much smaller (that is a contradiction in terms: I mean since they have become smaller.)

May the Lord bless you with His Light and His joy, and may the whole Church exult in His true Victory, which may not always consist in what the faithful think it to be. And may we be faithful ourselves to the grace of Easter and its liberty. I will remember you especially at the Altar on Easter Morning.

Very cordially and fraternally yours in Christ,

## HLS from Benedict Duss, OSB to Merton

+                                                  Monday in Holy Week[51]

Pax

Dear Father,

A wonderful fraternal letter from you a year ago – + the generous sharing of your essays since – and not a word from me . . .

---

49. Thomas Merton, "The Monk in the Diaspora," *Commonweal* 79 (20 March 1964) 741-45, included in augmented form in Thomas Merton, *Seeds of Destruction* (New York: Farrar, Straus & Giroux, 1964) as part two (199-213) of "The Christian in the Diaspora" (184-220); subsequent references will be cited as "*SD*" parenthetically in the text.

50. The reference is to Fr. Ronald Roloff, OSB of St. John's Abbey, Collegeville, MN, from whom Merton had received a letter concerning the article on March 20: see Merton's March 21, 1964 letter to Roloff with its mention of "Christian optimism" and assertion that "I do not place the knife anywhere between Teilhard and Rahner" (*SC* 210); the much longer letter entitled "Letter to a Priest" and published in *Seeds of Destruction* (318-26) was also a response to Roloff's critique of the article.

51. April 12, 1965.

This might assure you of special union + thought during these days.

Years since the beginning of this foundation (1946) have been packed with concern – but none more than the four last when through circumstances – mainly the architectural studies for a permanent monastery – we have had to think through practically every concrete issue of our monastic life.[52]

A sequence of "crises" – + now a rather decisive phase.

There would be too much to report.

But I entrust our present needs to your brotherly understanding + know that with your help, we will open ourselves to the Lord's victory.

Un grand merci for the Eremitical installment,[53] this way looming at a [decisive time][54] here!

Wishing you Peace in the Gaudium Paschale.

Devotedly yours + gratefully

S͏ʳ Benedict Duss pr OSB

## TLS from Mildred Wilson, OSB to Merton[55]

PAX                                  Regina Laudis
                                Easter Monday 1967[56]

Dear Father,

As soon as I saw the sun this morning, I knew I wasn't going to get through the day without writing to you. A lot of days have been like this and, as a result, there is a file folder in our cell stuffed with "Dear Father" letters, most of which I never dreamed of sending you. I keep them because they have a meaning for me. For you, their message could be summed up briefly: To the man who has everything – thank you for having it.

Fortunately, every expression of gratitude doesn't have to be committed to writing, else I'd need a file cabinet instead of a manila folder. But, the Easter joy has got mixed up with two things that happened last evening and this letter has become a must. Listening

---

52. See Bosco 273-89 for various aspects of this planning process.

53. The reference is probably to Thomas Merton, "For a Renewal of Eremitism in the Monastic State," *Collectanea Cisterciensia* 27 (1965) 121-49; reprinted as "The Case for a Renewal of Eremitism in the Monastic State" in Thomas Merton, *Contemplation in a World of Action* (Garden City, NY: Doubleday, 1971) 294-327 (subsequent references will be cited as "*CWA*" parenthetically in the text).

54. Reading conjectural due to frayed edge of paper.

55. Ruth Wilson entered Regina Laudis as a postulant on March 21, 1949, one of the earliest American vocations, and was clothed in early October in the presence of the Abbot of Solesmes, Dom Germain Cozien (see Bosco, 226, 228).

56. March 27, 1967.

to the refectory reading of Teilhard's "Building the Earth"[57] without experiencing any of the terrible inner tension his works, his followers and pseudo-followers used to create in me. What a relief. Listening to my sister at recreation saying that she doesn't really believe in the articles of faith and answering quite simply that I do – no anxiety to explain that my faith lies in the inexpressible Reality that the articles indicate but cannot contain – no fear lest my admission result in automatic excommunication from the modern, thinking, totally involved Church. This, Father, is FREEDOM.

Well, maybe the freedom is only relative, but it is real enough to have kept me dancing for the last four months. The actual dancing is confined to the woods and the attic, but the song-and-dance mood is remarkably persistent. Dancing in the clarity of perfect contradiction. Dancing in hope conceived of absurdity. Dancing to wisdom neither sacred nor secular. Dancing in the harmony at the heart of conflict. Dancing in praise of the inconsistent God. There is a regular litany. I won't bore you with it. The ideas are all yours anyway – but the expression is highly personal to me.

Only one idea I have that is not yours nevertheless seems to be worth having. After living for eighteen years with a bunch of women (many of them very intelligent) and having beaten my brains out searching for something that just isn't there, I have come to a conclusion. Wise men may be few, wise women are non-existent. We can look to ourselves for some pretty good intuitions and insights and even for a certain originality of thought. But for true wisdom, if we don't have the sense to receive it as man's gift to us, we'll never have it at all. Right here, we are very close to St. Paul's "the head of the woman is man".[58] And, right here, we are very, very close to the source of my gratitude to you.

Still, that's only part of it. I am grateful for all the words of wisdom that you have poured into my mind in the last four months. But, I'm even more grateful for the words that stagger my mind and stun it so that your thoughts slip past it and disappear in the parched ground deep down where there are no words or thoughts. It is here that you have touched me and brought me back to life. It's here that the Easter mystery becomes a reality and life and love merge into one. Though I suppose the mystery is that the one could ever have been divided to make two.

But it is silly of me to try to put it into words – all the sillier since I've decided to send this letter instead of filing it. And that, Father, is freedom.

So, since whether you like it or not, you have a new spiritual daughter,

---

57. Pierre Teilhard de Chardin, *Building the Earth*, trans. Noel Lindsay (Wilkes-Barre, PA: Dimension Books, 1965).

58. 1 Cor. 11:3.

give her an Easter blessing.

Respectfully in Christ,
Sister Mildred, O.S.B.

**TLS from Mildred Wilson, OSB to Merton**

PAX                                                      Regina Laudis
May 27, 1967

Dear Father,

How does one be a "dear friend" to an overworked hermit? I'm so overwhelmed to have heard from you directly,[59] I've been in a state of awed paralysis. Considering the crowded condition of your desk, writing to you could be construed as an unfriendly act, but if I am altogether silent, I might risk losing my coveted place on your mailing list. It's a dilemma.

I took your advice and got permission to subscribe to Theoria to Theory[60] but haven't heard anything yet. I don't mind. After eighteen years of utter neglect, I still have a lot of Thomas Merton to catch up on. And the more I read, the slower I go and the more reluctant I am to decide I have finished with a particular book or article. Then there is the

---

59. Merton's reply to Sr. Mildred's first letter does not seem to be extant.

60. *Theoria to Theory: An International Journal of Science, Philosophy, and Contemplative Religion*, fourteen volumes issued from 1966 to 1981; see Merton's description and recommendation of this British Anglican journal in his Easter 1967 circular letter (Thomas Merton, *The Road to Joy: Letters to New and Old Friends*, ed. Robert E. Daggy [New York: Farrar, Straus, Giroux, 1989] 101). Merton published two articles in this journal: the first is "The Death of God and the End of History," *Theoria to Theory* 2 (October 1967) 3-16; reprinted in Thomas Merton, *Faith and Violence: Christian Teaching and Christian Practice* (Notre Dame, IN: University of Notre Dame Press, 1968) 239-58 (subsequent references will be cited as "*FV*" parenthetically in the text); the second is "A New Christian Consciousness" (the same essay Sr. Mildred refers to in mimeograph form in her letter), *Theoria to Theory* 3 (January 1969) 5-8, which had appeared earlier as "The Self of Modern Man in the New Christian Consciousness," *R. M. Bucke Memorial Society Newsletter-Review* 2 (April 1967) 1-7, reprinted as "The New Consciousness" in Thomas Merton, *Zen and the Birds of Appetite* (New York: New Directions, 1968) 15-32.

outside reading – some of it way out – Camus,[61] Baldwin,[62] Pasternak,[63] Flannery O'Connor,[64] Julian of Norwich[65] (wonder what she thinks of the company she keeps).

Of all your writings I have read, there is only one I would not like to see published to the ends of the earth. And it is positively brilliant. It's your mimeographed article "A New Christian Consciousness?" What disturbs me about it is that you seem to be placing yourself in opposition to the new consciousness. But, no. You're right in the middle of it. Absolutely dead center. The Church right now is like a huge cyclone. All sorts of people and things are caught up in it and there is a lot of dust obscuring vision. No one seems to know where we're headed, but all seem determined to get there by going around in circles as fast as possible, liberals getting more radical and conservatives getting more reactionary each time around. In the center is the eye where the air is clear and still, and that's where you are. Maybe there are others in there with you, but you're the only one I know – the only one with the depth and breadth of vision to cope effectively with the situation. Every time I think of you, I get a great big bubble of joy inside, and I want to laugh right out loud with delight, because you exist.

I've had considerable experience with the new Christian consciousness. I was hit over the head by it for so long and from so many different directions, nothing seemed to make any sense. One conclusion was inevitable. If what people were saying was true, I didn't exist. The only person I could recognize as myself was an illusion, the product of an illusion, and quite incapable of distinguishing reality from fantasy. I was like a demented child desperately trying to get my hand inside a glove. I was determined it should fit, but the glove was turned inside out with all

61. See Merton's seven essays on Camus (not all of which had yet been written at the time of this letter) in Thomas Merton, *The Literary Essays of Thomas Merton*, ed. Patrick Hart, OCSO (New York: New Directions, 1981) 179-301 (subsequent references will be cited as *"LE"* parenthetically in the text). Sr. Mildred is perhaps thinking particularly of "Terror and the Absurd: Violence and Non-Violence in Albert Camus" (mimeograph dated August 1966) (*LE* 232-51); "Albert Camus and the Church," *The Catholic Worker* 33 (December 1966) 4-5, 8 (*LE* 261-74); and/or "Can We Survive Nihilism? Satan, Milton and Camus," *Saturday Review* 50 (15 April 1967) 16-19 (*LE* 252-60, under the title "Prophetic Ambiguities: Milton and Camus").

62. See Merton's letter to Baldwin (*SD* 302-306).

63. See "The Pasternak Affair" in Thomas Merton, *Disputed Questions* (New York: Farrar, Straus and Cudahy, 1960) 3-67.

64. See "Flannery O'Connor: A Prose Elegy," in Thomas Merton, *Raids on the Unspeakable* (New York: New Directions, 1966) 37-42; subsequent references will be cited as *"RU"* parenthetically in the text.

65. See "The English Mystics" (*MZM* 128-53).

the fingers bunched up inside. I had just about decided I would have to cut off my fingers or throw away the glove when you came along. Simply and gently, you turned the glove right side out and give it back to me. What's more – bless you – you did it with a sense of humor, something I never expected to see again in Catholic circles. Well, I really don't mind going around in these circles anymore as long as I can keep my eyes on the center and be reminded that many of the attractive ideas floating around out here are really good in themselves. It's just that people keep turning them wrong side out. (And mixing them up with equally attractive, highly questionable ideas.)

Being a Titan was always a lonely, thankless occupation.[66] Our Kentucky Titan can't expect to be an exception to the rule. (Maybe I like this better than the cyclone bit.) We can't expect you to enjoy holding our world on your shoulders, but heaven help us if you should give up on the Moves Watching. Some of the walls may be very thick, but your aim is amazingly accurate, and walls do fall down when you move. Besides, the old Christian consciousness was no better at explaining contemplation than the new. No mystic was ever really understood except by another mystic. The wonderful part about you is not that you are understood but that you understand.

All at Regina Laudis are grateful for your love. We need it. We're held together by a miracle – the only thing that could possible unite such a highly diversified group of people.

My own gratitude doesn't fit into words.

Respectfully,<br>
Sister Mildred

### TLS from Mildred Wilson, OSB to Merton

PAX

Regina Laudis<br>
Bethlehem, Conn.<br>
August 11th

Dear Father,

Someday, when I stop being cellarer and have time to sharpen up the dulled edges of my mind, I'm going to write an article entitled "Thomas Merton: An Appraisal". However, I won't send it to the American Benedictine Review.[67] Obviously, if they would publish Clifford Stevens', they

---

66. The reference is to Merton's "Atlas and the Fatman" (*RU* 91-107).

67. Fr. Clifford Stevens (1926- ) a priest of the Archdiocese of Omaha, NE who had earlier spent time at the Cistercian Abbey of New Melleray in Iowa but left because of dissatisfaction with the direction the Order was taking, wrote an article entitled "Thomas

would never publish mine.

I suppose I should be writing this to Mr. Stevens, but he might take it amiss if I pointed out that although he has the sense to see that you are "thoroughly the contemporary man" his own contemporariness seems to have atrophied in the mid-fifties. I am willing to praise you for the golden writings of your first years and hail you as the voice and symbol of the postwar years. He does this part rather well; those early books are excellent and will no doubt secure you a place with Newman and Augustine in the eyes of men in the twenty-fifth and fiftieth centuries. And perhaps, as Mr. S. says, your greatest work is yet to be written. But, if I ever get around to really praising you, it will be for those "hurried", "unsure", "forced and plodding" "afterthoughts and vague commentaries on unrelated subjects" that you have had the courage to write and publish in the last eight years.

And I do mean courage. It takes courage to be a thoroughly contemporary man in this fast-moving, complex, enigmatic decade. Thank you for that. Thank you for being unsure where any pretense of certainty would be absurd. Thank you for being in a hurry, for recognizing the urgency and extent of our need. Thank you for plodding along ahead of us and forcing a path through ground that most people spend their time trying to bypass. Thank you for your afterthoughts, your forethoughts and all your thoughts. Thank you for the quick, sure thrust of your insight that synthesizes unrelated subjects at a level of awareness which defies literary criticism.

Well, anyway, thank you. Lacking a sharpened mind, that seems to be all I have to say. Forgive the monotonous regularity with which I keep repeating it. But this time, blame Clifford Stevens.

A blessing please,

In Christo,
Sister Mildred

---

Merton: An Appraisal," *American Benedictine Review* 18.2 (June 1967) 223-26; in 1962 he had earlier sent an essay on St. Stephen Harding, one of the founders of the Order of Cîteaux, to Merton, who had responded with an unpublished letter of December 19, 1962; after learning of this article in *ABR* Merton wrote to Stevens on August 11, 1967; Stevens responded on August 20, and subsequently wrote two more letters to Merton, one from Japan on November 22, 1967 about the favorable reception of Merton's *Mystics and Zen Masters* there, and another on January 8, 1968, in response to a Christmas note from Merton (not extant) and enclosing a poem, "For an Archbishop Going to the Council" (TMC archives). He would subsequently write five more articles in Merton between 1972 and 1982.

## TALS from Miriam Benedict, OSB to Merton[68]

21 August 1967

Pax

Dear Father Louis,

We are reading your, <u>Monastic Vocation and Modern Thought</u> from the Advent 1966 issue of Monastic Studies[69] and I would like to tell you how grateful I am for it. Would you have any spare copies? I would like one for the Novitiate files and one which could be shared with active Sisters engaged in Religious Formation.[70] Some of the programs I have seen for "Formation" of Postulants and Novices seem to miss the whole point and ignore the problems of the young.

I am Postulant Mistress here and find the problem of "identity crisis" very much as you have presented it. As a matter of fact, if the paper were not being read in the Refectory, I would applaud. My own thoughts on so many of the aspects you mention are too many to write of now. I would like so much to speak of them with you!

This morning Josie, my "next youngest" Postulant and I were listening to <u>The Man of La Mancha</u>[71] and a record of folk-songs by a 15 year old called Janis Ian.[72] <u>The Man</u> – was a real spiritual experience but the other record tore me apart. I have heard Joan Baez and other moderns but this little girl sang only of violence, rape, prostitution, all kinds of anxiety. The teen agers whose <u>life is through</u> at 21 will be applicants for monastic

---

68. Mother Miriam Benedict was another of the Regina Laudis nuns who were founding members of Our Lady of the Rock Priory on Shaw Island, WA in 1977 (see Bosco 328); in 1989 she was sent to Italy to reestablish a Benedictine presence at the historic site of the monastery of San Vicenzo in Volturno, where she continued to serve as prioress until 2016.

69. Thomas Merton, "Monastic Vocation and Modern Thought," *Monastic Studies* 4 (Advent 1966) 17-54; reprinted as "Vocation and Modern Thought" (*CWA* 26-55).

70. The reference is probably to the Franciscan Sisters of the Eucharist, a newly formed group with a principal focus on counseling that developed a close relationship with Regina Laudis (see Bosco 319-20, 388 n. 2).

71. *Man of La Mancha*, the hit musical about Don Quixote, featuring the song "The Impossible Dream," opened in New York in 1965 and won the Tony Award for best musical in 1966.

72. Janis Ian (b. 1951) released her first of more than thirty albums, *Janis Ian* (Verve) in 1967; it featured her best known song, "Society's Child," about a doomed interracial romance; her autobiography, with the same title, was published by Penguin in 2008.

life in a few, a very few years.

And I think the Hippies and Tinnie-Boppers, the young who have grown up in this flavored culture will find their Identity in monastic life if it is lived with integrity and vitality by those who accept their sexual role as men and women consecrated to God.[73] I think they hunger for the Stability, the Way of Union with God and Man that the monastic life is. And I think that perhaps the role of monastic life is to preserve the values of Love – human and Divine – in all its aspects just as it once preserved the humanities.

Rabbi Zalman Schachter has been urging me to write to you for several years now.[74] There has never been real reason to write, but these past days that we have been reading your article, I have been impelled to send you a note of gratitude and affirm: "Yes, it is so".
Thank you and love,
Sr. Miriam Benedict osb

Dear Father

This little cluster of notes is a welcome echo of much of my thinking –
But there is so much beyond what you are being told – so very much . . .
Time for formulation + explicit exchange does not seem to have come yet. But it is joy to see many of your insights reaching out.

Where is the work of Synthesis + Healing of the Spirit beginning to take Full Possession? Perhaps clues are gathering . . .

In Christ, the Active Process of Assimilation to Himself.
Sr Benedict Duss
pr OSB

---

73. This comment proved to be prophetic: not only were some of the strongest vocations at Regina Laudis in the 1970s former hippies, but a vibrant lay community of young people influenced by the counterculture developed at the abbey (see Bosco 295-97, 302-308, 313-15).

74. Rabbi Zalman Schachter has been the guiding force of the Jewish Renewal Movement in North America; born in Poland in 1924 and educated in Vienna, he came to the United States in 1941 and was ordained a rabbi in the Lubavitcher (Chabad) Hasidic movement in 1947, and has been a chief proponent of Jewish mysticism and its relationships with contemplative teaching in other religious traditions. See Merton's letters to Schachter (*HGL* 533-41) and "An Interview with Rabbi Zalman Schachter-Shalomi" conducted by Edward K. Kaplan and Shaul Magid in Beatrice Bruteau, ed., *Merton & Judaism: Holiness in Words – Recognition, Repentance, and Renewal* (Louisville, KY: Fons Vitae, 2003) 301-25.

## HLS from David Serna, OSB to Merton[75]

+

Peace

Aug. 21st

Dear Father,

Mother Miriam mentioned to me that she had written to you in response to the article you wrote for the last issue of Monastic Studies which we are presently reading in refectory. I told her I had had the same desire and she invited me into her envelope. Actually my response was stimulated more by the evening reading which is your Seeds of Destruction. It was chosen to be read now because of the recent riots which have proven so much of what you wrote several years ago to have been accurate predictions . . . . . more's the pity! This whole question is like a heavy weight on my heart. How can we be so blind?

I know that our life seeks to be a response to the truth of our oneness in Christ and that in trying to live that oneness here we somehow contribute to the coming into unity of all men but sometimes it is so hard to watch so much injustice and to feel so frustrated to help.

I suppose what I am trying to say is that both at noon and in the evening you have given voice to so many thoughts in my own heart and I am grateful . . . . . . grateful that in your search you have remained alive and open, clear-sighted and forcefully articulate. Also, I am grateful for all you have written against war and the present war in Vietnam in particular. Why won't anyone hear?

In any case, dear father, you see that you have provoked lively response among us. May God continue to bless you, lead you and give you voice to speak.

With love,

M. David

## TL[c] from Merton to Miriam Benedict, OSB[76]

Sept 15, 1967

Dear Sister Miriam Benedict:

This is really a sort of round robin reply to all the various letters and

---

75. Daughter of immigrants from Peru and from England, Anne Serna grew up in Greenwich, CT and joined the Regina Laudis community in 1959, three years after graduating from the College of New Rochelle with a degree in sociology. Given the name David, she served the community as cellarer and subprioress, and became prioress when the monastery was raised to the rank of abbey; she succeeded Mother Benedict as the second abbess in 2001 (see Bosco 266-67, 270-71, 358-59, 392-93 n. 4), retiring in 2015.

76. This letter is found in slightly abridged form in *SC* 347.

notes, including a letter from Sr Mildred, as well as the notes of your two novices[77] and the note of Mother Benedicta. First, to Sr Mildred about Fr Clifford Stevens: the trouble with him is that he is an air force chaplain and that means that anything I have written on war or remotely like that becomes not only inacceptable but invisible as far as he is concerned. And the invisibility extends to everything else in that neighborhood, therefore to everything I write these days.[78]

I'd like very much to hear the songs of Janis Ian. Can I borrow it, or better, can you put it on tape? (I have a quarter track Sony, which in fact is stereo, don't be scandalized). While I am on that subject I have made tapes for various people and you might be able to get copies from them. I am just finishing one for the Carmel of Savannah[79] and I guess they'd send you a copy eventually if you asked them. Rev Mother Angela, Carmel, 11 West Back St, Coffee Bluff, Savannah, Ga 31406. Also another one[80] could be had from Sr Elaine Michael, the Cloister, St Elizabeth's, Allegany, N.Y. You might enjoy parts of them at least. I don't sing however.

The Hippy movement is a sort of pathetic children's crusade cum monastic movement, the joy is touching but under it all is a kind of despair that makes one sad. In the NCR[81] the other day there was a picture of a Hippy child on p. one for whom, we were told, the whole world was just one big flower etc etc. But the poor little thing had vacant eyes like an idiot. One big flower!!! Tell that one in Vietnam. Or in Harlem.

On Seeds of Destruction, Sr David, I have added a thing or two in this enclosed piece on the Hot Summer of 67.[82] Do you all know the magazine

77. These notes do not seem to have survived.

78. Interestingly one of Fr. Stevens' later articles on Merton is "Thomas Merton: Prophet of Peace," *Way* 31 (March 1975) 16-25; see also "The Contemplative Witness of Thomas Merton," *American Benedictine Review* 26.4 (December 1975) 295-305.

79. This recorded material is now available commercially as *Living Contemplatively: Address to the Carmelite Sisters of Savannah (1967)* [4 CDs] (Rockville, MD: Now You Know Media, 2013).

80. This material, sent to the Franciscan Sisters of Allegany, NY, is found on *"Man to Man": A Message of Contemplatives to the World (1967)* [3 CDs] (Rockville, MD: Now You Know Media, 2013), as well as on the last three segments of *Prayer and Growth in Christian Life* [6 CDs] (Rockville, MD: Now You Know Media, 2013).

81. *National Catholic Reporter*.

82. Thomas Merton, "The Hot Summer of Sixty-Seven," *Katallagete* 1 (Winter 1967-1968) 28-34; reprinted in *FV* 165-81.

Katallagete?[83] It will be in that. A radical Christian Southern mag. I'll send a copy herewith also.

Really I think that we who have sought our identity in the monastery and found it in the Cross of Christ (there is no other where) must be strong to defend our freedom against every wind of doctrine and the fashions of people who run in all directions and want us to run with them: we have our own way to go, a way of freedom and hiddenness and non-production, and we need to appreciate the peculiar joys and hazards of life in the desert, the paradise-wilderness, the loneliness and love which is our own special way. It is good to hear from the other pilgrims behind the hills of sand over there. I keep you all in my masses and prayers, in the hermitage where I am now. Pray for me too, I need your prayers and your company. Blessings and joy in the Lord and all love,

### TALS from Miriam Benedict, OSB to Merton[84]

Pax

24 September 1967
XIX Sunday after Pentecost

Dear Father,

Thank you for your letter of the 15th and the envelope with the enclosures. The letter has been shared with those for whom it was intended and after showing the enclosures to Reverend Mother I gave them to M. Mildred to read. She is recuperating from an operation so has the leisure to read them all at once. Besides, she was hounding me for them.

The little girl with the sad songs will soon be knocking at the door of your solitude.[85] (I would like to sit Reverend Mother down and play the songs for her before I send the record.) I think it best if I send you the record itself as I have not had very good luck in taping from records. Then too,

---

83. *Katallagete* ("Be Reconciled") was a journal published between 1965 and 1990, sponsored by the Committee for Southern Churchmen, organized by Merton's friend the radical Baptist preacher Will Campbell (1924-2013); four other pieces by Merton would appear in its pages between 1967 and 1975.

84. This letter was accompanied by a photocopy of an article by Stalin's daughter (Svetlana Alliluyeva, "To Boris Leonidovich Pasternak," *Atlantic Monthly* 219 [June 1967] 133-40) with an appended note; "In case your clipping service missed it. / Sm"; it is clear from the handwriting that the note was written by Sister Mildred, not Sister Miriam.

85. See Merton's journal entry for October 18, 1967: "the record of Janis Ian sent by a nun at Regina Laudis. Articulate, sensitive, vulnerable, disconcerting: a 15-year-old girl" (*OSM* 3).

the record jacket tells about Janis and the songs she sings. No, I am not scandalized that you have a quarter track Sony. I thought that you might be shocked that I would play such a record for one of my Postulants but it was her brother who sent it to her and she wanted to hear it so that she could thank him. But I am happy that her pain throbbed into the walls of my cell. Somehow my solitude is more chaste and vibrant for having heard these cries of anguish.

If you would like, I would be happy to share with you two tapes on the Sabbath meal which Rabbi Schachter made for me several years ago. They are very personal, very Zalman, very holy. I have shared them with many people and they have also been to Mount Savior. I am from Elmira and was practically raised at the Monastery.

I am grateful for your study on the <u>Cell</u>, (which we have and which appeared in <u>Sobornost</u>, Summer 1967[86]). It complements so many of my own thoughts on the "cell" which I had tried to put down for our building study. During my years as a Young Professed, the Name of God was so much a shelter to me – I was in a period of great suffering – that I used to run up into It as into a high tower. The Name is a Place for my soul and body where I love to dwell in my peculiar way as woman.

Thank you again for taking time to answer my letter and send your thoughts. It is good to have your word from across the sand . . .

With Love,<br>Sr. Miriam

A drink of water + palm dates for you, Father.
S. Benedict<br>OSB

KENRICK SEMINARY LIBRARY
5200 GLENNON DRIVE
ST. LOUIS, MO. 63119

---

86. Thomas Merton, "The Cell," *Sobornost* 5 (Summer 1967) 332-38; *CWA* 252-59.

# A Single Sacred Community:
# An Interview with Charles Brandt –
# Hermit, Bookbinder, Ecologist

*Conducted by Donald Grayston and David Chang*

Charles Brandt is a Roman Catholic priest and hermit, a bookbinder and paper conservator, and an award-winning ecologist. Since 1965, he has lived the hermit life, mostly at Merton House, his hermitage at Black Creek, British Columbia (a few miles north of Courtenay on Vancouver Island). When working elsewhere as a conservator, he would make his urban apartment his hermitage, always intending during those years to return to Black Creek. Now 93, he says this: "I'm looking towards eternity now. . . . I'm not going anywhere. I love this spot. I'm permanent. I feel steady, in a sense, with life, and with my calling." He is a beautiful old man.

Before the interview, he sent us a "Time Line," which provided us with many possibilities for questions. (This is why some questions in the interview appear without antecedent in the discussion; their antecedents are in the Time Line.) Born in Kansas City, Missouri, February 19, 1923, of Danish-English heritage, the child of Alvin Rudolph Brandt-Yde and Anna Chester Bridges, his family moved to a farm not far from the city when he was five years old. Between high school graduation in 1941 and 1951, he undertook post-secondary studies, interrupted by four years (1942-46) in the US Air Force. He encountered the Episcopal Church during his military service (the family was Methodist), and was confirmed in the Episcopal Church while at Cornell University. Over the next four years, he explored Anglican religious communities, and was ordained an Anglican priest in England in 1952. During this time of searching, however, he had been questioning the validity of Anglican ordinations; and in January 1956, at the age of 33, he was received into the Roman Catholic Church.

That Easter he visited the Abbey of Gethsemani and met Thomas Merton, who encouraged his contemplative vocation. In September 1956 he entered the Cistercian Abbey of New Melleray in Dubuque, Iowa. He remained there canonically for nine years, but without making final monastic profession, and continuing to explore other expressions of religious life. In 1965, he moved to Vancouver Island, the same year that Merton entered the hermitage at Gethsemani. Received there into the diocese of Victoria by Bishop Remi de Roo, he was ordained priest as a hermit-monk on November 21, 1966, at the age of 43, with his parents and sister in attendance. (Readers of Merton will note in the interview a number of points at which he connected with Merton.)

From 1973 until 1984, he lived away from Black Creek, undertaking advanced studies in bookbinding and archival paper conservation in the United States, Switzerland, Italy and England, then working in this field in Canada. Having returned to his hermitage in July 1984, he earns his living by bookbinding, and has also been active in ecological restoration work on the Oyster River, where his hermitage is located. He has received wide recognition for this, and a number of environmental awards. When people express a wish to keep in touch with him, he adds their names to his listserv, and regularly sends them photographs of birds, animals or plants from his immediate environs. He welcomes local people to visit him at the hermitage, and to share his life of contemplation and love of the natural order. He has arranged that on his death, the property will go to a nature trust, and the hermitage will be available for another hermit.

This interview took place on Friday, February 12, 2016.

\* \* \* \* \* \* \*

**Donald Grayston**: First of all, thank you very much for giving us your time, and let's cut right to the chase: why be a hermit? How do you explain yourself to yourself?

**Charles Brandt**: Part of it, I think, is tradition. You know I was a Trappist monk for eight years at New Melleray,[1] and I couldn't quite bring myself to making final vows. During Vatican II [1962-65], monks were trying to discover their roots. So there was a kind of a movement among the Trappists to explore their roots, and they discovered the hermits. We went back, just trying to discover our roots as monks.

**DG**: That was then, as the teenagers say, and this is now: so why be a hermit in the twenty-first century?

**CB**: It still has its place, and I think that anybody who prays benefits the whole body of Christ. Prayer touches everybody. The person next to me is affected by whatever I do. If I pray, that helps them, and it also helps the natural world. I'm very keen on the natural world, and I think that the human community and the natural world must go into the future as a single sacred community or perish in the desert, as Thomas Berry[2] says.

---

1. New Melleray Abbey, located near Dubuque, Iowa, founded in 1849 from Mount Melleray Abbey in Ireland.

2. Thomas Berry (1914–2009), a Catholic priest of the Passionist Order, cultural

Praying, living a life of solitude and stillness, quiet, is good for my soul; it's good for everybody, I think.

**David Chang**: Did your interest in spirituality and your interest in the natural world – matters of ecology – did they always go hand in hand, or did one come first and feed into the other?

**CB**: I was a Boy Scout, and I spent some time in the summer at Osceola Scout Camp in Missouri, where I was called into the tribe of Mic-O-Say.[3] The Osage Nation[4] lived in that part of Missouri; they [the Scouts] had braves and runners, and they called them Mic-O-Say. You would come down as a camper, and if you did well, and showed exemplary character, you were called into the Mic-O-Say; and so I was. Roe Bartle, the mayor of Kansas City, was the chief, and said to me, "You've been called, you do not know why, nor will you ever know, but thus far you've been considered worthy"; and then he gave me something to drink, bitter with the sweet, turned me around several times, and told me to keep absolute silence for 24 hours. Then I was to report to Blue-Eyed Otter, the medicine man of the tribe. He told me to go out and sleep in the wild, and to make medicine, and to take vows to God, to [my] mother, and [my] country. In terms of country, I wasn't thinking of Missouri or America; I thought of the earth, and that was a revelation to me. So it was through birding and Scouting that I got into contact with the natural world, and it always seemed to go hand-in-hand with what I was thinking about. And when I was about five years old, we moved out of Kansas City to a farming area, in the countryside, in the wilderness. Every tree had a bird's nest in it. It was amazing to me, my real first contact with the natural world, moving from the city to a farming area.

**DG**: So it was important for you to grow up on a farm, and then have this

---

historian and eco-theologian (although cosmologist and geologian – or "Earth scholar" – were his preferred descriptors), is considered a leader in the tradition of Teilhard de Chardin. Brandt's approach, strongly akin to Berry's, advances the concept of sacred or sacramental commons to frame the human relationship to the earth (see his article: https://throughtheluminarylens.wordpress.com/2014/12/01/father-charles-brandt-the-land-as-sacred-commons/).

3. The Tribe of Mic-O-Say is an honor society maintained by two local councils of the Boy Scouts of America, Heart of America Council and Pony Express Council; it is not a program of the National Council of the BSA. Mic-O-Say's ceremonies, customs and traditions are based on the traditions of the Osage people. Founded in 1925, it still functions.

4. The Osage are a Midwestern Native American nation of the Great Plains which historically ruled much of Kansas, Oklahoma, Missouri and Arkansas. Forced onto reservations in the nineteenth century, they are now based in Oklahoma.

exposure through Scouting.

**CB**: Very much so. And were you asking about the natural world and the spiritual?

**DC**: Yes.

**CB**: When I was quite young, I felt that we should have contact with God, that we should be able to communicate with God. Nobody told me anything about that, it was just kind of an intuition. I would ask pastors, do you know God? And it was kind of embarrassing, you know, it was sort of hem and haw, and I took it for granted that they should be able to communicate with God.

**DG**: Do you know *The Way of a Pilgrim*?[5]

**CB**: Yes.

**DG**: The pilgrim goes to his priest and then the bishop and neither knows what to say; finally he meets somebody who teaches him the Jesus prayer. You had a similar experience.

**CB**: Then somebody told me about *The Man Nobody Knows*, by Bruce Barton;[6] and it was the first time I realized that Christianity was more than just an ethical thing, that Jesus was really Son of Man, Son of God, he *was* God, and that was a revelation to me that he was divine. He never says he's God [laughs], but that's the theology . . .

**DG**: Divinity and humanity together.

**CB**: That's right.

**DG**: You did tell us in your Time Line that you started reading Thoreau[7] when you were 13. Now, what kind of a kid reads Thoreau at the age of 13?

**CB**: My mother's brother's wife, my Aunt Hildred, did book reviews for *The Kansas City Star*. She did one on *Walden*,[8] and I read it, and I

---

5. A classic of the Russian spiritual tradition. The best current edition is *The Pilgrim's Tale*, edited and introduced by Aleksei Pentkovsky, translated by T. Allan Smith, with a Preface by Jaroslav Pelikan (New York: Paulist Press, 1999).

6. Bruce Fairchild Barton, *The Man Nobody Knows* (Indianapolis: Bobbs-Merrill, 1925). Written by an advertising executive, it presents Jesus as the "Founder of Modern Business," in an effort to make the Christian story accessible to businessmen of the time. It was one of the best-selling non-fiction books of the twentieth century.

7. Henry David Thoreau (1817–1862) was an American author, poet, philosopher, abolitionist, naturalist, tax resister, development critic, surveyor and historian.

8. *Walden, or Life in the Woods* (Boston: Ticknor and Fields, 1854): Thoreau's

got interested then in Henry David Thoreau. He went to the woods to find out what life was all about, and that was really quite exciting, and a real challenge for me; and I wanted to do something like that. That was probably my first inroad into the hermit life. Then again in high school, we had to do a project on what was our vocation; and I wanted to be a fire-watcher, to live in a tower. So again, I guess that was sort of leaning toward a solitary life.

**DG**: Which was something that Merton discussed with Dom James about doing at one point.[9]

**CB**: That's right. Dom James thought that would give him kind of a footing.

**DC**: I want to ask a question about Thoreau. The first time I read Thoreau, I had a particular view of him. A couple of years later, I read him again, and I appreciated him differently. Did you find that? Or, have you revisited him?

**CB**: I think the big thing about Henry David Thoreau – I've been to Walden Pond, and I saw where the hermitage was – was that he went to the woods, and gave us a deeper appreciation of the natural world, what's out there. We take it for granted, when they [the colonists] first came to America, they came to use it, and to conquer the First Nations[10] people, and to use the land. But Henry David Thoreau went out just to appreciate what was there. I think that's perhaps his great contribution, and I think that's a big thing we could do today: show people the natural world so they fall in love with it. That's the only way we're going to save the world: to appreciate it. It's sacred, and we only love what is sacred. I think Thoreau helped us, along with John Muir[11] and Emily Dickinson.[12]

**DG**: In your second year in high school, you became quite interested in bird study, and you had a very special experience with a stream of warblers.

**CB**: It was Sunday morning. My Dad was not very appreciative of my not going to church, but I really became interested in bird study, and

---

best-known book.

9. See Michael Mott, *The Seven Mountains of Thomas Merton* (Boston: Houghton Mifflin, 1984) 286-88.

10. The Canadian term for those whom Americans refer to as Native Americans.

11. John Muir (1838-1914), also known as "John of the Mountains," was a Scottish-American naturalist, author, environmental philosopher and early advocate of preservation of wilderness in the United States. He was instrumental in the designation of Yosemite as a national park.

12. Emily Dickinson (1830-1886), notable American poet.

I was out along the Blue River. I saw birds of different colors, maybe five or seven different species. These were warblers of different species which migrate though in the spring, different species each with its own coloration, oftentimes moving through together. It was a quite amazing thing to me that that should exist, and that I should see that, and it was kind of a breakthrough for me. It was an experience that lifted me out of the ordinary run of life.

**DG**: After a year at William Jewell,[13] you went to the University of Missouri,[14] and met the son of Aldo Leopold.[15]

**CB**: That's right. I finished the first year at William Jewell, and then realized that my real interest was in natural history and biology; and at the University of Missouri, they had a course in wildlife conservation, taught by Dr. Rudolf Bennett. I wasn't a graduate student, I was just in second-year university, and one of my compatriots in my rooming house was Starker Leopold. He was studying wild turkey down in the Ozarks in Missouri, and I would see him from time to time at breakfast. I didn't get to really know him, but later on, looking back, Starker was quite an outstanding person.

**DC**: He never mentioned anything about his father during that time?

**CB**: No. His father died in 1948, and his book, *A Sand County Almanac*, was published a year later.

**DG**: Aldo Leopold spent a lot of time observing birds. Do you still do bird-sound recording at all?

**CB**: I don't, but I have a friend in the valley who does. You need some really special equipment for that. At Cornell, we had a sound truck with a parabolic reflector. When I was at Cornell, I won a scholarship in bird-sound recording. When I was in the Air Force, I learned to build radios, so I did a lot of work with preamplifiers, built a couple of those. That was my primary work for the bird-sound recording at Cornell. At the time, they had finished pretty much all the birds, and they were getting into recording amphibians, voices of the night, frogs and toads and crickets

13. William Jewell College is a private, four-year liberal arts college in Liberty, Missouri. Founded in 1849, it was associated with the Missouri Baptist Convention until 2003, when it became an independent institution.

14. The University of Missouri was founded in 1839 in Columbia, where its flagship campus remains. Charles Brandt attended its Kansas City campus.

15. Aldo Leopold (1887-1948) was an American author, ecologist, forester, conservationist and environmentalist. A professor at the University of Wisconsin, he is best known for his book *A Sand County Almanac* (New York: Oxford University Press, 1949).

and things like that.

**DG**: That's what Merton calls "the huge chorus of living beings." It's a wonderful passage, in which he describes the sounds of the night.[16]

**DC**: What is it about birds that provide an entry point to a larger ecological consciousness?

**CB**: There's something really magical about birds. The fact is, they can fly, they can move. That's really an enchanting thing, but I think once you get interested in any part of natural history, then it opens you up to everything, to rivers and trees and plants.

**DG**: Because it's all connected.

**CB**: It's all connected . . . our community here by extension includes plants and soil and all sentient life, so it's everything that's connected.

**DG**: Do the Buddhists have something to teach us about that?

**CB**: Oh, absolutely. What do they call it? . . . dharmakaya?[17] . . . everything is connected, everything is compassion, and everything is emptiness,[18] but I think the big thing that Thomas Berry – I've read a lot of Thomas Berry – would say is that the big thing with the Buddhists is their respect for life; that all life is precious, and that's really influenced me. I'm a fisherman, and I used to do fishing, catch and release, and I've given that up now, because I realized that once that hook gets into that mouth, they feel some pain, and the Buddhists want all pain to cease, all suffering. Thomas Berry was quite keen on Buddhists because of that.

**DG**: When I was in India, I met Chatral Rinpoche; and every year, he had a ceremony where he would release fish, not having caught them, just farmed them.

**DC**: They were otherwise destined for somebody's plate.

**DG**: Freeing the fish. He was noted for that.

**CB**: Did Thomas Merton meet Chatral Rinpoche?[19]

---

16. Thomas Merton, *The Sign of Jonas* (New York: Harcourt, Brace, 1953) 360.

17. In the glossary of *The Asian Journal*, ed. Naomi Burton Stone, Brother Patrick Hart and James Laughlin (New York: New Directions, 1973), dharmakaya is defined as "the cosmical body of the Buddha, the essence of all beings" (372); subsequent references will be cited as "*AJ*" parenthetically in the text.

18. "The rock, all matter, all life, is charged with dharmakaya . . . everything is emptiness and everything is compassion" (*AJ* 235).

19. See *AJ* 142-44 for Merton's encounter with Chatral.

**DG**: Yes. He talked with him for two hours.

**CB**: Yes, I remember now. He thought he was really an outstanding person.

**DG**: Yes. Much more so than the Dalai Lama. Everybody thinks of the Dalai Lama as he is today, but then he was very young. I asked Chatral Rinpoche's assistant, who was a Canadian, that when Chatral Rinpoche told Merton that he, Chatral, was on the edge of the great realization, was he speaking the literal truth, or was he just saying that to be polite to Merton? And he said, he was just being polite.[20]

**CB**: Really.

**DG**: Yes. He didn't want to discourage Merton by placing himself ahead of Merton on the spiritual path. But back to you. You entered active service in the US Army Corps, and later the Air Force, and you had a number of military experiences, including bombardier training.

**CB**: I was a navigator officially, but I did have bombardier training. You had to have bombardiering to be a navigator, so you could understand what the bombardier was [doing] . . .

**DG**: How do you feel about that now, looking back on that military period?

**CB**: You know, I never thought much about it. The war was going on when I was in high school. My father was an officer in the Air Force and I'd hear a little bit about the war. I never took it seriously; I never thought about it. Went to William Jewell College, went to the University of Missouri, joined the reserve corps, then I was drafted. I finally wound up training as a navigator, and then about halfway through the course, I began to think, well what is this about war? Is this really right? Should we be dropping these bombs? So I went in to see the chaplain – and this wasn't really down on my record, I know that. I said I may be a conscientious objector, I don't really know, I haven't really thought it out. So the chaplain said well, you go and think about it for a while. Then, I was shipped out to gunnery training and then finally navigation training. Things were really moving right along, and I really didn't have time [to think about it]. Today, I don't say I'm a conscientious objector, but I'm nonviolent. That's what Merton was. Merton was nonviolent. That's where I think I would stand. Merton might say there might be a necessity to take a stand, but he was really nonviolent. So that's where I stand, and I would be there from the very beginning, I think, had I realized what was taking place.

---

20. See *AJ* 143; the conversation about this was with Konchok Tashi (Steve Brown), December 12, 2000.

**DG**: Then you encountered the Episcopal Church.

**CB**: Yes, in Clovis, New Mexico. I picked up a copy of *The Clovis News Journal*, and there was a column in there called "The Parson." It was written by Ross Calvin, who was the rector of St. James Episcopal Church in Clovis.[21] He was describing a trip he had made to a place called Tucumcari, a town in New Mexico, and some of the plants and birds he had seen there; and I thought, well here was a pastor who knows something about science. I was trying to bring the two together and relate the two, so I went in to see him, and met his wife, and had a lot of good conversations. I sat through a confirmation class with him, but I wasn't confirmed. Ross Calvin had been a Harvard professor in English. He had to go to New Mexico because of his health. Then I went from there after I was discharged, to Cornell, in Ithaca, and started going to St. John's Episcopal Church; and then I was confirmed. I went to Cornell because of ornithology; they had a department. Then the first year, I decided I wasn't going to go ahead with ornithology, and I didn't know what I was going to do. I talked to the pastor and said, I think I might have a vocation. So the second summer I was at Cornell I spent at St. Barnabas Brotherhood.[22] That was founded by Gouverneur P. Hance, the uncle of Dr. Ross Calvin's wife, and they had told me about him. There was a deacon there from Philadelphia, Francis P. Voelcker, making a retreat. We started talking, and he thought I was a likely candidate for the Anglican priesthood. He thought I could think abstractly.

**DG**: [laughs] You have to do that to be an Anglican.

**CB**: [laughs] That's what he said. So, after the summer, he invited me to stop by in Philadelphia, which I did, at St. Mark's Church, where Dr. William Dunphy was.[23] I don't know if you've ever heard of him . . .

**DG**: No, but wasn't that a famous Anglo-Catholic parish?

---

21. Ross Calvin (1889–1970), rector of St. James (1942-57), was a noted naturalist. A recent book about him is Ron Hamm, *Ross Calvin: Interpreter of the American Southwest* (Santa Fe: Sunstone Press, 2016).

22. An Episcopal religious order for lay men only, devoted to the care of "incurable" men and boys, founded in 1902 and based in Gibsonia, PA. It is no longer in existence as an order; however, the work it began has developed into the St. Barnabas Health System, also in Gibsonia. Its work includes retirement communities, assisted living communities, nursing homes, an outpatient center and a rehabilitation facility. As of 2016, it provides more than six million dollars of free care annually.

23. Ninth rector of St. Mark's; no further information available.

**CB**: It was. The Wanamakers[24] went to church there. I met Mrs. Madelene Hart Jenkins, the wife of Judge Jenkins,[25] and she helped me a lot. I was thinking very seriously then, and I talked to the pastor at St. John's in Ithaca and decided that I was going to go for holy orders. Voelcker had gone to Seabury-Western,[26] and he thought it was a good place. I visited Seabury-Western, but Nashotah House[27] is out in the country, lake country, beautiful country, and that really appealed to me. I think that was the main reason I went to Nashotah House, just because of the ecology. At Nashotah they put a lot of emphasis on apostolic succession. The first time I ever heard of apostolic succession was through Dr. Calvin. I remember once talking to him about succession and bishops and he said, "I'm a priest," and I never realized the possibility of having a priesthood outside of the Roman Catholic Church. I remember walking out of the rectory – there was a hedge along that walk, and I was grabbing some of the leaves – and I said, that means I maybe have to become a Roman Catholic. I was very fearful of that, because I'd been brought up with certain prejudices against the Catholic Church, but that was the first time I ever considered the idea of becoming a Catholic, not a priest, but just a Catholic.

**DG**: I don't see the connection there. Calvin was an Episcopalian, and you could be a priest as an Episcopalian . . .

**CB**: Yes. But I had never realized there were priests outside of the Catholic Church; so when we think of priests, well, that's Catholic . . .

**DG**: That took your mind to the Roman Catholic Church.

**CB**: I made that jump, I don't know why.

**DG**: So, 1948: you were 25, and you decided to seek ordination. What were your feelings around that?

**CB**: I think that, at the time, first of all I'd got some sort of inkling of it from Ross Calvin and his family, the idea that I might have a possible vocation, and then Voelcker and Judge Jenkins encouraged me. I was ordained to the diaconate, my second year at Nashotah House, in Denver. My father came out, and my mother didn't. I think my mother had kind

---

24. Wealthy owners of a chain of department stores in Philadelphia and New York.

25. Theodore Finley Jenkins (1849-1940), lawyer and judicial reformer; he was a judge himself only for one year (1905-06), but retained the title.

26. Seabury-Western, founded in 1933 by the union of two older Episcopal seminaries, has been united with Bexley Hall, in Bexley, Ohio, since 2013.

27. Founded in 1842, at Nashotah, Wisconsin, Nashotah House is the most conservative of Episcopal seminaries.

of a prejudice against [my being ordained]; probably she thought it was Catholic or something.

**DG**: But you weren't estranged from your mother.

**CB**: Not at all, no. I love her very much; she's a great person.

**DC**: Did she eventually make peace with the idea of your being Episcopalian?

**CB**: Oh, she did. When I was ordained [in the Roman Catholic Church], here in Courtenay, in 1966, she came out and spent a week here, spent time at the hermitage. She was quite proud of me.

**DG**: In the beginning of your second year at Nashotah, somebody told you about *The Seven Storey Mountain*,[28] and loaned you his copy.

**CB**: That's right. He was a seminarian from Florida. We were walking from the refectory down to the dormitory; it was a long walk. He said, "Have you heard about this new book, amazing book? It's called *The Seven Storey Mountain*." So when I read *The Seven Storey Mountain*, that was what I was looking for; that really answered my question. I wanted to know if it was possible to really experience God in this lifetime, to talk to him, as a person? That was really a revelation, *The Seven Storey Mountain*, and it changed my whole thinking. From then on, I was thinking in terms of the monastic life. At Nashotah House, I was having some questions about Anglicanism and priesthood. Anglican orders were condemned by some Roman Catholic writers. There were conversations about this, the Malines conversations.[29] One person who took part in these was Dom Lambert Beauduin, from Chevetogne.[30] Voelcker and I went to Chevetogne, and actually talked to Beauduin. He spoke only French, but Voelcker also did [speak French], and he [Beauduin] said yes, they

---

28. Thomas Merton, *The Seven Storey Mountain* (New York: Harcourt, Brace, 1948); subsequent references will be cited as "*SSM*" parenthetically in the text.

29. The Malines Conversations were a series of informal discussions exploring possibilities of corporate reunion between the Roman Catholic Church and the Church of England. They were held at Malines, Belgium (now normally called Mechelen) between 1921 and 1927, largely on the initiative of Cardinal Mercier, primate of the Roman Catholic Church in Belgium, but with tacit support from the Vatican and from the archbishops of Canterbury and York. *Apostolicae curae*, the 1896 bull of Leo XIII, had declared Anglican ordinations "absolutely null and utterly void," and this remains the official position of the Roman Catholic Church – hence Brandt's scrupulosities.

30. Lambert Beauduin (1873-1960) was the founder, in 1925, of the monastery of Chevetogne, in Belgium. A monastery dedicated to Christian unity, it includes both western-style and eastern-style churches, and offers worship daily in both traditions.

[Anglicans] have valid orders. Then, I visited the Cowley Fathers[31] and and then I went to Mirfield . . .[32]

**DG**: . . . which is where I went to seminary . . .

**CB**: . . . and I told them that I wanted to spend time in meditation, contemplative prayer, and they said yes, you can come here and do that. You can follow your own *attrait*, do what you do, which wasn't really true in the long run.

**DG**: They told you what you wanted to hear.

**CB**: That's right. Then the idea of ordination came up, and the US group, Holy Cross[33] and Jenkins, were putting pressure on me to get ordained. I was really hesitant about ordination and priesthood, Anglican priesthood, and even though I was already a deacon, I still had this real doubt in my mind about it. But [in any case] I was ordained by the Bishop of Wakefield – I have a Bible upstairs signed by him – and I said my first mass at Mirfield.

**DG**: At one of those little chapels around the church. When I was a student there, we would serve those private masses, but after Vatican II, that all vanished.

**CB**: You'd seldom get to celebrate at some of the better altars; those were reserved for priests who had been in the community for years . . .

**DG**: A certain amount of preferential treatment?

**CB**: There was, yes. After leaving Mirfield in 1953, I spent ten days at Assisi, then spent a couple of weeks in Rome, and stayed at San Girolamo.[34] Then I went back to America, to the US, not knowing what I was going to do. I had met, through Mrs. Jenkins, Father Paul Weed, who had been rector at St. James the Less Episcopal Church in Philadelphia, and I went to confession to him as an Anglican. And it was amazing. He talked about prayer and meditation and I thought I could just remain there for

---

31. Officially, the Society of St. John the Evangelist, an Anglican religious community founded in the Oxford suburb of Cowley in 1866 by Richard Meux Benson. Now extinct in the UK, it continues in the US with a monastery at Cambridge, MA.

32. The Community of the Resurrection, Mirfield, West Yorkshire, founded in 1892 by Charles Gore and Walter Frere, both later bishops in the Church of England.

33. The Order of the Holy Cross is an Episcopal religious community based at West Park, New York. It was founded in 1884 by James Otis Sargent Huntington. Father Shirley Carter Hughson (1867-1949), mentioned below, a prolific author and spiritual director, was for two terms superior of the order.

34. A church in Rome, near the Palazzo Farnese and the Campo de' Fiori.

ever and ever. He was a real contemplative, I think. He had some land in Connecticut at Gaylordsville, about a hundred acres. There was a Miss Emily Babcock, who was being directed by Father [Shirley Carter] Hughson from Holy Cross; and Father Weed had encouraged her to set up a hermitage on his property. He had a chapel there, and he encouraged me to go there.

**DG**: Then after a while . . .

**CB**: . . . I realized that wasn't where I was supposed to be; and the only other place that I could think of was Three Rivers, Michigan.[35] I was received as a novice there: Benedict Reid was the novice master. I liked him a lot. He had a big blackboard, with all of his notes on it (chuckling). He was a methodical person, with a sense of humor.

**DG**: So how did you find Three Rivers?

**CB**: I didn't really know Latin, so I spent a lot of time studying Latin while I was there. Again, everything we read had to have an imprimatur, Roman Catholic approval;[36] so while I was there, I read Bede Griffiths' book – what was it called?

**DG**: *The Golden String?*[37]

**CB**: "I give you the end of a golden string; only wind it into a ball; it will lead you in at Heaven's gate, built in Jerusalem's wall."[38] *The Golden String*, I read that, and about his conversion. Then I also read *Apologia pro Vita Sua*, Cardinal Newman.[39] I really was convinced I should go into the Catholic Church. The only person I knew who was a Catholic priest was Dom Bede O'Leary; he was down in Louisiana at a parish. So I took the bus down to Louisiana, and talked to him about my thoughts that I might become a Catholic. Father Bede was going to go on his holiday to Mexico [City], to [the Shrine of] Our Lady of Guadalupe, and he invited me to go with him. So I did. It was really a great experience. They have this huge image of Our Lady of Guadalupe above the high altar.

---

35. Location of an Episcopal Benedictine community, founded in 1939; since 1946 it has been at Three Rivers.

36. A mark of the "papalist" tendency in Anglicanism; not a characteristic of mainstream Anglicanism.

37. Bede Griffiths (1906-1993), Camaldolese monk, swami in the Indian tradition, author of *The Golden String* (London: Collins, 1954).

38. From "Jerusalem" by William Blake (1757-1827), English poet, painter and mystic.

39. A defense of his religious opinions (London: Longman, Green, 1864) by John Henry Newman (1801-90), English Roman Catholic cardinal, canonized in 2016.

**DG**: It's the original one, isn't it, the cloak of St. Juan Diego?[40]

**CB**: I think there's some question about it. You know, the first [Roman Catholic] Mass I ever served was in the shrine. Father Bede wanted to say Mass at the cathedral, and the only time he could say it was really early in the morning, five o'clock. I knew all of the [Latin] responses from Three Rivers, so I served that Mass, and that was a great moment.

[*Excursus. On the table in his living room is a small brass bell which was the* sanctus *bell used by Charles de Foucauld*[41] *at his hermitage in Tamanrasset (or Tamanghasset), in Algeria. It came into the possession of a French family, and they gave it to Charles Brandt.*]

**DG**: *May I ring this? [bell sound].*

**CB**: *There isn't much sound to it. That's the bell that they found in his hermitage, in a trunk; and the French family used it as a dinner bell.*]

**DG**: Serving the Mass at Our Lady of Guadalupe was a critical moment, I take it, for you in deciding to be a Roman Catholic.

**CB**: I think it was. Most of my ordination cards as a Roman Catholic have her image on the front of them.

**DG**: You told us that you learned bookbinding at Shawnee, Oklahoma.[42] This was just after you'd been to Guadalupe.

**CB**: On my way home, I stopped in Santa Fe, and somebody there thought I should go down to Jemez Springs, in southern New Mexico, and visit a Father Gerald Fitzgerald.[43] He had opened a monastery there, primarily for alcoholic priests. This friend drove me down, and I met him, and told

---

40. St. Juan Diego Cuauhtlatoatzin (1474-1548), recipient of visions of the Virgin Mary, whose image, according to the tradition, is imprinted on his *tilma*, or cloak. It is the focus of devotion in the Basilica of Our Lady of Guadalupe in Mexico City. St. Juan Diego was canonized in 2002.

41. Charles de Foucauld (1858-1916), French Roman Catholic priest and hermit, linguist of the Tuareg language; beatified in 2005. His writings inspired the formation, after his death, of the Little Brothers of Jesus and a number of related groups.

42. A reference to St. Gregory's Abbey, founded under that name at Shawnee in 1929, a member of the American Cassinese Benedictine Congregation.

43. Gerald Michael Cushing Fitzgerald (1894-1969), American priest of the Congregation of Holy Cross, founder of a network of treatment centers for priests struggling with substance abuse or pedophilia. He was a pioneer in calling for a change in the practice of moving pedophile priests from one parish to another. Some bishops listened to him; most didn't. It is arguable that had the official church listened to him, the endemic problem of sexual abuse by priests could have been dealt with many years earlier than it has been.

him that I was thinking of becoming a Catholic. He took me out in the hall where there was a statue of Our Lady, and said, kneel down, and I knelt down, and he said, "At one time all of England knelt at the feet of Our Lady."[44] And he said, "I know where you should probably go. Some of my men are studying theology with the Benedictines in Oklahoma, at Shawnee." And I said, "Well I know somebody there, Dennis Statham; I met him in Rome." That clicked it; he got on the phone and called. I went to Oklahoma, and I was there for a full year, as a choir monk. I said the office with the monks, and during that year, I was received into the Roman Catholic Church. That's where I really learned bookbinding. Then at Easter, I had a mind to enter Gethsemani Abbey. The abbot was really upset about that, because he had just taken it for granted that since I'd been a whole year there, that I was going to remain. So at Easter I went to Gethsemani. I knew Merton was the novice master. I didn't realize I was going to meet him. I was in the guest house for about a week. So [knocking] I hear this knock on the door, and in enters Thomas Merton. You know, he sat down there, just the most ordinary person in the world. Immediately, I liked him, really liked him as a person, and we talked. My intent was to enter the novitiate there, but he said, "Don't come here. We could make a good monk of you, but not a good contemplative." He knew my history and my whole background.

**DG**: You don't think he said that to everybody, then.

**CB**: I don't think so. I had a different background.

**DG**: Yes, with your pre-existing interest in contemplative life. You were 33, whereas most of the novices that came to Merton were 18, 19, 20. Did your discussions with him align with your own impressions of Gethsemani?

**CB**: I didn't have much of an impression. I could hear the monks, see them, chanting the office. I'd read a lot about it, but I didn't really have any kind of impression about what it would be like to be a monk at Gethsemani, or to enter there.

**DC**: And when Thomas Merton said, we can't make a contemplative of you here, did you feel disappointed, or were you okay with that advice?

---

44. Cf. "Lady, when on that night I left the Island that was once your England, your love went with me" (*SSM* 129). Both the moment with Father Fitzgerald and Merton's comment reflect the then still active ill feeling about the separation of the Church of England from papal authority four centuries earlier. (Our thanks to Jonathan Montaldo for locating this reference for us.)

**CB**: I think I just accepted it because he's the great teacher, and he said it in just such a nice sort of way, just like ordinary people talking to one another.

**DG**: So then you ended up going to New Melleray. Did Merton recommend New Melleray?

**CB**: No he didn't. Bede O'Leary knew some Poor Clares, and I heard about New Melleray through them. So I made a visit to New Melleray, and spent some time in the guest house. They accepted me as a novice, and encouraged me to come at a time when another novice was going to enter.

**DG**: And you were in charge of the book bindery there.

**CB**: After a time. I was a novice for two years. Then later, I was put in charge of the bindery.

**DG**: You were still uncertain about making your final profession in 1964, by which time you were 41. You were attracted to the hermit life while there at New Melleray, and Merton had told you about the Camaldolese. Now, a question here. When Merton became the novice master in 1955, he promised Dom James that he wouldn't talk to the novices about the Camaldolese [CB laughs] or the hermit life.[45] Yet he did speak to you about the Camaldolese. Strictly speaking, he kept his promise, because you weren't a novice, but he was skating near the edge. What's your thought about that?

**CB**: I think it was quite courageous of him. He actually told me he thought that the biggest thing that was coming to the American Church were the Camaldolese . . .

**DG**: And he had wanted to be part of that [in Italy].

**CB**: That's right. The abbot would pigeonhole me from time to time and say, "So what are your plans?" I talked to him about the Camaldolese, and he drove me down there.[46] I have a really bad back problem, and I discovered that the Camaldolese stand for the whole office. As a Trappist, you chant a psalm and you sit, and you stand and you sit, and I could do that. So I found out after about 15 minutes that I couldn't live that life. There was an English Camaldolese there who told me about Father [Pierre]

---

45. See Donald Grayston, *Thomas Merton and the Noonday Demon: The Camaldoli Correspondence* (Eugene, OR: Wipf and Stock, 2015) 26-27; subsequent references will be cited as "Grayston" parenthetically in the text.
46. This was Holy Family Hermitage, Bloomingdale, Ohio, founded in 1959.

Minard,[47] down in North Carolina, a French primitive Benedictine, who was interested in the eremitic life. So I telephoned the abbot and asked him if I could go down to visit Father Minard. He gave me permission, and I went down, and was quite impressed. I said I'm really interested in the hermit life, and he said that's a real possibility. I went back to New Melleray, and I still didn't know what to do. The abbot said, "Well, write to Thomas Merton." Merton wrote back[48] and encouraged me to join that group. He did say, "You may find it a little uncomfortable, after your life [at New Melleray]." The abbot gave me his letter, and so I got the approval. I was still a monk of New Melleray when I went down and entered into that life. And I was there for maybe a year. Then I saw that really what Father Minard was looking for was somebody to run the farm. I had heard that there were hermits out on Vancouver Island [the Hermits of St. John the Baptist, at Merville]. Minard knew Father Winandy,[49] and so he gave me permission – a permission within a permission – to go out and visit the hermits; I was still a monk of New Melleray. I went out and arrived in Courtenay and entered the hermitage in March 1965. Never looked back.

**DG**: So here you are in Courtenay, or in Black Creek. And you've been here for a little more than 50 years. You were at Merville first, weren't you?

**CB**: I was on the Tsolum River, near Merville. It's about four miles west of Merville, and this building here, the one we're in, I built down there, and moved it here by low-bed truck. This is a new addition out here [points to the large deck], but this part, this 20-foot area, I built – my original hermitage. I tore down a house to get most of my lumber.

**DG**: Father Winandy: what sort of a person was he?

**CB**: He spoke in a very gruff voice. He knew very little English . . . you

---

47. There is a letter from Merton to Father Minard in Thomas Merton, *The School of Charity: Letters on Religious Renewal and Spiritual Direction*, ed. Patrick Hart (New York: Farrar, Straus, Giroux, 1990) 262-63 [1/9/1965]; subsequent references will be cited as "*SC*" parenthetically in the text.

48. See *SC* 241-42 [9/27/1964], for Merton's letter, addressed to "Brother C."; his exact words are: "Fr. Minard's group . . . might offer the best solution, if you are ready to take it" (242).

49. Jacques Winandy (1907-2002), friend and correspondent of Merton, Belgian-born, sometime Abbot of Clervaux in Luxembourg; for Merton's letters to him see *SC* 289-90 [8/30/1965], 293-94 [9/21/1965], 295-96 [11/13/1965], 343 [8/19/1967], 397 [9/8/1968], 403-404 [10/11/1968]. With eight or nine others, he established a hermit colony near Merville, BC, in 1964; Charles Brandt joined this colony in 1965. Winandy returned to Clervaux in 1972, and the members of the colony scattered, with Charles Brandt moving to his present hermitage, on the Oyster River at Black Creek.

met him.

**DG**: Yes [in 1967]: it was not a long conversation.

**CB**: I think that he was under the impression that the hermits wanted the kind of obedience they had had in monasteries, but some that came after me were more the free or roaming type. They didn't want a lot of official . . .

**DG**: Supervision?

**CB**: That's right. He was a little bit disappointed in that, I think. And then eventually, before I left Merville to come up here, he left to go to Mayne Island to live in a hermitage there. He wanted to be more solitary. But then he found that he couldn't take it. He had to have more contact.

**DG**: Which contradicts the public image of a hermit. Of course a hermit is still part of the larger human community.

**CB**: He is. But I could communicate with him, probably better than most of the hermits, because I would speak slowly and enunciate [clearly]. He tried to learn a little English from me, but his English was really very limited.

**DC**: I was just wondering, whether bookbinding, as a form of practice, has any contemplative value for you.

**CB**: I think it does. Probably the best contemplative part of bookbinding is sewing the book. It's a very relaxing, I think a very meditative, contemplative aspect of binding. Literature is disappearing at a great rate from our libraries all over the world, and it's our written record of humanity. So if you're preserving that, as I am, you're preserving humanity, the culture, and I think that's really quite worthwhile. It's like preserving the earth. It's not just a job, it's something that's conducive to the prolongation of civilization.

**DC**: It's an act of beneficence.

**CB**: Yes, and it's a slow, methodical work. You're not in any hurry, not working with heavy machinery. Merton, that was one of his big gripes at Gethsemani.[50]

**DG**: Here's one more question. You spent a number of years away from here, doing archival and preservation work. How does that fit with being

---

50. See on this Grayston 207, and Thomas Merton, *Entering the Silence: Becoming a Monk and Writer. Journals, vol. 2: 1941-1952*, ed. Jonathan Montaldo (San Francisco: HarperCollins, 1996) 335 [7/11/1949].

a hermit?

**CB**: After I'd been doing some bookbinding for a couple of years, I realized I didn't have a lot of experience working with paper conservation, and I wanted to get more experience. I had a friend who had a friend in Massachusetts at the New England Document Center,[51] Dr. Cunha. I wrote to him and asked if I could come, that I knew a little bit of bookbinding, and that I would offer that skill if he would teach me paper conservation. So I was there for about a year, and I kept getting jobs. I became head of the bindery. But it wasn't what I came for, and I wanted to learn how to do fine binding, you know what I mean? You do binding, then you put designs on it with tools, and it's called finishing. I wanted to learn that. They had said, we can teach you that, but they didn't have anybody there to do that. So I went to Ascona,[52] in southern Switzerland. While I was in Ascona, I got a telephone call from Ottawa, from the Canadian Conservation Institute, asking me if I would like to be interviewed for a job as conservator. That was a big chance, you know? So they flew me to Ottawa, and I got the job, and then they flew me back to Europe and I finished what I planned to do, and started working for the Canadian Conservation Institute.[53] I did that for five years, and got a pension from that. Then I went from there to Winnipeg, and set up a conservation centre for the [provincial] government there.

**DG**: During this time, what about the hermit life?

**CB**: Well, in Ottawa, I had a flat. I didn't do much parish work, and when I got to Winnipeg, I said a daily Mass at the cathedral there for a couple of years. When I was in Ottawa, I spent most of my weekends in Combermere: that's where the Baroness[54] was. So I was really in contact with the life. I wasn't just secular, and I was, like St. Paul, a tent maker. I was a bookbinder, and trying to live a contemplative life in a busy world.

---

51. Now called the Northeast Document Conservation Center, it was established in 1973, with Dr. George Martin Cunha as its first director.

52. To the Centro del bel Libro; Ascona is in the Italian-speaking canton of Ticino.

53. Based in Ottawa, it is a specialized agency of the federal Department of Canadian Heritage.

54. Combermere is the headquarters of the Madonna House Apostolate, founded in 1947 by Catherine de Hueck Doherty (1896-1985) – "the Baroness" – and her husband, Eddie Doherty (1890-1975), a famous reporter when he met Catherine; later, at Combermere, a priest of the Melkite rite. She was a major influence on the young Thomas Merton (see *SSM* 340-60 and *Compassionate Fire: The Letters of Thomas Merton and Catherine de Hueck Doherty*, ed. Robert A. Wild [Notre Dame, IN: Ave Maria Press, 2009]).

**DG**: Did you feel stretched by that experience? Did you have a sense of pull back to this place?

**CB**: Oh yes. I was always moving back. I was always coming back.

**DC**: At this point in your life, how you would say you've grown or changed in your appreciation of spirituality in relation to ecology, and in relation to your place here in Black Creek?

**CB**: In a way, I'm looking towards eternity now. I'll be 93 on February 19, [2016], so I'm not going anywhere. I love this spot. I'm permanent. I feel steady, in a sense, with life, and with my calling. And this is my place. I walk out and I know the trees, and I know the birds and the animals. They're my friends. As I said, the human community and the rest of the natural world has to go into the future as a single sacred community. I feel that I'm part of this community where the natural world and people come and go; and if we don't, as Thomas Berry says, we'll perish.

**DC**: So, you know the birds: do the birds know you? Do they have a sense you are a person who lives in their neighborhood?

**CB**: I think the deer know me more than the birds, because the birds are more skittish. But in a way, I'm sure they accept me into their community.

**DG**: It's wonderful to hear your story. Many thanks.

# From Clairvaux to Mount Olivet:
# Thomas Merton's Geography of Place

*Paul M. Pearson*

Dakota is where it all comes together, and surely that is one definition of the sacred.

Kathleen Norris[1]

The shape of the individual mind is as affected by land as it is by genes.

Barry Lopez[2]

## Introduction

Thomas Merton could never be accused of being indifferent to place. The
story of his life which he recorded so meticulously is the record of a journey
characterized by place – places he either loved or hated. In *The Seven Storey
Mountain* Merton has a tendency to set up pairs of places, one good, the
other bad – Montauban and Cambridge fall into the bad category while his
descriptions of St. Antonin and Columbia contain virtually no bad images.
In this essay I want to examine a little of Merton's attraction to place. It will
begin by tracing some of the major developments in his thought beginning
with his rediscovery of place in *The Sign of Jonas* after having thought
it would be of no more interest to him after his entry to the monastery,
through its transforming effect on him, especially in *Conjectures of a Guilty
Bystander*, to some final reflections on place in his writings of 1968. Hope-
fully, it will become clear from this why place is important to spirituality, a
topic of growing interest as seen in books like Kathleen Norris's *Dakota:
A Spiritual Geography*, *Spaces for the Sacred* by Philip Sheldrake,[3] *Place
and Belonging in America* by David Jacobsen,[4] *Landscapes of the Sacred*
by Belden C. Lane[5] or, his most recent book, *Backpacking with the Saints:
Wilderness Hiking as Spiritual Practice.*[6]

---

1. Kathleen Norris, *Dakota: A Spiritual Geography* (Boston: Houghton Mifflin, 1993) 131.

2. Barry Lopez, *Crossing Open Ground* (New York: Scribner's, 1988) 65.

3. Philip Sheldrake, *Spaces for the Sacred: Place, Memory, and Identity* (Baltimore: Johns Hopkins University Press, 2001).

4. David Jacobsen, *Place and Belonging in America* (Baltimore: Johns Hopkins University Press, 2002).

5. Belden C. Lane, *Landscapes of the Sacred: Geography and Narrative in American Spirituality* (New York: Paulist Press, 1988).

6. Belden C. Lane, *Backpacking with the Saints: Wilderness Hiking as Spiritual*

## Merton and Place – The Early Years

Merton's attitude to place was no doubt inherited from his parents, Owen and Ruth Merton. Ruth wrote that "there is no more fascinating subject in the world than the influence of surroundings on human character,"[7] and Thomas Merton draws our attention to this aspect of his father's work in the opening pages of *The Seven Storey Mountain*: "His vision of the world was sane, full of balance, full of veneration for structure, for the relations of masses and for all the circumstances that impress an individual identity on each created thing."[8] Clearly this thinking set the scene for Merton's own interest in place and for the influence it would have on his life.

The first half of Thomas Merton's life is marked by instability and wandering. Recall, for example, the innumerable journeys he records in his autobiography. He also imagined that with his entry into the Abbey of Gethsemani in December 1941 his geography would be limited to the "four walls" (*SSM* 372) of the monastic enclosure, imagining: "there will be no more future – not in the world, not in geography, not in travel . . . new work, new problems in writing, new friends, none of that: but a far better progress, all interior and quiet!!!"[9] In a poem written about this time, Merton expressed a similar sentiment, writing:

> Geography comes to an end,
> Compass has lost all earthly north,
> Horizons have no meaning
> Nor roads an explanation.[10]

The poem offers a contrast to the "terrific sense of geography" (*RM* 456) that Merton had claimed in his journal to have developed since he was sixteen years old.

As Merton's wanderings stopped in the limited enclosure of the novitiate, an enclosure within the enclosure, so he began, for almost the first time in his life, to put down roots and to notice the world around him:

---

*Practice* (New York: Oxford University Press, 2014).

7. Michael Mott, *The Seven Mountains of Thomas Merton* (Boston: Houghton Mifflin, 1984) 1; subsequent references will be cited as "Mott" parenthetically in the text.

8. Thomas Merton, *The Seven Storey Mountain* (New York: Harcourt, Brace, 1948) 3; subsequent references will be cited as "*SSM*" parenthetically in the text.

9. Thomas Merton, *Run to the Mountain: The Story of a Vocation. Journals, vol. 1: 1939-1941*, ed. Patrick Hart (San Francisco: HarperCollins, 1995) 458; subsequent references will be cited as "*RM*" parenthetically in the text.

10. Thomas Merton, *The Collected Poems of Thomas Merton* (New York: New Directions, 1977) 24.

All the hills and woods are red and brown and copper, and the sky
is clear, with one or two very small clouds. A buzzard comes by and
investigates me, but I am not dead yet. This whole landscape of woods
and hills is getting to be saturated with my prayers and with the Psalms
and with the books I read out here under the trees, looking over the
wall, not at the world but at our forest, our solitude.[11]

Biographer Monica Furlong says that for Merton, Gethsemani "began
to feel like home, a deeply consoling experience to a man who had not
really belonged anywhere since he was six years old; enclosure and stability were the antithesis of the wandering that had taken up so much of
his young life."[12]

### Place in *The Sign of Jonas*

As a monk at Gethsemani Merton continued to chart his journey by significant places. *The Sign of Jonas*, his journal for the years 1946-1952,
traces Merton's search for the solitude he was not finding within the
regimented communal life at Gethsemani at that time. Each new step on
Merton's path to a more solitary life in *The Sign of Jonas* is associated with
a particular place, and his descriptions of these places are very detailed.
Over the course of the book Merton gradually discovers a new geography,
a very solitary geography, whereas later on, his solitude would expand
to include other people and, in his final years, the whole of humanity.

In *The Sign of Jonas* Merton's physical horizons expand as his abbot
provides new opportunities for him to find the solitude he so desired. In
June 1947 he is given a room of his own for sleeping, a rare luxury after
the common dormitory (see Mott 240). Later in the year he is asked to
prepare a list of manuscripts held by the monastery in its rare-book vault,
and Merton found this also to be a place of solitude for him. As the monastic community expanded, largely as a result of the success of his own
writings, so Merton was at the forefront of pushing the boundaries of the
enclosure out further to allow for the solitude he believed necessary to the
monastic life. In 1951 Dom James Fox created the position of forester to
give Merton further opportunities for solitude in the Gethsemani woods.

As Merton's physical horizons expanded, so a new place for solitude
became available to Merton, a place that inspired him in a way the rare-
book vault never did. Early in *The Sign of Jonas*, after noting that "landscape seems to be important for contemplation" and "I have no scruples

---

11. Thomas Merton, *The Sign of Jonas* (New York: Harcourt, Brace, 1953) 69
[10/12/1947]; subsequent references will be cited as "*SJ*" parenthetically in the text.

12. Monica Furlong, *Merton: A Biography* (San Francisco: Harper & Row, 1980) 129.

about loving it," Merton writes in his journal: "Didn't Saint John of the Cross hide himself in a room up in a church tower where there was one small window through which he could look out at the country?" (*SJ* 109). The new place that Merton discovers fits almost exactly his description from Saint John of the Cross – in a barn at Gethsemani Merton "found a fine place to read and pray." On the top floor of the barn, under the roof, he writes, "is a chair and there is a beautiful small rectangular window which faces south over the valley . . . . It is the quietest and most hidden and most isolated place I have found in the whole enclosure." The solitude of this place serves to reinforce Merton's stability:

> I am happy – perfectly happy to be a Cistercian – not a Carmelite or Carthusian or Camaldolese but a Cistercian and sit in the top of a barn with more beautiful stove-pipes and strawberry boxes and lovelier old junk than a Carthusian ever saw, all alone and *suspenso en el aire* [suspended in the air]. (*SJ* 250-51)[13]

This new place of solitude is a place of epiphany for Merton, a place where he experiences the unity of place and time in what has been described as a "spot of time."

The phrase "spots of time" is "a curious phrase that fuses time and place into one intense, intimate explosion of meaning."[14] It is a term used in the study of autobiography to describe epiphanies "when the internal expands qualitatively and the instant becomes the eternal now";[15] the Romantic Poets called it the experience of the sublime. The actual phrase "spots of time" was first used by William Wordsworth in Book XII of *The Prelude*:

> There are in our existence, spots of time,
> That with distinct pre-eminence retain
> A renovating virtue, whence . . .
> . . . our minds
> Are nourished and invisibly repaired;
> A virtue, by which pleasure is enhanced,
> That penetrates, enables us to mount,
> When high, more high, and lifts us up when fallen. (ll. 208-18)[16]

---

13. Merton is quoting here from *The Spiritual Canticle* by St. John of the Cross.

14. Monica Weis, SSJ, "Beyond the Shadow and the Disguise: 'Spots of Time' in Thomas Merton's Spiritual Development," *The Merton Seasonal* 23.1 (Spring 1998) 22.

15. Jerome Hamilton Buckley, *The Turning Key: Autobiography and the Subjective Impulse Since 1800* (Cambridge, MA: Harvard University Press, 1984) 59; subsequent references will be cited as "Buckley" parenthetically in the text.

16. William Wordsworth, *The Prelude: 1799, 1805, 1850*, ed. Jonathan Wordsworth,

"Spots of time," moments of epiphany, describe "the moment of insight that transforms the soul or, less dramatically, alters the mental perspective" (Buckley 70). They are a phenomenon which recurs "throughout serious autobiography," confirming purpose and redirecting the author's energy. The importance Thomas Merton gives to some of the places where he was finding solitude in *The Sign of Jonas* can be described in this way and is a trait that will become more pronounced in later passages in *The Sign of Jonas*, as in *Conjectures of a Guilty Bystander* and other of Merton's autobiographical writings.

With Merton's growing awareness of place over the course of *The Sign of Jonas* there are frequent references to nature – to the Gethsemani woods, to the rain and the wind, to the birds and the other creatures who inhabit the woods, to the Kentucky knobs, the sky and the stars (see *SJ* 43, 62-63, 201-202, 203, 209-10, 263-64).[17] These references reflect a Franciscan side to Merton's character, a trait which was, no doubt, an element in his attraction in applying to join the Franciscans back in 1940 and to which he refers specifically again in *The Sign of Jonas*, saying, "The Franciscan side in me . . . continues to grow" (*SJ* 211).[18] This "Franciscan" view of nature, though, Merton was also finding evident in the life and work of the early Cistercians whom he was reading and studying at this time.

## The Early Cistercians

While Merton was making the entries in his diary that would eventually become *The Sign of Jonas*, he was also working on a history of the Cistercian order and its American foundations, a history which was published in 1949 as *The Waters of Siloe*.[19] Merton's early descriptions of the order in this book are very "Franciscan" and a far cry from the strict observance

M. H. Abrams and Stephen Gill (New York: W. W. Norton, 1979) 429, 431 (1850 version; the identical text is found in Book XI of the 1805 *Prelude* [428, 430]).

17. For a comprehensive overview of this aspect of Merton's writings, see Thomas Merton, *When the Trees Say Nothing: Writings on Nature*, ed. Kathleen Deignan, CND (Notre Dame, IN: Sorin Books, 2003).

18. In his December 1967 retreat for contemplative prioresses Merton recalls wandering outside the enclosure during his April 1941 retreat at Gethsemani and thinking to himself that he could never live at Gethsemani as a monk because he would not be allowed to get out in the woods! See Thomas Merton, *The Springs of Contemplation: A Retreat at the Abbey of Gethsemani*, ed. Jane Marie Richardson, SL (New York: Farrar, Straus, Giroux, 1992) 25-26.

19. Thomas Merton, *The Waters of Siloe* (New York: Harcourt Brace, 1949); subsequent references will be cited as "*WS*" parenthetically in the text. In editing the British edition, published as *The Waters of Silence* in 1950, Evelyn Waugh perceptively moved Merton's chapter on "Cistercian Life in the Twelfth Century" from its place in the closing chapters of the American edition to become chapter two of the British edition.

followed at Gethsemani under Dom Frederic Dunne at the time Merton was writing. Merton's descriptions of the early Cistercians also mirror his own growing experience of place and nature. For example he writes in *The Waters of Siloe*: "Forest and field, sun and wind and sky, earth and water, all speak the same silent language, reminding the monk that he is here to develop like the things that grow all around him . . . . even the site of a Cistercian monastery is, or ought to be, a lesson in contemplation" (*WS* 274); and: "When the monks had found their homes, they not only settled there, for better or for worse, but they sank their roots into the ground and fell in love with their woods. Indeed, this love of one's monastery and its surroundings is something integral to the Cistercian life. It forms the object of a special vow: stability" (*WS* 273).

This attitude toward nature and place that Merton writes of in *The Waters of Siloe* is reflected in his own journal entries as he became, in words used to describe the second abbot of Cîteaux, St. Alberic, "a 'lover of the brethren and the monastery, the *place*,' *amator fratrum et loci*" (*WS* 273). For example in *The Sign of Jonas* Merton notes, "I found a bower God had prepared for me like Jonas's ivy. It had been designed especially for this moment. . . . There I sat in silence and loved the wind in the forest and listened for a good while to God" (*SJ* 264). Nature, place and geography were providing Merton with a new and different sense of stability, a stability not related solely to a vow but to a sense of rootedness (as opposed to rootlessness), of home and of family, a stability which had not been present in his life prior to his entry into the Abbey of Gethsemani.

### Fire Watch, July 4, 1952

Merton's conclusion to *The Sign of Jonas*, "Fire Watch, July 4, 1952," is a journey through the times and places associated with his monastic life at Gethsemani and brings together the sense of place and home he has developed over the course of the book, presenting a very different image of himself than the one he'd wished to leave behind at the cloister door in December 1941. Beginning in the cellar of the monastery, Merton gradually progresses to the belfry of the abbey church and parallels once again his earlier reference to the place discovered by St. John of the Cross, the room in a church tower from where he could look out on the surrounding countryside. At the end of the fire watch, Merton is looking out from the steeple of the church at Gethsemani, thus paralleling his reference to St. John of the Cross more closely than in his earlier discovery of the "fine place" he found in the attic of the barn. Having found this new "fine place," Merton's final words at the end of *The Sign of Jonas* suggest it was a place of epiphany for him, a "spot of time," connecting nature, time and place in a paradise, an "eternal now" (Buckley 59), and there he hears the voice of God addressing him as Jonah: "*I have always overshadowed Jonas with My mercy, and cruelty I know not at all. Have you had sight of Me, Jonas My child? Mercy within mercy within mercy. I have forgiven the universe without end, because I have never known sin*" (*SJ* 362).

### Stability in a Peaceful Place

The effect of place and environment on Merton continues to play an important role throughout the course of *Conjectures of a Guilty Bystander*,[20] his journal covering the late fifties and early sixties. Every section of this book contains frequent references to place and to the nature surrounding Merton at Gethsemani. The increasing importance of place and nature to Merton can be seen to stem from his vow of stability. In the period covered by *The Sign of Jonas*, as Merton sought to find the solitude he desired by looking at orders such as the Carthusians or the Camaldolese, stability seemed like a problem Merton had to come to terms with; by contrast, in *Conjectures of a Guilty Bystander*, it is his liberation.

The vow of stability serves the purpose of stopping the monk from running and forces him to start an inner journey.[21] In Merton's case his vow of stability forced him to stop running, especially the wandering of his youth, and to delve into his own inner self and to journey towards God. For much of his monastic life, paradoxically, Merton appears as fairly unstable – moving from one crisis to the next, searching for more and more solitude, or for permission to travel, or to do other things which many did not consider particularly monastic. Speaking of this side of Merton's character, Matthew Kelty has suggested it was part of Merton's character to be constantly coming up with new plans, and Merton needed the figure of Dom James to keep his plans under control.[22] Through being forced to stop running and to face his inner self, Merton came to terms with himself and discovered a deeper inner stability.

The stability of place Merton found at Gethsemani, especially contrasted with the sense of homelessness and exile of his youth, was es-

---

20. Thomas Merton, *Conjectures of a Guilty Bystander* (Garden City, NY: Doubleday, 1966); subsequent references will be cited as "*CGB*" parenthetically in the text.

21. Philip Sheldrake has suggested "an engagement with 'place' (as, for example, in desert monasticism's mystique of 'the cell' or St Benedict's teaching on stability) may enable a spiritual, inner journey" (Philip Sheldrake, *Living between Worlds: Place and Journey in Celtic Spirituality* [London: Darton, Longman & Todd, 1995] 8).

22. See Matthew Kelty, "Looking Back to Merton: Memories and Impressions – An Interview," ed. Dewey Weiss Kramer, *Merton Annual* 1 (1988) 63. The authoritarian figure of Dom James replaced the lack of an authoritarian figure in Merton's youth.

sential to his development as a whole person. The Cistercian monk and writer Charles Cummings has pointed out the importance of stability to this development. Cummings writes that "reaching one's full human and spiritual potential seems to be facilitated by some degree of stability in a peaceful place where one can be at ease, sort things out, and develop a feeling of being a fully existing, unique individual."[23] Over the course of *Conjectures of a Guilty Bystander* it is possible to see Merton's growing sense of having discovered that "stability in a peaceful place" and the effect this has on Merton, making him increasingly aware of both his surroundings and the natural life he shared with those surroundings.

In one entry contained in the pivotal section of *Conjectures of a Guilty Bystander* entitled "The Night Spirit and the Dawn Air," dating from the very early sixties, Merton begins by describing "the 'way' up through the woods" and how he "appreciate[s] the beauty and the solemnity" of it, going on to describe the sunrise before stating: "It is essential to experience all the times and moods of one good place. No one will ever be able to say how essential, how truly part of a genuine life this is" (*CGB* 161) – to experience all the times and moods of one good place.

Merton's statement about "one good place" seems to be brought about by the effect upon him of his natural surroundings and by being allowed to spend a limited amount of time in solitude at the hermitage. The influence of these two factors on Merton can be seen in an entry in his personal journal from December 1960 in which Merton records, in words I would describe as a "spot of time" (Buckley 52), one of the first evenings he spent at the hermitage:

> Lit candles in the dusk. *Haec requies mea in saeculum saeculi* [This is my resting place forever] – the sense of a journey ended, of wandering at an end. *The first time in my life* I ever really felt I had come home and that my waiting and looking were ended. A burst of sun through the window. Wind in the pines. Fire in the grate. Silence over the whole valley.[24]

In this passage Merton combines the natural surroundings and the solitude of the hermitage to give a sense of having at last found a home. Merton's

---

23. Charles Cummings, *Monastic Practices*, Cistercian Studies Series 75 (Kalamazoo, MI: Cistercian Publications, 1986) 177; subsequent references will be cited as "Cummings" parenthetically in the text. For a more detailed exploration of the relationship between journey and stability in Merton's life, see Paul M. Pearson, "The Whale and the Ivy: Journey and Stability in the Life and Writings of Thomas Merton," *Cithara* 54.2 (May 2015) 18-32.

24. Thomas Merton, *Turning Toward the World: The Pivotal Years. Journals, vol. 4: 1960-1963*, ed. Victor A. Kramer (San Francisco: HarperCollins, 1996) 79-80.

vow of stability allowed him to notice the physical space around him, space that, as he said elsewhere, he never noticed when he was in the world and more mobile. Dwelling "for long periods in one place among familiar, congenial surroundings"[25] was essential for Merton to come to know God and to know himself; it was integral to his spiritual quest.

In September 1962, after returning to the monastery following a spell in hospital, Merton records his feelings towards Gethsemani:

> Once again I get the strange sense that one has when he comes back to a place that has been chosen for him by Providence. I belong to this parcel of land with rocky rills around it, with pine trees on it. These are the woods and fields that I have worked in, and in which I have encountered the deepest mystery of my own life. And in a sense I never chose this place for myself, it was chosen for me. (*CGB* 234)

Merton's reflection here is very much in line with Cummings's comments on the effect of "stability in a peaceful place" and the way it enables a person to "be at ease, sort things out, and develop a feeling of being a fully existing, unique individual" (Cummings 177).

It is in the same section of *Conjectures*, the section called "The Night Spirit and the Dawn Air," that Merton records one of his most famous "spots of time" – his experience in Louisville on the corner of Fourth and Walnut Streets (*CGB* 140-42). This epiphany has been discussed by a variety of commentators on Merton, so I will not explore it further here except to suggest that it came about as a result of Merton's new-found sense of stability and its effect on his spiritual development.

The "Night Spirit and the Dawn Air" section of *Conjectures of a Guilty Bystander*, like *The Sign of Jonas*, concludes with Merton once more on the Fire Watch at the monastery. In *The Sign of Jonas* Merton's reflections as he patrolled the monastery are introspective and related to the events of his own monastic life and to his spiritual development. The Fire Watch at the end of "The Night Spirit and the Dawn Air" is vastly different. As he passes through the novitiate, it "no longer speaks to" him of his "own past" but "more of the present generation of novices." He found that "their love and their goodness had transformed the room and filled it with a presence curiously real, comforting, perfect: one might say, with Christ. Indeed, it seemed to me . . . that He was as truly present here . . . as upstairs in the Chapel" (*CGB* 193). Having found a stable place, Merton is now able to turn outwards to others and to the world. "The Night Spirit and Dawn Air" section of *Conjectures* describes a truly

---

25. James McMurry, "On Being 'At Home': Reflections of Monastic Stability in the Light of the Philosophy of Gabriel Marcel, " *Monastic Studies* 4 (1966) 82.

pivotal moment in Thomas Merton's life, transforming his soul, confirming his purpose, and redirecting his energy for the remainder of his life.

As Merton began to spend longer periods of time at the hermitage, his rituals and the rhythms of life and nature around him led him to ponder further his stability, writing how "One has to be in the same place every day, watch the dawn from the same window or porch, hear the selfsame birds each morning to realize how inexhaustibly rich and diverse is this 'sameness.' The blessing of stability is not fully evident until you experience it in a hermitage."[26] By the end of *Conjectures* Merton conveys a very strong sense of being at home with himself, of having found a stability that enabled him to truly know himself and to go out to others and to the world.

### Place on a Journey

Merton's sense of place continued to develop through the final years of his life and is especially noticeable in the entries in his personal journal as the Merton Room at Bellarmine College was being set up, an event that coincided with his reading of Gaston Bachelard's book *The Poetics of Space*.[27] Merton's sense of place is also evident, in this same period, in some of the writing in his epic poem *The Geography of Lograire*[28] and, lastly, in his journal entries recalling his travels of 1968. It is to those journal entries, specifically entries from his time in Asia, that I now want to turn.

In *The Asian Journal*,[29] place, geography and journey are central motifs for Merton, and a number of times his spiritual journey and his physical journey come together in an important way for him, which he describes in considerable detail. This integration of the inner and outer journeys happens a number of times, and I would like to draw the reader's attention to four occurrences where Merton relates it to a specific place on his travels.

Firstly, at Dharamsala, in northern India, where many Tibetans were living in exile around the mountain on which the Dalai Lama had made his home, Merton "instinctively [saw] the mountain as a mandala, slightly

---

26. Thomas Merton, *A Vow of Conversation: Journals 1964-1965*, ed. Naomi Burton Stone (New York: Farrar, Straus, Giroux, 1988) 185 [5/28/1965]).

27. See in particular his journal entry for October 2, 1967 in Thomas Merton, *Learning to Love: Exploring Solitude and Freedom. Journals, vol. 6: 1966-1967*, ed. Christine M. Bochen (San Francisco: HarperCollins, 1997) 296-98.

28. Thomas Merton, *The Geography of Lograire* (New York: New Directions, 1969).

29. Thomas Merton, *The Asian Journal*, ed. Naomi Burton Stone, Brother Patrick Hart and James Laughlin (New York: New Directions, 1973); subsequent references will be cited as "*AJ*" parenthetically in the text.

askew no doubt, with a central presence and surrounding presences more or less amiable" describing it as a spiritual mountain and as the "'mandala awareness' of space" (*AJ* 105-106). Up until Merton's visit to Dharamsala in November 1968, he had been pondering the meaning of the mandala concept, yet feeling, he writes, that "all this mandala business is, for me, at least, useless" (*AJ* 59). But by the end of October, Merton's understanding of the mandala is changing. He sees everything he thinks or does as entering "into the construction of a mandala" (*AJ* 68) and records advice given to him by Sonam Kazi that "one meditates on the mandala in order to be in control of what goes on within one instead of 'being controlled by it'" (*AJ* 82). Gradually Merton moved from an approach to the mandala that was theoretical to one that touched on his own personal development until, in his encounters with the Tibetans at Dharamsala, he came to an experiential understanding of the mandala through the geography of the mountain on which the Tibetans were living "clinging precariously to a world in which they have no place" (*AJ* 93).

Secondly, there is Merton's fascination when he is in Darjeeling with the mountain Kanchenjunga. Merton had come across pictures of Kanchenjunga before he left for Asia, and he saw it for the first time from a plane in October 1968. In mid-November, when Merton was at Darjeeling, Kanchenjunga was also visible, or not visible depending on the cloud cover. He found the sight "incomparable," saying he needed "to go back for more" (*AJ* 135) and over the following ten days he made frequent references to the mountain in his journal. He found himself tired of it, "tired of icebergs 30,000 feet high" and of a "28,000-foot post card" (*AJ* 146, 148). For a few days at the Mim Tea Estate, within sight of Kanchenjunga, Merton had the use of a bungalow for a time of quiet. As he argued with Kanchenjunga he also had time to reflect on his Asian trip up to this point and felt he was not called to settle in Asia but in either Alaska or near the Cistercian convent of the Redwoods in California and acknowledged his desire to remain a part of the Gethsemani community. In this time of quiet Merton could reassess his Indian experience as "Too much movement. Too much 'looking for' something: an answer, a vision, 'something other.' And this breeds illusion" (*AJ* 148). In his bungalow at the tea estate Merton realized he could be anywhere; everything he had found in Asia, so far, he could have found anywhere – except for one thing, his own "illusion of Asia," which, he questions, "needed to be dissolved by experience? *Here?*" (*AJ* 150). After having made this entry in his journal Merton had a dream that night of Kanchenjunga in which he realized "there is another side of Kanchenjunga and of every mountain" (*AJ* 153).

In Kanchenjunga Merton sees an answer to his questions – the mountain holds paradoxes together, a theme central in Merton's own work. It has a side that is seen and a side that is not seen; it is a "palace of opposites in unity . . . impermanence and patience, solidity and nonbeing, existence and wisdom." Developing his reflection on the mountain Merton adds: "The full beauty of the mountain is not seen until you too consent to the impossible paradox: it is and is not. When nothing more needs to be said, the smoke of ideas clears, the mountain is SEEN" (*AJ* 156-57). After this passage Merton appears to have resolved his argument with Kanchenjunga and subsequently makes only a couple of minor references to it.

Thirdly, Merton is impressed with a visit to Mahabalipuram near Madras, where he finds "a sense of silence and space" (*AJ* 202), a sense he records in his journal:

Mahabalipuram is the remains of a culture such as I have not seen before. A complex of shrines carved out of, or built into, a great ancient rock formation – not cliffs but low rambling outcrops and boulders, smoothed and shaped by millions of years. Caves, porches, figures, steps, markings, lines of holes, gods and goddesses – but spread around without too much profusion. (*AJ* 198)

In *The Asian Journal* Merton recalls in particular the sea temples at Mahabalipuram and the Shiva lingam:

I'm curious to read again after so many years [D. H. Lawrence's] "Virgin Youth" when today I have seen the Shiva lingam at Mahabalipuram, standing black and alone at the edge of the ocean, washed by spray of great waves breaking on the rocks.

> He stands like a lighthouse, night churns
> Round his base, his dark light rolls
> Into darkness, and darkly returns.
>
> Is he calling, the lone one? Is his deep
> Silence full of summons?

There is no "problem," however, in the black lingam. It is washed by the sea, and the sea is woman: it is no void, no question. No English anguish about Mahabalipuram. How right the "lighthouse" stanza of Lawrence is, though, for this lingam on the rocky point! Night and sea are the same: so they are transferable. (*AJ* 197)

A few days later, Merton refers to Mahabalipuram after his visit to a fourth important place for him, Polonnaruwa, and says of them both:

"Surely, with Mahabalipuram and Polonnaruwa my Asian pilgrimage has come clear and purified itself. I mean, I know and have seen what I was obscurely looking for" (*AJ* 235-36).

At Polonnaruwa Merton experienced the ancient giant carved statues of the Buddha at the Gal Vihara as a "Zen garden," a place of unity in his life, where stillness and movement, geography and journey, came together: "the great figures, motionless, yet with the lines in full movement." As described in his *Asian Journal,* Merton's visit to Polonnaruwa reads like a moment of illumination for him. Only a couple of days later did he feel he could write about his experience there, in which he found "All problems are resolved and everything is clear, simply because what matters is clear. The rock, all matter, all life, is charged with dharmakaya . . . everything is emptiness and everything is compassion" (*AJ* 235). A week later Merton was dead.

## Conclusion

It is impossible to reach any conclusions from reading *The Asian Journal* about where Merton was headed. His time in Asia seemed to be affirming his own experience of solitude; affirming he had made progress in the solitary life and was recognized as having done so by people whom he went to see, somehow believing they had something he did not have; affirming that Asia did not have any more answers than North America and that all he needed for a solitary life could be found in his monastery. He also affirmed his movement from a place of solitude out towards others in love and compassion. If anything, Asia helped Merton once again to break through the illusion that the answer he was looking for was elsewhere. This was a message Dom James had been trying to tell him for many years; it is part of the message of the vow of stability and was something Merton had learned many times in his life but needed to learn in new and different ways. Writing to John Howard Griffin, just two days before his death, Merton said: "I have not found what I came to find. I have not found any place of hermitage that is any better than the hermitage I have . . . at Gethsemani, which is after all places, a great place."[30]

There is a great contrast between the travels of Merton's early years and those he undertook in the final year of his life. His early travels were an aimless wandering from place to place, unlike his travels of 1968, which were a part of his journey into solitude, his spiritual pilgrimage in search of the next stage on his spiritual journey. The major difference between Merton's early travels and those of 1968 is that by the latter year,

---

30. John Howard Griffin, *Follow the Ecstasy: Thomas Merton, The Hermitage Years, 1965-1968* (Fort Worth, TX: Latitudes Press, 1983) 206.

Merton had attained an inner stability and a sense of home, of rootedness, which allowed him to travel in a new way: "It was because he had by now found a home that he was ready to go out. He knew that he belonged at Gethsemani, and that this rootedness gave him a place from which to set out and to which to return."[31] Place, and stability in a peaceful place, enabled Merton to overcome his early alienation from self and from the world and to see the Divine manifesting itself in all times and places.

---

31. Esther de Waal, *A Seven Day Journey with Thomas Merton* (Ann Arbor, MI: Servant Publications, 1992) 29.

# "This Terrific Sense of Geography": Spatial Thinking in Merton's Journals

*Kathleen M. Baker*

## Introduction

Merton's journals show that he regularly engaged in what geographers refer to as spatial thinking. Forms of thinking (verbal, logical, mathematical, etc.) are distinguished by their representational system or their reasoning system. Spatial thinking is a system of cognitive skills that uses knowledge of the meaning and properties of space as a framework for understanding.[1] For Merton, the various modes of spatial thinking become vehicles to document both his sensory experience of the world and his contemplative experience of transformation of heart. At times Merton presents concrete descriptions of the landscape in tandem with abstract concepts, making the spatial connection between these observations explicit. This article examines the varied contexts in which spatial thinking is apparent in Merton's journals and discusses the potential impact of this form of thinking on the reader. Neuroscientists have associated spatial thinking with distinct regions of the brain[2] and recent research seems to support the idea that memories are more likely to last if they involve links among multiple brain regions working collaboratively to solve an intuitively important problem. This suggestion has implications in terms of Merton's ability to touch his readers by providing a spatial framework for understanding personal transformation that simultaneously engages multiple regions of the brain.

From 1939 to 1968, with varying frequency, Thomas Merton recorded spontaneous expressions of his thoughts, experiences and reactions to life-events in his journals. The journals show that Merton's patterns of thought often had a spatial bent.[3] Merton had a strong sense of awareness

---

1. Discussion of spatial thinking refers to: *Learning to Think Spatially: GIS as a Support System in the K-12 Curriculum*, "Part I: The Nature and Functions of Spatial Thinking" (Washington, DC: The National Academies Press, 2006).

2. The neuroscience of spatial thinking modes is summarized in Philip J. Gersmehl and Carol A. Gersmehl, "Spatial Thinking by Young Children: Neurologic Evidence for Early Development and Educability," *Journal of Geography* 106.5 (2007) 181-91.

3. See the seven volumes of journals: Thomas Merton, *Run to the Mountain: The Story of a Vocation. Journals, vol. 1: 1939-1941*, ed. Patrick Hart (San Francisco: HarperCollins, 1995) (subsequent references will be cited as "*RM*" parenthetically in the text); Thomas Merton, *Entering the Silence: Becoming a Monk and Writer. Journals, vol.*

of his physical surroundings and regularly used spatial-thinking meta-phors to convey images and ideas by pointing to geometries and shapes of objects around him, both material and illusory, and describing their interrelationships in space and time. In "Cuban Interlude," he describes dancers moving "in concentric circles like the souls of the prudent in heaven" (*RM* 175). At the hermitage, he notes that the storms that pass the monastery "go over to Loretto" (*LL* 270). On hearing of the death of Dr. Martin Luther King, Jr., he feels the presence of this death in space and time and describes that death "lay on the top of the traveling car like an animal, a beast of the apocalypse" (*OSM* 78). These few examples illustrate Merton's facility with pattern and presence in space.

Merton's frequent use of spatial-thinking mechanisms in his journal is an important part of his communication with himself and his readers. For Merton, each of the eight modes of spatial thinking becomes a vehicle to document both his sensory experience of the world and his contemplative experience of transformation of heart. Conveying his experiences in spatial language throughout his journals, Merton provides a spatial framework for understanding personal transformation that simultaneously engages multiple regions of the brain, creating lasting memories for himself and for the reader. For readers engaged in the "problem" of personal trans-formation, these memories can become touchstones by which they may come to understand their own experience.

## Spatial Representation and Reasoning

During spatial thinking, the properties of space are used in each stage of problem-solving, from describing situations and formulating problems to analyzing options and expressing solutions. These functions of spatial

2: *1941-1952*, ed. Jonathan Montaldo (San Francisco: HarperCollins, 1996) (subsequent references will be cited as "*ES*" parenthetically in the text); Thomas Merton, *A Search for Solitude: Pursuing the Monk's True Life. Journals, vol. 3: 1952-1960*, ed. Lawrence S. Cunningham (San Francisco: HarperCollins, 1996) (subsequent references will be cited as "*SS*" parenthetically in the text); Thomas Merton, *Turning Toward the World: The Pivotal Years. Journals, vol. 4: 1960-1963*, ed. Victor A. Kramer (San Francisco: HarperCollins, 1996) (subsequent references will be cited as "*TTW*" parenthetically in the text); Thomas Merton, *Dancing in the Water of Life: Seeking Peace in the Hermitage. Journals, vol. 5: 1963-1965*, ed. Robert E. Daggy (San Francisco: HarperCollins, 1997) (subsequent references will be cited as "*DWL*" parenthetically in the text); Thomas Merton, *Learning to Love: Exploring Solitude and Freedom. Journals, vol. 6: 1966-1967*, ed. Christine M. Bochen (San Francisco: HarperCollins, 1997) (subsequent references will be cited as "*LL*" parenthetically in the text); Thomas Merton, *The Other Side of the Mountain: The End of the Journey. Journals, vol. 7: 1967-1968*, ed. Patrick Hart (San Francisco: HarperCollins, 1998) (subsequent references will be cited as "*OSM*" parenthetically in the text).

thinking are relevant in each spatial context of human existence: life space, physical space and intellectual space. In Merton's unique way of carefully considering his own modes of thought, he comments briefly on differences he recognizes in his own use of the logic of mathematics versus the logic of language, indicating that language grows into a shape that it wants to be, not a geometric shape like mathematics (see *RM* 83). This passage illustrates that even in Merton's earliest journal entries he expresses what he considers verbal and mathematical forms in terms of spatial properties such as shape.

Shape and spatiality have a long tradition in the discussion of contemplation. In the fourth century Gregory of Nyssa expounded on what is meant by the "back of God" in Moses' vision, for "front and back pertain to a shape, and shape pertains to a body."[4] Gregory was troubled by the fact that bodies can be decomposed, while God must remain incorruptible and incorporeal. He concludes that it is more fitting to explain the text in light of the relationship between Moses and God, rather than the physical reality of God. His logic moves from physical space to an intellectual space, which, as described above, is now accepted as a purposeful act in spatial problem-solving by neuroscientists and science educators.

The logic of spatial relationships between phenomena, whether it be the I-Thou relationship between God and man or the relationship between a city and a storm cloud, follows three basic forms. The relationships include intersection, the place where two objects meet; proximity, the distance or lack of distance between objects; and containment, when one object is completely included or excluded from the other. These three types logically subsume other common designations of spatial relationships such as adjacency and directional relationships of movement such as through, across, towards, etc. The three spatial relationships in geographic theory are frequently mirrored in scriptural and liturgical language. In the Roman Catholic Eucharistic Prayer, as one example, the priest offers the sacrament "through Him, and with Him, and in Him." "Through" denotes a point of intersection, "with" indicates a lack of distance, and "in" is clearly a reference to containment. This language prepares an intellectual place where the theology of aesthetics championed by Hans Urs von Balthasar can be understood. Considered one of the most important Catholic theologians of the twentieth century, von Balthasar emphasizes experiences in which "we are confronted simultaneously with both the figure and that which shines forth from the figure."[5] The figure makes

---

4. Gregory of Nyssa, *Life of Moses*, trans. Abraham J. Malherbe and Everett Ferguson (New York: Paulist Press, 1978) 112.

5. Hans Urs von Balthasar, *The Glory of the Lord: A Theological Aesthetics: Seeing*

present that which is through, with and in the figure. In a further step, von Balthasar concretely makes the figure's relationship to space the test of genuineness, explaining that "only the form that stands within this spiritual space . . . only such form is genuine form" (von Balthasar 23).

The logic of shape, spatiality and spatial relationships between phenomena has been studied extensively by neuroscientists who now recognize neurologically distinct areas for spatial thinking in the brain, as noted above. These areas are developmentally critical for children. For adults, the more brain areas that are activated during thought, the better understanding gained when dealing with complex concepts. The eight modes of spatial thinking include the following: comparison – relating a new place to a familiar place; aura – recognizing a zone of influence; region – grouping similar connected locations; hierarchy – identifying nested organization of areas; transition – noticing change between places; analogy – drawing similarities between spatially separated locations; pattern – understanding arrangement; and association – correlating features that occur together. The breakdown of spatial thinking into distinct modes further clarifies the ways in which spatial representation and reasoning can be used in a contemplative context.

## Conveying Contemplative Experience
## with Modes of Spatial Thinking

Because of Merton's attraction to spatial thinking and his prolific use of spatial metaphor throughout his journals, he clearly models for his readers the use of each mode in describing and solving contemplative issues. He uses the modes not only in isolation, but often in concert with one another. Merton presents a spatial way of thinking about life and prayer without logically explaining his spatial framework, as Gregory of Nyssa and von Balthasar do. In the context of his journals, Merton is completely free to wander between life, physical and intellectual spatial metaphors with impunity and thus leaves the reader free to directly experience these metaphors without the added burden of metacognition. Examples of Merton's use of each mode of spatial thinking are described below.

*Comparison.* Throughout the journals Merton describes sites and situations from his present and past in detail. He uses spatial comparison, in which a new place is typically related to a familiar place, across spaces and times and frequently relates new locations to New York or the landscapes of Europe. This practice primes the reader for moments when he employs complex comparisons between intellectual and physical space.

---

*the Form* (San Franscisco: Ignatius Press, 1982) 20; subsequent references will be cited as "von Balthasar" parenthetically in the text.

In one instance, he compares the act of reading with the experience of a specific type of interior space, compelling the reader to visualize the relationship between word and symbol. Merton explains that these familiar "texts are beautiful in the same way that romanesque architecture is – filled with sap and life and sense of symbol and order. They have a rich unexpressed content that one gets from between the lines if one is a 'knower'" (*OSM* 9). In Madras, just a few days before his death, Merton explicitly compares types of experience in a similar manner after a discussion with Dr. Raghavan on Indian aesthetics, poetry and contemplative peace. Merton summarizes the discussion by writing that the "difference between aesthetic experience and religious experience" is that "the aesthetic lasts only as long as the object is present" (*OSM* 305). The reader is provided with a concrete spatial and sensory association between self and object that can be used in the understanding of personal experience just as Merton's journals come to an end.

*Aura.* Merton uses the term "aura," or recognizing a zone of influence around a particular phenomenon, with characteristic precision in detailing his need for continuing transformation. He dismisses the merely spatial aspects of his own aura in favor of a change in space and time, saying "I must sacrifice this diffuse aura of benevolence . . . . It is not a 'movement'" (*TTW* 87). The transformative aura of physical objects, too, is felt by Merton. On receipt of a new icon, he recognizes that its aura affects his entire day at the hermitage, exclaiming: "What a thing to have by you! It changes everything! Transfigures everything!" (*TTW* 315). In a curious discussion of his life space as an American citizen, Merton picks up René Daumal's idea that the "curvature of space around Mount Analogue makes it possible for people to live as though Mount Analogue did not exist" (*OSM* 107) as a way to discuss the influence of the aura of country in which one lives.

*Region.* The ability to identify regions is the ability to intellectually group similar, connected locations. Merton identifies such regions of both physical feeling, "a small area of raw and inflamed and infected thought and emotion" (*ES* 248) and spiritual designation: "go out into that particular desert which the Spirit has provided for our century" (*DWL* 103). He consciously attempts to combine these two types of regionalization as he prepares for his final pilgrimage, explaining a need "to try to establish the shape of an experience, a pilgrimage" (*OSM* 118). This passage illustrates how Merton's thoughts have developed a deep spatiality at this stage in his life. His vision for the future is a spatial region whose parameters he probes.

*Hierarchy.* The understanding of spatial hierarchy is the understanding that areas are often organized in a nested manner. Merton compares the nested physical setting of the monastery with the hierarchy of the holy of holies, "the basilica sitting in the carpet of fields, like a reliquary containing all that is most precious in the world" (*ES* 359). He also recognizes the hierarchy of self in love both with God and other. He places his "own deepest self" (*TTW* 146) in God and his love for M. in that self at "the very heart of my aloneness, and not just on the periphery" (*LL* 302).

*Transition.* Early in his monastic career, Merton notices that reading scripture changes the light and color around him and "all nature seems renewed around" him (*ES* 350) at these moments. Noticing such gradual change is spatial transition. He identifies the scriptures themselves as causal in the transition that he experiences. In his long walks, he also recognizes the transition from the monastery proper to the outer fields, saying: "I appreciate the beauty and solemnity of the 'Way' up through the woods" (*TTW* 122). He remarks too on the transformative quality of light as morning transitions to afternoon, noting that the "same hills as always" become "a new discovered continent" (*TTW* 321) at a different time of day. During this same time, Merton undergoes a transition from an internal focus to an external awareness of and engagement with "the world," which he turns toward for the rest of his life.

*Analogy.* One of Merton's most practiced spatial skills is analogy, drawing similarities between spatially separated locations. Even in the earliest journals he draws analogy between physical sensation and prayer. When he first sees Fra Angelico's *Temptation of St. Anthony*, he writes: "Looking at this picture is exactly the same sort of thing as praying" (*RM* 53) and continues with a long passage of explicit analogy between the act of appreciating the space and time represented in the painting and the perfect praise of God in heaven. At times Merton presents concrete descriptions of the physical landscape in tandem with abstract concepts, making the spatial analogy between these observations explicit. For example, he considers the "problem of contemplation vs. action – clear as the line of the landscapes of Southern France" (*ES* 344). Merton also draws direct analogy between his own experience and scriptural events. In the fields he begins to "think of Isaac, meditating in the fields at evening" (*ES* 362), and he writes that the monastery "is the burning promised land ... the place of peace ... the place of wrestling with the angel" (*ES* 473). When gathered with friends he feels suddenly that "we were sitting in Emmaus" (*DWL* 87).

*Pattern.* Merton's artistic side is fascinated with the understanding of arrangement, or pattern, as it is revealed in shadows, snow, fields, trees and his Zen garden, "calligraphies of birds and oxbows and lakes and flooded fields" (*OSM* 117). At a more complex level, Merton identifies and examines global economic patterns and dependencies, deciding that he is "responsible to those of the other country" (*SS* 150) because of those patterns. He also examines the patterns in his own spiritual development and feels the spatiality of such patterns, hypothesizing at one point that "the development from here is not linear but a spiral deepening" (*DWL* 223).

*Association.* Merton is also adept at association, the act of correlating features that occur together. In one telling passage, the sight of flying chimney swifts reminds him of the last time that he saw chimney swifts flying and this spatial association reminds him of his exact thoughts during that previous experience (see *SS* 206). As he matures as a monk, Merton begins to experience spatial association as a type of spiritual imperative. The guns at Ft. Knox become a part of his prayer. Because of their association with his location he decides that he is "supposed to hear them" (*DWL* 182). He also correlates physical conditions, "when rain encloses [his] solitude" (*DWL* 300) with his happiest times at the hermitage. Finally, in perhaps Merton's most forceful application of spatial thinking to a tangible problem, he directly associates the "Derby Day place" (see *LL* 54, 74, 108, 114, 117, 122, 129, 346) with M.'s love, seeking it out, avoiding it, and letting it melt back into the general landscape as his love progresses.

## Conclusion

Given the documented effects of multimodal spatial thinking on brain activity, memory and problem-solving ability, Merton's preference for using spatial metaphor to write about contemplative experiences certainly affected his capacity to remember and learn from such experiences. Merton's spatial-thinking tendencies affect the reader as well, not only in the ability to understand Merton's experiences, but in providing a spatial framework by which readers may verbalize, examine and learn from their own experiences. Immersed in Merton's spatial metaphors, the reader learns to compare aesthetic and religious experience, to recognize the aura of the I-Thou relationship, to delimit personal regions of experience, to feel the nested hierarchy of holiness, to savor moments of transition, to draw direct analogy from personal experience to events across space and time, to examine internal patterns in prayer and relationships, and to associate spatial co-location with gift. Readers are not so much encouraged to approach God as Merton approached God, but to recognize the unique metaphors that tell the story of their own experience of spiritual development. Merton's words activate the readers' spatial imaginations, opening them to a new way of seeing and understanding stability, travel and transformation. In his own words he has "this terrific sense of geography" (*RM* 456).

# Thomas Merton, Wildness and
# the Sacramental Power of Place

## Jason M. Brown

### Introduction

In *The Environmental Vision of Thomas Merton*, Monica Weis documents the roots and progression of Thomas Merton's love for creation, which she considers to have culminated in Merton's reading of Rachel Carson's groundbreaking critique of pesticides, *Silent Spring*.[1] Interpreted as a sort of environmental "Fourth and Walnut" experience, Weis suggests that Merton's "budding ecological consciousness"[2] was fully awakened by this timely book. While it is certainly true, as Weis shows, that Rachel Carson's book had an impact on the way Merton saw himself in relation to the environment[3] – he joined the Wilderness Society, and stopped using DDT to spray his hermitage for mosquitoes – Merton was already an accomplished nature writer well before his encounter with environmentalists like Carson.

Along with triggering Merton's own sense of ecological justice, Carson's book has been credited with starting the modern environmental movement. Shortly after its publication, the Environmental Protection Agency was formed, DDT was banned, and the US Wilderness Act was passed. Thus modern environmentalism, which has descended from Carson's critique of techno-modernism, very much in line with Merton's own criticisms, sought to reduce the harm of toxic chemicals, clean our air and water, and set aside areas for conservation and protection. The environmental movement has seen many successes. Interestingly, however, in the twenty-first century, a growing number of scholars are questioning the bedrock assumptions of the main stream of the environmental movement, now viewed by some as perpetuating the perceived separation between humans and nature it has sought to mitigate. Clearly the gains of the environmental movement deserve nothing but praise, but

---

1. Rachel Carson, *Silent Spring* (Boston: Houghton Mifflin, 1962).

2. Monica Weis, SSJ, *The Environmental Vision of Thomas Merton* (Lexington: University Press of Kentucky, 2011) 3; subsequent references will be cited as "Weis" parenthetically in the text.

3. See also Merton's January 12, 1963 letter to Carson in Thomas Merton, *Witness to Freedom: Letters in Times of Crisis*, ed. William H. Shannon (New York: Farrar, Straus, Giroux, 1994) 70-72; subsequent references will be cited as "*WF*" parenthetically in the text.

in an era of climate change and a shifting understanding of the nature of ecosystems, many are beginning to call for a deepening of what might be referred to as a non-dual approach to nature and ecology.[4]

The following discussion will propose that Merton's later essays, exposed to the power of Carson's work, take on the beginnings of a dualist perspective, whereas his earlier writings harmonize better with this emerging non-dual approach to ecology. Concepts familiar to Merton scholars such as *le point vierge* and his attention to place put Merton in the company of not only our greatest nature writers, but also some contemporary authors who are calling for an ecology without nature, or a wildness without wilderness.

## The Trouble with Wilderness

Although Carson's *Silent Spring* represents the birth of the modern environmental movement, environmentalism does not lack founding fathers as well. John Muir, Henry David Thoreau and Aldo Leopold were just a few of the nature writers that sought to address the destructive consequences of colonization and capitalism. It was Thoreau who wrote that in wildness comes the "preservation of the world"[5] and Aldo Leopold who added, "Our salvation."[6] In his ramblings through Yosemite Valley, Muir wrote: "Thousands of tired, nerve-shaken, over-civilized people are beginning to find out that going to the mountains is going home; that wildness is a necessity."[7] The conservation movement, inspired by Thoreau's and Muir's spiritual sensibilities, sought to set aside places of outstanding and transcendent beauty so that (mostly wealthy) people could experience the grandeur of the natural world, an experience that was seen as a tonic for the soul. This national project contradicted the spirit of Manifest Destiny, which sought to develop and exploit resources, but the project was also contrary to the ethic of Gifford Pinchot, who wanted to manage resources sustainably and saw no reason to set places aside completely.

This ethic of setting aside places of outstanding natural beauty has saved some of America's most iconic landscapes from industrial exploitation. However, as some have argued, it has also contributed to the perception that nature is somehow separate from culture. The culmination of

4. See for example Emma Marris, *Rambunctious Garden: Saving Nature in a Post-wild World* (New York: Bloomsbury, 2013).

5. Henry David Thoreau, "Walking," in Henry D. Thoreau, *Excursions*, ed. Joseph J. Moldenhauer (Princeton, NJ: Princeton University Press, 2007) 202.

6. Aldo Leopold, *A Sand County Almanac* (New York: Oxford University Press, 1949) 133.

7. John Muir, "The Wild Parks and Forest Reservations of the West," in *John Muir: Nature Writings* (New York: Library of America, 1997) 712.

the many successes of the preservation movement came with the passing of the Wilderness Act in 1964, which institutionalized our ideas about nature as *wilderness*, a term defined as "an area where the earth and its community of life are untrammeled by man, where man himself is a visitor who does not remain."[8] Human beings were to be kept separate from these places so as not to inflict the damages being relentlessly executed in other places. Thus, though a major win, the wilderness preservation movement could be said to have unwittingly proposed a dualistic response to a dualistic problem. And yet, this model of setting aside large areas of land has been referred to as "America's best idea."[9] However, as we have learned more about the functioning of ecosystems, discovered our impact on the climate through the emissions of $CO_2$, and begun to understand the role the First Peoples had on the pre-colonial landscape, many are beginning to call for a paradigm shift.

With many of the nineteenth-century nature writers, and with the Wilderness Act, it was assumed that these areas could be preserved in the state they were in for perpetuity. Without human interference, these majestic places would serve as monuments to the beauty of untouched nature. However, as ecological science has advanced, we have learned that ecosystems do not exist in stable states, but are in fact complex webs of relationships undergoing constant flux and change. For example, for much of the last century, fire was treated as an outside threat to be fought like a foe in war. However, much of the intermountain West is actually adapted to frequent low-intensity fires. With fire suppression, forests grow more densely, and fuels build up in the understory. When a fire does occur, it rages out of control with infrequently high intensity. This fact came home clearly in the fires that devastated Yellowstone National Park in the 1980s. A hands-off approach to wilderness neglected this fact, and now we are faced with millions of acres that are in need of fuels management. Photos of the intermountain West from the nineteenth century reveal a landscape that is much patchier, more open. Photographs today show a more uniform, densely vegetated landscape that is the result of fire suppression.[10]

Climate change is another factor that is challenging our ideas about wilderness. As species adapt and migrate north with the temperatures,

---

8. *The Wilderness Act*, Public Law 88-577 (16 U.S. C. 1131-1136) 88th Congress, second session: September 3, 1964.

9. This expression is probably most familiar from the Ken Burns documentary *The National Parks: America's Best Idea* (Florentine Films, 2009).

10. See Stephen J. Pyne, *Fire in America: A Cultural History of Wildland and Rural Fire* (Princeton, NJ: Princeton University Press, 1982).

protected areas are not following suit. In addition, as climate change makes some species more vulnerable to disease, managers are not sure if they should take a more active management approach even in untouched wilderness, or remain hands-off. For example, whitebark pine (*pinus albicaulis*) in northern California is succumbing to a blister rust that could cause it to go extinct if managers do not intervene, but this would mean modifying the definition of wilderness, which is where these rare trees thrive.[11]

Lastly, environmental historians are piecing together the historical ecology of pre-colonial landscapes, and while there were certainly vast stretches of land relatively un-impacted by human beings, many of the areas now under protected status, including Yosemite, were intensively managed by First Peoples using fire, selective breeding and horticulture. Much of what early nature writers and explorers saw as untouched wilderness was in fact the gardens, pastures and food forests of First Peoples.[12] The creation of these parks required the expulsion of many indigenous peoples from their traditional territories.

This body of evidence ultimately suggests that there is no stable "nature" out there, no separate domain of reality apart from culture to be preserved. The earth's systems are dynamic, always changing, sometimes in dramatic ways; and they constitute the very processes that gave rise to human beings as a species; and while it is clear that we must dramatically alter our path if we are to avoid ecological and civilizational catastrophe, the answer, apparently, does not restrict itself to simply designating more protected areas. In fact, it was thinking of our protected areas as examples of pristine nature that contributed to the problem in the first place. For this reason, many are beginning to call for an ecology *beyond* Nature, a wildness *without* wilderness.

One thinker who urges us to move past our traditional ideas about nature as a separate domain of reality is literary theorist Timothy Morton. Morton takes the environmental crisis seriously, but he finds the idea of nature problematic because ironically the idea has gotten in the way of overcoming the crisis. Morton points out that even nature writing has failed in its central task of breaking down the culture–nature dualism. He states: "Nature writing partly militates against ecology rather than for it. By setting up nature as an object 'over there' – a pristine wilderness beyond

---

11. See David N. Cole, "Paradox of the Primeval: Ecological Restoration in Wilderness," *Restoration* 18.2 (2000) 77-86.

12. See Charles C. Mann, *1491: New Revelations of the Americas before Columbus* (New York: Vintage, 2006); and William Cronon, *Changes in the Land: Indians, Colonists, and the Ecology of New England* (New York: Hill and Wang, 2003).

all trace of human contact – it re-establishes the very separation it seeks to abolish."[13] By meditating on nature as separate, and then designating wilderness as a separate institution, we have unwittingly adapted to the idea that it is also a separate domain of reality. The fact that wilderness as an institution has led us to develop a bifurcated view of reality is curious. As Morton writes, nature writing has sought to overcome this bifurcation by attempting to heal this divide. And yet, ironically, the writings that most reinforced this view were almost all written in places that had already been heavily modified by human culture or enterprise: Henry David Thoreau wrote *Walden* in a second-growth forest owned by Ralph Waldo Emerson that was less than two miles from Concord; John Muir's early essays were penned while operating a saw mill in Yosemite Valley; Aldo Leopold's *A Sand County Almanac* was written in a family cabin on a reclaimed dust bowl farm; Wendell Berry's *Long Legged House*[14] was written in a cabin on his uncle's Kentucky farm. And even Thomas Merton's hermitage was in a forest that the Trappists had long since been cutting and were just getting around to replanting.

Environmental historian William Cronon articulates another critique of wilderness in his controversial essay "The Trouble with Wilderness." Cronon points out that "only people whose relation to the land was already alienated could hold up wilderness as a model for human life in nature, for the romantic ideology of wilderness leaves precisely nowhere for human beings actually to make their living from the land."[15] Moreover, the idea of wilderness as a domain of authentic nature ("over there") has led us to undervalue places that do not fit within a narrow aesthetic. Cronon begs readers not to misunderstand his love for *wild* places. Cronon hopes we might start to see the beauty, usefulness and wildness of the places closer to home. He states: "If wildness can stop being (just) out there and start being (also) in here, if it can start being as humane as it is natural, then perhaps we can get on with the unending task of struggling to live rightly in the world – not just in the garden, not just in the wilderness, but in the home that encompasses them both" (Cronon, *Ground* 90). For Cronon, wildness is a kind of interior encounter with the beauty and fecundity of life, wherever we may find it: on a mountain peak, in a garden or on a

---

13. See Timothy Morton, *Ecology without Nature* (Cambridge, MA: Harvard University Press, 2009) 125.

14. Wendell Berry, *Long-Legged House* (New York: Ballantine Books, 1971).

15. William Cronon, "The Trouble with Wilderness, or, Getting Back to the Wrong Nature" in *Uncommon Ground: Rethinking the Human Place in Nature* (New York: W. W. Norton, 1996) 80; subsequent references will be cited as "Cronon, *Ground*" parenthetically in the text.

city street. To heal the perceived alienation from the rest of the world, we need a different kind of strategy, one that starts where we are, and does not divide the world into culture and nature, sacred and profane.

## Merton, Wilderness and Wildness

As Monica Weis shows, Thomas Merton was familiar with the nature writers of the nineteenth century: his master's thesis was written on the poetry of William Blake. But as Weis points out, it was writers like Rachel Carson and Aldo Leopold that set Merton thinking about the environment as something to be preserved. Certainly Merton would have continued writing in this vein had he lived beyond 1968. But already in a review essay published in 1967,[16] we get a hint that Merton is beginning to adopt the language of modern environmentalism:

> If the monk is a man whose whole life is built around a deeply religious appreciation of his call to wilderness and paradise, and thereby to a special kind of kinship with God's creatures in the new creation . . . then we might suggest that the monk, of all people, should be concerned with staying in the "wilderness" and helping to keep it a true "wilderness and paradise." The monk should be anxious to preserve the wilderness in order to share it with those who need to come out from the cities and remember what it is like to be under trees and to climb mountains. (*MJ* 150)

The words "stay" and "preserve" are reminiscent of the Wilderness Act's language of the human being as visitor to Nature. The phrasing in the last sentence is lifted from John Muir's previously quoted words. It was in this passage, other essays[17] and his letters to Barbara Hubbard (*WF* 72-75) that we might say Merton "discovered" wilderness and perhaps envisioned an army of hermit park rangers spreading out over the landscape to protect the wilderness. In one of the notes to a review essay, Merton even imagines how this might work: "Obviously the life of forest ranger or fire guard in the vast forests of North America offers a natural opportunity for the hermit life today, and some of the hermit vocation have adopted it" (*MJ*

---

16. Thomas Merton, "Wilderness and Paradise," in Thomas Merton, *The Monastic Journey*, ed. Brother Patrick Hart (Kansas City: Sheed, Andrews & McMeel, 1977) 144-50 (subsequent references will be cited as "*MJ*" parenthetically in the text); first published in *Cistercian Studies* 2 (1967) 83-89.

17. See in particular "The Wild Places," his review-essay of Roderick Nash's *Wilderness and the American Mind*, in Thomas Merton, *Preview of the Asian Journey*, ed. Walter H. Capps (New York: Crossroad, 1989) 95-107, and in more complete form in Thomas Merton, *Selected Essays*, ed. Patrick F. O'Connell (Maryknoll, NY: Orbis, 2013) 442-51 (subsequent references will be cited as "*SE*" parenthetically in the text).

184). In this note to his review essay, Merton is probably referring to Gary Snyder, with whom Merton corresponded,[18] who after his serious studies in Buddhism, spent several summers as a fire watcher in the remote North Cascades National Park.

## *Le Point Vierge*

Writers like William Cronon and Tim Morton have asked the environmental movement to pay more attention to the wildness all around us and the places closer to home. It is my view that Merton's earlier writings in fact illustrate a much stronger ability to see all of creation as sacred, without an appeal to bifurcating humans and nature. Merton, like many contemplatives before him such as Saint Francis of Assisi, saw all of creation as being a sacred manifestation of God in the world. In *New Seeds of Contemplation*, chapter 4 is entitled "Everything That Is, Is Holy"[19] and Merton often expressed this sacramental quality to creation as *le point vierge*, or the virginal point. By this he means the place where God and creation come together, the place where we might find the "true self." In *Conjectures of a Guilty Bystander*, Merton writes about *le point vierge* manifest in the first moments of monastic dawn: "The first chirps of the waking birds mark the '*point vierge*' of the dawn under a sky as yet without real light, a moment of awe and inexpressible innocence, when the Father in perfect silence opens their eyes. They begin to speak to Him, not with fluent song, but with an awakening question that is their dawn state, their state at the '*point vierge*.'"[20] This awareness of Merton to the present, to the true self, is in my view the spiritual language that Cronon hints at when he asks us to look for wildness rather than wilderness. This distinction could be the one pointed out between religion and spirituality: the experience and the institution.

For Merton, this inner sanctity pervaded all of creation regardless of its ecological purity:

> The forms and individual characters of living and growing things, of inanimate beings, of animals and flowers and all nature, constitute their holiness in the sight of God. Their inscape is their sanctity. . . . The

---

18. See Ross Labrie, "Nature and the Sacred in Merton and Snyder," in Ron Dart, ed., *Thomas Merton and the Counterculture: a Golden String* (Abbotsford, BC: St Macrina Press, 2016) 50-69.

19. Thomas Merton, *New Seeds of Contemplation* (New York: New Directions, 1961) 21; subsequent references will be cited as "*NSC*" parenthetically in the text.

20. Thomas Merton, *Conjectures of a Guilty Bystander* (Garden City, NY: Doubleday, 1966) 117 (subsequent references will be cited as "*CGB*" parenthetically in the text); for a discussion of this passage see Weis 55-63.

special clumsy beauty of this particular colt on this April day in this field under these clouds is a holiness consecrated to God by His own creative wisdom and it declares the glory of God. . . . This leaf has its own texture and its own pattern of veins and its own holy shape, and the bass and trout hiding in the deep pools of the river are canonized by their beauty and their strength. The lakes hidden among the hills are saints, and the sea too is a saint who praises God without interruption in her majestic dance. The great, gashed, half-naked mountain is another of God's saints. There is no other like him. He is alone in his own character; nothing else in the world ever did or ever will imitate God in quite the same way. That is his sanctity. (*NSC* 30-31)

Here Merton sees the minute details of a leaf, the particular being of a horse, or the patterns of erosion on a nearby mountain as expressing the goodness and uniqueness of God. A horse is not a wilderness creature, but it is wild. Even the minutest roadside flowers are holy in Merton's eyes. This attention to the sacred beyond the extraordinary is the instinct of an ecology without nature. It is the *haecceitas* (this-ness) of Scotus, the inscape of Gerard Manley Hopkins,[21] and I would suggest, the Wildness of William Cronon as discussed above. Wilderness, then, is not a quality of ecology, perceived as nature, but the very habitat of the Divine encounter always present and before us.

### Merton on the Sacramental Power of Place

Neither would the early Merton see wildness as separate from human dwelling. As a Trappist, Merton was involved in the aggressive management of his landscape. In its most positive interpretation, the monk could be seen as seeking (not always successfully) a cooperative relationship between human beings and God in the making of a living. For Merton, human beings occupied a unique though not superior role in creation. As *dwellers* in the wilderness, rather than visitors, Merton sees monks as called to "actively participate in [God's] creative freedom" (*NSC* 32). As the monastery forester Merton would cut timber, gather firewood, plant trees, clear brush, and occasionally watch for fire from the Vineyard Knob tower. Merton's work was a prayer:

> Now all our saws sing holy sonnets in this world of timber
> Where oaks go off like guns, and fall like cataracts,
> Pouring their roar into the wood's green well.[22]

---

21. See Patrick F. O'Connell, "The Traditional Sources of Thomas Merton's Environmental Spirituality," *Spiritual Life* 56.3 (Fall 2010) 154-71.

22. Thomas Merton, "Trappists, Working," ll. 1-3, in *The Collected Poems of Thomas*

Work is the way in which human beings make a living, as Cronon suggests, and also how we come to know a place intimately.

The power of place is the power of belonging to it. In *Conjectures*, Merton shows how a place constitutes our very being: "I belong to this parcel of land with rocky rills around it, with pine trees on it. These are the woods and fields that I have worked in, and walked in, and in which I have encountered the deepest mystery of my own life. And in a sense I never chose this place for myself, it was chosen for me" (*CGB* 234). Rather than seeing ecology as a domain of reality (nature), Merton's sense of place suggests that the world around us is not a background, not a space we visit and then leave, but the container of who we are. As Weis suggests, Merton's daily weather reports also showed his vivid connection to place: "I myself am part of the weather and part of the climate and part of the place."[23] Merton was not a visitor, or an observer of the exterior environment, but an interlocutor in "dialogue with [his] surroundings."[24] This notion of place constituting our being is corroborated by contemporary ethnographers such as David Abrams, who show that place is not just empty space given meaning by human culture, but a participant in the meaning we make from the beginning: "The world and I reciprocate one another. The landscape as I directly experience it is hardly a determinate object; it is an ambiguous realm that responds to my emotions and calls forth feelings from me in turn."[25]

This reciprocal notion is evident in Merton's essay *Day of a Stranger*, written in May 1965, about a day in the life at the hermitage. Reflecting on his daily walks to the monastery for meals and liturgy, Merton notes: "Here is the place on the path where I killed a copperhead. There is the place where I saw the fox run daintily and carefully for cover carrying a rabbit in his mouth."[26] Places themselves elicit a response in us by carrying our memories. Our experiences are not simply a cognitive process of remembering, but an intimate interconnection between perceiver and perceived.

---

*Merton* (New York: New Directions, 1977) 96; see the discussion of this poem by Patrick F. O'Connell later in this volume (115-19).

23. Thomas Merton, *Turning Toward the World: The Pivotal Years. Journals, vol. 4: 1960-1963*, ed. Victor A. Kramer (San Francisco: HarperCollins, 1996) 300 (cited in Weis 83).

24. Thomas Merton, *Dancing in the Water of Life: Seeking Peace in the Hermitage. Journals, vol. 5: 1963-1965*, ed. Robert E. Daggy (San Francisco: HarperCollins, 1997) 48.

25. David Abrams, *Spell of the Sensuous* (New York: Vintage, 1997) 33.

26. Thomas Merton, *Day of a Stranger* (Salt Lake City: Gibbs M. Smith, 1981) 55; *SE* 238.

## Conclusion

Through his readings of writers of the emerging wilderness movement, Merton was certainly in favor of the legal designation of more wilderness areas (as am I). But Merton's earlier writings point to the deep possibilities of dwelling in particular places and getting to know particular species in the stillness of contemplation. While nature writers seek to draw us toward the vast wildernesses of National Parks and Forests, may we *also* deepen our sense of the wildness in the places we call home.

# The Persistence of Harlem in the Life and Legacy of Thomas Merton

*Michael N. McGregor*

One summer night in a year America would go to war, Thomas Merton stood in an unfamiliar and probably dingy room in upper Manhattan, sorting women's dresses and shoes. The room was a clothing-strewn, street-level storefront in a tenement building on 135th Street in Harlem, and by the time Merton had finished his sorting, his hands were "thick with the gray dirt" left by the whitening used on the shoes.[1] In his journal the following day, he wrote: "You don't get sentimental or exalted, sorting dresses in an old store in a tenement. You work . . . there is nothing aesthetic about it" (*RM* 385).

In many ways Merton's life had been more aesthetic than practical up to that point, more abstract and philosophical than concrete and real. Even the previous work he had done – writing and teaching – had been more mental than physical. And his previous experiences of Harlem had all been, to some extent, "aesthetic." During his days at Columbia College in the 1930s, he'd traveled the short distance north to Harlem's Apollo Theater to listen to jazz musicians. Later, while living in lower Manhattan, he'd wandered the Harlem nights in the footsteps of poet Federico Garcia Lorca, listening as "black men, befuddled, went wailing" in a place where "under the skins, blood is raging."[2] Garcia Lorca's depictions of African-American life were gritty in places, even grotesque, but mostly they were surreal. They left an impression on Merton, but it was an intellectual impression, an "aesthetic" impression, not the kind that comes from personal experience – the kind that can change a life.

It wasn't until Merton touched those dresses, felt the dirt from those shoes, and saw the people his sorting efforts were helping, that he understood at a deeper level – the level of empathy and compassion – what actual poverty and degradation were like: the unsentimental conditions of daily Harlem life. It wasn't until he saw with his eyes and felt in his heart what it meant to be truly broken in spirit that he could let go of his

---

1. Thomas Merton, *Run to the Mountain: The Story of a Vocation. Journals, vol. 1: 1939-1941*, ed. Patrick Hart (San Francisco: HarperCollins, 1995), 384 [8/15/41]; subsequent references will be cited as "*RM*" parenthetically in the text..

2. Federico Garcia Lorca, *Poet in New York*, trans. Ben Belitt (New York: Grove Press, 1955) 21.

theoretical view of himself and others. Harlem, he saw, like the monastery he was longing to enter, was a world set apart, but "it was a world more real and more concrete than a monastery, in which the imitation of Christ was literal and actual."[3] Merton spent only a handful of nights in Harlem that summer of 1941, but what he experienced there deeply impacted his life, altering his understanding not only of poverty but also of what sociologists call *the other*.

In *The Life You Save May Be Your Own*, Paul Elie calls Merton's announcement to his friends in the fall of 1941 that he was going to "live in Harlem for good. . . . certainly the most surprising twist in *The Seven Storey Mountain*. After two hundred pages of medieval Catholicism, grounded in the distinctions of scholastic philosophy," Elie writes, "suddenly Merton is asking blunt questions: Shouldn't the imitation of Christ consist in living the way Christ lived, nothing less, nothing more? Why don't Christians love their neighbors as themselves, as the Gospel instructs? Where are the saints, not to minister to the poor, but to do away with poverty?" (Elie 129).

Suddenly poverty, which Merton has hardly touched on before, has become the most important consideration in his life. This is even truer in the journal entries written during and after his time in Harlem. On September 1, 1941, for example, shortly after leaving Harlem, he sets down a long reflection on laws meant to feed the poor (see *RM* 389-91). And on September 4, after musing about suffering and tribulation, he writes: "I am disgusted to read myself writing like an ascetic when I have never suffered anything or denied myself anything" (*RM* 401). Later in this same entry he tells himself that he should seek to become "totally, voluntarily" poor before asking God to bless him with the kind of suffering that will make him rely on God alone. In a brief amount of time poverty has become his shorthand, his touchstone, for faith itself, a sign of one's willingness to give himself freely and absolutely to God.

So how did the change, the "surprising twist" Elie notes, come about? And how did it affect Merton's life? It began in a confluence of events. Merton had spent Easter week in 1941 on retreat at the Abbey of Gethsemani and emerged wanting to become a Trappist – if that was God's will and if the past that had prevented him earlier from becoming a Franciscan didn't keep him out of this order, too. His desire to become a Trappist was so strong that he was afraid to ask either the Gethsemani abbot or his own spiritual director, Father Philotheus Boehner, to render a ruling on his fit-

---

3. Paul Elie, *The Life You Save May Be Your Own: An American Pilgrimage* (New York: Farrar, Straus & Giroux, 2003) 129; subsequent references will be cited as "Elie" parenthetically in the text.

ness for becoming a monk. He feared, as he writes in the *The Seven Storey Mountain*, "an ultimate refusal."[4] And so he returned to his teaching at St. Bonaventure College and bided his time, until a woman who worked in Harlem, a formidable figure with steely convictions, thrust her cause and her presence into his life. Faced suddenly with the chance and the challenge to move beyond his comfortable life, he felt compelled to act.

As he tells the story in his autobiography, Merton was climbing the stairs in St. Bonaventure's Alumni Hall to see who the campus lecturer was that evening when he heard someone "speaking with great vehemence" (*SSM* 340). Stepping into the theater on the second floor, he saw a woman "dressed in clothes that were nondescript and plain, even poor," whose strong opinions were having a powerful effect on the priests and nuns in attendance. He knew right away that this was the Baroness Catherine de Hueck, "who was working among the Negroes in Harlem" (*SSM* 340).

Whatever Merton thought working among that population meant, he was unprepared for the Baroness's message, which she delivered in simple, blunt words. If Catholics "were able to see Harlem, as they ought to see it, with the eyes of faith," she said, "they would not be able to stay away from such a place. Hundreds of priests and lay-people would give up everything to go there and try to do something to relieve the tremendous misery, the poverty, sickness, degradation and dereliction of a race that was being crushed and perverted, morally and physically, under the burden of a colossal economic injustice" (*SSM* 341).

Her arguments alone were convincing, but it was the Baroness's manner, her *presence*, that made the greater impact on Merton. Here, he thought, was a woman living "the pure essence of the Franciscan apostolate of poverty, without the vows taken by the Friars Minor" (*SSM* 343). Here was a woman risking her life for the Gospel – a woman truly living her faith. When he ran into her again the next day, he asked if he could join her that summer. "'Sure,' she said, 'come on'" (*SSM* 344).

Although she was born into a wealthy Orthodox family in Russia, Catherine de Hueck always felt a particular compassion for the poor. While still a young girl, she took down a crucifix and tried to clean the blood from Jesus's body, hoping thereby to alleviate his suffering – a suffering she came to associate with that of the poor. After seeing the horrors of World War I up-close as a nurse and then fleeing the Bolshevik Revolution, she converted to Catholicism in England and worked in Canada as a laundress, a maid and a waitress, striving to feed her son and her ailing husband. When troubles in her marriage led to divorce (and then

---

4. Thomas Merton, *The Seven Storey Mountain* (New York: Harcourt, Brace, 1948) 333: subsequent references will be cited as "*SSM*" parenthetically in the text.

annulment), she found herself able to earn much more than she needed giving lectures about her life. She could have settled into a comfortable routine, but the thought of Jesus' call to the rich man to sell all he had and give it to the poor tormented her until she did exactly that. Moving into a Toronto slum, she committed herself to serving whatever needs were right in front of her. In time she moved to Harlem to do the same thing there and her efforts grew into the wide-ranging services of the lay mission called Friendship House.[5]

But Friendship House wasn't just another Christian charity helping the poor. According to historian Karen Joy Johnson, the Baroness and those who gathered around her believed that the primary duty of American Catholics was, as the Baroness put it, to "liberate Christ in the Negro."[6] It was more than being poor that made the African Americans in Harlem her target; it was their societal condition, their unique position as America's most destitute and despised.

"It is quite conceivable," she wrote, "that [Christ would say to an American Catholic] I was hungry for the justice of my Father and you did not give me to eat. And I was thirsty for friendship and understanding and you did not give me to drink. And I was naked of any privileges and rights belonging to me as a human being such as the right to work, the right to the pursuit of happiness, and you did not clothe me with them. And I was in prison, the bars of which were made not of iron or steel but prejudice and discrimination, and you neither broke those bars nor visited me. And I was sick with despair and loneliness and you did not minister unto me" (Johnson 58). In answer to the sinner's question of when he had seen these needs and left them untended, Christ would then say, "I was in the American Negro, and you – you were a white American Catholic" (Johnson 59).

During the two weeks he worked in Harlem, Merton was immersed in this spirit as well as a related belief: that one could only truly serve the black poor – the person of Christ – if one became indigent oneself. In the days and then weeks after he left Harlem at the end of that August, Merton felt an almost unbearable pressure to do something other than what he was doing. Teaching at St. Bonaventure, he wrote, was only "a sort of harmless hobby: about on the plane of stamp-collecting."[7] Although he

---

5. See madonnahouse.org/doherty (accessed 14 June 2015).

6. Karen Joy Johnson, "Healing the Mystical Body: Catholic Attempts to Overcome the Racial Divide in Chicago, 1930-1948," in *Christians and the Color Line: Race and Religion After* Divided by Faith (New York: Oxford University Press, 2014) 58; subsequent references will be cited as "Johnson" parenthetically in the text.

7. Thomas Merton to Catherine de Hueck, Nov. 10, 1941, in Thomas Merton and

appreciated the peacefulness in his life, the chance to pray quietly and go to Mass without the world's needs intruding, he felt increasingly that he had to give himself more completely to God, to lose the things that kept him from living by faith alone. He still held out hope that he could become a Trappist, but under the Baroness's influence, he began to believe that he was being called to Harlem. "It is no use waiting now," he wrote in his journal on November 4; "I desire very much to begin to live in poverty, more than anything on earth. And this is a chance, and I pray that I may take it, and not lose it, and begin now to really follow Christ as He told us to" (*RM* 451).

Six days later, he sent a letter to the Baroness, implying without clearly stating that he would be returning to Harlem. "This is all the more remarkable because my body is terrifically afraid," he wrote.

Afraid of bedbugs. Afraid of exchanging this nice healthy mountain for a slum full of pestilences. Afraid of being cold and hungry. Afraid of losing all the nice consolations, the quiet and good and fruitful kind of prayer that is possible here. Afraid I may never write anything decent again. Afraid of being beaten up. Etc. You can't guess the number of things I am afraid of, or maybe you can. I guess everybody is afraid of the same things. But none of these fears have any power as a reasonable argument as to what is God's will, which seems to be quite clearly that I must face them: and if it is God's will that I face them, He will make it His affair to see that I get through things that I would run a million miles from, left to myself. Saying it all over bluntly: my whole nature is completely horrified at the idea of living in Harlem, and yet what my nature has to say on this subject does not seem, right now, to have much meaning.[8]

Merton, of course, didn't return to Harlem to face his fears or learn to rely solely on God in that place. On November 27, after numerous journal entries about his desire to give himself over to Holy Poverty and "prayer, meditation, writing, work" (*RM* 451; see also *RM* 447-48) – usually in that order – he finally put the question to himself straight: "should I be going to Harlem or the Trappists?" He still didn't know if becoming a Trappist was even an option, but he seemed ready at last to face his fear of an

---

Catherine de Hueck Doherty, *Compassionate Fire: The Letters of Thomas Merton and Catherine de Hueck Doherty*, ed. Robert A. Wild (Notre Dame, IN: Ave Maria Press, 2009) 18.

8. Thomas Merton to Catherine de Hueck, Nov. 10, 1941, Merton Archives, Thomas Merton Center, Bellarmine University, Louisville, KY (section omitted in published version of letter).

"ultimate refusal" and find out. On November 27 he wrote in his journal:

> If I really had a choice, what would send me to Harlem rather than the Trappists? Would it be the following combination of good and bad reasons: that there would be real poverty (insecurity) but also I would be independent, continue to write, be able to circulate in the world and its life . . . but be able to help people and work in a place which cries out for help. The good reasons do not apply only to Harlem. I would have to renounce perhaps *more* to enter the Trappists. That would be the one place where I would give up *everything*. Also, anyone who believes in the Mystical Body of Christ realizes I could do as much for the Church and my brothers in the world at Gethsemani, as in Harlem. (*RM* 455-56)

The poverty he ultimately gave himself over to was an absolute poverty lived in physical isolation from, rather than proximity to, those in the world who weren't fellow monks – a devotion to God in solitude and contemplation rather than charity and ministry. But as his descriptions of Harlem in *The Seven Storey Mountain* (descriptions the Black Panther leader Eldridge Cleaver thought as powerful as "the words of any spokesman of the oppressed in any land"[9]) and his later turn back toward the world make clear, Harlem and the manner of serving Christ it offered had lodged themselves deeply inside him. They had, in fact, profoundly transformed him, showing him that poverty meant more than simply not having possessions, that following Jesus meant more than saving his own soul, and that he could not look for the answers to existential questions only in his own experience and understanding.

Perhaps nothing he wrote about Harlem expressed its effect on him as well as his description of an old black woman – "thin, quiet, worn out, dying of cancer" – who lived in the same building as many of the Friendship House workers and was said to have visions of the Virgin Mary (see *SSM* 348). It was this woman, he says in his November 30 journal entry, who made him think about staying in Harlem in the first place (see *RM* 464). "The only time I spoke to her and got a good look at her," he wrote,

> I realized one thing: she possessed the secret of Harlem, she knew the way out of the labyrinth. For her the paradox had ceased to exist, she was no longer in the cauldron, except by the pure accident of physical presence, which counts for nothing since the cauldron is almost entirely of the moral order. And when I saw her and spoke to her, I saw in this tired, serene, and holy face the patience and joy of the

---

9. Eldridge Cleaver, *Soul on Ice* (New York: Dell, 1968) 35.

martyrs and the clear, unquenchable light of sanctity. She and some other Catholic women were sitting on chairs by the doorsteps of the building, in the relatively cool street, in the early evening: and the group they made, there, in the midst of the turmoil of the lost crowd, astounded the passer-by with the sense of peace, of conquest: that deep, deep, unfathomable, shining peace that is in the eyes of Negro women who are really full of belief! Seeing the boys and girls in the library, I had got some insight into the problem of Harlem. Here, just across the street, I saw the solution, the only solution: faith, sanctity. It was not far to seek. (*SSM* 348)

The solution Merton found in the woman's face wasn't just to the problems of Harlem but also, and even more, to the question of how to live in a world that is selfish, discriminatory, corrupt and violent. It wasn't an abstract solution, an intellectual solution, or even a corporate one. It was an individual solution, for both the woman and for him: patience and faith and joy and sanctity. And it was significant, both then and later, that he had found it in the face of a sick old woman in the most neglected neighborhood in the country, the black face of one of the least exalted people he had ever seen: poor, despised and other. Merton's most powerful descriptions of Harlem – the ones that impressed Eldridge Cleaver – are general and synoptic, but his description of this one woman without a name is singular and specific. Her face was still vivid to him when he wrote his autobiography five years later and, I believe, in the years after that when he turned again toward the world.

Merton never directly credited his time in Harlem with helping him see the needs of the oppressed people who, in the '50s and '60s, rose up in Asia and Latin America and on the streets of our own country to fight for equal rights. But there can be little doubt that his Harlem encounters with the poor and despised, like the unnamed woman, fueled his call for a sympathetic, moral response. It wasn't just that he'd had flesh-and-blood encounters with people his native culture – the dominant American white culture – had long defined, generally and abstractly, as inferior. It was also that he had come to understand what true poverty and humility were, and he had embraced them, thereby relinquishing the supposed superiority and authority his whiteness gave him.

In *Orientalism*, the 1978 book that helped establish the post-colonialist concept of "the other" in sociological and literary circles, Edward Said calls "the idea of European identity as a superior one in comparison with all the non-European peoples and cultures" the main reason for the "us" vs. "them" mentality that has long dominated relations between developed and developing countries.[10] This is more than a political identity, Said says. It is also a cultural one, embedded so securely in our Western thinking that we cannot see those of other races and geographical areas as anything but inferior, no matter how enlightened we think we are. In fact, he writes, this idea is central to our understanding of ourselves. "European culture gained in strength and identity," he writes, "by setting itself off against the Orient as a sort of surrogate and even underground self" (Said 3). It doesn't take much thought or transference to see that his description of European ideas about and relations with the Orient also describes white America's attitudes and approaches to black America. Central to this kind of superior self-definition is the idea that those who differ from "us" in some external way are also different from us in constitution and ability: we are we, an exceptional country and culture, and they are "other."

It is clear from how Merton described his encounters at Friendship House and the thoughts that flowed from them that Harlem helped him see black America as both the suffering extreme of what white American culture does to people and an alternative culture that, despite all it has had to endure, is already superior to white culture. "The most terrible thing about it," he writes in *The Seven Storey Mountain*, "is that there is not a Negro in the whole place who does not realize, somewhere in the depths of his nature, that the culture of the white men is not worth the dirt in Harlem's gutters. They sense that the whole thing is rotten, that it is a fake, that it is spurious, empty, a shadow of nothingness" (*SSM* 345-46).

Merton spent only two weeks of evenings in Harlem, yet his time there – his only real exposure to those at the bottom of our economic, social and racial scales – galvanized his understanding of true poverty and humility, the oneness of humanity at the level of the personal encounter, and the often superior contributions those we think of as "other" can make when we allow them equal agency and respect. Even a cursory look at books such as *Seeds of Destruction*,[11] *Faith and Violence*[12] or his collected journals will show that these understandings came to full flower in later life. In writing about Martin Luther King, Jr. and his nonviolent approach to the African-American fight for equality, in particular, he states repeatedly that King and his followers were sacrificing themselves for the advancement not only of black Americans but also of white Americans,

---

10. Edward W. Said, *Orientalism* (New York: Vintage Books, 1979) 7; subsequent references will be cited as "Said" parenthetically in the text.

11. Thomas Merton, *Seeds of Destruction* (New York: Farrar, Straus & Giroux, 1964); subsequent references will be cited as "*SD*" parenthetically in the text.

12. Thomas Merton, *Faith and Violence: Christian Teaching and Christian Practice* (Notre Dame, IN: University of Notre Dame Press, 1968).

allowing whites to recognize and embrace their better selves. These better selves were not superior to or even different from those of their black sisters and brothers but rather capable of being changed and bettered by their equal participation with others in the Mystical Body of Christ. "To have a vow of poverty seems to me illusory," Merton writes in his author's note for *Seeds of Destruction*, "if I do not in some way identify myself with the cause of people who are denied their rights and forced, for the most part, to live in abject misery. To have a vow of obedience seems to me to be absurd if it does not imply a deep concern for the most fundamental of all expressions of God's will: the love of His truth and of our neighbor" (*SD* xvi).

# Trappists, Working – Trappists, Praying:
# The Earliest Monastic Poetry of Thomas Merton

*Patrick F. O'Connell*

Readers of Thomas Merton are of course familiar with the retrospective account in his autobiography of his earliest days at the Abbey of Gethsemani,[1] where he arrived on December 10, 1941: his entrance into "the four walls of my new freedom" (*SSM* 372); his initial interviews with the master of novices and with Dom Frederic, the abbot (see *SSM* 375-79); his immersion in the Advent monastic liturgy as he "tried to sing my first few notes of Gregorian chant with the worst cold I had ever had in my life" (*SSM* 379); his deep sense of having discovered his true vocation (see *SSM* 383). It is noteworthy however that there survives very little contemporary documentation of this crucial period of transition in his life. He had continued writing the journal he had been keeping at least since the beginning of May 1939,[2] but only brief fragments survive of this "novitiate journal long since torn up," as he described it to his friend and unofficial archivist Sr. Thérèse Lentfoehr[3] – nine typed pages of reflections on the Christmas season, dated from December 23 through December 30, 1941,[4] sent on April 14, 1942 to his friend and Columbia professor Mark Van Doren,[5] and fourteen handwritten pages dating from December 13, 1941 through Good Friday, April 3, 1942 (*ES* 3-12), which were preserved because they contained drafts of seven poems that were later sent to Sr. Thérèse. This handful of early monastic poems was written mainly during "the interval after the night office, in the great silence," a time when "[w]hole blocks of imagery seem to crystallize

1. See Thomas Merton, *The Seven Storey Mountain* (New York: Harcourt, Brace, 1948) 372-93; subsequent references will be cited as "*SSM*" parenthetically in the text.
2. Thomas Merton, *Run to the Mountain: The Story of a Vocation. Journals, vol. 1: 1939-1941*, ed. Patrick Hart (San Francisco: HarperCollins, 1995), which concludes with an entry of December 5, 1941 (470-71); subsequent references will be cited as "*RM*" parenthetically in the text.
3. Thomas Merton, *Entering the Silence: Becoming a Monk and Writer. Journals, vol. 2: 1941-1952*, ed. Jonathan Montaldo (San Francisco: HarperCollins, 1996) xv; subsequent references will be cited as "*ES*" parenthetically in the text.
4. Thomas Merton, "Meditations, December 23-30, 1941," introduced by Jonathan Montaldo, *The Merton Seasonal* 25.4 (2000) 3-11.
5. "I enclose a page or two of a Journal I have been keeping: it is completely to do with religious experience" (Thomas Merton, *The Road to Joy: Letters to New and Old Friends,* ed. Robert E. Daggy [New York: Farrar, Straus, Giroux, 1989] 14).

99

out as it were naturally in the silence and the peace, and the lines almost write themselves" (*SSM* 389-90), until his father master told him that this period before daybreak should be reserved for reading and reflecting on the scriptures. He notes, "After the poems I wrote the first Christmas, and one or two in January, and one at the Purification, and one more in Lent, I was glad to be quiet. If there were no other reason for not writing, summer is too busy a season" (*SSM* 390). These poems, then, provide a rare and privileged source of insight into Merton's mind and heart during his first weeks as a new member of the Gethsemani community. A consideration of three of the poems first recorded in these journal fragments, along with a pair of other poems from the same period that seem to serve as a kind of diptych linking the days just before and just after his entrance into the monastery, can thus give some sense of Merton's immediate response to the place itself and to the way of life he was in the process of discovering and participating in: the rhythm of prayer and work, the disjunctions and continuities between life within and beyond the monastery walls, between the world he had left behind and the world he had chosen, or for which he had mysteriously been chosen.

* * * * * * *

The logical place to begin this exploration is, not surprisingly, the chronological place to start as well. What is almost certainly the earliest of the poems written at Gethsemani, "A Letter to My Friends," subtitled "On entering the Monastery of Our Lady of Gethsemani, 1941,"[6] was initially entitled "Poem for My Friends, Dec 12-13" (*ES* 3-4) – thus begun two days after arriving at the abbey and completed in its first draft on the Feast of St. Lucy, the day Merton was officially enrolled as a Cistercian postulant.[7] The opening lines identify the abbey with the home of the boy Christ:

> This holy House of God,
> Nazareth, where Christ lived as a boy,
> These sheds and cloisters,
> The very stones and beams are all befriended
> By cleaner sun, by rarer birds, by lovelier flowers. (ll. 1-5)

---

    6. Thomas Merton, *A Man in the Divided Sea* (New York: New Directions, 1946) 54-55 (subsequent references will be cited as "*MDS*" parenthetically in the text); Thomas Merton, *The Collected Poems of Thomas Merton* (New York: New Directions, 1977) 90-92 (subsequent references will be cited as "*CP*" parenthetically in the text).
    7. See *SSM* 377: "It was the Feast of St. Lucy and a Saturday. I went back to the room . . . and copied out a poem I had just written by way of a farewell to Bob Lax and Mark Van Doren."

Thus the focus is particularly on the obscurity of the speaker's new home, likened to the place where Christ dwelt in the "hidden years" preceding his public life – unnoticed, uncelebrated, yet the "House of God," a phrase used in the Benedictine *Rule* to describe a monastery.[8] There may also be an implicit suggestion of a dwelling shared with the Mother of God,[9] alluding to the Cistercian custom of naming all monasteries after Our Lady. The phrase "House of God" originally appears in Genesis 28:16-17, when Jacob comes to recognize the divine presence at Bethel ("truly this is the house of God [Beth-el], the gate of heaven"), so that this unpretentious site is above all a place of epiphany, of divine manifestation. The juxtaposition of "sheds and cloisters," with the sheds mentioned first, indicates that it is not just the more formally monastic "regular places" but the humble outbuildings (comparable to the carpenter shop of Joseph) that are to be recognized as the divine dwelling place, that Christ is to be found in the places of work as surely as in the places of prayer. The subsequent pairing of "stones and beams" completes a progression from the abbey as a whole to its particular constituent parts to the raw materials out of which the monastery has been constructed. Only at this point does the verb of this introductory sentence finally appear: the site is "befriended" by the natural elements – there is a sense of integration, of intimacy between the human and the natural, incorporating the celestial and the terrestrial, the avian and botanical, in a harmonious balance without estrangement or dissonance. The comparative adjectives make an implicit contrast with the rest of the human world – the sun is "cleaner" (a favorite early Merton word), the birds "rarer," and the flowers "lovelier."[10] Such a comparison has both objective and subjective aspects: there is an actual, factual difference because here the place is what it should be: it hasn't lost – or has regained – its proper relation with the wider creation; but there is also the suggestion that the perception of this relationship is clarified, sharpened, more vivid, a kind of Edenic awareness that the original divine plan for creation is being realized here. It is also noteworthy that the natural elements are described as taking the initiative – sun, birds and flowers

8. Chapter 31.19 (*RB 1980: The Rule of St. Benedict in English*, ed. Timothy Fry, OSB [Collegeville, MN: Liturgical Press, 1982] 55).

9. See Merton's journal entry for November 29, 1941, the day before the beginning of Advent and the day after he had consulted Fr. Philotheus Boehner about his "impediment" to becoming a priest, a conversation that led to his departure for Gethsemani less than two weeks later: "I give this whole Advent, every minute to the Blessed Virgin, begging her to help me to bring me to her house at Gethsemani to be her loving child and servant, a child of God in silence and labor and sacrifice and obscurity" (*RM* 462).

10. In the original draft the flowers are said to be "humbler," but that has a different focus; here the common emphasis is on heightened experience.

welcome the abbey (and implicitly its newest resident) into their midst.

The lines which follow go on to align the monastery with the next stage of Christ's incarnate life:

> Lost in the tigers' and the lions' wilderness,
> More than we fear, we love these holy stones,
> These thorns, the phoenix's sweet and spikey tree. (ll. 6-8)

The monastery is both domestic and wild, both Nazareth and the desert where Jesus is "with the wild beasts" (Mk. 1:13) – an ambiguous detail that can be interpreted either as a threat of hostile attack or as a promise of eschatological reintegration, transcending the estrangement of the fallen world. The following line reflects this conflicted response, but asserts that for the monks who risk a journey into the wilderness where there is no clear path, love is ultimately more powerful than fear. The reference to the stones suggests the first of the three temptations undergone by Christ, to turn stones into bread (Mt. 4:3; Lk. 4:3), but here they are recognized not as objects to be changed into something else but as "holy stones" that can be used to build the house of God, the "very stones" befriended by the natural world into which the monastery is integrated. Likewise the thorns, conventional symbols of barrenness, can be loved more than feared because of their association with Christ's Passion – they are an integral element of redemption. Finally the "sweet and spiky tree," an image of the cross on which Christ the phoenix dies and returns to life, thus a sign of both suffering and consolation, is fearful but even more it is loveable. Thus "lost" in this pathless wilderness of tigers and lions, the monks experience both the beginning and the fulfillment of Christ's salvific mission.

The following section begins by recapitulating what has just been said and then turns its attention from the setting to the persons concerned, the monks themselves:

> More than we fear, we love the holy desert,
> Where separate strangers, hid in their disguises,
> Have come to meet, by night, the quiet Christ. (ll. 9-11)

The first line here repeats line 7, with the substitution of "desert" for "stones" – and by extension for the other two objects loved more than feared. The desert, incorporating all of these elements, is the place of encounter with Christ in darkness ("by night"), in solitude ("separate"), in silence ("the quiet Christ"), perhaps to be connected particularly with the period of prayer that follows the night office. The monks are initially described as "separate strangers" (as they certainly would have been for Merton himself two days after his arrival at Gethsemani!), but at the same time consistently identified with the corporate "we" – members of a community sharing a common purpose, a common experience, a common goal. The phrase "hid in their disguises" may be a way of describing the monks with their hooded cowls up, concealing their faces and so their identities, but it also suggests the story of Nicodemus coming to Christ by night (Jn 3:1-21), not yet ready to acknowledge Christ openly and so likewise involved in a dialectic of fear and love which will be fully resolved only when he openly joins Joseph of Arimathea in burying the dead Christ (cf. Jn. 19:39), bringing the myrrh and aloes that may be considered as corresponding to the "sweet and spikey" tree of the phoenix. In any case, the climax of the first part of the poem comes in this meeting with Christ; though it is still only a beginning, still marked by concealment of some sort, the whole purpose of entering monastic life centers on just such an encounter.

With the following lines the focus now turns back to the world left behind:

> We who have some time wandered in those crowded ruins,
> (Farewell, you woebegone, sad towns)
> We who have wandered like (the ones I hear) the moaning trains,
> (Begone, sad towns!)
> We'll live it over for you here. (ll. 12-16)

The journey described now, unlike that into the desert, is an aimless one, without direction or purpose, through towns implicitly contrasted with Nazareth, towns described as "crowded ruins," a figurative way of indicating the disorder and transience of the Augustinian city of man, but in December 1941 not an exclusively metaphorical image, as the literal ruins of London and other cities being bombed in the blitz had become a sign of the consequence of spiritual and moral turmoil, as Merton had described in his novel *My Argument with the Gestapo*.[11] The comparison to the train in the parallel pair of lines that follow suggests not just aimless wandering within towns but from place to place, looking in vain for meaning and for rest, a hopeless quest to escape the sorrow and pain expressed in the "moaning" of the whistle that announces the train's passage through the

---

11. Thomas Merton, *My Argument with the Gestapo: A Macaronic Journal* (Garden City, NY: Doubleday, 1969); for a summary, see Patrick F. O'Connell, "*My Argument with the Gestapo*" in William H. Shannon, Christine M. Bochen and Patrick F. O'Connell, *The Thomas Merton Encyclopedia* (Maryknoll, NY: Orbis, 2002) 311-14; for further discussion see also Patrick F. O'Connell, "Merton's Earlier *Commedia*: Dante and *My Argument with the Gestapo*," *The Merton Journal* 21.1 (Easter 2014) 28-38.

towns along the track.[12] Now the towns are not merely bid "Farewell" but "Begone" – as though cast out, banished even from the speaker's memory, yet the final line here is crucial. The monastic community is not in fact simply abandoning the world to its own disintegration – the sad towns are dismissed so that a new start can be made, not merely in place of the fallen, broken world but for the sake of that very world. Life at the monastery is to be understood as an agent of renewal "for you" – for the "woebegone, sad towns" that are incapable of renewing themselves because they have lost contact with the spiritual power that makes such a transformation possible.

This claim is elaborated in the passage that follows, still addressing the towns[13] and linked with the previous section by the immediate repetition of its concluding "here":

> Here all your ruins are rebuilt as fast as you destroy yourselves,
> In your unlucky wisdom,
> Here in the House of God
> And on the holy hill,
> Where fields are the friends of plenteous heaven,
> While starlight feeds, as bright as manna,
> All our rough earth with wakeful grace. (ll. 17-23)

Monastic life is not simply building an alternate, separate system – a city of God over against the city of man – but engaged in a countermovement to the disintegration of the secular world, a creative agency that models God's will for all creation and functions as a sacramental sign and instrument of the restorative, transforming power of Christ. The vision is similar to that expressed by Merton when during his initial visit to Gethsemani he called it "the only real city in America" (*RM* 333), a source of inner creative dynamism for the whole world. The self-destructive tendencies of the "sad towns" with

---

12. See the similar image of the train which "runs, lost, / Baying in eastward mysteries of distance" in Merton's poem "The Trappist Abbey: Matins" (Thomas Merton, *Thirty Poems* [Norfolk, CT: New Directions, 1944] [15] [subsequent references will be cited as "*TP*" parenthetically in the text]; *CP* 45-46), which was written at the time of Merton's first visit to Gethsemani during Holy Week 1941; for a discussion see Patrick F. O'Connell, "Sacrament and Sacramentality in Thomas Merton's *Thirty Poems*" in Patrick F. O'Connell, ed., *The Vision of Thomas Merton* (Notre Dame, IN: Ave Maria Press, 2003) 180-84.

13. It is important to recognize here that although the revised title of the poem originally called "Poem for My Friends" has become "A Letter to My Friends," the second-person references here are not to be understood as addressed to them. Note also that Merton alters the phrasing of the first line here from "as fast as you destroyed them," which thus awkwardly refers to destroying what were already "ruins."

their "unlucky wisdom," the wisdom of this world (cf. 1 Cor. 1:19-31) that not only brings misfortune but suggests that from its own perspective such misfortune is merely a matter of chance, with no assumption of personal responsibility – an attitude that perhaps has specific applicability to the war now raging. The rest of this section, with its further repetition of "Here" and subsequent indication of "Where," makes the reference to place explicit: it is "the House of God," as in the opening line; "the holy hill," a parallel to "the holy desert" of lines 9-11 but suggestive of all those meeting places between God and humanity, most importantly Calvary but perhaps also Gethsemani itself (on the Mount of Olives); as in lines 4-5, there is a sense of integration, but here with a focus on unity with the transcendent, the friendship of the fields with heaven itself, described as "plenteous" in the abundance of its gifts as detailed in the two final lines of this section: the starlight shining in the midst of darkness (suggesting the star of Bethlehem in particular) that nourishes the spirit in a way comparable to the gift of manna to the People of God on their desert journey, a parallel reinforced by the transfer of epithets, as "bright" is applied to the manna to balance the use of "feeds" to describe the starlight, which is not exclusive to the monastery but is directed to "All our rough earth." Again the monastery is considered as a paradigm rather than simply as an alternative – a sign of contradiction to "the world" but more fundamentally a sign of potential transformation and renewal. Even in the midst of the world's crisis, the promise of enlightenment and nourishment is given to overcome a temptation to discouragement or despair, directed to the world beyond the monastery generally and in particular to the friends mentioned in the title whom the poet has left behind but not forgotten or abandoned. The offer is one of "wakeful grace," a free gift that cannot be earned yet one that can be received only by those who are themselves awake and attentive, who have heeded the summons of Christ to "stay awake – you know not the day nor the hour," like the wise virgins in the parable of the Bridegroom's coming (Mt. 25:1-13), and unlike the disciples in the Garden of Gethsemani (Mt. 26:36-46).

The poem concludes with a prophetic, eschatological vision, in two parts:

> And look, the ruins have become Jerusalems,
> And the sick cities re-arise, like shining Sions!
> Jerusalems, these walls and rooves,
> These bowers and fragrant sheds,
> Our desert's wooden door,
> The arches, and the windows, and the tower! (ll. 24-29)

The first two lines foresee a final transformation, the ruined cities as New

Jerusalems, the sick cities as "shining Sions" (themselves "holy hills"), healed and "lit by the radiant glory of God" (Rev. 21:23). This vision of a future restoration (with the prophecy of Deutero-Isaiah as the background) is made possible by the realized eschatology of the monastic Jerusalem, already participating in the divine plan for a renewed creation, but tellingly described not with romanticized, idealistic imagery, but with reference to ordinary, unadorned, even "prosaic" components of the monastic complex. Thus the poem concludes with an expanded recapitulation of the catalogue of lines 3-4 – the "walls and rooves" of the monastic buildings; the bowers[14] and sheds (the only item actually repeated, here "fragrant" with whatever has been gathered from the abbey's fields and paired with the naturally sweet-smelling bowers); the "wooden door" providing an entryway into the desert of lines 6-11, but a plain wooden door, neither ornate nor magical; and finally the cloister with its arches and the church with its windows and tower, "Jerusalems" par excellence.

This poem, evidently Merton's first written response to the new home he has chosen, is obviously filled with the enthusiasm of a true believer, that will of course be tested, tempered, challenged and modified by the experience of the twenty-seven years to follow. Yet if Gethsemani fails to live up fully to its identity as House of God, holy desert, radiant Jerusalem, as perceived in Merton's first two days of permanent residence, his evolving view of monastic life will continue to find it, in all its ordinariness, a sacramental instrument, a sign of God's kingdom, not only for its own participants but for the wider church and world. "A Letter to My Friends" reveals that despite the recurring temptation to a simplistic "world rejection" during his early years at Gethsemani, such a reductive dualism was never intrinsic to Merton's vision of authentic monasticism. Concern for the world beyond the cloister, in which those he loved continued to live, and a hope for its renewal, was perceived from the very beginning as an integral dimension of any genuine monastic vocation, especially his own.

* * * * * * *

In *The Seven Storey Mountain* Merton writes: "Liturgically speaking, you could hardly find a better time to become a monk than Advent. You begin a new life, you enter into a new world at the beginning of a new liturgical year" (*SSM* 379). But of course when he arrived at Gethsemani Advent was already mid-way into its second week, having begun on November 30 that year, so that it represents an underlying continuity in the Church's liturgical cycle that transcends the momentous change in Merton's own personal circumstances. Two closely related poems were the products of

---

14. The original draft reads "flowers" – perhaps a transcription error.

this season.[15] The first, entitled "Advent" (*MDS* 51; *CP* 88), was almost certainly written while Merton was still at St. Bonaventure, since it resembles quite closely in some of its details journal passages written at the very outset of Advent.[16] The second, "Carol" (*MDS* 52; *CP* 89), might possibly also have been begun before Merton left the college, sooner than expected in the wake of Pearl Harbor, but as it is more properly a Christmas poem than an Advent poem it is likely that it was composed close to the feast itself and therefore at the monastery, particularly given the busyness that would have occupied Merton in his few days of preparation before heading off to Kentucky on the evening of Tuesday, December 9.[17] Thus taken together, this pair of poems connect Merton's "new life" with what preceded it, this "new world" of religious life with the world into which Christ entered to identify with and redeem all humanity

The first of these poems begins with three pairs of parallel lines describing, or rather invoking, the winter skies:

> Charm with your stainlessness these winter nights,
> Skies, and be perfect!

15. Bonnie Thurston provides brief but insightful reflections on "Advent" and "Carol" in "The Sacrament of Advent: Thomas Merton's Lessons and Carols," *The Merton Journal* 16.2 (Advent 2009) 50-51.

16. Two drafts of the poem are found in a typescript, now in the archives of the Butler Library at Columbia University, of *Man in the Divided Sea* pieces that otherwise includes only poems written before Merton's entrance into Gethsemani. All the poems are in the same order as in the published volume except this one, which precedes rather than follows "The Peril," suggesting that it was written before the latter poem. The two texts, the second a fair copy of the first, are virtually identical to one another and to the published version, other than in punctuation and the phrase "feed by" (l. 15), which reads "fed at" in the first version and "fed by" in the second, and "Skies; . . . lovely" in the first version (but not the second) rather than "You skies: . . . gentle" (l. 17). In this line the phrase "and travel like the lovely Virgin" is interlined in pencil above the cancelled "go slowly to the setting of your stately planets;" followed by the cancelled "And travel like the lovely Virgin out of Nazareth" and "Toward the appointed setting" added in pencil and then cancelled.

17. Merton's rather general reference in the autobiography to "the poems I wrote the first Christmas" (*SSM* 390) might plausibly be considered to include this specifically Christmas piece. Note also that no draft of this poem is included in the Columbia typescript of pre-monastic poems that would appear in *A Man in the Divided Sea*. Most conclusively, in the chronology found in Ross Labrie, "The Ordering of Thomas Merton's Early Poems," *Resources for American Literary Study* 8 (1979) 115-17, which draws on a 1951 letter, written by Merton's secretary, providing the year of composition of almost all the poems in Merton's first three collections of verse, "Carol" – but not "Advent" – is followed by the notation "Gethsemani" in parenthesis (116); the same notation is found in Merton's personal copy of *A Man in the Divided Sea*, now at the Thomas Merton Center, Bellarmine University, Louisville, KY.

> Fly vivider in the fiery dark, you quiet meteors,
> And disappear.
> You moon, be slow to go down,
> This is your full! (ll. 1-6)

The initial command in this set of imperatives presents the darkness not as hostile or threatening but as attractive, fascinating, and perhaps also as casting a spell, but a beneficent one. As stainless, the night sky symbolizes the heavenly realm, and may be implicitly associated with Mary, conceived without the stain of original sin. It is called upon to "be perfect," a command familiar from the Sermon on the Mount (see Mt. 5:48), suggesting here a completely clear night sky that is "*teleios*," totally what it is supposed to be, completely realizing its identity and serving as a sign of its perfect Creator the heavenly Father. Its interaction is to be not with human observers but with "these winter nights," a temporal referent that complements the spatial focus of the skies themselves, thus calling for the whole cosmos, the world of space and time, to come together in complete integration during this auspicious time of preparation, implicitly being made ready specifically for the coming appearance of the angelic messengers in the winter sky. The summons that follows is to the heavenly bodies that traditionally serve as omens, portents of propitious births. The initial command to be more "vivid," brighter than usual, makes them signs of a uniquely significant birth, but then they are to "disappear," for the event to come transcends all natural hopes and expectations. As "quiet meteors" they are not a disruptive presence, do not break the stillness of the night sky, and so represent both a completion and a cancellation of "pagan" traditions. The last of the three commands is exactly the opposite, asking that the full moon, the maximum reflection of light in darkness, "be slow to go down" rather than "disappear" like the meteors, for it makes the light of the sun itself available even in the darkness.

The lines that follow change the focus from the celestial to the earthly, or rather situate the latter in the context of the former, and do so in three declarative rather than imperative statements:

> The four white roads make off in silence
> Towards the four parts of the starry universe.
> Time falls like manna at the corners of the wintry earth.
> We have become more humble than the rocks,
> More wakeful than the patient hills. (ll. 7-11)

Again the images are both spatial and temporal. The image of the crossroads (one that the early Merton particularly appreciates[18])

---

18. See "The Evening of the Visitation," ll. 1-2 (*TP* [13]; *CP* 43); "In Memory of the

presents a design of perfect order, in which paths ray out from a central organizing point not just to the rest of the earth but to the entire cosmos. White from the moonlight, they "make off" as though sent on mission, but their message is a silent one, akin to the "silent meteors": what is to take place will have cosmic consequences affecting all creation, but as yet the Word is not ready to be spoken. The simile that follows likens time to manna, heavenly nourishment, because the *kairos*, the time of fulfillment (cf. Mk. 1:15), is almost at hand. The line recalls the scriptural phrase "*stillabunt montes dulcedinem*" ("the mountains will drip sweetness") (Amos 9:13; Joel 4:18), which Merton quoted and commented on in his journal entry of November 29: "In the long quiet night of Advent, (*dulcedo*) sweetness falls from the skies of Time's darkness like a radiance that is just beyond our vision! O Holy Grace! The Lord is coming!" (*RM* 459); it also suggests the similar phrase "*Rorate caeli desuper et nubes pluant justum*" ("Drop down dew, you heavens from above, and let the clouds rain the just") (Is. 45:8) quoted in the entry for the following day, the First Sunday of Advent (*RM* 463). The gift extends to the margins of "the wintry earth," recalling the "winter nights" of the opening line but also juxtaposed with the "starry universe" of the line immediately preceding; it is an all-encompassing "right time" for creation as a whole, in which *kairos* transcends *chronos*, the lifelessness and darkness of the December night being infused with new vitality. The phrase is also a reminiscence of John Donne's Holy Sonnet "At the Round Earth's Imagined Corners,"[19] but here referring not as in Donne's poem to the final judgment but to the Incarnation, not to the culmination but the initiation of the drama of salvation. The section concludes with the brief appearance of "We" in line 10, the very center of the poem, in which the human community surpasses the rocks in humility – a paradoxical superiority in lowliness that recalls the root of "*humilis*" in "*humus*," the dust of the earth, and thus a reminder of the origin of humanity in the creation story of Genesis 2; and likewise it surpasses the hills in wakefulness – a comparison that suggests the identification of hills as symbolizing earth reaching out to heaven, and perhaps con-

---

Spanish Poet Federico Garcia Lorca," l. 21 (*TP* [15]; *CP* 45); "St. Agnes: A Responsory," l. 25 (*TP* [22]; *CP* 55); "The Widow of Naim," ll. 15, 27 (*MDS* 58, 59; *CP* 94, 95); "St. John's Night," ll. 7-8 (Thomas Merton, *Figures for an Apocalypse* [New York: New Directions, 1947] 58 [subsequent references will be cited as "*FA*" parenthetically in the text]; *CP* 171).

19. *The Complete Poetry of John Donne*, ed. John T. Shawcross (Garden City, NY: Doubleday Anchor, 1967) 340-41.

nected as well with the proclamation of Isaiah 40:4, in which the hills made low are themselves signs of humility. In either case the shared patience of creation and humanity is about to be rewarded.

The line which follows is a reprise of the opening line, with two significant alterations, beginning a variation of the triple invocation in lines 1-6 that will then continue through the rest of the poem:

> Charm with your stainlessness these nights in Advent, holy spheres,
> While minds, as meek as beasts,
> Stay close at home in the sweet hay;
> And intellects are quieter than the flocks that feed by starlight.
>
> (ll. 12-15)

Here "winter nights" becomes "nights in Advent" – a transition from natural, seasonal identification (*chronos*) to liturgical identification (*kairos*), and the first specific indication in the poem of its actual thematic focus;[20] and the imperative is now addressed to "holy spheres" rather than simply to "Skies," a reference to the planets but using a term borrowed from the old cosmology of concentric spheres with angelic intelligences found in Dante as elsewhere, holy because obedient to the divine will and upholding divine order. The human element is now compared with other living creatures, not as a generalized "we" but as personified faculties. Preparation for the (re)birth of Christ in the soul requires minds to take the meek role of the beasts in the stable – i.e. not to dominate the scene by logical analysis but to recognize the inadequacy of rational investigation to comprehend the miracle of the Incarnation, to bow in humility before the divine mystery to be revealed. There is also the willingness to withdraw from outward activity, from the distractions of exterior business, to await God's epiphany in a state of recollection. The second comparison, of the "quieter" intellect to the shepherds' flocks, reinforces the sense of stillness, silence, receptivity and expectancy, while the reference to feeding connects with the earlier manna imagery, the starlight with the "starry universe" of line 8, and the flocks' location with the "patient hills" waiting attentively for the angelic proclamation to the shepherds watching their flocks by night.

In the second invocation of this concluding set, the skies, displaced by the "holy spheres" in the previous lines, are now addressed in lieu of the meteors, which have indeed disappeared:

---

20. The two earlier drafts of the poem lack the final title: in the first it is untitled, and simply "Poem" in the second.

Oh pour your darkness and your brightness over all our
    solemn valleys,
You skies: and travel like the gentle Virgin,
Toward the planets' stately setting,
Oh white full moon as quiet as Bethlehem! (ll. 16-19)

The paradox of the request suggests the "dazzling darkness" of Dionysius and Henry Vaughan,[21] that what is darkness and obscurity to the intellect is brightness to the spirit, as the divine light of the Word of God is concealed in human form. The "solemn valleys," complementing the "patient hills" previously mentioned, are to be raised with the coming of the Lord, as Isaiah and the Baptist proclaim in the Advent liturgy. Only here at the very conclusion of the poem does the Christmas context become explicit, and still only in the form of similes, as befits the time of preparation that is not yet completed. Whereas the moon was first instructed to "be slow to go down" (l. 5), now in the final invocation it is told to "travel . . . / Toward the planets' stately setting," for the night is almost over, the dawn is about to break, the sun to rise. The completion of the moon's journey across the sky is comparable to the completion of the gentle Virgin's journey to the child's birthplace, an especially apt connection as Mary is also a "moon" that reflects the light of the Son rather than shining with her own brightness.

This journey, described with particular effectiveness in the series of trochaic words ("darkness," "brightness," "solemn," "valleys"; "travel," "gentle," "Virgin"; "planets," "stately," "setting"), concludes with a shift of rhythm in the final line, set off by itself, with its three stressed monosyllables in a row ("white full moon"), the assonance of "white" and "quiet" and then the double stress of the final "Bethlehem!" It may seem as though the moon is doing incompatible double duty in being compared both to the Virgin and to Bethlehem, but each in turn is the place where the Light of the World is to be found. The moon in motion reflects the journey of Mary to the birthplace (the temporal dimension), while its final appearance, its momentary comparison to the stillness of Bethlehem (the spatial dimension), allows the heavenly quiet of the moon and the earthly quiet of Bethlehem to reflect and reinforce one

---

21. See Henry Vaughan, "The Night," ll. 49-50: "There is in God (some say) / A deep, but dazling darkness" (*The Complete Poetry of Henry Vaughan*, ed. French Fogle [Garden City, NY: Doubleday Anchor, 1964] 325); Vaughan's reference is almost certainly to the *Mystical Theology* of Pseudo-Dionysius, which considers "the mysteries of God's Word . . . in the brilliant darkness of a hidden silence" (Pseudo-Dionysius, *The Complete Works*, trans. Colm Luibheid, Classics of Western Spirituality [New York: Paulist Press, 1987] 135).

another, to share the sense of expectancy at the point of equilibrium, as the balance between sky and earth, night and day, is about to change. For this final line transfers attention from heaven to earth, from the cosmic to the intimate. The moon's role is completed: the light which has been reflected from the moon is now ready to shine in and on and from the City of David.

*       *       *       *       *       *       *

"Carol,"[22] the companion poem to "Advent," switches from a cosmic to an incarnational focus as the time of Christ's birth arrives. As the poem opens, what had been a figurative referent for the quiet intellect in the previous poem (l. 15) is now presented in its literal actuality:

> Flocks feed by darkness with a noise of whispers,
> In the dry grass of pastures,
> And lull the solemn night with their weak bells. (ll. 1-3)

The scriptural background is of course immediately evident here – these are the flocks which the shepherds were watching by night in Luke 2:8 immediately before the appearance of the angel proclaiming the good news of the new birth, though the shepherds themselves will not be mentioned until later in the poem. The phrase "by darkness" is both a variant of the scriptural "by night" and a contrast to the phrase "by starlight" found in "Advent." Moon and stars from the previous poem have disappeared; a complete absence of light precedes the coming dawn, both natural and spiritual. The presence of the flock is known only by the "whispers" of their movement through the dry grass of the pastures and the barely perceptible sound of the bells around their necks. While there is no overt suggestion of the transformative event that is about to take place, the key word here is "lull," suggesting the soothing, even soporific effect of the "weak bells" but also, playing on the meaning of "lull" as a noun, that this calm is a temporary pause that is to give way to the paean of exultation signaling the arrival of the Word, just as the darkness is about to be banished by the arrival of the Light of the World.

There is no evident expectation on the part of the flocks of what is to come, but the reference to "the solemn night" (a variant of the "solemn valleys" in

---

22. A typed draft of "Carol" now in the Columbia University Butler Library was sent, along with numerous other poems, in a November 7, 1945 letter to Mark Van Doren; its text is very close to the published version, with minor punctuation variants and "some hay" for "the hay" in line 9 and "straw-built" for "straw-roofed" in line 10; x'd out "prayers and tears," precedes "penances" in line 16. This version of the text was also published in *The New Yorker* 20 (Dec. 23, 1944) 36.

line 16 of "Advent") as being lulled for the moment signals that despite the seemingly unremarkable routine being described this is no ordinary time – it is not *chronos* but *kairos*, as the following section makes explicit:

> The little towns upon the rocky hills
> Look down as meek as children:
> Because they have seen come this holy time. (ll. 4-6)

As in the previous lines, the figurative details, the "rocks" and "patient hills," of "Advent" (l. 16), have now become literal, the location of the "little towns" (of Bethlehem and its neighbors), themselves personified, which unlike the flocks are presented as attentive and aware of what is about to happen. Their act of "look[ing] down" could be an indication of an assumption of superiority, but such an interpretation is immediately countered by the comparison "as meek as children" (a reworking of "as meek as beasts" in "Advent," line 13), recalling the beatitude "blessed are the meek" who are to inherit the earth (Mt. 5:4) as well as Christ's words that only those who "become as little children" will inherit the kingdom of God (Mt. 18:1-4), and that what has been hidden from the wise has been revealed to "little children" (Mt. 11:25 – a passage immediately following Christ's excoriation of the proud cities of Chorazin, Bethsaida and Capernaum). Here, then, to "look down" is both to observe from a privileged standpoint for witnessing epochal events and to lower one's gaze before a superior. It is to see clearly, precisely because one's eyes do not look too high (cf. Ps. 131:1), that the "time is fulfilled, the kingdom of God is at hand" (Mk. 1:14) that it is now "the acceptable time, the day of salvation" (2 Cor. 6:2).

The three parallel statements that follow explain both in what "this holy time" consists and why it is as yet not perceived by the world at large:

> God's glory, now, is kindled gentler than low candlelight
> Under the rafters of a barn:
> Eternal Peace is sleeping in the hay,
> And Wisdom's born in secret in a straw-roofed stable. (ll. 7-10)

Now, at the time of birth, God's glory, the perceptible presence of the divine in space and time, is manifested in a unique way in the Incarnation according to the prologue to the Gospel of John, verse 14 ("The Word became flesh and dwelt among, us, and we have seen his glory"), and associated with light in the same passage (cf. Jn. 1:4-5, 9) and in the iden- tification of Christ as the Light of the World later in this Gospel (cf. 8:12, 9:5). The focus here is on the gentleness of the light, itself a manifestation of the same meekness of children found in the onlooking towns, and its unobtrusive, easily overlooked presence in an insignificant outbuilding. As glory and peace are linked in the song of the heavenly host in Luke 2:14 ("Glory to God in the highest, and on earth peace to people of good will"), so here the Christ Child is proclaimed as Peace personified, his tranquil sleep itself a kind of icon of this transcendent shalom enfleshed in time. Finally he is recognized as divine Wisdom itself, hidden from the wise of this world (cf. 1 Cor. 1:17-31) in this humble setting.

It is only at this point that the events related in Luke 2:8-14 take place. As in "Advent" (see ll. 1-6, 12, 16-19), the poet serves as a kind of herald, calling upon angels, shepherds and flocks to fulfill their appointed roles in the drama of the Incarnation:

> And O! Make holy music in the stars, you happy angels.
> You shepherds, gather on the hill.
> Look up, you timid flocks, where the three kings
> Are coming through the wintry trees; (ll. 11-14).

The "holy music in the stars" is of course the hymn of glory and proclamation of peace sung by the heavenly host (Lk. 2:14), with perhaps a suggestion of the *trisagion* of Isaiah 6:3 as well ("Holy, holy, holy, Lord of Hosts"); the angels are happy because they bear "good news of great joy for all the people" – the birth of the Savior (Lk. 2:10-11). The shepherds are called to gather to hear this good news from the angel, their location suggesting a revelation shared with the childlike towns, whose action of looking down is now complemented by the command to the "timid flocks" to "Look up" and so to notice the "coming through the wintry trees" (reminiscent of the "wintry earth" of "Advent," l. 9) of the Magi, whose arrival will complete the traditional nativity scene.

The directive to the flocks here forms an inclusion with the opening lines, and so might appear to be a fitting culmination to the poem, but it is followed by an unexpected coda in which speaker and audience (and all humankind) join the procession to the stable:

> While we unnumbered children of the wicked centuries
> Come after with our penances and prayers,
> And lay them down in the sweet-smelling hay
> Beside the wise men's golden jars. (ll. 15-18)

"Unnumbered" – in contrast with the precise tally of the three kings that precede them – these children of unredeemed time might appear to be differentiated from the meek children referred to earlier in the poem, but in fact the penances and prayers they bring, readily associated with the preparatory exercises of Advent in particular, are signs of genuine humility. Placed in the "sweet-smelling hay" (an echo of the "sweet hay" of "Advent," l. 14), these gifts to the Child Jesus are implicitly linked by that detail to the Eternal Peace brought by and embodied in the newborn Savior asleep there, just as the "golden jars" of the wise men (presumably filled with frankincense and myrrh, themselves traditionally associated with prayerful worship and penitential practice) are an appropriate response to the presence of Wisdom incarnate. Thus the poem ends not simply with a reminiscence and representation of a historical event but with participation in the present in the salvific power of this event. *Chronos* once again gives way to *kairos*, and time itself is experienced as redeemed, transformed; the "wicked centuries" no longer control their erstwhile children, who in company with the childlike hill towns now "have seen come this holy time."

* * * * * * *

The initial draft of "Trappists, Working" (*MDS* 61; *CP* 96), originally titled "The Woodcutters and the Harvesters" (*ES* 7), is dated January 25, 1942, approximately six weeks after Merton's arrival at Gethsemani. Its origin is evident from a passage in *The Seven Storey Mountain*: "In January the novices were working in the woods near the lake which the monks made by throwing a dam across a gulley. The woods were quiet and the axes echoed around the sheet of blue-grey water sleek as metal among the trees" (*SSM* 385). The focus of the poem is on the manual labor of Benedictine life as another form of praise of God, though its initial expression will require some further precision and specification:

> Now all our saws sing holy sonnets in this world of timber
> Where oaks go off like guns, and fall like cataracts,
> Pouring their roar into the wood's green well. (ll. 1-3)

From the very start the work is perceived and described in terms of worship rather than simply of practical usefulness, the procuring of wood for some utilitarian purpose such as heating or building. The image of the saws as singing is an indication that this expression of reverence does not merely accompany the work but is intrinsic to the activity itself. Yet it should be noted that the specification of the songs as "holy sonnets," rather than, for instance, psalms, leaves unresolved for the moment whether they are to be considered a manifestation of personal devotion only or are a form of communal prayer.[23] Certainly the "holy sonnets" of John Donne, with

---

23. The original draft says the saws "make holy sonnets"; it also has, as a separate line: "And elms come down like cataracts" – a differentiation between the two species of trees that seems to create a distinction that distracts from the point Merton is evidently

whom the term is most familiarly associated, were not liturgical verse but introspective meditations. The lines which follow seem to problematize the description still further, as the subsequent sounds are certainly incongruous with the lyrical quality of the opening image, with the noise of the fall of the trees compared first to gunshots (heard from a distance, presumably, as would frequently have been the case in the Gethsemani woods), then, more close at hand, to the "roar" of cataracts (amplified by the internal rhyme with "Pour-") that would certainly be more than capable of drowning out (to extend the water image) the peaceful sound of the saws' song. There seems to be implied a suggestion of danger that the spiritual focus of the work could quite possibly be lost amid the din and hurly-burly of the strenuous demands of the task being performed.

It is the presence of Christ that is able to bring a clarity to the monks' efforts and reveals their true significance. The speaker prays:

> Walk to us, Jesus, through the wall of trees,
> And find us still adorers in these airy churches,
> Singing our other Office with our saws and axes.
> Still teach Your children in the busy forest,
> And let some little sunlight reach us, in our mental shades,
>     and leafy studies. (ll. 4-8)

The call to Jesus to join them in the forest suggests a parallel with the only scene in the Gospels where the Lord "walks" to meet his disciples, crossing the water to encounter them in their boat – their workplace – in the midst of a storm (see Mt. 14:22-33; Mk. 6:45-52; Jn. 6:16-21). The added detail that he is to walk "through the wall" also calls to mind the appearance of the risen Christ in the locked upper room on Easter night (see Lk. 24:36-43; Jn. 20:19-23), penetrating any barrier that could separate the disciples from himself. Only at this point is the full meaning of the opening line articulated: the woods are "airy churches," places of adoration; nature is recognized as sacred space, creation as a temple. Manual labor (*"opus manuum"*) is "embodied" prayer, an essential aspect of the monastic vocation of encountering and worshipping God that complements the formal prayer of the liturgy of the hours (*"opus Dei"*) in the abbey church. The "holy sonnets" sung by the saws in the opening line are now identified with "our other Office" sung by the monks themselves with the accompaniment of their tools, a participation that interiorizes the worship and so makes it less dependent upon – or subject to distractions from – exterior sense impressions.[24] The sense of continu-

---

trying to make here.

24. Merton's description in the autobiography, written with more than five years

ity between communal prayer and communal labor found in the phrase "still adorers"[25] is echoed by the request that Christ's teaching "still" continue in the woods, probably in reference to two famous passages in St. Bernard where the great Cistercian Father cites nature as a primary source of knowledge of the Creator,[26] but here it is specifically "the busy forest," not just the quiet stillness of a solitary woodland retreat, that is to be the site of Christ's instruction. That teaching is described as an illumination, an image suggested of course by the very activity in which the monks are engaged as they open up the forest to light by thinning out the trees. These divine rays of insight are to touch "our mental shades, and leafy studies," parallel phrases but actually referring to two distinct levels of experience. The first is figurative, pertaining to the interior life and indicating the need to bring light to shadowy places, both intellectual and moral. The second could refer both to place – the woods as a study, a place of learning – and to activity – the study of the natural world as revelatory; in either case it points to the actual, literal forest as the site of potential enlightenment.[27]

---

of experience of monastic manual labor, is considerably less idealized, perhaps even a bit sardonic: "You are not supposed to *pause* and pray when you are at work. American Trappist notions of contemplation do not extend to that: on the contrary you are expected to make some act of pure intention and fling yourself into the business and work up a sweat and get a great deal finished by the time it is all over. To turn it into contemplation you can occasionally mutter between your teeth: 'All for Jesus! All for Jesus!' But the idea is to keep on working" (*SSM* 385).

25. The original draft refers to "Your faithful" rather than "adorers" here; it also makes no reference to saws in the following line, which might suggest an unintended distinction between this activity and that described in the opening line.

26. See Bernard's Letter 107 to the English Cistercian abbot, later Archbishop of York, Henry Murdac: "Believe me who have experience, you will find much more labouring amongst the woods than you ever will amongst books. Woods and stones will teach you what you can never hear from any master. Do you imagine you cannot suck honey from the rocks and oil from the hardest stone; that the mountains do not drop sweetness and the hills flow with milk and honey; that the valleys are not filled with corn? So many things occur to me which I could say to you that I can hardly restrain myself" (*The Letters of St Bernard of Clairvaux*, trans. Bruno Scott James [London: Burns & Oates, 1953] 156); see also William of Saint-Thierry's comment in the first book of the *Vita Prima* of St. Bernard, c. 23: "His exterior work did not form a barrier to the sweetness of his interior contemplation. To this day he confesses that whatever he gains from the Scriptures, whatever he finds spiritually in them, comes chiefly from the woods and fields, and he has no teachers besides the oaks and beeches; he was accustomed to make a good-humored joke of this among his friends" (William of Saint-Thierry, Arnold of Bonneval, Geoffrey of Auxerre, *The First Life of Bernard of Clairvaux*, trans. Hilary Costello, OCSO [Collegeville, MN: Cistercian Publications, 2015] 27).

27. Of course "leafy" is not literally accurate for the actual time of year when the

The final section of the poem looks forward to another important occasion of manual labor having both literal and symbolic significance, the time of harvest (which of course the author had not yet experienced in his brief residence at the abbey at the end of 1941 and beginning of 1942), and repeats the earlier request for Christ's presence in the midst of their work:

> When time has turned the country white with grain
> And filled our regions with the thrashing sun,
> Walk to us, Jesus, through the walls of wheat
> When our two tractors come to cut them down:
> Sow some light winds upon the acres of our spirit,
> And cool the regions where our prayers are reapers,
> And slake us, Heaven, with Your living rivers. (ll. 9-15)

Whereas the woodcutting was taking place "Now" – the very first word of the poem – the corresponding temporal indicator here is "When" – followed by the present perfect of "has turned . . . / And [has] filled . . ." in a subordinate clause rather than the complete sentence of lines 1-3. This clause is also linked with the lines immediately preceding by the contrast between "some little sunlight" there and the summer landscape "filled . . . with the thrashing sun" here; "thrashing"[28] is simply a variant of "threshing" – the sun itself imaged as a winnower, separating wheat from chaff – but perhaps suggesting also the sun beating down upon the monk-harvesters themselves, who are therefore in need of relief from the summer heat. Again the speaker prays in almost identical words for the coming of Jesus into the midst of the laborers, with only "walls of wheat" replacing the earlier "wall of trees," though more than a touch of humor marks the projected simultaneous arrival of the Lord and of the two tractors[29] sent to cut down the wheat, an apparently deliberate juxtaposing of the supernatural and the mechanical. The specificity of the number of tractors suggests both an awareness of the incongruity of this literal preciseness with a prayer for the presence of one who has no need of machines to cut down these walls, and a recognition that this

poem was composed, but the season is not specified in the text itself.

28. This adjective is not found in the original draft.

29. The original draft reads "clean scythes go out" rather than "Two tractors come" – the change presumably made for the sake of greater accuracy; Merton of course had no experience of the harvesting process in January 1942 when the poem was originally written; in describing the wheat harvest of July 1942 in *The Seven Storey Mountain* Merton does not mention the tractors cutting down the grain but does note both the "big threshing machine . . . drawn up at the east end of the cow barn" and the "wagons loaded with sheaves . . . constantly coming in, from all directions, from the various fields" (*SSM* 392).

transcendent presence is not incompatible with even the most prosaic of factual details.

The concluding three-fold prayer for spiritual relief, analogous to a physical alleviation of the effects of the heat at harvest time, indicates how bodily experience can serve as a stimulus to an awareness of a parallel spiritual situation. First is the paradoxical request that Christ "sow" on the fields of their spirits "light winds" – gentle but perhaps light-bearing as well – and suggesting the gift of Spirit to spirit, of the mysterious creative and sanctifying "wind" that blows where it wills, as Jesus tells Nicodemus in John 3:8. The second petition, to "cool the regions where our prayers are reapers," pointing to the role of prayer in gathering the spiritual harvest, with all the salvific and eschatological associations of that imagery in the Gospels (see Mt. 9:37, 13:18-23, 36-43; Lk. 10:2; Jn. 4:35-38; Rev. 14:15-16), is particularly applicable to Trappists, not engaged in direct apostolic work, for whom prayer for the full realization of the Kingdom of God is their way of participating in this harvest. The imagery here bears a striking resemblance to the lines "In hard labor You are rest, / In the heat You refresh best" from the sequence for the Feast of Pentecost,[30] reinforcing the impression that the speaker is asking Jesus for the gift of the Holy Spirit, a conclusion that receives further corroboration from the final appeal for "living rivers" to slake the monks' spiritual thirst (or to "Lave our dryness" in the words of the Pentecost sequence), a clear reminiscence of Christ's reference to "living water" in his conversation with the woman at the well in John 4:10-15 and of the "fountains of living water" to flow from the breast of Christ that are explicitly identified with the Spirit in John 7:37-39. The specification of "living rivers" rather than just "living waters" gives this imagery an eschatological resonance parallel to that of the harvest, pointing toward ultimate fulfillment of the divine plan in the New Jerusalem, where the river of life flows from the throne of the Lamb for all to drink (see Rev. 21:6, 22:1-2, 17). Work, then, if done in continuity with prayer, can be experienced both as an emblem of transcendent completion in the hereafter and as an encounter with Christ in the Holy Spirit here and now – an intersection of time and eternity indicated by addressing Christ as "Heaven" in this final line. *Opus manuum* is both a participation in God's own creative activity on the literal level and a sign of the full realization of that process on the moral (tropological) and cosmic (anagogical) levels. Hence the particular appropriateness

---

30. *Saint Joseph Daily Missal*, ed. Hugo H. Hoever, SOCist, rev. ed. (New York: Catholic Book Publishing Co., 1959) 430; subsequent references will be cited as "*Missal*" parenthetically in the text.

of including this second scene, which has not yet actually taken place since Merton's arrival at Gethsemani, but is an imaginative projection of an experience still to come, not only in a few months in the abbey's wheatfields, but in the fullness of time when the final harvest is gathered in and when all who thirst may come to the water of life.

*     *     *     *     *     *     *

"The Candlemas Procession" (*MDS* 56; *CP* 92-93) presumably was written on or close to February 2, 1942, the Feast of the Purification of Mary (or Presentation),[31] a week after the previous poem, though the surviving draft is dated April 3, Good Friday (*ES* 11-12). Whereas "Trappists, Working" considered manual labor as a continuation of the work of liturgical worship, in this poem Merton turns for the first time to the celebration of the liturgy itself as the focus for his poem. It begins simply with the Latin antiphon sung before the traditional procession on Candlemas Day,[32] "*Lumen / Ad revelationem gentium*" (ll. 1-2)[33] – "a light of revelation for the Gentiles" (*Missal* 781) – borrowed from the *Nunc Dimittis*, the hymn of Simeon in response to encountering the Child Jesus in the temple and recognizing him as the long-awaited Messiah (Lk. 2:29-32), the light not only of Israel but of all humanity, the "Light of the World" as Christ will identify himself in John's Gospel (8:12, 9:5).

The speaker then turns to address Christ, serving as spokesman of the entire monastic community:

> Look kindly, Jesus, where we come,
> New Simeons, to kindle,
> Each at Your infant sacrifice his own life's candle. (ll. 3-5)[34]

These lines, particularly musical with their linking by consonance of "kindly," "kindle" and "candle" (to be joined in line 8 by "kindred") – along with the further alliteration of "come" – also draw on the liturgy of the feast, as both the introit and the gradual are taken from Psalm 47:10: "we ponder Your kindness within Your temple" (*Missal* 783, 784). The monks are identified as "new Simeons," but unlike the original, who prays that having seen the Savior he may now depart this life in peace

---

31. Merton says in *The Seven Storey Mountain* it was written "at the Purification" (*SSM* 390).

32. For a detailed description of the traditional Cistercian Candlemas procession around the cloister, see Terryl Kinder, *Cistercian Europe: The Architecture of Contemplation* (Kalamazoo, MI: Cistercian Publications, 2002) 67-75.

33. The draft version of the opening line, "*Lumen!* The life, the holy light of men!" is flatter and less effective than this citation of the scriptural and liturgical text.

34. This final version drops as unnecessary the words "to Church" at the end of line 3.

(Lk. 2:29-30), they represent not the end of the period of expectation but the beginning of the new age – they are not leaving but coming. But like Simeon they too are called to witness, to share the light of Christ in their own lives, symbolized by the lighted candles they carry. The source of the light is specified here as "Your infant sacrifice," a reference to the ceremony that has brought the child and his parents to the temple, in which the first-born son is symbolically offered to God, an offering that in this unique instance serves as a foreshadowing of the redemptive sacrifice that will be the culmination of Christ's earthly mission. There is thus an implicit connection made between this feast and the Easter vigil, when candles will again symbolize the illumination brought by Christ's sacrificial self-gift.

This paschal context is extended even further in the following lines, which identify the light with the tongues of fire on Pentecost:

> And when Your flame turns into many tongues,
> See how the One is multiplied, among us, hundreds!
> And goes among the humble, and consoles our sinful kindred. (ll. 6-8)

The entire process of redemption is recognized as already present in this event of Christ's infancy, forty days after his birth. The fire of the Holy Spirit (whose "radiance" is mentioned in the third prayer of blessing for the feast [*Missal* 780], and power to enlighten in the fifth [*Missal* 781]) is presented as a result of "Your flame," recalling Christ's words: "I came to cast fire on the earth, and would that it were already kindled" (Lk. 12:49) (with perhaps a reference as well to the "refining fire" of Malachi 3:1-4, the epistle for the feast [*Missal* 784]). The single flame becomes multiple as it is distributed among the worshippers, visibly represented by the hundreds of candles in the procession, but it remains the same fire, as indicated by the singular verb forms in line 8. The light "goes among the humble" – first the monastic community itself but then all those who humbly recognize that they are not themselves the source of light but must receive it as a free, undeserved gift, the "sinful kindred" – related to the monks in their shared awareness of sinfulness – who, like Simeon himself, were awaiting "the consolation of Israel" (Lk. 2:25) and find it in the coming of the Messiah.

The first half of the poem ends with a summary recapitulation of what has preceded, the description of the reception of the candles, forming an inclusion by the repetition of line 2, which is now placed in a new, more particular context:

> It is for this we come,

> And, kneeling, each receive one flame:
> *Ad revelationem gentium.* (ll. 9-11)

The first line here may be an allusion (or perhaps an unconscious echo) of one of Merton's favorite poems, the sonnet of Gerard Manley Hopkins that begins "As kingfishers catch fire, dragonflies draw flame" and concludes its octave with *"What I do is me: for that I came"* – that is, in order to be a unique manifestation of the divine image, sharing in the identity of the one Christ who "plays in ten thousand places."[35] Similarly the reason why "we come" to receive the light of Christ is to become that very light, to be "the light of the world" as identified in the Sermon on the Mount (Mt. 5:14-16), not instead of Christ, or in addition to Christ, but as participating in that same illumination of which he is the sole source.[36] As Christ is a sign *"Ad revelationem gentium,"* so the community is to be this sign as well, called to witness to that same light for that same purpose, to receive the "one flame" in order to reveal Christ's redemptive presence to the entire world.

The second half of the poem turns to a meditative reflection on the meaning of the candles, introduced by the single line "Our lives, like candles, spell this simple symbol:" (l. 12), that is, spell out, express through their actions, the meaning of the symbolism of the candles, which are now apostrophized:

> Weep like our bodily life, sweet work of bees,
> Sweeten the world, with your slow sacrifice.
> And this shall be our praise:
> That by our glad expense, our Father's will
> Burned and consumed us for a parable. (ll. 13-17)

The phrase "work of bees" is borrowed from the first blessing prayer of the feast (*Missal* 779) but is also found in the *"Exultet"* of the Easter vigil, which also mentions the "odor of sweetness" of the wax (*Missal* 345, 346),

---

35. Gerard Manley Hopkins, *Poems and Prose*, ed. W. H. Gardner (Baltimore: Penguin, 1953) 51. In the anthology of religious poetry that he was assembling in the summer of 1941, Merton included this sonnet among seven Hopkins poems (see Patrick F. O'Connell, "Thomas Merton's Projected Anthology of Religious Poetry," *The Merton Seasonal* 25.3 [Fall 2000] 20-28), and he echoed it repeatedly in his own verse: see "The Sowing of Meanings," ll. 28-30 (*FA* 85; *CP* 188-89); "Canticle for the Blessed Virgin," ll. 75-76 (*FA* 46; *CP* 163); *Hagia Sophia* III (Thomas Merton, *Emblems of a Season of Fury* [New York: New Directions, 1963] 64; *CP* 366); "The Ladies of Tlatilco" 12 (Thomas Merton, *The Geography of Lograire* [New York: New Directions, 1969] 29; *CP* 485).

36. The replacement of "receives his flame" in the draft with "receive one flame" in the final version sharpens the focus on the single source of light that is Christ.

another connection of the Feast of the Presentation with paschaltime. The dripping of the wax is compared to tears of repentance as the literal and figurative terms of the simile of the previous line ("lives, like candles") are here reversed: the candles weep "like our bodily life" – or rather are bidden to do so in order to "Sweeten the world" through the aroma of the "slow sacrifice" of the melting wax (echoing the "most sweet love" mentioned in the second blessing prayer of the feast [*Missal* 780]). Dying in order to give life, the candle recalls of course the self-sacrifice of Christ already foreshadowed in the ritual of presentation itself, but the gradual character of its decrease reflects particularly the pattern of monastic life, especially Trappist asceticism, the slow process of death to self. The monks' way of praising God (and perhaps of praising the candles as well) is to go and do likewise, to expend themselves joyfully, "burned" in the fire of repentance and "consumed" to nourish the flame of love. The focus here is no longer specifically on the illumination the flame provides but on the power of the purifying fire to bring about a salutary diminishment, as the monks disappear in conformity with the divine will and in so doing become a "parable," a dynamic expression of complete self-surrender and self-gift, a participation in the paschal mystery.

The poem concludes by returning the focus to the illuminative power of the candles and of the monks who carry them:

> Nor burn we now with brown and smoky flames, but bright
> Until our sacrifice is done,
> (By which not we, but You are known)
> And then, returning to our Father, one by one,
> Give back our lives like wise and waxen lights. (ll. 18-22)

The speaker makes clear that the burning mentioned in the previous line does not produce a murky obscurity, evidence of impurity, but shines brightly and thus is able to provide light to others, illumining not the self but God, as Jesus emphasizes in calling his disciples the light of the world ("Let your light so shine before others that seeing your good works they may give praise to the Father in heaven" [Mt. 5:16]). This brightness lasts a lifetime, in so far as the sacrifice that makes it possible does so as well. But the final lines also suggest that in returning to the Father one returns the light of life given by Christ, the Light of the world, to its source, an image not of extinguishment but of eternal fulfillment. The final comparison of lives to "wise and waxen lights" implies that these modifiers may be applied to the lives as well, suggesting that the monks can be likened to the wise virgins with their lamps lit to meet the

Bridegroom and enter into the eschatological banquet (Mt. 25:1-13),[37] and perhaps even that "waxen" refers not simply to the material composition of the candles but to the paradoxical truth than in the end the light of the spirit, unlike the candles of the flesh, has not diminished at all, has not in fact waned but waxed, and is now revealed to be completely one with the infinite, eternal Light, "the true Light that enlightens all" (Jn. 1:9).

\* \* \* \* \* \* \*

The poems discussed here are not the only ones Merton wrote in his first weeks at Gethsemani. "How Long We Wait" (*MDS* 53; *CP* 89-90), the first version of which is dated Epiphany 1942 (*ES* 4-5), uses the image of waiting for the dawn to suggest waiting for the coming of the Lord.[38] The other three poems surviving in early drafts[39] are verse reworkings of scriptural narratives, an application of the monastic practice of *lectio divina*, the third foundational practice of Benedictine spirituality along with liturgical prayer and manual labor. They merit a separate study of their own.[40] But the five poems discussed here, Merton's well-crafted reflections on his new home, on the liturgical season that marked his arrival, and on the complementary dimensions of work and communal prayer that would be essential elements of his vocation for the rest of his life, are a particularly appropriate focus for consideration as we mark the seventy-fifth anniversary of Merton's arrival at Gethsemani and entrance into Cistercian life. They provide perspectives on key aspects of this momentous decision that are not otherwise available and so appreciably deepen our understanding of his initial response to his new environment and his new commitment.

---

37. See Merton's use of this parable in "The Winter's Night," ll. 15-17 (*TP* [9]; *CP* 38); "The Trappist Abbey: Matins," ll. 10-17 (*TP* [15]; *CP* 46); "The Holy Sacrament of the Altar," ll. 10, 14, 19 (*TP* [19]; *CP* 50-51); "The Peril," ll. 8-9 (*MDS* 50; *CP* 87); "Figures for an Apocalypse" epigraph and I.34-44 (*FA* 12, 14; *CP* 134, 136). Merton returns to this parable in his late poem in French, "Les Cinq Vierges," written for Jacques Maritain (*CP* 819; English translation *CP* 826-27).

38. For a discussion see Patrick F. O'Connell, "Thomas Merton's Wake-Up Calls: Aubades and Monastic Dawn Poems from *A Man in the Divided Sea*," *The Merton Annual* 12 (1999) 146-52.

39. "Cana" (*ES* 5-6; *MDS* 57; *CP* 93); "St. Paul" (*ES* 6-7; *MDS* 60; *CP* 95-96); "The Ointment" (*ES* 8-10; *CP* 777-79).

40. "Cana" and "St. Paul," along with four other early poems based on scripture passages, are discussed in Patrick F. O'Connell, "From *Lectio* to Lyric: Thomas Merton's Early Poems on Scriptural Narratives," *Cistercian Studies Quarterly* 52.2 (May 2017) [forthcoming]; "The Ointment," which was never revised or published during Merton's lifetime, is not considered in this article.

# Was Thomas Merton Merely Dabbling in Early Irish Poetry?[1]

*Monica Weis, SSJ*

Why, hermit Marvan, sleepest thou not
Upon a feather quilt?
Why rather sleepest thou abroad
Upon a pitchpine floor?[2]

Readers of Thomas Merton's journals are well aware of his interest in the Russian Orthodox theologians exiled in Paris such as Sergius Bulgakov and Nicholas Berdyaev, his avid conversations with D. T. Suzuki examining the resonance between Buddhism and Christianity, and his attraction to anthropology, especially the Cargo Cults in the South Pacific islands. We continue to be amazed at his ability to embrace multiple intellectual views while at the same time maintaining his commitment to solitude, contemplation and the monastic *horarium*. We might even wonder: what else could his active (over-active?) mind find to preoccupy it?

Known to only a limited number of scholars is Merton's fascination – I even dare to say "passion" – for early Celtic monasticism and, in particular, early Irish hermit poetry. As testimony to this fascination, I offer Merton's June 2, 1964 journal entry in which he mentions that reading Celtic monastic history is "A new world that has waited until this time to open up."[3] And, indeed, for Merton, this was a whole new world opening up. A curious and serendipitous convergence of events during the last four years of his life persuaded Merton to spend extended

---

1. This essay is a condensed and significantly reorganized version of chapter five of my study of Merton's interest in Celtic spirituality: *Thomas Merton and the Celts: A New World Opening Up* (Eugene, OR: Wipf and Stock, 2016).

2. "King and Hermit," *Selections from Ancient Irish Poetry*, translated by Kuno Meyer (London: Constable, 1911) 47 (subsequent references will be cited as "Meyer" parenthetically in the text); the first poem in Thomas Merton's "Anthology of Irish Poetry," unpublished mimeograph (September 1964) included in volume 2 (232-54) of Merton's "Collected Essays," the 24-volume bound set of published and unpublished materials assembled at the Abbey of Gethsemani and available both there and at the Thomas Merton Center, Bellarmine University, Louisville, KY (subsequent references will be cited as "'Anthology'" parenthetically in the text).

3. Thomas Merton, *Dancing in the Water of Life: Seeking Peace in the Hermitage. Journals, vol. 5: 1963-1965*, ed. Robert E. Daggy (San Francisco: HarperCollins, 1997) 107; subsequent references will be cited as "*DWL*" parenthetically in the text.

time reading and thinking about Celtic monastic history. First, Merton's meeting in 1963 and subsequent correspondence with A. M. (Donald) Allchin[4] awakened in him a desire to reclaim his Welsh heritage – his father Owen Merton being partly Welsh on the Grierson/Bird side of the family.[5] Second, Allchin encouraged Merton to read not only Russian Orthodox theologians of the diaspora, but also contemporary Welsh poetry and early Celtic myths. Third, with a keen mind that always wanted to read everything on a subject that grabbed him, Merton initiated a four-year correspondence (1964-67) with medieval and Celtic history expert Nora K. Chadwick[6] who provided him with lists of critical texts on early Celtic history and Christianity. Merton's notes – housed in the archives of the Thomas Merton Center at Bellarmine University – fill several notebooks with outlines of texts, quotations, cross-references to notable sources such as Bede, Anthony, Columba and Colmcille, and comprise more than one hundred-eighty holograph pages. To read through this voluminous material is to realize just how deeply Celtic Christianity of the fourth to the eighth centuries became a preoccupation for Merton between 1964 and 1968 and how much time he must have devoted to this focused study.

While Merton was entranced by accounts of early monasteries and their founders, stipulations of the Rule of Tallaght, the Celtic propensity for *peregrinatio*,[7] and tales of the monks' wanderings, as well as their unique Celtic spirituality that was rooted in the mysteries of the Incarnation and the Trinity, he was particularly fascinated by early Irish hermit poetry. This essay, due to space constraints, will narrow its focus to this material, relying primarily, as did Merton, on the scholarship of Kuno Meyer, Robin Flower and Kenneth H. Jackson, quintessential experts in

---

4. Arthur MacDonald (Donald) Allchin (1930-2010), an Anglican theologian, canon at Canterbury, and librarian at Pusey House, was a prolific writer, expert on Orthodox theology, advocate for East-West dialogue and Christian unity and close friend of Thomas Merton.

5. Merton mentions in a May 27, 1964 letter to his Aunt Kit that he is reading "about hermits and recluses in early Celtic Christianity" and that because of their Welsh background, "we all have some of this in our blood" (Thomas Merton *The Road to Joy: Letters to New and Old Friends*, ed. Robert E. Daggy [New York: Farrar, Straus, & Giroux, 1989] 62).

6. Nora K. Chadwick (1891-1972), specialist in Anglo-Saxon and Old Norse, was a University Lecturer at the University of Cambridge and noted scholar of Celtic history. Her 1961 book *The Age of Saints in the Early Celtic Church* is still considered to be an essential source for Celtic monastic history.

7. *Peregrinatio* or pilgrimage was a unique feature of Celtic Christianity in which a monk chose "white martyrdom," that is, exile to "seek the place of one's resurrection." Often a monk would set out in a leather-bound *currach* (small boat) allowing God to choose his destination.

this early literature.[8] To set the context, however, I need to offer readers a brief introduction to the Celtic worldview, early Celtic Christianity, and the characteristics of Irish hermit poetry as an art form.

## The Celtic World View

The most pervasive and startling characteristic of the early Celts, acknowledged by all historians and critics of Celtic culture, is their gift of imagination and their distinctive way of seeing. For the Celts, there is no distinction between the sacred and the profane, between the spiritual and the material. There are not two worlds, but one integrated life. This Celtic worldview, Donald Allchin has argued, is grounded in the two doctrines of creation/redemption and the Trinity.[9] As Allchin has aptly phrased it: "God comes out of himself into his world both in creation and redemption" (Allchin 22). Jesus is, as Colossians 1:15-20 affirms, the creative Word of God who reconciles the entire cosmos that is forever being created. The Trinity, the second doctrine defining the Celtic worldview, celebrates the mystery of *relationship* among Persons. The Celts honor the Father *through* the Son, and *in* the Holy Ghost – one Being ceaselessly creating, saving and sanctifying humans and non-humans alike. For the Celts, the Divine is both here and there, both immanent and transcendent. Everything is infused, saturated with Presence, so that all elements of creation are to be reverenced as unique expressions of the Divine, each coming into being as an outpouring of Creative Love. Although early Celtic Christianity was primarily monastic in its configuration, the centrality of these two doctrines infused both ecclesiastical and domestic spheres. Monks, rising to greet the dawn, celebrated hymns and psalms in honor of the Trinity and the creation of the new day; similarly, housewives on rising blessed the Three Persons of God, stoked the embers three times, and engaged in multiple household tasks with a tri-fold blessing.[10] Historically, Celtic

---

8. Kuno Meyer (1858-1919), a German scholar distinguished in Celtic philology and literature, was considered the "father" of Celtic and Gaelic scholarship. Robin Flower (1881-1946) was an English poet, Celtic scholar and translator, perhaps best known for his translation of "Pangur Bán," the famous ninth-century poem identified as "The Monk and His Pet Cat" or "The Scholar and His Cat." Kenneth H. Jackson (1909-1991) was an English linguist and translator specializing in Celtic languages and concentrating on tales and poems traceable to the third and fourth century CE. He was a student of Nora Chadwick, mastering six Celtic languages and conducting fieldwork in Scotland and Wales.

9. A. M. Allchin, *God's Presence Makes the World* (London: Darton, Longman & Todd, 1997) xi-xii; subsequent references will be cited as "Allchin" parenthetically in the text.

10. See Esther de Waal, *The Celtic Way of Prayer: The Recovery of the Religious Imagination* (Garden City, NY: Doubleday, 1997); subsequent references will be cited

spirituality can be traced to *theoria physike*,[11] that is, natural contemplation practiced by the fourth-century Egyptian desert fathers and mothers and elucidated in the writings of Pelagius, John Scotus Eriugena, the Greek Fathers and Maximus the Confessor – all of whom regard creation as a theophany of God. With such a worldview, it is understandable that Celtic poetry – and in particular Irish hermit poetry – would celebrate the interplay between and among the Triune Persons, as well as the trinity of the Divine, the human and the earth.

### Early Celtic Christianity

Springing from the influence of fourth-century Egyptian monasticism, a unique form of monastic life developed during the fourth and fifth centuries in Cornwall, Wales and Ireland. It is important to reiterate that the practice of early Celtic Christianity – for both church and society – was essentially monastic. During the sixth century, there were well-established monasteries at Bangor, Derry, Durrow, Kildare, Clonfert, Lismore and Kells. At the same time – and perhaps paradoxically, as historian David Knowles notes – "a vivid Latin culture" and "remarkable artistic achievement," supported by the Celtic gift of imagination, arose that puts "Celtic monastic illuminations and metalwork among the masterpieces of art-history."[12] Despite this Eastern influence, Knowles maintains, the *spirit* of the Celtic monks was far different from that of their Egyptian models, primarily because of their deep-seated pre-Christian belief in the unity of matter and spirit, their incorporation of druidic elements into their celebrations, and their "predilection for exile (*peregrinatio*) as a form of renunciation or exile," in which monks set sail in a small boat (*currach*) seeking the place of one's resurrection (Knowles 32). Although many monks desiring the "white martyrdom"[13] of exile or *peregrinatio* took to

---

as "de Waal" parenthetically in the text.

11. Merton frequently refers to *theoria physike* in his writings; see in particular Thomas Merton, *An Introduction to Christian Mysticism: Initiation into the Monastic Tradition* 3, ed. Patrick F. O'Connell (Kalamazoo, MI: Cistercian Publications, 2008) 121-36.

12. David Knowles, *Christian Monasticism* (New York: McGraw-Hill, 1969) 31; subsequent references will be cited as "Knowles" parenthetically in the text.

13. Dating from a seventh- or eighth-century homily, the Celts identified three kinds of martyrdom: "red" involving violent death for the sake of Jesus; "white" referring to desert hermits who choose exile or pilgrimage modeled on Abraham's obedience to God to "go to the land which I will show you"; "green" martyrdom for those committed to fasting and penance without implying a journey or exile. Additionally, in Frederick Buechner's historical novel, *Brendan* (New York: Atheneum, 1978), Bishop Erc mentions a fourth category of "blue martyrs" who are "*currach* martyrs" with beards of seaweed,

the sea, others retreated to the woods, occupying their time with prayer, copying manuscripts and writing poetry – often in the margins of sacred manuscripts.

Living so closely with nature, these early monks saw the beauty of their God revealed in the elements and the flora and fauna surrounding them. Each day was an acclamation of praise to the Creator, parallel to the hymns and psalms they chanted in their cell or outside in the woods. Celtic scholar Kuno Meyer acknowledges the Celtic love of nature in his introduction to *Selections from Ancient Irish Poetry*. He writes: "To seek out and watch and love Nature, in its tiniest phenomena as in its grandest, was given to no people so early and so fully as to the Celt" (Irish or Welsh) (Meyer xii). Both Meyer and Kenneth Jackson agree that because no manuscripts exist from the early days of Celtic literature – comprising six languages and thirteen centuries – "gross misinterpretation" has occurred, namely the Celts' literary adherence to magic and their lack of emotion.

Although some critics regard the "Celtic mind as something mysterious, magical, filled with dark broodings over a mighty past . . . in some strange way in direct contact with a mystical supernatural twilight world which they would rarely reveal to the outsider," Jackson, who studied under Nora Chadwick, is adamant that the Celts were *not* "given to mysticism or sentimentality . . . ; their most outstanding characteristic is rather their astonishing power of imagination."[14] Merton resonated with this evaluation of these early people and was, we know, fond of exploring the power of the imagination. In *Contemplation in a World of Action*, for example, he applauds "the creative task of making symbols, joining things together . . . [to] throw new light on each other" and praises human imagination as "something which enables us to discover unique present meaning in a given moment in our life."[15]

This vivid power of imagination that was part of the Celtic mindset made early Irish hermit poetry fresh and original. It strengthened the poet's ability to see in new ways – a unique characteristic of the Celtic worldview finely honed in all of the monks. British scholar and Irish translator Robin Flower remarks that "the poets of the old Irish time had always a keen and unaffected delight in the beauty of their country, its hills and rivers,

---

barnacled cheeks, and "eyes bleared with salt from scouring the blue storms of the sea for the peace of God" (86).

14. Kenneth H. Jackson, *A Celtic Miscellany* (Cambridge: Harvard University Press, 1951) 12; subsequent references will be cited as "Jackson, *Miscellany*" parenthetically in the text.

15. Thomas Merton, *Contemplation in a World of Action* (Garden City, NY: Doubleday, 1971) 345.

lakes and forests, the cleared plains, and the vast surrounding sea."[16] As illustration of his point, Flower recounts the ancient tale of Lady Poverty who asks to see the monks' monastery. Happily they escort her to the brow of a hill with its vista of the countryside. "This," the monks exclaim, "is our monastery, lady!" (Flower 64-66). The best of the hermit poems, argues Flower, "are all fire and air, praise and prayer and dedication of the heart, touching little upon dogma or miracle, but content and eager with a new joy and a young revelation" (Flower 47). As historian Esther de Waal phrases it in her discussion of Celtic hermits: "They saw the world through eyes washed miraculously clear by continual spiritual exercise; they saw with 'rinsed eyes' . . . . They saw with such clarity because the seeing came out of their contemplative vision. And their writing reflects this, with its distinctive freshness and immediacy, its attention to detail" (de Waal 96). De Waal bases her position on Robin Flower who claims the monks "brought into that environment an eye washed miraculously clear by a continual spiritual exercise" (Flower 42). It is not surprising, as de Waal remarks in a footnote, that Merton also has been described as seeing with "rinsed eyes" (de Waal 221 n. 2). Certainly, as a fruit of his own contemplation, Merton developed a sense of clean non-attachment and the ability to allow every creature its own voice.

A second and related area of misinterpretation about Celtic nature poetry – which included Irish and Welsh poetry – is the question of emotion. Contrary to critics such as E. Sieper, who argues that the Celtic imagination is objective and "infinitely primitive," Kenneth Jackson maintains that poems are "concerned vitally with the singer's own reaction to his surroundings, not with making a descriptive catalogue [as found in earlier Latin poems] about the various things he sees, but with telling us how he feels about them and how they harmonize or clash with his own particular mood."[17] Using as an example oft-quoted lines from a hermit-scribe – "Pleasant is the glittering of the sun today upon these margins because it flickers so" – Jackson quotes his predecessor Robin Flower as remarking: "It is the emotion, not the sun, that matters here" (Jackson, *Studies* 80). In short, Jackson and Flower would have us understand that early Celtic poetry is "the work of literary artists, not the crude chant of primitive man" (Jackson, *Studies* 80-82).

---

16. Robin Flower, *The Irish Tradition* (Oxford: Clarendon Press, 1947) 50; subsequent references will be cited as "Flower" parenthetically in the text.

17. Kenneth H. Jackson, *Studies in Early Celtic Nature Poetry* (Cambridge: Cambridge University Press, 1935) 80; subsequent references will be cited as "Jackson, *Studies*" parenthetically in the text. Jackson makes the point that catalogues were acceptable in Welsh gnomic poetry and seasonal poems, but not in hermit poems.

By examining early Celtic poetry, one can sense that in every case, the Celtic poet was an astute craftsman, adept at presenting not an "elaborate or sustained description" of a scene, but a succession of crisp pictures and precise colorful images with implied emotional overtones, similar to the brush strokes of French impressionism or the subtlety of the Japanese haiku.[18] Consider this brief illustration of Celtic artistry that Merton copied into his own notes and later included in his "Anthology" of favorite Irish hermit poems (250):

> There is here above the brotherhood
> A bright tall glossy yew
> The melodious bell sends out a clear keen note
> In St. Columba's church. (Jackson, *Studies* 10)

As Kuno Meyer explains: "the Celts were always quick to take an artistic hint; they avoid the obvious and the commonplace; the half-said thing to them is dearest" (Meyer xiii). Robin Flower evaluates their flair for the precise word this way – which Merton included in his handwritten notes: "The extreme correctness of the Irish way of thought is reflected in the idioms of their language and determines the effect of their literature upon any mind that is at all attuned to distinctions of style." Merton also copies Flower's comment that the elder Cato offers a telling critique: "Celts were distinguished for their aptitude for fighting and for subtle speech. The Irish have well maintained these two characters . . . a sharp and homely brevity of epigrammatic speech eminently calculated for the rapid thrust and return of contentious talk" (Flower 110).[19] For Nora Chadwick, the Celts' special poetic gifts could be attributed to "the simplicity and integrity of the spiritual elite," men who lived a Spartan "life purified from material desires in simple communion with nature."[20]

### A Brief Look at the History of Irish Hermit Poetry

Kuno Meyer offers us valuable insight into the somewhat cloudy history of the genre. Once the Romans conquered and influenced the life of continental Europe, native people lost not only their liberty, but their language and vernacular literature as well, so that by the fifth century,

18. Jackson, *Studies* 177. Jackson makes the point that there is fine Irish nature poetry as early as the ninth century that tends to be impressionistic; however, there are no early Welsh nature poems – their writing tends to be sententious and epigrammatic.

19. This quotation can be found in Merton's *Working Notebook #48* (no date – 1966?); unpublished holograph, archives of the Thomas Merton Center (TMA) at Bellarmine University, Louisville, KY.

20. Nora K. Chadwick, *The Age of Saints in the Early Celtic Church* (Oxford: Oxford University Press, 1961) 165; subsequent references will be cited as "Chadwick" in the text.

most of these cultural expressions were extinct. This, maintains Meyer, did not happen in Ireland, partly because of its insularity, but primarily because Celtic Christianity can be traced not to Rome, but to Britain and Gaul.[21] Indeed, Meyer believes that the Irish are the earliest voice from the dawn of Western European civilization, and that it was "the influence and example of those Irish missionaries who converted Northumberland that taught the Anglian monk to preserve and cultivate *his* national treasure" [emphasis added] (Meyer ix). The sixth century, dubbed "The Golden Age of Celtic Saints" by Nora Chadwick, is for Meyer the "The Golden Age of Irish Civilization" (Meyer ix) – a time when "vernacular literature received a fresh impulse from the new faith" and "flourishing primitive Christian literature arose" (Meyer ix). Sadly, despite a rich "oral literature, handed down by many generations of bards and story-tellers . . . first written down in the monasteries" (Meyer x), most manuscripts were destroyed by the Viking invasion in the eighth century; however, many manuscripts attributed to the eleventh century onward – as Meyer, Jackson, Flower and Chadwick have established – were undoubtedly composed in the seventh and eighth centuries. Meyer believes that as Irish scholarship advances, "it is not unlikely that fragments of poetry will be found which, from linguistic or internal evidence, may be claimed for the sixth century" (Meyer xi).

### Shapes and Themes of Irish Hermit Poetry

Irish poets generally did not write epic poetry. Prose was their choice for the hero-narrative. Lyric poetry was written either by professional bards attached to a court or king, or by unattached itinerant poets or monks. Their subjects were primarily religious topics, the seasons and nature, but rarely love poems (at least from extant examples). Composed generally in quatrains of four heptasyllabic lines with rhyming couplets, derived from earlier Latin meters, religious poetry provides a unique window into the early Christian Church. Poems, which give us a "fascinating insight into the peculiar character of the early Irish Church," might feature the "hermit in his lonely cell, the monk at his devotions or at his work of copying in the scriptorium or under the open sky" (Meyer xii-xiii). On occasion they might spotlight the ascetic, praying in the woods, on mountains or on an isolated island. The religious fervor and asceticism of the monk or hermit are central to the text, as illustrated in these two different examples from Robin Flower, the first a prayer, the second a comment on the austerity of "the beehive cells of the monks, built of dry stones":

---

21. Meyer viii–x. Meyer notes that only three groups left behind some record of their pagan civilization in a vernacular literature – the Irish, Anglo-Saxons and Icelanders.

Christ keep me safe, Christ guard me lowly,
Christ bring me to his dwelling high . . .
. . . This hope I have.

Cells that freeze,
The thin pale monks upon their knees,
Bodies worn with rites austere,
The falling tear – Heaven's king loves these. (Flower 49)

With the development of the anchorite movement in the eighth to tenth centuries (as reconstructed by Robin Flower with his research on the Tallaght and Finglas monasteries), so too was there an "intimate affection for wild life and wild nature, such as we may find elsewhere in Christian sources perhaps only in the story of St. Francis" (Jackson, *Miscellany* 306). Thus, Irish hermit poetry – a subset of Celtic monasticism – reinforces the ideal of the solitary life: "a little cell in woods and wild," simple fare and an ascetic way of life, harmony with one's surroundings, clarity of vision, and "love and sympathy for wild life" such as the "trilling of birds" (Jackson, *Studies* 96-99). Kenneth Jackson makes the important distinction that the third-century BCE Greek poet Theocritus "only listened to birds and noted that their song was pleasant, but the hermits did more than this; they lived so much among the wild creatures that they became almost one with them, almost own brother to them, as it were hardly conscious that there was any distinction of genus" (Jackson, *Studies* 100).

This tendency to celebrate wild life was integral to the tales of early Celtic saints who befriended animals and found in them acceptable companions for praising God.[22] St. Maedoc, for example, is mentioned in Charles Plummer's *Lives of the Saints* as meeting a she-wolf who was "piteous, exhausted, starving." Securing some bread and fish from a lad on the road, Maedoc "cast them to the wolf" to satisfy her hunger.[23] Likewise, Saint Ciarán of Saighir is said to have met a wild boar who "at first fled in terror," but "becoming calm by God," returned to become his first pupil, cut saplings for his first cell, and joined other animals gathered around Ciarán. One of these pupils, a fox, stole the monk's shoes, but with the urging of the wild boar, repented and returned the shoes. This same sympathy with animals is found in the more tame and celebrated ninth-century "The Monk and his Pet Cat" (translated by Robin Flower

---

22. See Jackson, *Studies* 103; he makes the point that the hermits had an instinctive need for society and animals often became the substitute for monastic brothers; see also *Beasts and Saints* translated by Helen Waddell (London: Constable, 1934).

23. Jackson, *Studies* 101-102, quoting from Charles Plummer, "Maedoc," *Lives of the Irish Saints*, 2 vols. (Oxford: Oxford Univesity Press, 1922) 2.xxxiv.

as "The Scholar and His Cat, Pangur Bán"[24]) – so well known that Jackson claims it needs no quoting – which highlights the "'childish craft' of Pangur's mousing" compared to the monk's more challenging "attempt at solving problems of scholarship" (Jackson, *Studies* 101).

Merton, who thought of himself primarily as a poet, was tempted to try his hand at his own lyrics: "St. Maedoc (Fragment of an Ikon)" appears in handwritten form in Working Notebook #14 (June 1964)[25] after several pages of notes about Celtic high crosses, the Rule of Tallaght, books on ancient Irish poetry, and an outline of the events of St. Brendan's sea journey (*Navigatio Sancti Brendani*), which was Merton's favorite epic. His original poem celebrates an early sixth-century Irish or Welsh monk, founder of the monastery of Ferns and legendary miracle worker noted for his benevolence and hospitality.[26]

Merton's poem[27] refers to several of the miracles associated with the saint: the "floating stone" that ferried him as an infant across a lake when no boat was available, the transformation of the visage of "Aed Duv, son of Fergus" who "Prayed and slept / In Maedoc's cowl" and the saint's power in stopping a warring king and his army. Notable is the triplet of images that constitute the King's decision to turn back: "No fighting the saints / The Blessed Trinity / Or Maedoc's wonders." Sr. Thérèse Lentfoehr, the earliest interpreter of Merton's poetry, questions whether Merton had access to a real ikon fragment or whether the poem is a symbol of Maedoc's life. She discussed the connotative links between images that give the poem a surrealistic pattern by juxtaposing nature and war, reality and miracles.[28] Certainly the Celtic love of nature is evidenced in this poem which grounds its celebration of a trinity of miracles in the "floating stone," "fresh hazel," "wolves," a "green shore," "sunlight in spring rain," "Water and Spirit / Bright wave and flame / at the wood's edge."

---

24. See www. ling.upenn/edu/~beatrice/pangur-ban.html for Flower's translation of the poem. "Pangur" appears also as one of Samuel Barber's "Hermit Songs," Op. 29 and was originally performed at the Library of Congress in 1953 by Leontyne Price with Barber at the piano.

25. Thomas Merton, *Working Notebook #14* (June 1964); unpublished holograph (TMA).

26. Also known as Mogue or Aidan, Maedoc was educated in Wales at St. David's monastery, taking with him a "cartload of beer" to this notoriously abstemious monastery, and later returned to Ireland.

27. Thomas Merton, *The Collected Poems of Thomas Merton* (New York: New Directions, 1977) 752-53; subsequent references will be cited as "*CP*" parenthetically in the text.

28. Thérèse Lentfoehr, *Words and Silence: On the Poetry of Thomas Merton* (New York: New Directions, 1979) 67.

A few pages later in this same *Working Notebook #14*, Merton sketches out another poem – "Merlin and the Deer" (*CP* 736-37) – perhaps now more well-known, although the poem was not published during his lifetime, nor is it mentioned in Sr. Thérèse's analysis of Merton's poetry.[29] George Kilcourse, however, featured the poem in his 1991 article in *The Merton Annual* as an illustration of the process of discovering the "true self."[30] What intrigues me, in addition to the poem being based on a real episode of Merton seeing a deer temporarily trapped in the water of the monastery reservoir (see *DWL* 158-59) is the figure of Merlin.[31] In Welsh mythology Merlin is considered, among other things, to be a Master of Breath. Breath, that animating principle and portal to higher consciousness, is nature's tool for finding the "self." In Merton's poem, "The deer swims beautifully / And so escapes / Limping across the country road into the little cedars." Merlin, the Welsh magician, "awakes," becomes a "gentle savage / Dressed in leaves" and hums to himself – audible breathing – while saying psalms in the woods. Sidetracked by the deer episode, Merlin "pulls out / Of all that icy water" of distraction and allows nature to capture him "in many spells" as a "Willing prisoner of trees and rain." But wait. Is this Merlin or Merton we are talking about? Thomas Merton was at this time transitioning to more extended time in the hermitage in the woods and choosing to be that "prisoner of trees and rain." Yet in the poem he – Merlin/Merton – is not totally alone. "The invisible people // Visit his jail / With forest stories / Tales without sound / And without conclusion." This Merlin/Merton magic initiates "Clear fires without smoke / Fumbled prophecies / And Celtic fortunes." With the merging of Merlin/Merton, the woods become one of those "thin places" that reveal secrets of the solitary life, the Otherworld, and – we might add – secrets of the "hidden wholeness" (*CP* 363) or "true self" deep within the human person.

Readers of Merton will recall his fondness for the deer that often appeared at twilight in the meadow outside his hermitage. Between January 1965 and June 1966 there are thirteen references to deer in Merton's

---

29. Because the poem is handwritten in *Working Notebook #14* – June 1964, it was presumably composed sometime that year.

30. See George A. Kilcourse, "A Shy Wild Deer: The 'True Self' in Thomas Merton's Poetry," *The Merton Annual* 4 (1991) 97-109.

31. The figure of Merlin has many predecessors, including Myrddin, the "Wild Man of the Woods" who fled to the forest after the battle of Arfderydd (573), lived with animals and was given the gift of prophecy. His legend is identified with the twelfth-century figure of Laioken, and later with Merlin in the fifteenth century.

journals.[32] They reveal his initial superficial fascination with these mysterious beings – "suddenly realized that there were beings there" (*DWL* 189 [1/8/1965]) – that over time evolves into deeper insight and reverence. Merton exclaims over the "deerness" that "reveals to me something essential in myself!"

> The thing that struck me most: one sees, looking at them directly in movement, just what the cave painters saw – something that I have never seen in a photograph. It is an awe-inspiring thing – the *Mantu* or "spirit" shown in the running of the deer . . . A contemplative intuition! . . . I could sense the softness of their coat and longed to touch them. (*DWL* 291 [9/6/1965])

Not surprisingly one doe becomes quite used to Merton's pacing back and forth outside the hermitage reciting compline (*DWL* 292 [9/10/1965]) and, again not surprisingly, Merton writes: "Yesterday, Feast of St. Francis, I made a holiday of it. In the morning (bright and cold) walked through the hollow then to the long field and in and out the wood where the deer sleep" (*DWL* 300 [10/5/1965]). It is this intimate connection with nature that contemporary philosopher John O'Donohue celebrates as a veritable conversation among all the creatures and elements: bird, tree, water, rock, vegetation and soil.[33] If matter and spirit interpenetrate one another, there is a kinship to be recognized, acknowledged and acclaimed.

## Kinship with Nature as an Act of Praise

Kinship with particular birds is often cited in Merton's journals and appears frequently as well in early Celtic poetry and Irish hermit poetry.[34] In Celtic lore, there are many stories of birds and humans sharing praise of God, even oral reports of bards wearing bird feathers (de Waal 14). To this end Robin Flower maintains that "hermit poetry is never so lovely as when it has to tell of the bird's song that cheered the scribe at his meticulous labours and the anchorite at his long prayers and vigils." As example, Flower offers this delightful piece:

> The tiny bird
> Whose call I heard

---

32. See my discussion of deer in "Afterword," *The Environmental Vision of Thomas Merton* (Lexington: University Press of Kentucky, 2011) 157-65. There is a total of twenty-two references to deer in Merton's journal beginning in 1963 and continuing until 1968.

33. John O'Donohue, *A Celtic Pilgrimage with John O'Donohue* [DVD] (New York: SoundsTrue, 2009).

34. A cursory glance at the poetic selections included in Merton's "Anthology of Irish Poetry" offers a broad list: lark, blackbird, ousel, cuckoo, herons, seagulls, wild goose.

I marked his yellow bill;
The ousel's glee
Above Lough Lee
Shakes golden branches still. (Flower 61)

Birds were also significant in early Celtic culture as a way of marking time. As far back as Hesiod the first cry of the cuckoo marked the beginning of a season. Early birdsong calendars, as both Robin Flower and Kenneth Jackson agree, suggest a shared tradition between the English and the Irish and "are one way in which the passing of the seasons was noted in the almanac literature of these islands at an early period" (Jackson, *Studies* 165-66). Merton copies into *Working Notebook #14* Jackson's reference to birdsong calendars and adds his own comment about the Calendar of Pseudo-Bede from the Durham MS in the *Patrologia Latina* that February 11 or 12 was the "day when the birds begin to sing" and they cease on June 17. The *Navigatio Sancti Brendani* – well read by Merton – also picks up on this bird imagery. The welcoming monks on one island remain in their cells after compline until cockcrow; on another island, the birds join in singing the office with them, answering the call to prayer – "Thou shalt open my lips, O Lord" – with the response "Praise the Lord, all his angels; praise him, all his virtues."[35] Merton, too, often, refers to the birds as accompanying his recitation of the divine office, teaching him the value of practicing contemplation,[36] and heralding the dawn of day. Certainly these references to birds are more than simply being *simpatico* with God's creatures. Rather, they reinforce an understanding of the Celtic worldview and celebration of the elements: rock, sea, earth, fire, seasons and annual patterns (de Waal x) – a notion the ancient Greeks described as "the breathing together of all things."[37] In *Working Notebook #15*, dated 1965-August 1966, Merton sketches ideas for, among other things, a long anti-poem, *Cables to the Ace* – a concise reflection that effectively becomes his own marginalia, pulling together the beauty of nature, the solitude of the hermit and the prayer of the contemplative:

---

35. See Charles Kingsley, "The Celtic Hermits," *The Hermits* (Charleston, SC: BiblioLife, 2008) in which he recounts at length the "Navigation of St. Brendan," based on the French version of the tale. Kingsley's text was originally published by Macmillan in 1868.

36. Thomas Merton, *Entering the Silence: Becoming a Monk and Writer. Journals, vol. 2: 1941-1952*, ed. Jonathan Montaldo (San Francisco: HarperCollins, 1996) 407-408.

37. See Noel D. O'Donoghue, "Saint Patrick's Breastplate," in *An Introduction to Celtic Christianity*, ed. James Patrick Mackey (Edinburgh: T & T Clark, 1989) 50: "his marvellous creation of earth and sky and ocean is a living intimate presence, the 'divine milieu' of Teilhard de Chardin, the 'breathing together of all things' of which the first philosophers of the West spoke so feelingly."

My worship is a blue sky and ten thousand
crickets in the deep wet grass of the field.
My vow is the silence under their
Sound. I support the woodpecker & the dove.
Together we learn the norms. The plowed & planted field
says: *it is my turn*. And several of us
begin to sing.[38]

The bottom line, as Donald Allchin and Esther de Waal have said repeatedly, is that early Celtic poetry was, in a very real and deep sense, an
act of praise, bringing the "whole world together as participants in the
singing of one great hymn of praise. The hermit who might seem to be
most alone in his or her cell praying the canonical hours and singing the
Psalms is least alone" (de Waal 199; see also Allchin 7-11).

Kenneth Jackson makes the point that bird songs are also an apt
example of the distinction between the Greeks and the Celtic hermits:
distance versus emotional engagement. "The Greeks stopped short of the
wilderness. The hermits did not; they were 'Simple Lifers' who really did
live the simple life, and that in its simplest form." The Celtic "hermits
sought spiritual purity in nature . . . . Yet the ultimate significance of the
hermit's relationship with nature is something that transcends both nature
and hermit alike" (Jackson, *Studies* 108). It is no wonder that Thomas
Merton copies this quotation from Jackson into his *Working Notebook
#14* with these subsequent sentences from the scholar:

> The woodland birds might sing to him around his cell, but through
> it all, rarely expressed, always implicit, is the understanding that the
> bird and hermit are joining together in an act of worship; to him the
> very existence of nature was a song of praise in which he himself took
> part by entering into harmony with nature. (Jackson, *Studies* 109)

Merton, however, does *not* copy Jackson's next sentence: "It was from
this harmony with nature, this all-perceiving contemplation of it, that the
Irish hermits reached to a more perfect unison with God" (Jackson, *Studies*
108-109). Perhaps this insight is too obvious to Merton – from both his
study and his personal experience of prayer. For good measure, however,
Merton *does* copy into his notebook an apt summary from Jackson: "The
solitary hermitage in the wilderness, the life of ascetic purity and humble
piety, the spare diet of herbs and water, and the companionship of wild
creatures, are the distinguishing marks of the Irish hermit poetry" (Jack-

---

38. Thomas Merton, *Working Notebook #15* (1965-August 1966); unpublished
holograph (TMA).

son, *Studies* 103). From Merton's point of view, Jackson captures it all: solitude, asceticism of spirit and diet, kinship with creatures.

Merton himself had a few years earlier offered a startling description of his own interaction with creation in solitude. In his journal entry for June 5, 1960, Pentecost, he writes: "The other day (Thursday) – the *full meaning* of lauds, said against the background of waking birds and sunrise." He goes on to itemize the genesis of the creatures and the dawn: the bullfrog who some mornings "says Om," the whippoorwill, sometimes "close," sometimes "in the distance," and the "first chirps of the waking birds – *'le point vierge* [the virgin point]' of the dawn, a moment of awe and inexpressible innocence, when the Father in silence opens their eyes and they speak to Him, wondering if it is time to 'be'? And He tells them 'Yes '" Merton's editorial comment after this list of waking is also enlightening: "With my hair almost on end and the eyes of the soul wide open I am present, without knowing it at all, in this unspeakable Paradise, and I behold this secret, this wide open secret which is there for everyone, free, and no one pays any attention."[39]

Not only birds and animals, but also the sea and its related weather figured repeatedly in Irish hermit poetry. Because of its island geography, the sea, according to Esther de Waal, became a "place of revelation" (de Waal 180). Many of the hermits, living among rocks at the edge of the sea, meditated on the mighty ebb and flow of the tides. Kenneth Jackson is of the opinion that the most remarkable treatment of the sea is found not in Welsh or British tales, but in Irish poetry, where "the sea was regarded with genuine delight mingled with terror" – a true experience of the sublime for these "amazingly adventurous sailors" (Jackson, *Studies* 91). The epic voyages of early sea adventurers such as Bran and Brendan, most likely recited by local bards, highlight the dangers and mystery of the sea. Other early poems celebrate the "fierce exultation in the storm at sea, worthy of the Vikings for whom tradition says it was composed." The tale of the drowning of Conaing refers to the "sea's hair," whereas "Columba's Farewell" boasts of a calm sea (Jackson, *Studies* 91-92).

Weather, of course, is important not only to seafaring people, but to all those who live on the land. In Ireland and Wales, weather and fertility auguries often existed in prose almanacs that foretell the character of the seasons, yet "prognostications in short phrases about the seasons, weather, fertility and prosperity were given in early chant-metre" (Jackson, *Studies*

---

39. Thomas Merton, *Turning Toward the World: The Pivotal Years. Journals, vol. 4: 1960-1963*, ed. Victor A. Kramer (San Francisco: HarperCollins, 1996) 7; subsequent references will be cited as "*TTW*" parenthetically in the text. See also my discussion of this event in *Environmental Vision* 55-63.

170). Kenneth Jackson offers the noun-adjective or noun-verb formula from a prophecy of Néde as illustrative of a weather chant:

> Good tidings (scela)
> Sea fruitful,
> Strand wave-washed,
> Woods smile,
> Witchcraft flees,
> Orchards prosper,
> Cornfields flourish,
> Bee-swarms abundant,
> The world cheerful,
> Joyous peace,
> Happy summer. (Jackson, *Studies* 170)

Merton himself was fascinated by weather. Often in his journals, he comments on the temperature, rain, sky or clouds at the beginning or end of an entry. Sometimes he inserts such a comment in the middle of an entry after a discussion of his current reading project. But weather for Merton is more than a meteorological report; it is a recognition of the very rhythm of his life. In his journal entry for Ash Wednesday, 1963, he confides:

> Our mentioning of the weather . . . [is] perhaps not idle. Perhaps we have a deep and legitimate need to know in our entire being what the day is like, to *see* it and *feel* it, to know how the sky is grey, paler in the south, with patches of blue in the southwest, with snow in the ground, the thermometer at 18, and cold wind making your ears ache. I have a real need to know these things because I myself am part of the weather and part of the climate and part of the place, and a day in which I have not shared truly in all this is no day at all. It is certainly part of my life of prayer. (*TTW* 299-300)

### Merton's "Anthology of Irish Poetry"

It should not be surprising, then, that Merton's immersion experience in Celtic thought and early Irish hermit poetry prompted him in September 1964 to put together his own twenty-three-page "Anthology of Irish Poetry." In looking over Merton's selections to try to second-guess his choice and arrangement of poems, it is clear that he is using primarily two translations: Kuno Meyer's *Selections from Ancient Irish Poetry* for the first fourteen poems – many of which also appear in Jackson's anthology but in a different order and slightly different translation – and, for the next twelve poems, Kenneth Jackson's *Studies in Early Celtic Nature*

*Poetry* (1935) with poems #13 and #14 coming from Jackson's *A Celtic Miscellany* (1951).[40]

Merton's eclectic assortment of Irish poems follows a loose thematic pattern: a first section featuring vocation to the hermit life, celebration of the seasons, tribute to sacred places, short quatrains about different subjects that evidently captured his fancy, and a second section entitled: "Ten Celtic Hermit Poems" from Jackson's *Studies* (Merton's numbering actually goes to twelve poems). His anthology concludes with "St Columba's Island Hermitage" and "The Hermit," taken from the Religion section of Jackson's later text, *A Celtic Miscellany*. Following is a brief overview of Merton's choices with pertinent quoted phrases so that the reader may glean something of the poems' charm and power. For those with access to the Merton Archives at Bellarmine University, this little anthology can offer inspiration for one's own prayerful reflection.

Section I: the first selection is "King and Hermit" (Meyer 47-50), a long dialogue – really a monologue – in which Marvan renounces his life as a warrior for a "tiny shieling" [an isolated hut] in the woods with birds, deer and the voice of the wind that constitutes a "Beautiful spot! . . . Without an hour of fighting, without the den of strife / In my house." In a brief response, the king sighs that he would give his "glorious kingship" as well as his inheritance "To be in thy company, my Marvan" ("Anthology" 232-34). While I have identified this somewhat facilely as a vocation poem, it is more of a rhapsodic colloquy on the hermit life that presents the hermit – as part of the promised hundred-fold here on earth – with all the richness of creation that comes "From my good Christ."

Nature is celebrated in the next three poems ("Anthology" 235-37): 1) summer with its bees, light swallows, peat-bog and the "timorous, tiny, persistent" lark whose song surpasses "summer-time of delicate hues!" (Meyer 54-55); 2) a lament for the departure of summer with the "sea running high" and an icy temperature that "has caught the wings of birds" (Meyer 56); and finally 3) the cold of winter with its tidal sea, roaming fish, wolves, and "Ice in heaps on every ford" (Meyer 57-58). Tribute to the sea is then highlighted in two poems that function as bookends for the famous "The Monk and His Pet Cat" (Meyer 81-82; "Anthology" 239) in which the monk muses about his scholarly challenge that is so akin to the cat Pangur's challenge of catching mice. "Arran" (Meyer 59) is a celebration of the sea around the island of Ireland as well as the animals

---

40. Jackson's 1935 book includes Irish hermit poetry as well as Welsh gnomic poetry. The latter book of translations by Jackson is a much broader collection of Irish literature ranging from hero-tales to descriptions, to humor and satire, to elegies and poems about religion.

and plants of every season that cause the poet to conclude: "Delightful at all times is Arran" ("Anthology" 238). The second sea poem is "Colum Cille's Greeting to Ireland" (Meyer 83-85) which, despite the frequent use of the word "delightful," is a lament for not only the Hill of Howth which the sailor, "rowing one's little coracle" is leaving, but also for his home in Derry, far behind him to the west. Even with his acknowledgement that "Grievous is my errand over the main / Travelling to Alba" (England) and his tears for his beloved home in Derry, the poet seems to reconcile himself to the beauty of the present moment in the last stanza: "Delightful it is, / The deep-red ocean where the sea-gulls cry. / As I come from Derry afar, / It is peaceful and it is beautiful" ("Anthology" 240-41).

Next Merton has selected two poems about historical figures: "On Angus the Culdee" (hermit) (Meyer 86) praises the hermit who lived in the latter half of the eighth century on the banks of the Nore River and is known for his austerity and love of solitude; "Alexander the Great" (Meyer 95) celebrates a leader whose friends, standing around his grave, comment on the fleetingness of power and material goods ("Anthology" 242). Then follow five short poems selected from Kuno Meyer's collection of "Quatrains" (Meyer 99-101). Merton seems taken with "The Scribe" (Meyer 99), above whose "lined booklet / The trilling birds chant"; "The Crucifixion" (Meyer 99), when the "cry of the first bird" heralded the torment of Christ and "the parting of day from night"; "The Blackbird" (Meyer 100) who, satisfied in his nest, "clinkest no bell" only a "sweet, soft" peaceful" note; and "The Church Bell in the Night" (Meyer 101) that signals a tryst with God in church preferred by the monk to one "with a foolish woman." (This phrase is sometimes translated as "wanton woman.") In the middle of this group of five quatrains is the famous "The Pilgrim at Rome" (Meyer 100), thought to be ninth-century Irish marginalia, often quoted in discussions of Celtic *peregrinatio* and copied out by Merton in his meticulous notes from Nora Chadwick's *The Age of Saints in the Early Celtic Church*: "To go to Rome / Is much of trouble, little of profit: / The King whom thou seekest here, / Unless thou bring Him with thee, thou wilt not find" ("Anthology" 243).

Section II: the "Ten Celtic Hermit Poems," that comprise the second half of Merton's "Anthology" (although there are actually twelve poems) are chosen from Jackson's 1935 translations and continue this theme of finding solace in the woods with the animals and birds for companions, culminating in two longer poems from Jackson's more comprehensive text, *A Celtic Miscellany*: "St Columba's Island Hermitage" and "The Hermit." Poem number X in Merton's anthology: "Ah, blackbird, it is well for thee / where thy nest is in the brake . . ." ("Anthology" 250) is a translation by Jackson of a quatrain from Meyer's 1911 collection ("Ah, blackbird, thou art satisfied / Where thy nest is in the bush") printed earlier in Merton's "Anthology" (243). Was Merton aware of this duplication? Or was he taken with the crispness of Jackson's final line: "melodious, soft, and peaceful is thy call" over Meyer's earlier "sweet, soft, peaceful is thy note"? His preference must remain an unanswered question that the reader is free to ponder.

| | |
|---|---|
| Ah, blackbird, thou art satisfied | Ah, blackbird, it is well for thee |
| Where thy nest is in the bush: | where thy nest is in the brake; |
| Hermit that clinkest no bell | hermit that dost not clang a bell, |
| Sweet, soft, peaceful is thy note. | melodious, soft, and peaceful is thy call. |
| (243) | (250) |

One of the two concluding poems, "St Columba's Island Hermitage," attributed to an unknown twelfth-century author, is also a duplicate of Merton's poem VI (translated by Meyer as "Colum Cille's Greeting to Ireland" [83-85]), but now translated by Jackson, beginning: "Delightful I think it to be in the bosom of an isle, on the peak of a rock that I might often see there the calm of the sea." The poem applauds the hermit's isolation and adds a list of what else would be delightful: "the voice of the wondrous birds," "its mighty whales," "its ebb and its flood-tide," "that I might bewail my many sins," "that I might bless the Lord," "pore on one of my books," "while meditating upon the Kingdom of Heaven," "a while at labour not too heavy." Both versions begin and end with the word "delightful," the deliberate classical literary technique of epanalepsis, effective for a kind of "bookending" emphasis ("Anthology" 249, 258). The speaker in the final poem, "The Hermit," thought to be of eighth- or ninth-century composition, rejoices to be "Alone in my little hut" to pursue various ascetic practices in atonement for sin, concluding: "If of my own I have done wrong at all, through the pride of this world, hear my wail for it all alone, O God!" ("Anthology" 254).

## Concluding Thoughts

While there are many other Irish hermit poems Merton might have chosen for his anthology, these selections bespeak not only his general interest in Celtic monasticism, but also his pleasure in discovering a strong resemblance between the hermits' celebration of nature, their longing for contented solitude in a little hut, and Merton's own desire to spend more time in his hermitage in the woods. Certainly the Celtic kinship with nature, reinforced by their gift of imagination and sense of the unity of all things, enabled these Celtic hermits to experience a deeper and deeper communion with the Divine, the human and the earth. This, for Merton, was the essence of hermit spirituality. No wonder the writings of the Celtic monks, and especially the poetry of the Irish hermits, captured his attention. Was Merton merely dabbling in Irish hermit poetry and following another curious intellectual tangent? I don't think so. Evidence from his notebooks suggests that Merton's sustained study of an ancient and tested vocation to solitude, as well as his fondness for their poetic expression, certainly satisfied his intellectual thirst for knowledge. But perhaps more important, Merton's immersion in "all things Celtic" reinforced his inner desire for more solitude. If Merton were seeking a seal of approval for his spiritual leaning toward the eremitic life and contemplative prayer in nature, these unknown early Irish monks provided that affirmation.

Despite the separation of centuries, the early Celts and Merton were coming from the same worldview, the same mystic experience, and seeking the same union with the Divine. Whether on pilgrimage at sea in a fragile *currach*, wandering the craggy terrain or choosing solitude in a woodland hut, these early monks had discovered the spiritual energy of "white martyrdom" (exile) and the Christian significance of becoming a cultural bystander. They had discovered the value of living in time yet in touch with eternity. For them and for Merton, St. Columbanus's oft-quoted wise counsel was an invitation to the heart: "Understand creation if you would understand the Creator" (de Waal 181).

# "What I Wear Is Pants. What I Do Is Live. How I Pray Is Breathe": Merton and the Spiritual Life in the Twenty-First Century

*Michael Plekon*

### The Voice of a Hermit

The hills are blue and hot. There is a brown, dusty field in the bottom of the valley. I hear a machine, a bird, a clock. The clouds are high and enormous. In them, the inevitable jet plane passes: this time probably full of fat passengers from Miami to Chicago, but presently it will be a plane with the bomb in it. I have seen the plane with the bomb in it fly low over me and I have looked up out of the woods directly at the closed bay. Like everyone else I live under the bomb. But unlike most people I live in the woods. Do not ask me to explain this. I am embarrassed to describe it. I live in the woods out of necessity. I am both a prisoner and an escaped prisoner.[1]

That's the voice of a hermit, a monk who has finally gotten out of the monastery proper and into a little cinderblock house, a hermitage that is a paradise really, not at all a prisoner. You have to be careful of how he's writing in describing a day in the life of a hermit, a stranger! Long after his death, Thomas Merton remains one of the most influential spiritual writers in America. What keeps his books being read and numerous articles and books being published each year is his honesty as well as his humanity. These are best seen in his effort to live the spiritual life and to share his struggles. Like others, from Augustine to Teresa of Avila, and his contemporary, Dorothy Day, there is an exuberance that makes him – and them – classics. Still very appealing, provocative even, is his determination to continue to seek God, to come to terms with his own gifts and defects, his commitment to continue to find his "true self," the person, the saint he was made to be.

His letters and journals are remarkable records of his experiments with ideas, his rants, as well as his coming to terms with crises and difficulties of which there were many. However there is a great deal of joy and beauty

---

1. Thomas Merton, *Dancing in the Water of Life: Seeking Peace in the Hermitage. Journals, vol. 5: 1963-1965*, ed. Robert E. Daggy (San Francisco: HarperCollins, 1997) 239; subsequent references will be cited as "*DWL*" parenthetically in the text.

in these writings. His musing on details of everyday life brings us back to America in the 1960s. In his journals for those years, Merton has a lot to say about the civil rights movement, about the anti-war movement, about the place of the Church in the turbulence of those days. When he speaks of the president he means LBJ. He is torn apart, as many were, by the assassinations, just in that last year of his life, 1968, of Robert Kennedy and Martin Luther King Jr.

By the time he finally was allowed to live at his hermitage, Merton had come a long way from the idealistic author of his best-selling auto-biography *The Seven Storey Mountain*.[2] Released decades after his death, his journals show the extent to which his faith and spiritual practice had evolved.[3] Listen to Jonathan Montaldo:

> Scholars of repute call Thomas Merton a "spiritual master," and publishers lace the back covers of his books with avowals that he is one of the most important spiritual writers of our century. Merton's own assessment of his achievement was more modest. He even insured a more complex reception of his spiritual legacy by writing journals that scandalize the reader who seeks in them a spiritual success story to emulate. . . . They reveal instead a disconcerting journey of his descent into an ever-deepening spiritual poverty. . . . They disclose . . . Merton's being mastered by the Spirit as his willfulness is purified in the furnace of failure, and his self-absorption is transfigured into compassion for everyone else. Merton's mature journals are a sustained narrative of redemption from his having to wear the self-fabricated public mask of holy monk. In them his readers have a final accounting of the "lucky wind / That blew away his halo with his cares" and of the "lucky sea that drowned his reputation." His journals elaborate his parable of hard-road enlightenment through a loss of status. Readers of his journals witness their "spiritual master's" deepening foolishness and the manner by which his polished ego arrived at tarnishment: an inveterate exhibitionist's happy fall from a public grace. (Montaldo, "Winter" 99-100)

Throughout his life, Merton's pilgrimage continued. Is this why his

---

2. Thomas Merton, *The Seven Storey Mountain* (New York: Harcourt, Brace, 1948).

3. See Victor A. Kramer, "'Crisis and Mystery': The Changing Quality of Thomas Merton's Later Journals," *The Vision of Thomas Merton*, ed. Patrick F. O'Connell (Notre Dame IN: Ave Maria Press 2003) 77-97; see also Jonathan Montaldo, "Loving Winter When the Plant Says Nothing: Thomas Merton's Spirituality in His Private Journals," *Vision of Thomas Merton* 99-117 (subsequent references will be cited as "Montaldo, 'Winter'" parenthetically in the text).

writing remains so compelling? Merton was never content but restless, constantly becoming. I have heard similar things from monks who lived with Merton and knew him well.[4]

## Day of a Stranger

While Merton had wanted more solitude, his hermitage, about a mile from the main monastery buildings, was never an isolated retreat. He complains about fans as well as stalkers who occasionally terrified him and became a nuisance. But journals, letters and photos witness to the many visitors he welcomed there.[5] It was the site for an important gathering of peacemakers in November 1964.[6]

I want to listen carefully to what Merton has to say about life, prayer and his identity as he moved to a new phase of his time as a monk, that of living at the hermitage. It is most valuable for us now – mindfulness, returning to simplicity, attention to the world and oneself, doing away with dualism, all while celebrating the ordinary, the everyday, and passing on what one has received. While much of this can be found throughout Merton's writings, I think they are in a special display during his hermitage years, in the journals, but also in other places such as retreats and talks he gave.

*"Sometime in May 1965,"* as Merton's journal has it (*DWL* 237), comes *Day of a Stranger*. Having recently moved into the hermitage, Merton wrote a description of his daily routine as a hermit. He had done a bit of this in a piece for *Holiday* magazine, "Rain and the Rhinoceros."[7] To begin with, he was allowed to spend part of the day at the hermitage, the rest at the monastery. Later on, more improvements would be made – plumbing, electricity and a small addition for a chapel. On August 20, 1965 he would retire as novice master, and by vote of the monastery council, be allowed to take up full-time residence at the hermitage, something his longtime nemesis and abbot, James Fox, had originally opposed, along

---

4. For a perspective very much in focus with what I am saying here, see Jonathan Montaldo, "To Uncage His Voice: Thomas Merton's Inner Journey toward *Parrhesia*," *The Merton Seasonal* 39.4 (Winter 2014) 9-20; subsequent references will be cited as "Montaldo, 'Voice'" parenthetically in the text.

5. See for example the photographs and commentary in *Merton/Meatyard – Meatyard/Merton: Photographing Thomas Merton* (Louisville, KY: Fons Vitae, 2014).

6. See Gordon Oyer, *Pursuing the Spiritual Roots of Protest: Merton, Berrigan, Yoder, and Muste at the Gethsemani Abbey Peacemaker Retreat* (Eugene, OR: Wipf and Stock, 2014).

7. Thomas Merton, *Raids on the Unspeakable* (New York: New Directions, 1966) 9-23; originally published in *Holiday* 37 (May 1965) 8, 10, 12, 15-16.

with much else in Merton's vision and activities.[8]

Merton wrote this essay in response to his friend, the Argentinian poet Miguel Grinberg's request for a description of a day in the life of a hermit (see *DWL* 87, 89-90). The first, shorter version is edgy, confrontational (*DWL* 239-42). There was to be a second and then later, a third, longer version. The final one[9] retains the intensity of the first but Merton adds reflection, even a short question-and-answer exchange, as well as detailed descriptions of everyday chores – "rituals," he calls them: washing the coffee pot, approaching the outhouse carefully because of the snake who likes to lodge inside, spraying for insects, closing and opening windows either for a cooling breeze or to shut out heat. These are elements of his daily liturgy of living – and lessons for all of us in mindful, prayerful existence!

Again, I am grateful to Jonathan Montaldo (see "Voice" 13-15), for pointing out Merton's very important letter to Ludovico Silva of March 13, 1965. In it he previews but also enlarges on what he would say in *Day of a Stranger*:

> The religion of our time, to be authentic, needs to be the kind that escapes practically all religious definition. Because there has been endless definition, endless verbalizing, and words have become gods. There are so many words that one cannot get to God . . . . [W]hen [God] is placed firmly beyond the other side of the words, the words multiply like flies and there is a great buzzing religion, very profit-able, very holy, very spurious. One tries to escape it by acts of truth that fail. One's whole being must be an act for which there can be found no word. . . . My whole being must be a yes and an amen and an exclamation that is not heard. Only after that is there any point in exclamations . . . . That is where the silence of the woods comes in. Not that there is something new to be thought and discovered in the woods, but only that the trees are all sufficient exclamations of silence, and one works there, cutting wood, clearing ground, cutting grass, cooking soup, drinking fruit juice, sweating, washing, making fire, smelling smoke, sweeping, etc. This is religion. The further one

---

8. For a comprehensive account of this complex relationship see Roger Lipsey, *Make Peace Before the Sun Goes Down: The Long Encounter of Thomas Merton and His Abbot, James Fox* (Boston: Shambhala, 2015).

9. Thomas Merton, *Day of a Stranger* (Salt Lake City: Gibbs M. Smith, 1981) (subsequent references will be cited as "*DS*" parenthetically in the text). This final version first appeared in English in *The Hudson Review* 20 (Summer 1967) 211-18.

gets away from this, the more one sinks in the mud of words and gestures. The flies gather.[10]

These lines bring to mind Bonhoeffer's "religionless Christianity," even if not precisely. But what he says here is far stronger, even brutal. This is Merton at his most discerning, recognizing the excessive, overly specialized verbiage passing for theological language and a religion that is distanced, dehumanized. He is also is aware of the entrapment of faith in the culture and sentimentality of the past, something of which he himself was guilty in earlier writings.

In all of the versions of *Day of a Stranger*, Merton lists writers who speak to him in the solitude, from the ancient Syrian mystic Philoxenus to contemporary poet Nicanor Parra. The list is greatly enhanced in the last, longer version. He adds Asian authors, more contemporaries like Ungaretti and Zukovsky, as well as almost half a dozen women writers, including Julian of Norwich and Flannery O'Connor (see *DS* 35).

In the introduction to his edition of *Day of a Stranger*, Robert Daggy makes much of the self-characterization by Merton as "stranger" (*DS* 12-19). The South American destination of the piece, *Papeles*,[11] would render this *extraño*, and there are layers of meaning here in the very title and self-image of one who is an alien. Merton is "stranger" to his own North American society and culture – this is stressed throughout, even though America would try to claim him as a citizen, consumer, supporter of government policy. As in the rest of his journals and other essays in the last decade of his life, he was anything but a booster of American values, politics, lifestyle or anything else. "Wealth is poison," he shouts in the text, also decrying the pollution of water and soil. There is affluence, but also hunger and poverty in the United States and the full bellies have produced "dementia" rather than peace and satisfaction (see *DWL* 240). In a passage that does not appear in either the first or the third drafts, this is put rather forcefully:

I do not intend to belong to the world of squares that is constituted by the abdication of choice, or by the fraudulent choice (the mass-roar in the public square, or the assent to the televised grimace). I do not intend to be citizen number 152037. I do not consent to be poet number 2291. I do not recognize myself as the classified antisocial and subversive element that I probably am in the file of a department in a department. Perhaps I have been ingested by an IBM machine

---

10. Thomas Merton, *The Courage for Truth: Letters to Writers*, ed. Christine M. Bochen (New York: Farrar, Straus, Giroux, 1993) 225.

11. Thomas Merton, "Día de un Extraño," *Papeles* 1 (July-Aug.-Sept. 1966) 41-45.

in Washington, but they cannot digest me. I am indigestible: a priest who cannot be swallowed, a monk notoriously discussed as one of the problems of the contemporary Church by earnest seminarists, wearing bright spectacles in Rome. I have not chosen to be acceptable. I have not chosen to be inacceptable. I have nothing personal to do with the present indigestion of officials, of critics, of clerics, of housewives, of amateur sociologists. It is *their* indigestion. I offer them no advice.[12]

Merton, while in important positions such as novice master and teacher of student monks, was also in many and fairly complicated ways a stranger to the Gethsemani monastery and to aspects of monasticism and the church more generally. One can read a great deal of Merton's conflict with all these but also of his own transformation from the idealistic, romantic monk of *The Seven Storey Mountain.* There were many aspects of monastic life but also of the Catholic Church, not to mention the United States government and its policies, that profoundly troubled him. Merton followed closely the paths of Catholics who spoke out for more freedom both in the church and the country. He sadly recognized the institutional power that saw such protest as great threats and so the ostracizing, and the removal of such voices of prophetic protest, both from the ranks of the clergy and from civil society.

The journals document a great deal of personal struggle, failure but also growth of the stranger in the years to follow, the hermitage years. There were the visitors, celebrities and lesser-knowns, the exchanges with other writers and critics, both in letters and in person, the falling in love with "M." and so much soul-searching and anguish that surrounded it. There was also, I believe, further movement toward integration. Whatever can be said about his relationship with this young woman, this was a life-changing encounter. It is true that we only know of it from his point of view. Nevertheless, Merton learned that he could be loved and that he could love. And imperfect as it was – isn't all love imperfect? – he did love her.

### Out in the Woods Yet Still in the World

Merton refuses to be part of the American dream and the crowd that runs to work in the morning, works frantically all day, only to also run home to yet more "leisure" time and conspicuous consumption. He had been turned inside out in the epiphany "In Louisville, at the corner of

---

12. "Day of a Stranger" [second draft]; typescript in the archives of the Thomas Merton Center, Bellarmine University, Louisville, KY; cited by Daggy in his introduction (*DS* 20).

Fourth and Walnut."[13] He was no longer the one who had run away to the paradise of the monastery. Such was his early infatuation. By May 1965 much had changed, not just in the larger world of which he is part but within Merton himself.

Even out in the woods, with the birds, foxes and snakes, in silence, the world is with him, in him. And so, he carries the world and the many people with whom he corresponds, whom he knows both at Gethsemani and beyond, with him in the early hours as he reads from the scriptures and from other writers. This is a huge realization for him, especially poignant in the start of this new life out in the hermitage. There is no longer separation of either the world or God from this poet-hermit. And this will become a theme as he talks about prayer in one's life.

Merton's "day" is punctuated by the world and its often threatening appearances. He sees and hears overhead the jetliners en route from Miami to Chicago. There had been no 9/11, but with the Cold War and Vietnam alive and well, he imagines the atomic weapons in the bomb bays of the SAC planes flying overhead. He lists words that penetrate the silence of his rising at 2:15 a.m. for praying the psalms and rest of the scriptures. *Magna misericordia* – great mercy; also "wash me," "destroy iniquity," "I know my iniquity," "I have sinned." "Concepts," he says cynically, "without interest in the world of business, war, politics, culture, etc. Concepts also often without interest to ecclesiastics" (*DS* 43).

Merton begins to sound as though he is writing in our time, not over fifty years ago – now, when we are tired of hate passing for politics, of remote, disconnected churches and overspiritualized religion. Onward the chain of vocabulary winds: "Blood, Guile. Anger. The way that is not good. . . . Out there the hills in the dark lie southward. The way over the hills is blood, guile, dark, anger, death: Selma, Birmingham, Mississippi" (*DS* 43). We are back in the 1960s, in the Civil Rights conflicts, and even closer is Fort Knox, with gold reserves and material for nuclear weapons. We are not back in the '60s at all! Quite a "day," especially for a monk, a hermit, poet, mystic! Just before all of this, the most memorable and cutting passage:

> This is not a hermitage – it is a house. ("Who was that hermitage I seen you with last night? . . .") What I wear is pants. What I do is live. How I pray is breathe. Who said Zen? Wash out your mouth if

---

13. See Thomas Merton, *Conjectures of a Guilty Bystander* (Garden City, NY: Doubleday, 1966) 140-42 (subsequent references will be cited as "*CGB*" parenthetically in the text); for the original journal version of this March 18, 1958 revelation, see Thomas Merton, *A Search for Solitude: Pursuing the Monk's True Life. Journals, vol. 3: 1952-1960*, ed. Lawrence S. Cunningham (San Francisco: HarperCollins, 1996) 181-83.

you said Zen. If you see a meditation going by, shoot it. Who said "Love?" Love is in the movies. The spiritual life is something that people worry about when they are so busy with something else they think they ought to be spiritual. Spiritual life is guilt. Up here in the woods is seen the New Testament: that is to say, the wind comes through the trees and you breathe it. Is it supposed to be clear? I am not inviting anybody to try it. Or suggesting that one day the message will come saying NOW. That is none of my business. (*DS* 41)

Such language, for a monk who says his hermitage is "full of ikons of the Holy Virgin" (*DS* 49)! This has to be the Merton that Jonathan Montaldo was talking about, not a "spiritual master" but one very much struggling with himself, with others, with God. He announces that "In an age where there is much talk about 'being yourself' I reserve to myself the right to forget about being myself, since in any case there is very little chance of my being anybody else. Rather it seems to me that when one is too intent on 'being himself' he runs the risk of impersonating a shadow" (*DS* 31). Irreverent. Smugly sarcastic. Playing the proverbial wiseguy, as in his letters to his friend, Robert Lax.[14] Maybe he would soon be in inner disarray, cut loose from the monastery and watchful eyes. Later, in the journal, as mentioned, he wondered if he'd returned to the wildness of his youth, drinking too much, talking too much, too many friends visiting. In the next year he would meet the nurse in the Louisville hospital, fall in love, write and write and write to her, about her, about finally having loved and been loved. Merton did struggle – with his abbot of many years, James Fox, and the limits imposed on him, with the visitors, his celebrating with them, with his concern about the future of the monastery and monastic life.

Of course, he could not know that in the last three years of his life he would be allowed a hermitage and solitude. He would never have thought he would fall in love. As for the world beyond the monastery and so much going on in it – the Cold War's aggressive nuclear arms race, then the Vietnam war and the Civil Rights movement, the growing cultural upheaval of the 1960s – Merton had long before returned to the world through reading, through his huge correspondence with writers, activists and like-minded critics of church and society. The previous year, almost a dozen peacemakers descended on both the hermitage and monastery

---

14. See Thomas Merton and Robert Lax, *A Catch of Anti-Letters* (Kansas City: Sheed, Andrews and McMeel, 1978); and the complete correspondence: Thomas Merton and Robert Lax, *When Prophecy Still Had a Voice: The Letters of Thomas Merton & Robert Lax*, ed. Arthur W. Biddle (Lexington: University Press of Kentucky, 2001).

for a memorable retreat on peace in troubled times.

However, here, in this narrative of his "day" at the hermitage, Merton shows himself to have returned to the world far more deeply and in an extraordinary way as a writer, a monk and priest, as a Christian and as a citizen. Of course he still wears the Trappist habit to the monastery, vestments at the liturgy. But beneath it all, not just literally, what he wears is pants, like everyone else. And what he does is the usual for him – unbelievably extensive correspondence, a volcano of writing – articles, reviews, essays, books, translations. He reads all the time, even while walking outside. But he also makes coffee in the predawn darkness, does rudimentary cooking to feed himself; cleans house, does dishes; cuts brush, stacks wood and feeds the fireplace – all that anyone living rurally, in the woods, would do.

### Mindful of the Everyday, the Little Things

A key feature of living, Merton shows us in *Day of a Stranger*, is *mindfulness*. One could also call it contemplative attention, but whatever the description, it is the product of the pattern of living he also describes as his existence there. This contemplative way of being includes cleaning away a lot of the baggage of institutionalized, stereotypical religion. Getting back to basics means the psalms, the rest of the scripture – "Up here in the woods is seen the New Testament." We don't need even the kind of elaboration Merton employed in earlier writing, like *Seeds/New Seeds of Contemplation*,[15] *No Man Is an Island*[16] and like books. His South American correspondent, a secular poet, would be able to understand the kind of "slow living," like today's "slow cooking," as more humane, basic, attuned to the most important things in one's faith and existence.

This is expressed through what Merton saw and chose to capture with his camera. In the many photographs he takes, one rarely finds any specifically religious images or objects. Merton was not interested in writing about such details of church or monastic life and observance, nor in stock photography of monastic piety. He still wears the Trappist habit, attends the services in the monastery church, lectures, but he is no conventionally pious monk. Rather, it is the simple, worn, everyday things inside the hermitage and around it and in the countryside that Merton most frames in his camera lenses and captures – barns, a woodpile, the chair on the hermitage porch, his desk, the top covered with books, magazines

---

15. Thomas Merton, *Seeds of Contemplation* (New York: New Directions, 1949); Thomas Merton, *New Seeds of Contemplation* (New York: New Directions, 1961) (subsequent references will be cited as *"NSC"* parenthetically in the text).

16. Thomas Merton, *No Man Is an Island* (New York: Harcourt, Brace, 1955).

and manuscripts. All these are the sacramental elements of his life (see *DS* 22-23). This I take to be another facet of the living, breathing prayer he engages in and tells us about. His prayer is as ordinary as the stool, the little hermitage kitchen, the water can, typewriter and other objects which are the markers of his space, the tools of his "day."

What he does is live. How he prays is breathing and it is the wind, the spirit, who blows where she wills, that he breathes, the New Testament that he sees. The spiritual life, Zen, love – all this does not get close to the life he experiences within the cinderblock walls and out in the woods. In the quiet, the words of the psalms, especially Psalm 51, are clear. Over against iniquity, sin, blood, anger, guile, death there is mercy – the mercy of God, mercy for us, mercy that becomes ours to give and be. It is the theme that winds its way through all of Merton's pages and life:[17]

> seeing the multitude of stars above the bare branches of the wood, I was suddenly hit, as it were, with the whole package of meaning of everything: that the immense mercy of God was upon me, that the Lord in infinite kindness had looked down on me and given me this vocation out of love, and that he had always intended this, and how foolish and trivial had been all my fears and twistings and desperation. (*DWL* 177-78)

In these few pages describing a typical course of the day in his hermitage, Merton says more than in many of his more focused pieces, ones on contemplation, what it is and is not. Quite directly, he shows how both integration and contemplation play out in daily life. In these pithy, extremely perceptive lines of *Day of a Stranger*, we find not so much a formula or program, but rather an example of prayer lived out and of the attitude or vision that such an everyday prayer creates.

### Simplicity

Another important aspect of life Merton shares with us is the return to basics, a radical *simplifying* of everything, from prayer to work, food, schedule. Entwined with this is an almost poetic awareness of not just one's own thoughts and actions but of the immediate surroundings, of others and then, the world beyond. From the start – "The hills are blue and hot" (*DS* 29) – there is attention to the world of creation, to the need to protect the environment, where Merton knows all the birds that are his neighbors, the snake in the outhouse as well. The woods and the foxes, the natural world, make for the "cool" that is his immediate existence, over against the "hot medium" (in Marshall McLuhan's terms) of the

---

17. See Thomas Merton, *The Sign of Jonas* (New York: Harcourt, Brace, 1953) 362.

monastery. This "hot" world is one of "ought" and "must" and "should," despite St. Benedict, who saw the best thing to do was to "cool it." Merton says his life is one in which he does not have to "bundle up packages and deliver them to myself" (*DS* 37, 39). Cryptic terms? not really. The "packages" are the trends, the traditions, the selves with which we are obsessed and over which we obsess with others.

The air is clean up on the hermitage hill. The Spirit is the wind that comes through the trees. Merton sensed that it had been blowing through his life for years, clearing away a lot of debris. Before his days' end, three years ahead, even more will be cleaned out, revealed, made simple. But there, in that small hermitage, in the simplicity of keeping a house, everything that is necessary becomes clear.

Throughout his writings, Merton uses the natural world to talk about contemplative prayer, that is, the utterly simple silence before and with God. A God "out there," or "up there" or anywhere else but in and with oneself too, became impossible for him. In *Thoughts in Solitude*, he says the sky, birds and wind in the trees have become his prayer.[18] All through *New Seeds of Contemplation* we hear much the same.[19] But by 1965, in *Day of a Stranger*, the more pious and theoretical tone is gone, while the substance is perhaps even more formidable. He doesn't waste his time with "spirituality" or "love" or Zen. "I am working on knowing myself, becoming myself, my true self," Merton seems to say, encouraging us to do the same. The "false and private self" that tries to exist outside God, reality and life, is an illusion (see *NSC* 34). It is in the "love and mercy of God" that the secret of identity is hidden and where it is to be found (see *NSC* 35). Even in his early work, Merton already disclosed the real heart of what we are shown in *Day of a Stranger*. We have to empty ourselves,

---

18. Thomas Merton, *Thoughts in Solitude* (New York: Farrar, Straus and Cudahy, 1958) 94; see also 99, 101, 113.

19. "A tree gives glory to God by being a tree. For in being what God means it to be it is obeying Him. It 'consents,' so to speak, to His creative love. It is expressing an idea which is in God and which is not distinct from the essence of God, and therefore a tree imitates God by being a tree. . . . The forms and individual characters of living and growing things, of inanimate beings, of animals and flowers and all nature, constitute their holiness in the sight of God. Their inscape is their sanctity. It is the imprint of His wisdom and His reality in them. The special clumsy beauty of this particular colt on this April day in this field under these clouds is a holiness consecrated to God by His own creative wisdom and it declares the glory of God. The pale flowers of the dogwood outside this window . . . the little yellow flowers that nobody notices on the edge of the road are saints looking up into the face of God. . . . For me to be a saint means to be myself. Therefore the problem of sanctity and salvation is in fact the problem of finding out who I am and of discovering my true self" (*NSC* 29-31).

radically simplify daily activities, possessions, even thoughts and prayer so that we can be with and in God. Merton would describe his prayer to his Pakistani correspondent Abdul Aziz: "Strictly speaking I have a very simple way of prayer. It is centered entirely on attention to the presence of God and to His will and to His love."[20]

I think this simplicity of prayer is one of the most important gifts of Merton to us today. Prayer is never just a formal, obligatory activity. Here he knows from hard experience, for when he entered the monastery, not only did the Trappists sing the canonical office, all the hours in Latin every day. They also did the little office of the Blessed Virgin Mary and often, the office of the dead. On some days the hours in choir for this formal prayer could have been six or seven if one also included the Mass. For Merton the prayer of the church was deeply integrated in his life. Even on his final trip to Asia, he was praying the daily psalms and readings.

So too did these prayer "hours" define his "day" at the hermitage. From the middle of the night – he rises at 2:15 a.m. for night vigils – the day is framed by prayer. He quotes from just one psalm, but there a hundred and forty-nine others he sings, along with Alleluia in the Gregorian second mode (see *DS* 59). At the time he writes this account of his daily activities, he is still trudging down to the monastery to finish his teaching of the novices, to take part in the daily community liturgy. He returns, water bottle filled (this is before his plumbing and power have been hooked up) and notices a bumblebee humming in the eaves, the larks singing as they rise from the tall grass. There is quiet for reading and reflection in the afternoon. He says he's married "the silence of the forest":

> The sweet dark warmth of the whole world will have to be my wife. Out of the heart of that dark warmth comes the secret that is heard only in silence, but it is the root of all the secrets that are whispered by all the lovers in their beds all over the world. So perhaps I have an obligation to preserve the stillness, the silence, the poverty, the virginal point of pure nothingness which is at the center of all other loves. I attempt to cultivate this plant without comment in the middle of the night and water it with psalms and prophecies in silence. (*DS* 49)

For all the quiet of the woods, the companionship of the animals and the release from all the demands of monastery life, Merton was no slacker in his "day." He continued to work, to produce – numerous reviews, articles, essays, letters. I counted over thirty authors mentioned in the various drafts of the piece, from Isaiah and Jeremiah to W. H. Auden, Camus

20. Thomas Merton, *The Hidden Ground of Love: Letters on Religious Experience and Social Concerns*, ed. William H. Shannon (New York: Farrar, Straus, Giroux, 1985) 63.

and Sartre. There are great voices of the tradition as well as doubters and critics of the same, visionaries and realists. Merton's "day" was a continual nourishment of inner life. And he was writing like crazy. He connected his monastic audience to a really diverse selection of writers and themes. Scripture and the monastic tradition were important, but he was constantly introducing authors and issues that made his listeners part of the larger world. The recordings of these talks over many years reveal the sheer breadth of Merton's learning, all of which he carefully shared with his community. There are the classical spiritual writers and less-known Cistercians. He introduced Sufism and Buddhism to his fellow monastics. He spoke on literary giants like Blake, on whom he wrote his master's thesis, Donne and Nietzsche, as well as Beckett, Camus, Joyce, Auden, Kafka, Weil and Foucault, among others. The death of John F. Kennedy is discussed, but also contemporary Russian writers like Pasternak, Bulgakov and Berdyaev, various approaches in Marxism, racism in the South and throughout the country, and the work of Martin Luther King, Jr. This is just the audio portion. Readers know well the enormous correspondence, all the reviews, essays and articles, and then the many volumes of notes and comments in his journals. Merton was a walking university. The hermitage may have been rural peacefulness, solitude and silence, but the world of ideas blazed there too.

### The Gate of Heaven Is Everywhere

If simplicity is a crucial gift Merton gives, then commitment to work, to service of others and the world are likewise gifts. There is no valuing of one action over another. All have their place – the psalms, scriptures, liturgy, the reading from all the writers mentioned and many more, the talks for the novices and the broader Gethsemani community, and then the work of writing about trying to find God and God's way, in the civil rights and anti-war movements, in the Vatican II renewal in the church, and much more. Oh yes, and the laundry, making coffee, a supper at day's end, sweeping, stacking wood, cutting grass and weeds and the rest.

If God is everywhere and fills all things, as a prayer of the Eastern Church puts it, then prayer, like God, finds a way into, around and through concern for ecology and peace, also the constant struggles of one's own person, feelings, disappointments, hope. When he was finally free to live at the hermitage, Merton did not know that he had only three more years, but full, productive and turbulent years they were. Describing his day as a stranger, one marginal but yet still present in his community and world, he unwittingly echoes both an ancient, scriptural perspective, namely that we are always strangers and pilgrims, that our real home is heaven.

Recognizing that heaven is not to be found "up there" or "after" this life, but here and now, that "paradise is all around us and we do not understand" (*CGB* 118) that "the gate of heaven is everywhere" (*CGB* 142), Merton's own search for home, orphan that he was as a child, was not just for a street address and a building. Much as he longed for and fought for his hermitage, he makes it clear not long before and even during his last Asian trip, that he needed greater solitude at least part of the time. "Home," for this "stranger" was his "true self." I believe he prayed his way to his true self. But this was because he prayed, as St. Paul said, everywhere and all the time. I close with Jonathan Montaldo's discerning and beautiful words:

> Merton gradually abandoned hope for a suddenly perfect life in some perfect place always elsewhere than where he actually was. He surrendered himself instead to the slow heart-work of seeking God one day and one night at a time in the place where his eyes opened and shut every morning and evening. He got up and fell down, he got up and fell down, and he got up over and over again. Merton's journals are a confession of the necessity for us all to move insistently forward through our daily experiences of both absence and presence to that Voice of Love calling each of us to Love's Self. As he acknowledged his road to Joy was as curved as everyone else's, and that, in the face of his life's contradictions, all he might really have had left was prayer and hope in God's mercy. . . . Thomas Merton might have stumbled home, but he has made it home. No longer an orphan or an exile, no longer solitary or a prodigal, Merton now waits in joyful hope for the complete and final epiphany of his Lord. . . . As each of us stumbles falteringly forward toward the one, true Voice of Love, calling us each by our names, may the Holy Spirit who is searching our hearts for us, hurrying like a mother toward the sound of all our cries, find us quickly. (Montaldo, "Winter" 117)

# Public Intellectual, Democratic Dissenter:
# Thomas Merton on Nuclear Weapons

*Donald Grayston*

"Public intellectual" – what, or who, is that? Definitions abound. According to American social critic George Steiner, an intellectual is simply someone "who has a pencil in his or her hand when reading a book."[1] Public intellectuals then are individuals who having read deeply in the humane learning of their culture choose to venture into the public sphere with their reflections, usually on matters of some urgency, in the hope of response and dialogue, even perhaps partnership and action. Noam Chomsky, for example, sees public intellectuals as persons who want to use their intellectual abilities to take part in movements for social change, in contrast to those who merely want to accept and serve the status quo.[2] In an earlier time, those whom we now call public intellectuals might more simply have been called philosophers, or, in the biblical tradition, prophets.

Edward Said (1935-2003) is an epitome of the public intellectual in recent times; he recorded his thoughts about the role of the public intellectual in his Reith lectures, *Representations of the Individual*.[3] For Said, "the intellectual's job is to 'question patriotic nationalism, corporate thinking, and a sense of class, racial or gender privilege'" (Said xiii). "There is no question," asserted Said, "that the intellectual belongs on the same side with the weak and unrepresented" (Said 22); and then he offers some criteria in using which we can hardly believe that he was not thinking about Thomas Merton when he wrote them. "The intellectual in exile is necessarily ironic, skeptical, even playful – but not cynical" (Said 62). Exile, playfulness, marginality, the need to create one's own path as one walks it – all these indicators mark the career and indeed the self-understanding of Thomas Merton.

J. S. Porter is a Canadian Merton scholar who has given substantial

---

1. George Steiner, *No Passion Spent: Essays 1978-1995* (New Haven: Yale University Press, 1996) 8; quoted in J. S. Porter, "Thomas Merton as Public Intellectual," *The Merton Seasonal* 29.2 (Summer 2004) 16 (subsequent references will be cited as "Porter" parenthetically in the text).

2. See Peter G. Prontzos, "Prescient professor Chomsky more right than wrong," vancouversun.com/entertainment/books/Review+prescient+professor+Chomsky+more+right+than/10755311/story.html (accessed 24 January 2015).

3. Edward Said, *Representations of the Individual* (London: Vintage, 1994) xiii; subsequent references will be cited as "Said" parenthetically in the text.

thought to Merton as public intellectual. Here he reflects on Said's views:

> If one goes through Said's extended definition of the intellectual . . .
> one finds how accurately it matches the intellectual life of Thomas
> Merton. Merton is the man in exile from a one-dimensional techno-
> logical society . . . the man on the margins, someone who is neither
> on governmental nor corporate payroll. The moneyed classes may
> expect monks to keep their mouths shut, particularly Trappist ones, but
> Merton seldom lives according to the expectations of the financially
> and politically or ecclesiastically powerful. He is in the Sartrean and
> Saidean sense, *l'homme engagé*. (Porter 17-18)

And why should Trappist monks especially be expected to keep their
mouths shut? because until the 1960s they had a practice of almost complete silence, communicating for ordinary matters through sign language.
Later we will hear how the authorities of the Trappist Order tried to see
to it that this talkative Trappist kept his mouth shut insofar as matters of
war and peace were concerned.

### Thomas Merton (1915-1968)

Thomas Merton himself, then – some basics: born January 31, 1915, in
Prades, in the Languedoc region of southern France, mother an American,
father a New Zealander, both artists. Because of World War I, the family
returned to the U.S. in 1916 to live with his mother's parents. When he
was six, his mother died, and he lived and traveled thereafter with his
father who was pursuing his painting career. When he was nearly 16, his
father died. His grandfather gave him a trust fund, and he became thereby
a wealthy orphan. He went to Cambridge, had a disastrous year there,
and was sent packing by his British guardian. Back in the U.S. he went
to Columbia University, where he was mentored by English professor
Mark Van Doren. Living the high life at university, he came close to a
nervous breakdown, searched for security, and found it in the Roman
Catholic Church, which in those days presented itself as the repository of
unchanging truth – not that this was ever the case, but it was the perception
strongly promoted by that Church. Having become a Roman Catholic, he
discovered its living monastic tradition through a visit in the spring of 1941
to Gethsemani, in Kentucky, the flagship abbey of the American Trappist
community. Here is what he said about it at the time: "This is the center
of America. I had wondered what was holding the country together, what
has been keeping the universe from cracking in pieces and falling apart.
It is places like this monastery . . . . This is the only real city in America.
. . . It is an axle around which the whole country blindly turns and knows

nothing about it."[4] It was of course his personal universe rather than the larger one that is in question here. He becomes a Trappist, and stays at Gethsemani for the next 27 years, holding important roles as master of students and master of novices. In his first 17 years there, he focuses on his own interior life and the life of the monastery. In 1948, he publishes his autobiography, *The Seven Storey Mountain*,[5] which becomes a bestseller and brings him to public attention. Then in March 1958 comes this experience, which some call his conversion to humanity:

> In Louisville, at the corner of Fourth and Walnut [now Muhammad Ali Boulevard], in the center of the shopping district, I was suddenly overwhelmed with the realization that I loved all those people, that they were mine and I theirs . . . . This sense of liberation from an illusory difference [between monks and other human beings] was such a relief and such a joy to me that I almost laughed out loud. . . . To think that for sixteen or seventeen years I have been taking seriously this pure illusion that is implicit in so much of our monastic thinking. . . . I have the immense joy of being *man*, a member of a race in which God Himself became incarnate. . . . There is no way of telling people that they are all walking around shining like the sun.[6]

With these last thoughts we come to Merton's foundational Christian convictions, which are at the root of his public role. Merton's belief was that since – as Christians believe – God took human form in Christ, "the form of a servant" (Philippians 2:7), all human life, and beyond this, the whole cosmos, was sacred. The spiritual basis of his thinking may be difficult for some of us, especially in Canada, given the widespread conviction in our essentially secular society that religious views are private matters best kept private, and are not to intrude into the public sphere. I acknowledge here that the American reality is different, with public figures regularly making faith-based statements in political and cultural contexts. Out of this conviction, then, came what he said in the last decade of his life about his major public concerns: nuclear weapons, technology, racism, the environment and interfaith dialogue. All of these, he asserted, had to be approached contemplatively, that is, prayerfully

---

4. Thomas Merton, *The Secular Journal* (New York: Farrar, Straus & Cudahy, 1959) 183.

5. Thomas Merton, *The Seven Storey Mountain* (New York: Harcourt, Brace, 1948).

6. Thomas Merton, *Conjectures of a Guilty Bystander* (Garden City, NY: Doubleday, 1966) 140-41. See also Thomas Merton, *Peace in the Post-Christian Era*, ed. Patricia A. Burton (Maryknoll, NY: Orbis, 2004) 10; subsequent references will be cited as *"PPCE"* parenthetically in the text.

and discerningly out of the contemplative's true self. After this decade of intense public engagement, he died accidentally at a conference in Thailand on December 10, 1968.

### Merton's View of Himself as Public Intellectual and Dissenter

John XXIII was elected pope on October 28, 1958. On November 10, Merton wrote to him, and in his letter sketched out what he called his "apostolate" in the intellectual community:

> It is not enough for me to think of the apostolic value of prayer and penance; I also have to think in terms of a contemplative grasp of the political, intellectual, artistic and social movements in this world – by which I mean a sympathy for the honest aspirations of so many intellectuals everywhere in the world and the terrible problems they have to face. . . . In short, with the approval of my Superiors, I have exercised an apostolate – small and limited though it be – within a circle of intellectuals from other parts of the world; and it has been quite simply an apostolate of friendship.[7]

Later in this letter he asks the pope for his blessing on his apostolate, but receives no direct response. Lawrence Cunningham[8] notes "the importance of this letter for understanding Merton's rationale for social engagement."[9] It was written during a period in American Catholic history when historian John Tracy Ellis and others were lamenting the "under-representation of American Roman Catholics in public life and in the world of public intellectuals" (Cronin 23). This changed with the election of John F. Kennedy to the presidency in 1960, an event that thrust the American Catholic reality into general public awareness, and in effect, provided context for Merton's work as a public intellectual.

Then in January 1960, writing to Cardinal Valerio Valeri, prefect of the Vatican congregation which supervises religious orders, about his desire to move to an experimental monastery near Mexico City, a desire abandoned after the Vatican's rejection of his request, he says that he had hoped to develop "certain limited contacts with intellectuals in Mexico City who are somewhat communistic in outlook, but who would have accepted me

7. Thomas Merton, *The Hidden Ground of Love: Letters on Religious Experience and Social Concerns*, ed. William H. Shannon (New York: Farrar, Straus, Giroux, 1985) 482; subsequent references will be cited as "*HGL*" parenthetically in the text.

8. See Lawrence S. Cunningham, *Thomas Merton & the Monastic Vision* (Grand Rapids, MI: Eerdmans, 1999) 64-65.

9. James G. R. Cronin, "Thomas Merton's Social Conscience in Formation," *The Merton Journal* 22.1 (Eastertide 2015) 23; subsequent references will be cited as "Cronin" parenthetically in the text.

with much goodwill as a person who would understand them."[10] Given the general American view of Communism at that time, during the Cold War, this comment, even with the qualifier "somewhat," would have set off loud alarm bells in the minds of most of his monastic confreres, to say nothing of his fellow Americans in general. A month later, on February 11, he sketches out in another letter to the pope what he has been doing or plans to do in leading retreats for theologians, psychiatrists and poets (see *HGL* 484-85). Again there is no direct response; but in his next letter, April 11, he thanks Pope John for the gift of a stole which the pope himself had worn, a gift which he took as a sign of the pope's approval of his project (see *HGL* 485-86). A few weeks later, perhaps prompted by the death of his correspondent Boris Pasternak, he records in his journal what Roger Lipsey calls "an informal vow"[11] in regard to the social and political commitment to which as both monk and intellectual he felt called:

To discover *all* the social implications of the Gospel not [simply] by studying them but by living them, and to unite myself explicitly with those who foresee and work for a social order – a transformation of the world – according to these principles: primacy of the *person* – (hence justice, liberty, against slavery, peace, control of technology, etc.). Primacy of *wisdom* and *love* (hence against materialism, hedonism, pragmatism etc.).[12]

American Merton scholar David Belcastro sees a prototype for Merton as public intellectual in Clement of Alexandria (150-215 CE), perhaps the first Christian public intellectual, one among many philosophers in pre-Christendom Alexandria, who spoke freely and publicly as a Christian in a time before the heavy hand of the Constantinian settlement descended on both church and state.[13] I see this as a germane characterization, in that Merton addressed his readership in the early post-Christendom period, meaning that like Clement, he could not be dismissed as speaking for a religious establishment. Unlike Clement, however, he had to take

---

10. Thomas Merton, *Witness to Freedom: Letters in Times of Crisis*, ed. William H. Shannon (New York: Farrar, Straus, Giroux, 1994) 217; subsequent references will be cited as "*WF*" parenthetically in the text.

11. Roger Lipsey, *Make Peace Before the Sun Goes Down: The Long Encounter of Thomas Merton and His Abbot, James Fox* (Boston: Shambala, 2015) 169; subsequent references will be cited as "Lipsey" parenthetically in the text.

12. Thomas Merton, *Turning Toward the World: The Pivotal Years. Journals, vol. 4: 1960-1963*, ed. Victor A. Kramer (San Francisco: HarperCollins, 1996) 9; subsequent references will be cited as "*TTW*" parenthetically in the text.

13. David Belcastro, "Praying the Questions: Merton of Times Square, Last of the Urban Hermits," *The Merton Annual* 20 (2007) 123-50.

cognizance of the views of many of his readers who would be critical of Christianity because of its history of persecution and its frequent inhibition of free speech during the Christendom era (roughly 313-1945 CE).

Merton has had the experience, he says, of how his reaching out to intellectuals has generated strong responses from many artists and writers who have become his friends without his having to leave the cloister. Here I believe he is thinking particularly of the many Latin American writers with whom he had been put in touch by his protégé and fellow poet, Ernesto Cardenal, later minister of culture in the Nicaraguan government. As he says to John XXIII, he has exercised an "apostolate of friendship," albeit a limited one, within the circle of intellectuals who were his correspondents. Beyond the many less well-known Latin Americans with whom he corresponded, we may mention Boris Pasternak, Erich Fromm, Rachel Carson, Nicanor Parra, Czeslaw Milosz, James Baldwin, Lawrence Ferlinghetti, Henry Miller, and Jacques and Raïssa Maritain. Some may indeed have experienced his friendship as "apostolic," others as something more collegial. This is not to say that he regarded his other correspondents as less important than his intellectual contacts, but simply to say that within the larger cohort of his 2100 correspondents, public intellectuals constituted an important subgroup.

On June 26, 1951, Merton had become an American citizen, something of great importance to him; previously, as the child of a father from New Zealand, he had been a British subject. Now he was a citizen of his chosen country, for which as time went on he felt increasing responsibility. This, I would assert, is where the democratic dissent which characterized his later life had its beginnings. He believed that as an American citizen, he had co-responsibility for his nation's actions and perspectives, and was ready both to affirm and to dissent from the policies of his government. Here is his comment on this, from his "Author's Note" in *Seeds of Destruction*:

> I speak not only as a monk but also as a responsible citizen of a very powerful nation. . . . [I]t is not my intention to imply that a state which is, and should be, secular, has to be guided by the perspectives of an eschatological Church. But I do intend to say at what point I and Christians who think as I do become morally obligated to dissent.[14]

---

14. Thomas Merton, *Seeds of Destruction* (New York: Farrar, Straus & Giroux, 1964) xv; subsequent references will be cited as "*SD*" parenthetically in the text. Another dissenting Roman Catholic writer of a slightly later period is moral theologian Charles E. Curran. In his memoir, *Loyal Dissent: Memoir of a Catholic Theologian* (Washington, DC: Georgetown University Press, 2006), he relates how his public dissent from official Vatican policies on contraception led to his firing from his teaching position at the Catholic

This statement brings together his American citizenship and his justice-oriented Christian world view. Together they form the grounds of his vocation as democratic dissenter.

## Merton and Nuclear Weapons

J. S. Porter's article on Merton as public intellectual focused on his thinking about technology (Porter 18-24); in this article, I will focus on another of his major concerns, nuclear weapons.[15] I see this as particularly apropos, given that on January 22, 2015, nine days before Merton's hundredth birthday, the *Bulletin of the Atomic Scientists* moved the hands of the Doomsday Clock two minutes forward. Taking climate change as well as nuclear weapons into consideration, the atomic scientists have now set the clock of our historical-political-social-environmental moment at three minutes to midnight.

Merton was not keeping a journal in August 1945; so there is no record of his response to the use of nuclear weapons at Hiroshima and Nagasaki. A letter of August 1961 gives the initial evidence of his frustration with his church in regard to its apathy about nuclear weapons: "why this awful silence and apathy on the part of Catholics, clergy, hierarchy, lay people . . . ?" he asked Catholic Worker founder Dorothy Day (*HGL* 139). The first entry in his journal about nuclear weapons, however, on October 23, 1961, indicates that he had already started to write about them. He had sent an article called "The Root of War Is Fear" to Dorothy Day for publication in *The Catholic Worker,* still selling now as then for one cent a copy.[16] He had felt impelled by the lack of strong Catholic

University of America, followed by the student and faculty protest which led to his reinstatement. Like Merton, he became a public figure; but his dissent concerned intra-church issues rather than issues that were political in a primary sense. His comment: "In the political realm, [dissent] has often been expressed as the highest form of patriotism, which consists in resisting one's country or one's government when it is in the wrong. In the context of the church, for me, dissent means speaking the truth in love, and that has always been my intention" (68).

15. Some contemporary resources on nuclear weapons include: Joseph M. Siracusa, *Nuclear Weapons: A Very Short Introduction* (Oxford: Oxford University Press, 2008); Gareth Evans, Tanya Ogilvie-White and Ramesh Thakur, *Nuclear Weapons: The State of Play 2015* (Canberra: Australian National University Press, 2015); Gareth Evans, "Challenges for the *Bulletin of the Atomic Scientists* at 70: Restoring reason to the nuclear debate" (16 November 2015), an update to his book (mail.google.com/mail/?ui=2&ik=c2e94 (m da103&view=pt&search=inbox&th=1515f16811dc096a&siml=1515f16811dc096a) (accessed 1 December 2015).

16. Thomas Merton, "The Root of War Is Fear," *The Catholic Worker* 28 (October 1961) 1, 7-8; Thomas Merton, *Passion for Peace: The Social Essays*, ed. William H. Shannon (New York: Crossroad, 1995) 11-19.

voices speaking about nuclear weapons and nuclear war to venture into the world of public debate. Here is what he said in his journal: "I am one of the few Catholic priests in the country who has come out unequivocally for a completely intransigent fight for the abolition of war . . . . Hence by implication not only against the bomb, against nuclear testing, against Polaris submarines but against all violence" (*TTW* 172). He goes on to bemoan the resistance of the authorities of his Trappist Order to his concern about what he sees as the greatest moral crisis in human history, an attitude which he calls "unrealistic and absurd" (*TTW* 172). A month later, on November 25, 1961, he records an important moment of decision. "Yesterday afternoon . . . surely a decisive clarity came. That I must definitely commit myself to opposition to, and non-cooperation with, nuclear war. . . . Not that I did not mean this before – but never so wholly and so definitely" (*TTW* 182). He was now fully engaged in anti-nuclear activity. He wrote a number of articles which he started to gather together for a book which he wanted to call *Peace in the Post-Christian Era.* He had picked up the term "post-Christian" from C. S. Lewis, who had used it in his 1954 inaugural lecture at Cambridge.[17] The term doesn't seem strange to most of us now; but at the time, when most people in the West, Christian or not, still thought of themselves as living in Christian societies, it had considerable shock value. Certainly Christendom, the state of political and religious affairs in which Christianity was normative and in some cases dominant, and which began with Constantine, had at least symbolically come to an end around 1945, marked by three factors in particular: the dropping of nuclear bombs by a nation seen as Christian on a nation seen as non-Christian (ironically, Nagasaki was the center of the Japanese Catholic community); by the beginning of the end of European colonialism, which had fostered and sheltered the missionary movement; and by the discovery as World War II ended of the Holocaust, of which a "Christian" nation was the perpetrator.

## Leo Szilard (1898-1964)

On April 12, 1962, Merton wrote to one of the fathers of the atomic bomb, the brilliant Hungarian physicist Leo Szilard (*WF* 49-50).[18] In 1919, Szilard had gone to Germany, where he studied with Albert Einstein. Fleeing as a Jew from the Nazis, he then went to England in 1933, then to the United States in 1938. On August 2, 1939, at Szilard's instigation,

---

17. *"De descriptione Temporum,"* in C. S. Lewis, *They Asked for a Paper* (London: Bles, 1962) 14; see also *PPCE* 72.

18. This letter is also found in Thomas Merton, *Cold War Letters,* ed. Christine M. Bochen and William H. Shannon (Maryknoll, NY: Orbis, 2006) 130-32.

Einstein wrote to President Roosevelt about the possibility that nuclear power could be generated from uranium, and about his conviction that the Nazis were actively researching this possibility for military use. Einstein's letter, and an accompanying explanatory memorandum, were given by banker and scholar Alexander Sachs on October 11 to Roosevelt, who on this first occasion showed no particular interest. Sachs asked for a breakfast meeting the next day, October 12, when he managed to persuade Roosevelt to take the action which led to the inauguration of the Manhattan Project, which in 1945 produced the atomic bombs. Until 1945, Szilard's fear was that Germany would create and use atomic weapons; but in that year it became clear that this was not happening. Szilard, who had up to this point assumed that the U.S., if it developed atomic weapons, would never use them except in self-defense, then began to fear that the U.S. would indeed use the bombs. By contrast, General Leslie Groves, the military supervisor of the Manhattan Project, was afraid that the war would end before the bombs could be used; and his view, as we know, prevailed. When he realized the likelihood of this, Szilard then obtained another letter from Einstein to Roosevelt, warning against any such use; it was found unread on Roosevelt's desk after his sudden death on April 12, 1945. Szilard, who had been so instrumental in the development of the bomb, then spent the rest of his life working for nuclear disarmament. In November 1961, he gave a major public address,[19] which concluded by asserting the necessity of a mass movement in opposition to nuclear weapons. It was this address which came to Merton's attention, and in response to which Merton wrote Szilard on April 12, 1962. In his letter Merton stated his support for what he called Szilard's "proposals about a peace lobby" (*WF* 49) and offered to contribute "a notable part of the royalties of a book I am currently writing" (*WF* 49-50) to Szilard's cause. This book was *Peace in the Post-Christian Era*, not so named in his letter. As we know, it was not published until 2004, 42 years after it had been prepared for publication, and so there were no royalties available to Szilard. Szilard replied to Merton on May 2,[20] expressing his gratitude for Merton's interest, and assuring him that he would be regularly informed of the progress of the "peace lobby." Szilard's proposals did result in the formation of such a lobby, the Council for Abolishing War, later called the Council for a Livable World (livableworld.org). This continues to function, and works to help elect members of Congress who will support its goal of the elimination of nuclear weapons. The two letters constitute the

---

19. "Are We on the Road to War?" in the archives of the Thomas Merton Center (TMA), Bellarmine University, Louisville, KY.

20. Letter in TMA.

only exchange between Merton and Szilard; there is nothing in writing which records any further contact between them.

## Merton and the Abbot General

By the spring of 1962, Merton had collected carbon or mimeographed copies of all the articles he wanted to include in *Peace in the Post-Christian Era*; and, writing to his longtime publisher and friend, James Laughlin, he records that Macmillan had offered him a $10,000 advance for the projected book.[21] Then on April 27, Merton's abbot, James Fox, gave him a letter from the Trappist-Cistercian Abbot General, Gabriel Sortais, which he, Dom James, had received in January, but had chosen not to pass on immediately – a very supportive gesture (see Lipsey 183). The letter required of Merton, as a Trappist monk, that he no longer publish on issues of war and peace, particularly nuclear weapons. As any Roman Catholic writer, Merton accepted the fact that his writing, to be acceptable to the Church, had to be free of anything which conflicted with core Roman Catholic teaching. But this issue was not one of doctrine. The Abbot General, and indeed many other Trappists, simply did not accept Merton's interest in war and peace as a fit subject for a monk. He was not told that his opinions were wrong, but that it was not his place as a monk to express them publicly. He had made a vow of obedience, and now he was expected to keep that vow, whatever it cost him. He could of course at any time have walked away from Gethsemani, as some of his friends urged him to do. But had he done this, he would have lost his status as a monk in good standing, and this he was unwilling to do. He believed that his words had more impact from his location of marginality and "exile" than they would have from a non-monastic place of utterance. He spoke and wrote, as Richard Rohr might say, from "the edge of the inside." With both humor and bitterness he wrote on June 4 about the Abbot General's letter to his good friend from Columbia days, poet Robert Lax, in their private language: "I have been silence [*sic*]. I have been nacht und nebel for my war book. I have been put in the calabozo. I have been shut up in a tin can. I have been shrewdly suppressed at the right moment. I have been stood in the corner. I have been made to wear the cap. . . . I have been told to shut up about the wars, wars is not for Christians except to support."[22] But he found a solution. He stopped trying to publish his writings in any

---

21. Thomas Merton and James Laughlin, *Selected Letters*, ed. David D. Cooper (New York: W. W. Norton, 1997) 196.

22. Thomas Merton and Robert Lax, *When Prophecy Still Had a Voice: The Letters of Thomas Merton & Robert Lax*, ed. Arthur W. Biddle (Lexington: University Press of Kentucky, 2001) 237.

*public* forum, and instead, in the year that followed the prohibition, 1963, sent mimeographed copies of the book to friends, for *private* circulation. He did check this out with his abbot, who, still supportive, agreed with him that private or personal communications did not contravene the ban from the Abbot General. In effect he embraced the practice of *samizdat*, the clandestine circulation of mimeographed materials, just as Soviet dissidents did in that period. The irony of an American needing to do what Soviet dissidents were doing in a time of intense anti-Communism in the United States was not of course lost on Merton and his friends. The Second Vatican Council began its work in October 1962, and it is known that in 1963, a number of copies of the mimeographed book reached some of the bishops at the Council, and some of the *periti*, their expert advisers. Whether Merton's views on nuclear weapons influenced any of the members of the Council cannot be exactly ascertained; but in the view of peace activist Jim Forest, he was a significant influence on what the Council eventually said about war and peace.[23]

In April of 1963, early in the Council and only six weeks before he died, John XXIII issued his encyclical letter, *Pacem in Terris* [Peace on Earth], important not only for what it said about war but important as well in that unlike previous papal encyclicals it was addressed not only to Roman Catholics but to all people of good will[24] (as was the recent encyclical of Pope Francis on climate change, *Laudato Si'*). In paragraph 112, Pope John says flatly that nuclear weapons must be banned, that the reaching of a general agreement on disarmament is a moral imperative. Soon after the encyclical appeared, Merton wrote to the abbot general, pointing out that he was saying nothing more than the pope was saying, and asking that the prohibition be lifted. Again the answer was no (the pope was not a monk – and Merton was not the pope), and on May 10, 1963, Merton recorded this response in his journal:

> Letter from the General came today categorically denying my request to publish *Peace in the Post-Christian Era* now that the Encyclical has said what I was saying myself! At the back of his mind obviously is an adamant conviction that France should have the bomb and use it

---

23. See Jim Forest, *The Root of War Is Fear: Thomas Merton's Advice to Peacemakers* (Maryknoll, NY: Orbis, 2016) 140-51; see also his foreword in *PPCE* (xviii).

24. See sandiego.edu/cctc/documents/readings/PaceminTerris.pdf, April 11, 1963 (accessed 19 August 2015). John was not the first pope to be concerned about nuclear weapons. On February 21, 1943, in an early word of warning, Pius XII, speaking to the Pontifical Academy of Science, called on the nations never to use nuclear energy destructively. See Robert Jungk, *Brighter Than a Thousand Suns: A Personal History of the Atomic Scientists* (New York: Harcourt, Brace, 1958) 174.

if [France deemed it] necessary. He says the Encyclical has changed nothing in the right of a nation to arm itself with nuclear weapons for self-defense, and speaks only of "aggressive war." I suppose the letter was composed by his secretary, Père Clément: it reflects his obtuseness. (*TTW* 317)

The abbot general, a French citizen, was clearly mistaken in what he said about *Pacem in Terris*, which says flatly that all nuclear weapons should be banned. But both the abbot general and his secretary were veterans of World War II, and of a continuing military cast of mind. As French patriots, they were unwilling to have France's nuclear *force de frappe* relinquished even if retaining it contradicted what the pope said: in this instance, nationalism trumped papal authority. This abbot general died in November 1963, and was succeeded by another patriotic French monastic, Ignace Gillet. Merton by this time was working on another book, *Seeds of Destruction*, in which he wanted to include some of the articles he had written for *Peace in the Post-Christian Era*. However, the new general, reading Merton's file in Rome, discovered what his predecessor had decided, and renewed the prohibition. I make some allowance for the abbots general in their response to Merton in that they were writing in the time of the Cold War, when an intense fear of the possible global triumph of Communism terrified many. Merton himself, although cognizant of the dangers of the Cold War, had removed beyond this binary Cold War mode of thinking, being ready to criticize both sides as appropriate.

However, in July 1964, four months after the new abbot general's renewal of his predecessor's prohibition, and with Merton's final article for *Seeds of Destruction*, "The Christian in World Crisis" (*SD* 93-183), on the abbot general's desk, waiting to be sent to the censor, a plea for a quick response arrived from the publisher, Farrar, Straus and Giroux, indeed from Merton's longtime friend and publisher, Robert Giroux. It happened that the abbot general's secretary, the "obtuse" Père Clément, was away from Rome, and the general, who did not read English, called in an American Trappist working in Rome, Laurence Bourget, and asked him to read the article and tell him if it was acceptable. Having read it, he told the general that the article was "pure gospel," and so publication of *Seeds of Destruction* went ahead.[25] Three years later, in 1967, the monastic censorship system was abandoned as a result of the reforms of Vatican II; and Merton was thenceforth free to write and publish whatever he wanted.

---

25. See Patricia A. Burton, "Introduction: The Book That Never Was" (*PPCE* xlvi-xlvii) and Jonathan Montaldo, "Thomas Merton: A Monk Who 'Succeeded': An Interview with Dom M. Laurence Bourget OCSO," *The Merton Annual* 12 (1999) 45-48.

## Merton and Vatican II (1962-65)

Vatican II was a historic event which Merton followed closely, taking particular interest in what it would say to the world on behalf of the Roman Catholic Church in regard to nuclear weapons.[26] The Council began its work in the fall of 1962, virtually simultaneously with the Cuban missile crisis, which of course turned the thoughts of many to the nuclear issue; it met four times, each time in the fall, with the final session ending on December 8, 1965. The issue of peace was dealt with in the document called in Latin *Gaudium et Spes* ["Joy and Hope"], *The Pastoral Constitution on the Church in the Modern World*. Foundational to what it would say was of course Pope John's encyclical, *Pacem in Terris*, in which he had written that nuclear weapons must be banned, and that any use of nuclear weapons in populated areas would constitute a crime against humanity. *Gaudium et Spes* came up for discussion at the third session of the Council, in the fall of 1964. Pope John's successor, Paul VI, took a much more hands-on approach to the Council's workings than John had. His speech in regard to peace at the UN, given on October 4, 1964, had a strong impact on the Council, which began its discussion of the issue only two days later, on October 6, with the Pope's call for peace fresh in their minds.

The first issue which arose was this: did the existence of nuclear weapons render obsolete the traditional distinction between just and unjust war? For a war to be just on the grounds of just-war theory, a line of thinking which goes back though St. Thomas Aquinas to St. Augustine, it was required that it be waged for a just cause, be declared by a duly constituted public authority, be waged with a right intention to do justice, have a reasonable probability of success, be undertaken only as a last resort, and be expected to do more good than harm. In its conduct, to be considered just, it must not attack non-combatants, act only out of military necessity, respect the rights of prisoners of war, and avoid what we now call war crimes.[27] But how relevant were *any* of these criteria if nuclear weapons were used in war? Merton was not a pacifist in the strict sense, but he was a *nuclear* pacifist. Given that in any war involving a nation possessing nuclear weapons that nation might decide to use them, as the United States had done near the end of World War II, the risk of global disaster was so great that no longer, he believed, could *any* war

---

26. For a comprehensive account of the Council, see John W. O'Malley, *What Happened at Vatican II* (Cambridge, MA: Belknap Press/Harvard University Press, 2008).

27. See *The Challenge of Peace: God's Promise and Our Response* (Washington, DC: National Conference of Catholic Bishops, 1983) nn. 80-110.

be considered just, given the risk of escalation.[28] Most of the bishops of the Council came to the same conclusion, that just-war theory was now obsolete, although at this intermediate stage, a persistent minority supported the continued possession of nuclear weapons on the grounds of deterrence.

The final text of *Gaudium et Spes*, hammered out in the fall of 1965, and promulgated by Paul VI in December of that year, affirmed the right of nations to defend themselves, and gave grudging acknowledgement to the possibility that the possession of nuclear weapons could be justified, although only as a deterrent to war. But it accompanied this with a strong call for the ending of the arms race, and the ultimate abolition of nuclear weapons. A number of American bishops, among them Francis Spellman (1889-1967), Archbishop of New York, who was chaplain-general for Roman Catholics in U.S. forces and a noted conservative among the bishops, ran a campaign in the very last week of the Council to persuade the bishops to vote against even these provisions, notably more modest, as some bishops noted, than what John XXIII had set forth in *Pacem in Terris*. But the majority supported the final draft, and this became the official position of the Roman Catholic Church. Merton's journal entry of December 11, 1965, gives us his view of the Council's position: "The Schema [draft] on the Church and the World [*Gaudium et Spes*] finally passed with the part on conscientious objection weakened, but the strong statement against total war unmitigated in spite of the efforts of Cardinal Spellman. . . . Really this Council has been a great thing."[29] I confess that I find the mildness of this response surprising, given Merton's absolute opposition to nuclear weapons. Yes, total war was condemned, but the retention of nuclear weapons was not forbidden. I can only speculate that having tried for so long to get nuclear weapons on the Church's agenda he was satisfied that since the issue had been given such substantial attention at the Council, it provided grounds for hope for stronger statements in the future. Ronald Powaski takes a sterner view, asserting that both Merton and the bishops who wrote the 1983 pastoral letter of which I speak in the next section were inconsistent in even considering the manifestly contradictory view that limited nuclear war was both theoretically possible and morally unjustifiable (Powaski 143-44).

---

28. See Ronald E. Powaski, *Thomas Merton on Nuclear Weapons* (Chicago: Loyola University Press, 1988) 32-33 (subsequent references will be cited as "Powaski" parenthetically in the text); see also *PPCE* 5-7.

29. Thomas Merton, *Dancing in the Water of Life: Seeking Peace in the Hermitage. Journals, vol. 5: 1963-1965*, ed. Robert E. Daggy (San Francisco: HarperCollins, 1997) 323.

### The Challenge of Peace

Roman Catholics after Merton's time, many of them influenced by him, continued to be concerned about nuclear weapons and the dangers both of their simple possession and their possible use. In 1983, after some years of public discussion, and many drafts, the Roman Catholic bishops of the United States issued a major document, *The Challenge of Peace: God's Promise and our Response.* Its only reference to Merton occurs in note 45, in a list of authors who had dealt with Christian pacifism and non-violence, a reference to Merton's *Faith and Violence*.[30] The pastoral letter occasioned a cover story in *Newsweek*, "and was selected as religious news story of the year in 1982 and 1983 by numerous publications."[31] Its moral critique of nuclear weapons alarmed the Reagan administration (there were, after all, 50 million Roman Catholic voters in the United States), which went to some lengths to influence its early drafts, or, once published, to discredit it. Gerard Powers points out that it was the work of the bishops of the generation of Vatican II, many of them appointed by Paul VI; a later generation of bishops, mostly appointed by John Paul II, shifted their prime concern to matters of what John Paul saw as the cardinal marks of "Catholic identity" – matters of sexual morality and a backing-away from the ecumenical openness that marked the sixties and seventies (Powers 74).[32] Thus *The Harvest of Justice Is Sown in Peace*, issued by the bishops in 1993 to mark the tenth anniversary of *The Challenge of Peace*, devotes only four pages to nuclear matters, and breaks no new ground (see Powers 75).

*The Challenge of Peace* gives thorough attention to the biblical, moral, social, cultural and political dimensions of the possession and possible use of nuclear weapons. It is simultaneously bold and prudent. However, it was prevented from advocating the end of Catholic support for the policy of deterrence by a statement made a year earlier by John Paul II in his message to that year's UN Special Session on Disarmament. "In current conditions 'deterrence' based on balance, certainly not as an end in itself but as a step on the way toward a progressive disarmament, may still be judged morally acceptable. Nonetheless, in order to ensure

---

30. Thomas Merton, *Faith and Violence: Christian Teaching and Christian Practice* (Notre Dame, IN: University of Notre Dame Press, 1968); see *Challenge of Peace* note 32.

31. Gerard F. Powers, "The US Bishops and War since the Peace Pastoral," *US Catholic Historian* 27.2 (Winter 2009) 73; subsequent references will be cited as "Powers" parenthetically in the text.

32. See also Frank Cordaro, "Americans or Catholics: On Then and Now," in *"The Challenge of Peace* 25 Years Later," catholicpeacefellowship.org/nextpage.asp?m+2565 (accessed 27 July 2015).

peace, it is indispensable not to be satisfied with this minimum which is always susceptible to the real danger of explosion."[33]

Commenting on this, the bishops state:

> In concert with the evaluation provided by Pope John Paul II, we have arrived at a strictly conditional moral acceptance of deterrence. In this letter we have outlined criteria and recommendations which indicate the meaning of conditional acceptance of deterrence policy. We cannot consider such a policy adequate as a long-term basis for peace.[34]

The Non-Proliferation Treaty of 1970 had invited non-nuclear nations to sign it on the understanding that the nuclear nations would move toward "progressive disarmament," to use the words of John Paul II, and thereby toward a relinquishment of deterrence, a policy which was essentially a justification of possessing weapons the use of which on any reckoning would be immoral if not insane. However, as the years went by, it became very clear that the nuclear-armed nations had (and have) no intention whatever of disarmament. Thus in 2008, when the twenty-fifth anniversary of *The Challenge of Peace* was commemorated by the Catholic Peace Fellowship, it took the position that any further justification of deterrence by Catholics was immoral and *passé*. As Tom Cornell, a co-founder of the CPF and a longtime member of the Catholic Worker community, says, "Either we intend to use them [nuclear weapons] or we do not and are lying. If we intend to use them, we are already guilty."[35] Since then, the United States and Russia have invested and continue to invest billions in the modernization of their nuclear arsenals.

### The Roman Catholic Church and Nuclear Weapons Today

It may be, in fact, that the Roman Catholic Church has now moved beyond John Paul's 1982 statement on deterrence. Pope Francis sent a strong message on the issue to the December 2014 conference in Vienna on the Humanitarian Impact of Nuclear Weapons. He restated what he called "the Vatican's long-standing advocacy for the global elimination of nuclear weapons" and asserted that a world without nuclear weapons is possible.[36] In a statement of April 10, 2015, the Vatican's ambassador to the UN,

---

33. *The Challenge of Peace*, Introduction, I.B.1.

34. *The Challenge of Peace*, Introduction II.B; see also nn. 162-99.

35. Tom Cornell, "The Church Needs You," in *"The Challenge of Peace* 25 Years Later."

36. Chaz Muth, "Pope Francis calls for solidarity in creating a world without nuclear weapons," *National Catholic Reporter*, ncronline.org, December 8, 2014 (interestingly, the anniversary of the promulgation of *Gaudium et Spes*) (accessed 14 January 2015).

Archbishop Bernardito Auza, made this further comment, published in *Time* magazine: "Today there is no more argument, not even the argument of deterrence used during the Cold War, that could minimally justify the possession of nuclear weapons. The 'peace of a sort' that is supposed to justify nuclear deterrence is specious and illusory."[37] A recent series of articles in the *National Catholic Reporter* has also taken the position that deterrence theory is outdated, and that full and prompt disarmament must be a geopolitical priority. As recently retired NCR publisher Thomas Fox asserts, "there is a growing consensus around the world that the nuclear weapons states have not met their obligations under Article VI [of the Non-Proliferation Treaty, which committed them to eliminate their nuclear stockpiles] and have no plans to do so."[38] However, while the Vatican grows increasingly insistent in its condemnation of nuclear weapons, the American bishops remain formally committed to their 1983 statement, which relied on the 1982 statement of John Paul II justifying deterrence as a step towards disarmament – which it has been clearly proven not to be. A strongly-worded editorial in NCR flatly states: "It's time to declare deterrence a failed strategy, and the possession of nuclear weapons immoral,"[39] asserting that the conditional acceptance which the bishops gave to deterrence in 1983 has lost whatever validity it ever had, as, therefore, has John Paul's statement of 1982. It concludes with this call to the Roman Catholic faithful of the United States to go over the heads of their bishops and show their support for Pope Francis in his opposition to nuclear weapons:

> In the absence of hierarchical consensus [among the U.S. bishops], it is imperative that we and other Catholics amplify the case the Vatican is clearly articulating and condemn U.S. nuclear policy. In expressing this condemnation from the heartland of the United States, we are buoyed by the hopes of countless millions around the world who are also demanding that nations possessing nuclear weapons give them up before they destroy us all.

Merton would be much encouraged to read these statements. Even so, it is clear that as his own work on this issue did not reach completion,

---

37. Elizabeth Dias, "Pope Francis' Latest Mission: Stopping Nuclear Weapons," *Time* (13 April 2015) (time.com/3817021/pope-francis-nuclear-disarmament) (accessed 13 April 2015).

38. Thomas C. Fox, "Nuclear nations meet at UN amid growing support for disarmament," *National Catholic Reporter* (ncronline.org, May 7, 2015) (accessed 9 May 2015).

39. "Editorial: Demand Nuclear Disarmament, not Deterrence," *National Catholic Reporter* (ncronline.org, May 20, 2015) (accessed 20 May 2015).

neither has ours.

## A Summary Word

At the beginning of this article I listed Merton's major concerns: nuclear weapons, yes, but also racism, technology, the environment and interfaith dialogue, as well as the need for human beings to learn how to live contemplatively, that is, as he understood it, in loving and discerning presence to the present moment. It can be argued that for Merton these challenges to the contemplative spirit are all one issue, humanity's alienation from its own well-being. Nuclear weapons could not have come about without technology. The willingness of a nation perceived as white to use nuclear weapons against a non-white nation brings in the issue of racism. The devastating effect of nuclear weapons on the environment would be incalculable. The great religions of the world increasingly see their mandate as promoting peace among the world's peoples and thereby making war and nuclear war less likely (although as we know, there are some in every religion who are prepared to do the opposite). The true contemplative, Merton would argue, is unable to justify or initiate nuclear war.

In conclusion, then, a summary word from Merton himself about how he saw his role as a contemplative public intellectual in our fractured world. He wrote it in August 1963 in his preface to the Japanese translation of *The Seven Storey Mountain*, with no explicit reference to nuclear weapons. However, it clearly states the position which he held to the end of his life. Written more than fifty years ago, I note here its contemporary character:

> by being in the monastery I take my true part in all the struggles and sufferings of the world. . . . It is my intention to make my entire life a rejection of, a protest against the crimes and injustices of war and political tyranny which threaten to destroy the whole race of man and the world with him. By my monastic life and vows I am saying NO to all the concentration camps, the aerial bombardments, the staged political trials, the judicial murders, the racial injustices, the economic tyrannies, and the whole socio-economic apparatus which seems geared for nothing but global destruction in spite of all its fair words in favor of peace. I make monastic silence a protest against the lies of politicians, propagandists and agitators, and when I speak it is to deny that my faith and my Church can ever seriously be aligned with these forces of injustice and destruction. But it is true, nevertheless, that the faith in which I believe is also invoked by many who believe in war, believe in racial injustices, believe in self-righteous and lying

forms of tyranny. My life must, then, be a protest against these also, and perhaps against these most of all.[40]

In this statement Merton declares himself a Christian believer who sees no contradiction between his faith and what he has to say as a public intellectual and democratic dissenter. Given the strong presence of Christian fundamentalists in the public discourse of the United States, some of them aspirants to high political office, what he had to say would now be unwelcome both to secularists who believe that religious conviction is a private matter, and to these Christian co-religionists of a very different stripe. We can trust, however, that Merton, articulate and passionate as he was, would, if he were with us in the flesh today, have no difficulty knowing what to say to either of these cohorts.[41]

### Coda

Since this paper was first drafted (in January 2015), Pope Francis has visited the United States, where he addressed both its Congress[42] and the General Assembly of the United Nations. In an article published four days before the pope addressed the UN, Catholic activists Joe Cirincione and Tom Collins floated the possibility that he might "declare that any possession of nuclear weapons is immoral."[43] In the event, what he said was this:

An ethics and a law based on the threat of mutual destruction – and possibly the destruction of all mankind – are self-contradictory and an affront to the entire framework of the United Nations . . . . There is urgent need to work for a world free of nuclear weapons, in full

---

40. Thomas Merton, *"Honorable Reader": Reflections on My Work*, ed. Robert E. Daggy (New York: Crossroad, 1989) 65-66.

41. In an earlier form, this article was first delivered on February 5, 2015, as a lecture for the Institute for the Humanities at Simon Fraser University, as part of the Institute's series on democratic dissent, and as part of the Vancouver celebrations of Merton's centenary. Here I wish especially to acknowledge my indebtedness to J. S. Porter for his article on Merton as public intellectual.

42. In his address to the Congress, Pope Francis mentioned the names of four notable Americans whom he sees as model representatives of contemporary response to continuing social challenges: Abraham Lincoln, Martin Luther King, Jr., Dorothy Day – and Thomas Merton. For the complete text of the address, see Pope Francis, "Address of the Holy Father to a Joint Session of the United States Congress – September 24, 2015," *The Merton Annual* 28 (2015) 16-23.

43. "The Pope is Lining Up to Ban Nuclear Weapons," September 21, 2015 (http://www.defenseone.com/ideas/2015/09/pope-lining-ban-nuclear-weapons 121589) (accessed 22 September 2015).

application of the Non-Proliferation Treaty, in letter and spirit, with the goal of a complete prohibition of these weapons.[44]

So he did not take the moral position that Cirincione, Collins, Fox and others wanted him to take. Yet given his recognition of the failure of deterrence as a permanent resting-place for the international order, and his reference to "the goal of a complete prohibition of these weapons," it seems to me that a declaration of the very possession of nuclear weapons by Pope Francis as immoral is a logical and highly desirable next step. He has emerged as a moral leader who for huge numbers of people transcends his designated but limited identity as the head of the largest Christian church. I am convinced that there is at this historical moment no one on the global level better placed than he is to declare the utter immorality of the possession of nuclear weapons and to receive a solid and supportive response to such a declaration from the millions who long for such a bold and timely word.

These hopes were encouraged by a conference on nonviolence and just peace held at the Vatican in April 2016,[45] cohosted by the Pontifical Council on Justice and Peace and Pax Christi International, which brought together bishops, theologians, laypersons, sisters and priests from around the world – many living in situations of extreme violence and social upheaval. Conference participants called on the Catholic Church to recommit itself to the centrality of Gospel nonviolence and proposed a six-point plan: 1) to continue to develop Catholic social teaching on nonviolence – in particular, Pope Francis was asked to write an encyclical on nonviolence and just peace; 2) to integrate Gospel nonviolence explicitly into the life, including the sacramental life, and work of the Church; 3) to promote nonviolent practices and strategies; 4) to initiate a global conversation on nonviolence within the Church, with people of other faiths and with the larger world in order to respond to the crises of our time with the vision and strategies of nonviolence and just peace; 5) no longer to rely on just-war theory and to continue advocating for the abolition of war and nuclear weapons; 6) to lift up the prophetic voice of the Church to challenge unjust world powers and to support and defend nonviolent activists whose work for peace and justice put their lives at risk. In response, Pope Francis has made "Nonviolence: a Style of Politics for

---

44. "Full text of Pope Francis' speech to United Nations," PBS NewsHour (pbs.org/newshour/rundown/full-text-pope-francis-speech-united-nations) (accessed 25 September 2015).

45. For extensive coverage of the conference and information on the subsequently formed Catholic Nonviolence Initiative, see https://nonviolencejustpeace.net (accessed 28 December 2016).

Peace" the theme for the fiftieth anniversary of the World Day of Peace, January 1, 2017, declaring: "In the most local and ordinary situations and in the international order, may nonviolence become the hallmark of our decisions, our relationships and our actions, and indeed of political life in all its forms."[46] The vision of shalom articulated by Merton a half-century ago may yet become a central dimension of the preaching and living of the gospel in a world desperately in need of a prophetic witness to peace rooted in justice and extending to all creation.

---

46. For the entire message, see: https://w2.vatican.va/content/francesco/en/messages/peace/documents/papa-francesco_20161208_messaggio-l-giornata-mondiale-pace-2017.html (accessed 28 December 2016).

# Thomas Merton and Henry Miller:
## A Correspondence in Vision

*Angus F. Stuart*

When Thomas Merton sent a picture of himself to Henry Miller in June 1964, Miller was struck by their physical resemblance; Merton's face to him seemed to combine his own and that of French author Jean Genet, he wrote in a response dated July 4, 1964: "You too have the look of an ex-convict, of one who has been through the fires."[1] Merton was clearly delighted, and replied commenting that he also had noticed their physical similarity, though adding that the person he was most often likened to was Picasso. "Still," he writes, "I think it is a distinction to look like Picasso, Henry Miller, and Genet all at once. Pretty comprehensive. It seems to imply some kind of responsibility."[2] To Miguel Grinberg, who was photographed with Merton and whom Miller likened to "a pugilist and a vagabond," Merton wrote (in a letter dated July 12, 1964), "only ex-convicts and vagabonds have any right to be moving about and breathing the air of night which is our ordinary climate" (*CT* 199). He said something similar in his August 16 response to Miller: "It seems to me that the only justification for a man's existence in this present world is for him to either be a convict, or a victim of plague, or a leper, or at least to look like one of these things" (*CT* 280). Merton and Miller see reflected in each other's faces their own understanding of themselves standing on the margins (or on the outside) of society.

In a letter dated October 6, 1965, Merton tells Chilean poet Hernan Lavin Cerda, "Miller is a very good friend of mine and has much to say, but he is old. Here he is very famous but he is read, above all, for 'kicks' because he has a reputation of being pornographic. Actually he is a kind of secular monk with a sexual mysticism" (*CT* 205). Thomas Merton and Henry Miller had been in correspondence with each other since April 1962 when Miller had written to Merton to say how "moved" he was by

---

1. Ken Shapero, "Dear Henry: Love Thomas*,*" *Louisville Today* 5 (May 1981) 36; subsequent references will be cited as "Shapero" parenthetically in the text. This article makes available in published form all six items of the extant correspondence from Henry Miller to Thomas Merton; the originals are held in the archives of the Thomas Merton Center at Bellarmine University, Louisville, KY.

2. Thomas Merton, *The Courage for Truth: Letters to Writers*, ed. Christine M. Bochen (New York: Farrar, Straus, Giroux, 1993) 280; subsequent references will be cited as "*CT*" parenthetically in the text.

Merton's satirical poem on Hiroshima, *Original Child Bomb*,[3] and how "stimulated" he is by Merton's writings, "especially by that one on the Desert Fathers!" (Shapero 36). Prior to this, messages and greetings to one another had been mediated by their mutual contacts James Laughlin and Robert MacGregor at New Directions who published both Miller and Merton.

In November 1961 Miller had written to MacGregor that he "Was happy to get the new annual with Merton's fragment on the Desert Fathers. . . . I feel closer to him, his way of thinking, than any other American author I know of."[4] Laughlin passed these comments on to Merton, who responded, "Well, that is a testimonial. I am really warmed by it. To me that is an indication that I am perhaps after all a Christian. I believe that this element of inner recognition that cuts right through apparent external barriers and divisions is of crucial importance today."[5] Both through reading one another and through their correspondence, Merton and Miller came to see that such "external barriers and divisions" are indeed illusory and that they had more in common than might be expected. In many ways Merton had more in common with the likes of Henry Miller than he did with many in the Catholic Church; and Miller, who could be quite dismissive of Christianity, was no doubt pleasantly surprised to find he had so much in common with Merton whom he initially regarded as a "Father Brown" figure, the priest-detective in a number of novels by G. K. Chesterton.[6]

Beyond some superficial parallels between Merton and Miller – both having spent significant periods of their lives in New York and France, both fluent in French and familiar with French literature, both having run into trouble with censorship – a deeper parallel is found in their relationship to "the world" as manifested in mid-twentieth-century America and Western civilization. Both became increasingly disenchanted with the world in which they had grown up, both rejected it in various ways, turning away from it and stepping outside the bounds of conventional society. Yet by the time they had begun to encounter one another's writing and

---

3. Thomas Merton, *Original Child Bomb: Points for Meditation to Be Scratched on the Walls of a Cave* (New York: New Directions, 1961); Thomas Merton, *The Collected Poems of Thomas Merton* (New York: New Directions, 1977) 293-302 (subsequent references will be cited as "*CP*" parenthetically in the text).

4. Henry Miller and James Laughlin, *Selected Letters*, edited by George Wickes (New York: W. W. Norton, 1996) 197-98; subsequent references will be cited as "Miller/Laughlin" parenthetically in the text.

5. Thomas Merton and James Laughlin, *Selected Letters*, edited by David D. Cooper (New York: W. W. Norton, 1997) 189.

6. Miller/Laughlin 186 [2/27/1961 from Miller to Robert MacGregor].

connected with each other through their letters, each had experienced a turning back towards the world and a re-engagement with it.

Merton entered the monastery in order to leave the world behind, including his life as a writer, and embrace the anonymity of a monk dedicated to God. As the years went by he came to realize that the idea of leaving the world was an illusion, culminating in his famous epiphany on the corner of Fourth and Walnut in Louisville in March 1958 which was "like waking from a dream of separateness."[7] Miller too had turned away from the bounds of conventional society in his early thirties when he quit his job in the personnel department at the Western Union Telegraph Company in New York to devote himself to writing. This was in the early 1920s; it was more than ten years before he found success, and only after he had moved to France where *Tropic of Cancer* was published but banned everywhere else, including America where it remained unpublished until 1961. At the end of his time in France, with gathering storm clouds over Europe, Miller travelled to Greece in 1939 at the invitation of his friend Lawrence Durrell who was living at the time on the island of Corfu. During these months in Greece Miller underwent a rebirth of his own and the beginning of a renewed turning back towards the world. Miller's account of his time in Greece was published by New Directions in 1941 as *The Colossus of Maroussi*, one of two books by Miller that Merton, who said he had often thought of writing to him, said he had read when he replied to that first letter from him on July 9, 1962, and which he described as "a tremendous and important book" (*CT* 274). In *Colossus* Miller contrasts the ancient world, or better, timeless or eternal world, of Greece with both old-world Europe and new-world America, both of which he saw as in decline. With an impending war, already described as a "world war," there is much the same ambivalence that we find in Merton's *Seven Storey Mountain*. Both writers see the deteriorating world situation as not simply to do with specific powerful individuals like Hitler, Mussolini and Stalin, but rather emanating from "civilization" itself, though Merton identified himself as part of the problem whereas Miller comes across as more detached from it.

Despite a number of negative comments about Christianity, at one point referring to it as "a blight," it is easy to see what impressed Merton about the book. As with much of Miller's other writing, it articulates a profound spiritual sensibility, often making use of striking Christian

---

7. Thomas Merton, *Conjectures of a Guilty Bystander* (Garden City, NY: Doubleday, 1966) 140; see also the original March 19, 1958 journal entry in Thomas Merton, *A Search for Solitude: Pursuing the Monk's True Life. Journals, vol. 3: 1952-1960*, ed. Lawrence S. Cunningham (San Francisco: HarperCollins, 1996) 181-82.

imagery, as in this piece in which Miller describes the effect of the light in Greece on him: "The light is no longer solar or lunar; it is the starry light of the planet to which man has given life. The earth is alive to its innermost depths; at the center it is a sun in the form of a man crucified. The sun bleeds on its cross in the hidden depths. The sun is man struggling to emerge towards another light. From light to light, from calvary to calvary. The earth song."[8] For Miller, the "man crucified" is an emblem for all humanity, as it is in Christianity too, rightly understood; but the "man struggling to emerge towards another light" is not only humanity in general but Miller himself as he struggles to be born anew. Miller journeys from one illumination to another. When he passes through the Straits of Poros he describes it as passing through a womb; his inner experience of re-birth is reflected in his outer journey. At Epidaurus the outward peace he finds reflects a deep inner peace, in which he is prepared to let go of the struggling and striving with the world and with himself:

> It is the morning of the first day of the great peace, the peace of the heart, which comes with surrender. I never knew the meaning of peace until I arrived at Epidaurus. Like everybody I had used the word all my life, without once realizing I was using a counterfeit. Peace is not the opposite of war any more than death is the opposite of life. . . . I am talking of course of the peace which passeth all understanding. There is no other kind. The peace which most of us know is merely a cessation of hostilities, a truce, an interregnum, a lull, a respite, which is negative. The peace of the heart is positive and invincible, demanding no conditions, requiring no protection. It just is. If it is a victory it is a peculiar one because it is based entirely on surrender, a voluntary surrender, to be sure. (Miller, *Colossus* 76)

Miller's move from New York to Paris and his writing of *Tropic of Cancer*, based on his experiences there, had been a journey of self-discovery as an artist. In the follow-up, *Tropic of Capricorn*, where he turned from the present to the past for literary inspiration, he wrote that his deepest desire was not to live, "but to express myself."[9] In contrast, *The Colossus of Maroussi* tells how he, as an artist, discovers a greater self as he makes the transition from art to *life*. Toward the conclusion of the book Miller writes, "I shall pass from art to life, to exemplify whatever I have mastered through art by my living." He speaks of "a growing liberation, supplemented more and more by a desire to serve the world in the highest

---

8. Henry Miller, *The Colossus of Maroussi* (New York: New Directions, 1941) 57; subsequent references will be cited as "Miller, *Colossus*" parenthetically in the text.

9. Henry Miller, *Tropic of Capricorn* (New York: Grove Press, 1961) 13.

possible way" (Miller, *Colossus* 205-206).

Just as Merton's turning away from the world by becoming a monk found its fulfillment in an increasing return towards the world in the late 1950s and 1960s, epitomized by the Fourth and Walnut experience, so also we see Miller turning back towards the world in his desire to find fulfillment not so much in art as in life. "To live creatively," Miller writes, "means to live more and more unselfishly, to live more and more *into* the world, identifying oneself with it and thus influencing it at the core, so to speak" (Miller, *Colossus* 206). He then goes on to compare the role of art to that of religion: "Art, like religion, it now seems to me, is only a preparation, an initiation into the way of life. The goal is liberation, freedom, which means assuming greater responsibility." Miller's journey of liberation, becoming free from the demands and expectations of the world, ultimately led him to assume a growing responsibility towards the world.

At the conclusion of *Colossus* Miller writes, "I was proud and arrogant, content to live the false, restricted life of the city man. The light of Greece opened my eyes, penetrated my pores, expanded my whole being. I came home to the world, having found the true center and the real meaning of revolution" (Miller, *Colossus* 241). All of this resonated with Merton, reading it at the very time when he was experiencing his own "real meaning of revolution" wherein a turning away from the world was working its way round to fulfillment in a turning back to the world, a return to the world with a renewed sense of vision.

The other of book of Miller's that Merton mentioned he had read in his first letter to him was *Big Sur and the Oranges of Hieronymus Bosch*, so titled because the oranges in a triptych by artist Hieronymus Bosch represent the fruit of paradise, and Miller came to experience Big Sur, on the California coast, where he settled after his return to America, as a paradise, albeit not without imperfections but, as he says, "Any paradise worth the name can sustain all flaws in creation and remain undiminished, untarnished."[10]

This was a new beginning for Miller, continuing the transition begun in Greece, as J. D. Brown writes, "from the civilized to the primitive, from art to life, from the air-conditioned nightmare to a back-country monastery."[11] Whether it is paradise or not depends on how you see it: "There seems to be an unwritten law here which insists that you accept what you find and like it, profit by it, or you are cast out" (Miller, *Big*

---

10. Henry Miller, *Big Sur and the Oranges of Hieronymus Bosch* (New York: New Directions, 1957) 25; subsequent references will be cited as "Miller, *Big Sur*" parenthetically in the text.

11. J. D. Brown, *Henry Miller* (New York: Ungar, 1986) 69.

*Sur* 26 ). Not that anyone is doing the casting out; it is the place itself. For those who have eyes to see, it is paradise; it is not about acceptance in a passive sense, but about embracing life and whatever it brings, to "profit by it" and so discover paradise. This echoes what Miller says about finding true peace through acceptance and surrender in *The Colossus of Maroussi*; it signifies a profound abandonment and trust in providence that is also found in Merton's monasticism: "all prayer, reading, meditation and all the activities of the monastic life are aimed at *purity of heart*, an unconditional and totally humble surrender to God, a total acceptance of ourselves and our situation as willed by Him."[12]

*Purity of heart*, Merton says, is the aim of the monastic life; *purity of heart* involves *surrender* to God and *acceptance* of ourselves and our situation. Blessed are the pure in heart, for they shall *see* God (Matthew 5:8). Purity of heart, this surrender and acceptance, is about a way of seeing – seeing the Divine at work in our life and situation. This new way of seeing, this purity of heart, leads to a new spiritual identity; one is transformed, becomes new, born again, through this new vision, this new way of seeing that is to do with acceptance and surrender. How we see affects how we are, or as Miller says in *Big Sur*, "To see things whole is to be whole" (Miller, *Big Sur* 144); and as Merton says in his prose-poem *Hagia Sophia*: "There is in all visible things an invisible fecundity, a dimmed light, a meek namelessness, a hidden wholeness" (*CP* 363).

In a striking passage, Miller writes, "I have come to believe that through being receptive, keeping one's mind and heart open – showing faith and trust, in other words – one's desires, or prayers, are realized. By prayer I do not mean asking, hoping, begging or bartering for that which one desires but, without formulating it, living the thought – 'Thy will be done!' In short, acknowledging wholeheartedly to ourselves that, whatever the situation we find ourselves in, we are to regard it as an opportunity and a privilege as well as a challenge" (Miller, *Big Sur* 205). In this articulation of "faith and trust" together with Miller's attitude of surrender and acceptance that began in Greece and came to full expression in his life at Big Sur it is easy to see how Merton could identify with Miller and characterize him as "a kind of secular monk."

At Gethsemani Merton discovered his "roots in eternity,"[13] and with such roots in eternity he was able to re-engage with the "world" in a new way, not as something separate from himself or itself cut off from

12. Thomas Merton, *Contemplative Prayer* (New York: Herder & Herder, 1969) 83.

13. Thomas Merton, *Sign of Jonas* (New York: Harcourt, Brace, 1953) 345; see also Thomas Merton, *Entering the Silence: Becoming a Monk and Writer. Journals, vol. 2: 1941-1952*, ed. Jonathan Montaldo (San Francisco: HarperCollins, 1996) 473.

eternity but as also being rooted in eternity, the "hidden wholeness." This re-engagement with the world, conscious of his own roots in eternity, enabled him not only to recognize that the world itself was rooted in eternity but to write from this perspective, offering the possibility of a new vision for those with eyes to see. Conscious of his roots in eternity, Merton was able to recognize others, like Miller, who also had "come home to the world" through a transcendent vision. Miller writes of his experience of coming to Big Sur and finding himself in paradise: "Seeking intuitively, one's destination is never in a beyond of time or space but always here and now. If we are always arriving and departing, it is also true that we are eternally anchored. One's destination is never a place but rather a new way of looking at things. Which is to say that there are no limits to vision. Similarly there are no limits to paradise" (Miller, *Big Sur* 25). The parallel between being "eternally anchored" and having "roots in eternity" is striking.

Merton enclosed the photo of himself in a letter to Miller in which he praised the latest New Directions collection of essays spanning Miller's writing, *Stand Still Like the Hummingbird*,[14] which bears resemblance in style and content to Merton's own collection, *Raids on the Unspeakable*,[15] published at around the same time. "I cannot let your hummingbird get away without a resounding shout of approval," Merton writes on June 22, 1964 (*CT* 279). In the same way that Miller recognized himself in Merton's face, Merton recognizes himself in Miller's writing: "All that you say seems to me as obvious as if I had said it myself and you have said it better than I ever could. It needs to be said over and over again." Merton further adds, "I resound to everything you say, Europe, Zen, Thoreau, and your real basic Christian spirit which I wish a few Christians shared!"

Merton recognizes himself in this "secular monk with a sexual mysticism," perhaps himself aspiring to the kind of integration of eternity in the world that Miller seems to embody; and Miller in turn recognizes in Merton an outsider like himself, an outlaw, "an ex-convict . . . one who has been through the fires" and bears the traces of it. Miller seems to admire Merton's monasticism, encouraging him to keep to his "(wonderful) way" in a letter on July 31, 1962 (Shapero 36) and to "Keep writing – and praying!" in another from January 12, 1963 (Shapero 36). Yet whilst reveling in the irony of their *simpatico* of spirit, Merton's embrace of formal religion remains an enigma for him. Following Merton's death in 1968, Miller concludes a letter dated April 22, 1969 to Bob MacGregor of New Directions: "By the way, I admired Merton greatly. He was a real

---

14. Henry Miller, *Stand Still Like the Hummingbird* (New York: New Directions, 1962).
15. Thomas Merton, *Raids on the Unspeakable* (New York: New Directions, 1966).

radical, a true anarchist, even if a Christian." No doubt this was meant as a supreme compliment. He then adds in parenthesis, "(Was St. Francis a Christian – or a great revolutionary spirit killed by the Church?)" (Miller/Laughlin 240).

# Finding Our Way: Thomas Merton, John Wu
## and the Christian Dialogue with Early China

*Anthony E. Clark*

Scholars of comparative religions, especially those who study Sino-Missionary exchange, have grown increasingly interested in what dialogue looks like when Christian intellectuals encounter views formed in a culture far distant from the cultures within which Christianity emerged, and views formulated by intellectuals who lived long before Christ was born. Religious and intellectual dialogue is always important, but it is also always difficult. Agatha Christie (1890-1976), in her novel *Towards Zero*, wrote that "It's extraordinary, the amount of misunderstandings there are even between two people who discuss a thing quite often – both of them assuming different things and neither of them discovering the discrepancy."[1] I would like to address here how Christians, mostly modern ones, have responded to one of the most popular and ambiguous world philosophies in Asia, Daoism.[2] We can gain much through honest dialogue, and perhaps if we are persistent and open-minded, we will actually discover and illuminate the discrepancies that Agatha Christie mentions in her book.

### Intellectual Intersections

In the fourth century a group of Christian men in Egypt, Palestine, Arabia and Persia abandoned society to find what Thomas Merton (1915-1968) refers to as "their own true self, in Christ."[3] It is astonishing to me how often these "desert fathers" imparted Christian principles that are nearly identical with the assertions of China's early Daoists. The famous Daoist philosopher Zhuangzi[4] (ca. 369-ca. 286 BC) recorded an account of the death of his wife:

---

1. Agatha Christie, *Towards Zero* (1944; New York: Pocket Books, 1972) 149.

2. Chinese characters are rendered in English according to the current pinyin system rather than the Wade-Giles system used at the time Thomas Merton and John Wu were writing: hence Daoism rather than Taoism, Zhuangzi rather than Chuang Tzu, etc.

3. Thomas Merton, *The Wisdom of the Desert: Sayings from the Desert Fathers of the Fourth Century* (New York: New Directions, 1960) 5; subsequent references will be cited as "*WD*" parenthetically in the text.

4. 莊子; also Zhuang Zhou 莊周.

When Zhuangzi's wife had died, [his friend] Huizi went to convey his condolences. But when he arrived he found Zhuangzi sitting with his legs sprawled out, pounding on a tub and singing a song. Huizi said: "You lived with her, she brought up your children and grew old. It's bad enough not weeping at her death, but pounding on a tub and singing – this is going too far, isn't it?"[5]

Zhuangzi is unperturbed by Huizi's criticism of his joyful singing after his wife's death. He replies: "Now my wife is going to lie down peacefully in a great room, and if I merely follow after her bawling and sobbing, it would show that I don't understand anything about fate. So I stopped weeping" (*Zhuangzi* 450).[6] In other words, Zhuangzi suggests that weeping when one dies expresses a profound misunderstanding of what death truly is – something more appropriately celebrated.

A story recorded in the sayings of the desert fathers recounts an exchange between an elder and a group of monks surrounding him as he lay dying. The monks dressed the dying elder in a shroud and began weeping, but the dying man opened his eyes and began to laugh. He then laughed two more times while his brothers continued to wail over his passing. They asked, "Tell us, Father, why you are laughing while we weep?" He responded: "I laughed the first time because you fear death. I laughed the second time because you are not ready for death. And the third time I laughed because from labours I go to my rest" (*WD* 50). Both the Daoist and Christian accounts of joyful merriment in the face of death represent well one of the many areas of intersection between how Chinese Daoists and early Christian monastics viewed the spiritual connotations of dying.

Another desert father, who was named Serapion, "sold his book of the Gospels and gave the money to those who were hungry." When justifying why he gave away his Bible, the monk exclaimed, "I have sold the book which told me to sell all that I had and give to the poor" (*WD* 37). This is precisely like the famous Daoist axiom expressed by Zhuangzi that, "A fish trap is for catching fish; once you've caught the fish you can throw away the trap" (*Zhuangzi* 725).[7] For Daoists, as well as the Christian desert fathers, once one has fully absorbed the teachings imparted by the sacred text, the sacred text is no longer needed. The entirety of the Daoist and Christian paradigms are pointers to a specific

---

5.莊子妻死，惠子弔之，莊子則方箕踞鼓盆而歌。惠子曰：與人居長子，老身死，不哭亦足矣，又鼓盆而歌，不亦甚乎 (Zhuangzi 莊子, *Zhuangzi jinzhu jinyi* 莊子今注今譯, ed. Chen Guying 陳鼓應 [Hong Kong 香港: Zhonghua shuju 中華書局, 1990] 450; subsequent references will be cited as "*Zhuangzi*" parenthetically in the text).

6.人且偃然寢於巨室，而我噭噭然隨而哭之，自以為不通乎命，故止也。

7.荃者所以在魚，得魚而忘荃.

message; the pointers themselves are not the message, and diminish once the message is apprehended. My intent in pointing out these similarities is to illustrate that religious and philosophical ideas often, at their highest levels of inquiry, intersect.

There is something about the human condition that compels us toward similar conclusions, but divergence as well as correspondence exists, and I would like to consider here how two Christian intellectuals, the Trappist monk and author Thomas Merton and the Chinese philosopher-diplomat John Wu[8] (1899-1986), engaged Daoism, and each other, in order to reflect on how one of Asia's most influential philosophical traditions contrasts with the teachings of Jesus Christ and the Christian Church. This will, perhaps, also serve to highlight how Christians have engaged with the principles expressed most acutely in the earliest Daoist texts, the *Daodejing*, or "The Classic of the Way and its Virtue,"[9] and the *Zhuangzi*, or "Master Zhuang."[10]

### The Epistolary Dialectics of Thomas Merton and John Wu

Sometime in 1937, John Wu visited a small Catholic Carmelite monastery at Chongqing, in Sichuan province, to find a few moments of respite and spiritual contemplation. One of the sisters there, Mère Élizabeth, OCD (née Marie Roussel [1903-1996]), remembered his "hesitant French," but also recalled a remarkable encounter the sisters had with Wu after Mass. In her memoir she writes: "the Holy Sacrifice was just coming to a close when there echoed the air raid alarm, long and lugubrious like a death knell."[11] The area was being attacked by Japanese planes, and Wu was ushered into the private enclosure of the nuns for safety. Once in their small bomb shelter, the sisters asked Dr. Wu about his conversion to Roman Catholicism, and he replied: "It was Confucius who brought me to Christianity, and Thérèse of the Child Jesus to Catholicism" (Mère Élizabeth 94). John Wu's understanding of Confucius[12] (551-479 BC) helped him better appreciate Christianity, and he became a Methodist; his encounter with St. Thérèse of Lisieux (née Marie Françoise-Thérèse Martin [1873-1897]) helped usher his soul into the Catholic Church.[13]

8. Wu Jingxiong 吳經熊.

9.道德經.

10.莊子.

11. Mère Élizabeth (Marie Roussel), OCD, *Leaving for, Living in, & Farewell to China: The Life Experiences of a Carmelite Nun, Mère Élizabeth* (Fairfax, VA: Eastern Christian Publications, 2010) 93; subsequent references will be cited as "Mère Élizabeth" parenthetically in the text.

12.孔夫子.

13. For John Wu's account of his conversion, see his memoir: John C. H. Wu,

John Wu was not the only Chinese intellectual to recognize how the thought of Confucius resonates with the teachings of Christianity; the Chinese diplomat who later became a Benedictine abbot in Bruges, Belgium, Dom Pierre-Célestin Lu Zhengxiang, OSB[14] (1871-1949) wrote in his memoir: "I am a Confucianist because that moral philosophy . . . profoundly penetrates the nature of man and traces clearly his line of conduct towards his Creator."[15]

That Confucius and Christ are well matched is quite apparent to those who have studied the Confucian classics, but when John Wu and Thomas Merton began their seven-year epistolary exchange in 1961,[16] Merton asked Wu to help him understand the *Daoist* writings of Zhuangzi. It did not take long, however, before they discovered their mutual interest in another topic, Chan[17] (or Zen) Buddhism. Our question is, then, how are scholars now, fifty years later, to assess their Christian interest in the Lao-Zhuang[18] (Laozi[19] and Zhuangzi[20]) strand of Daoist philosophy? That Confucianism harmonizes well with the Christian faith is not difficult to recognize, but where did Wu and Merton stand in their conviction that Daoism likewise complements Christianity? I am especially interested in how Wu and Merton understood the implications and applications of the Daoist "Way," or Dao,[21] in their dialectical exchange of letters. As a university professor trained in classical Sinology I view the greatest compliment an intellectual can pay to the ideas and publications of an important thinker, such as Thomas Merton, is engagement and analysis. My remarks here are thus intended to be more of a compliment than a criticism, and my conclusions are intended to add to the important discussion that Wu and Merton inaugurated fifty-five years ago about the Christian dialogue with early China's Daoist ideas.

---

*Beyond East and West* (New York: Sheed & Ward, 1951); subsequent references will be cited as "Wu, *Beyond*" parenthetically in the text. See also his work *The Interior Carmel: The Threefold Way of Love* (New York: Sheed & Ward, 1953).

14.陸徵祥.

15. Pierre-Célestin Lou Tseng-tsiang, *Ways of Confucius and Christ*, trans. Michael Derrick (London: Burns & Oates, 1948) 64.

16. The complete correspondence is now available in Cristóbal Serrán-Pagán, ed., *Merton & the Tao: Dialogues with John Wu and the Ancient Sages* (Louisville, KY: Fons Vitae, 2013) 171-346; subsequent references will be cited as "*Merton & Tao*" parenthetically in the text.

17. 禪.

18.老莊.

19.老子.

20.莊子.

21.道.

By way of an opening salvo, I'll begin with an examination of what is implied in the *Daodejing*[22] by the term Dao, and how this early Chinese text's usage of the term compares to the usage employed by Merton and Wu. In Thomas Merton's first letter to John Wu, in which he seeks Wu's assistance in preparing a book on the writings of Zhuangzi, the Trappist expresses his desire to immerse himself in "the mysticism of the early Taoists" (*Merton & Tao* 174 [3/14/1961]). This statement entreats us who have read the early Daoist texts in Chinese to ponder what Merton means by Daoist mysticism, and even what he means by this mysticism as a Christian. The theologian Louis Bouyer (1913-2004) describes mysticism as "God's uniting himself directly with us,"[23] and Heribert Fischer, who provided the entry on mysticism in Karl Rahner's (1904-1984) *Encyclopedia of Theology*, suggests that it is "the experience of uncreated grace as revelation and self-communication of the triune God."[24] In other words, mysticism is the experience of unsolicited union with the Triune God. In John Wu's lengthy response to Merton's first letter, Wu appears to confirm Merton's inclination that philosophical Daoism, or the early disputations on the Way expressed in the *Daodejing* and the *Zhuangzi*, is compatible with the Christian understanding of mysticism. Wu wrote, "Only when we are united with the Word incarnate can we be full-fledged Confucianists and thoroughgoing Taoists at the same time" (*Merton & Tao* 180 [3/20/1961]). Merton sees in early Daoism an alternative model for Christian mysticism and Wu submits that only in being united with God can one be a "thoroughgoing Taoist." Even more provocative is Wu's suggestion that the ideas of Laozi and Zhuangzi were "pointing at . . . [t]he *Logos* of God who enlightens everyone coming into this world" (*Merton & Tao* 178). I'll consider these points in sequence after a brief excursus regarding what the Dao meant to the "early Taoists" to whom Merton refers.

Perhaps the most prominent definition of the Dao in early Chinese texts derives from the first line of the most famous version of the *Daodejing*, the Wangbi[25] edition (AD 226-249) – a previous recension has the order reversed, placing the *De*[26] section before the *Dao*[27] section.[28] The

22. 道德經.

23. Louis Bouyer, *Dictionary of Theology*, trans. Charles Underhill Quinn (Tournai, Belgium: Desclée, 1965) 316.

24. Heribert Fischer, "Mysticism," in Karl Rahner, SJ, ed., *Encyclopedia of Theology: The Concise Sacramentum Mundi* (New York: Seabury Press, 1975) 1004.

25. 王弼.

26. 德.

27. 道.

28. This is the so-called Mawangdui Silk Edition, 馬王堆帛書 which dates to

original text reads: "*Dao ke Dao feichang Dao – ming ke ming feichang ming.*"[29] John Wu translates this passage as: "Tao that can be talked about, but not the eternal Tao."[30] Wu indulges here in what almost all experienced translators disparage as bad translation; he dodges the question of what the Dao is by refusing to translate it. He uses neither "Way" to render the character, which is the most common translation, nor does he attempt an explanation of its implication. Wu simply prefers to leave the term ambiguous, perhaps because the text itself is suggesting the ineffability of the term. But this is avoidance, and does not help the English reader arrive at even the slightest apprehension of what the original Chinese author is getting at.

The third-century BC philosopher Han Feizi[31] (d. 233 BC), explains the Dao in this way: "*Dao zhe, wanwu zhi suo ran ye,*"[32] or "The Dao is the thus-ness of all things" (*Laozi yizhu* 1). Said another way, the Dao is defined as the existential reality, or state, of all that exists; it is the pattern and meaning of everything. Embedded in the grammar of this opening line of the *Daodejing* is an intimation of its larger meaning. The first Dao in the sentence is nominal – it is a noun, "the Way" – and the second appearance is verbal – it is the action of Way-ing. I would thus translate this line as Angus Graham rendered it in his great work, *The Disputers of the Tao*: "The Way that can be 'Way'-ed is not the constant Way."[33] Implied in this assertion is that the Dao, or Way, includes all dualities, all apparent opposites, in a unified monad; all dyads are in fact only a unified monad. In other words, the Dao encompasses all binaries; if we use the provisional term "truth" to translate the Dao, then this "truth" would be comprised of both truth and non-truth, since one cannot exist without the other. The Dao would thus contain both "good" and "bad" since one cannot endure without its opposite. The Dao, then, has less to do with

---

approximately 168 BC. An even earlier version is the Guodian Edition, 郭店 which dates before 300 BC. The version used by Thomas Merton and John Wu was the much later version, which includes the organization – first Dao 道 and the De 德 sections – and commentary of Wang Bi.

29. 道可道非常道。名可名非常名. *Laozi yizhu* 老子譯注 [Modern Chinese Translation and Commentary of the *Laozi*], translation and commentary of Feng Dafu 馮達甫 (Taipei: Shulin chubanshe, 1995) 1; subsequent references will be cited as "*Laozi yizhu*" parenthetically in the text.

30. *Tao Teh Ching*, trans. John C. H. Wu (Boston: Shambala, 1989; originally published by St. John's University Press, 1961) 3.

31. 韓非子.

32. 道者萬物之所然也.

33. A. C. Graham, *Disputers of the Tao: Philosophical Argument in Ancient China* (Chicago: Open Court, 1989) 219.

a mystical encounter with the Triune God as it is a functional term to describe the ontological state of all being – or non-being. It is ineffable because no term can accurately define what defies definition; the Dao is meta-linguistic. This is perhaps what the *Daodejing* is insisting when it states that, "*Dao chang wu ming*,"[34] or "The eternal Way has no name" (*Laozi yizhu* 85). John Wu expressed his understanding of this idea when he corrected Merton's use of "philosophic monism," recommending the more accurate term "non-dualism" (*Merton & Tao* 319 [1/19/1966]). In any case, the early Daoist writers who used the term Dao to express non-dualism were chasms away from any notion of communing with God; the expression was merely a provisional term to help readers better apprehend Daoist ontology.

What is in my view even more intriguing than Thomas Merton's sense that early Daoism involves some form of mysticism is Wu's suggestion to Merton that the Daoist "Way" may be used as an analogue for the Logos, which appears in the Gospel of St. John. The Gospel's famous assertion states simply that "In the beginning was the Word [*Logos*]" (Jn. 1:1). The Greek usage of this term early on was related to mathematics, and by the time of the authorship of the Gospel it had acquired a more philosophical implication. As B. K. Gamel has suggested, "Since logos means an account (explanation) of something, some philosophers began to refer to the explanation for order and balance in the universe as a cosmic logos. According to these philosophers, humans can explain things through language because they share in this cosmic logos or rationality."[35] Logos is the illustrative principle of the cosmos, or all being. This is indeed quite close to what is intimated in the Daoist writers' meaning of the Dao. The first Western philosopher to apply a metaphysical meaning to the Greek word Logos (Λόγος) was Heraclitus of Ephesus (ca. 540-480 BC), a meaning that was carried into the canonical writings of the first Christians. Reginald E. Allen succinctly summarized Heraclitus' use of Logos:

[Logos] is the first principle of knowledge: understanding of the world involves understanding of the structure or pattern of the world, a pattern concealed from the eyes of ordinary men. The Logos is also the first principle of existence, that unity of the world process which sustains it as a process. This unity lies beneath the surface, for it is a unity of diverse and conflicting opposites, in whose strife the

---

34. 道常無名.

35. B. K. Gamel, "Logos, Greek Background," in J. D. Barry, D. Bomar, D. R. Brown, R. Klippenstein *et al*, eds., *The Lexham Bible Dictionary* (Bellingham, WA: Lexham Press, 2012-2015).

Logos maintains a continual balance. . . . The Logos maintains the equilibrium of the universe at every moment.[36]

Allen's description of Heraclitus' Logos accurately represents the early Daoist explanation of the Dao, especially his remark that the Logos can be viewed as "a unity of diverse and conflicting opposites."

Still, the early Daoist usage of the character Dao was not intended to describe the nature of God, but was rather hoped to better denote the nature of reality and to disengage the reader from her or his impulse to define reality in dichotomies. This is perhaps why the *Daodejing* asserts: "*Ren fa di, di fa tian, tian fa Dao, Dao fa ziran,*"[37] or "Humans are modeled from earth, earth is modeled from heaven, heaven is modeled from the Dao, and the Dao is modeled from what is self-so" (*Laozi yizhu* 60). Put more simply, the Dao is not modeled upon anything other than itself, which is a self-derived self without opposites or origins. While one may not wish to be overly pedantic here, or wearying with plodding philological and exegetical digressions, it is nonetheless important to note that whereas the Daoist Dao, or Way, as it is expressed in the original ancient Chinese sources, includes both aspects of all dichotomies in a unified monad, the God of the Bible is ineffable but not non-dualistic in the way the Daoist Way is. In Sacred Scripture God is described as complete goodness, complete perfection and complete justice; he is not good *and* bad, perfect *and* flawed, or just *and* unjust.[38]

The complications related to adopting the term Dao as an analogue to the Greek word Logos has led to a conscious reconsideration of how Logos is rendered by Chinese Bible translators today. The first complete Roman Catholic translation of the Bible, the so-called Studium Biblicum Version[39] accomplished by the Italian Franciscan scholar Gabriele Allegra, OFM (1907-1976), translates the opening of John's Gospel as "*Yuanshi zhi chu jiu you Dao*"[40] or "At the origin of the beginning there was the 'Dao.'"[41] And the character Dao, or Way, is cautiously placed in quotation marks in most current editions of the Studium Biblicum Version, highlighting the ambiguous and borrowed nature of the term. Recognizing the various problems with translating the Logos as "Dao," modern Chinese translators have translated "Logos" in an entirely different manner: "*Zai qichu*

36. Reginald E. Allen, ed., *Greek Philosophy: Thales to Aristotle* (New York: Free Press, 1985) 9-10.

37. 人法地。地法天。天法道。道法自然.

38. See for example Psalm 12:6, 18:30, 145:17; Revelation 15:3.

39. 思高本.

40. 元始之初就有'道'.

41. John 1:1: Studium Biblicum Version (思高本).

*yi you Shengyan,*"[42] or "In the beginning was already the Divine Word."[43] The term "Dao" – "Way" – and "Shengyan" – "Divine Word" – are quite different, and this new translation carefully distances the Christian understanding of Logos from the Daoist understanding of the Dao. Current Chinese scholars are reassessing previous attempts under the direction of foreign missionaries to adopt, or arrogate, extant Chinese religious and philosophical terms into the Christian lexicon. There is a suspicion that Christians, especially Christians from the West, such as Thomas Merton, sought confirmation of their own Christian ideas within China's existing traditions, and thus somewhat haphazardly employed terms, such as the Dao, into their own vocabulary without first understanding the nuances already present in the terms they borrowed.

The Eastern Orthodox writer Hieromonk Damascene (né John Christensen, b. 1961), who wrote an insightful book comparing the Dao of Daoism to the Logos of Christianity, shares Wu and Merton's admiration for the *Daodejing*. He argues that, "while Lao Tzu's *Tao Te Ching* represents the highest that a person can know through intuition, St. John's Gospel represents the highest that a person can know through revelation, that is, through God making Himself known and experienced in the most tangible way."[44] Like Wu and Merton, Hieromonk Damascene believes that the Dao can function as a substitute for the Christian Logos, but he limits the insights of the early Chinese Daoists to human intuition; and nowhere does he suggest that Daoism contributes to or facilitates what Christians understand to be mysticism. The traditional Chinese figure, Laozi, was, according to this Eastern Orthodox view, less of an example of mysticism than, as Hieromonk Damascene puts it, "a pre-Christian witness of Christ the Logos" (Damascene 44).

One other aspect of the *Daodejing* that must be addressed is its patent political message, which is interwoven almost furtively throughout the text; in fact, the earliest version of the text we know of, the Guodian[45] recension, was discovered in the tomb of the private tutor of the heir-

---

42.在起初已有聖言.

43. John 1:1, NRV, The Church Affairs Commission of the Bishops' Conference of the Catholic Church of China (中國天主教主教團教務委員會), 2008. This version is identified as the "Chinese: Studium Biblicum Version" in the front matter, but the Chinese translators have revised Allegra's translation to better match what they consider to be more appropriate Chinese characters for terms such as Logos.

44. Hieromonk (Igumen) Damascene, *Christ the Eternal Tao* (Platina, CA: Valaam Books, 1999) 35; subsequent references will be cited as "Damascene" parenthetically in the text.

45.郭店楚簡.

apparent of Chu.[46] The inherent political significance of the *Daodejing* can be seen in several passages, including the statement that "*Shiyi shengren zhi zhi, xu qi xin, shi qi fu, ruo qi zhi, qiang qi gu; chang shi min wu zhi wu yu, shi fu zhi zhe bug an wei ye,*"[47] or "The rule of a sagely man empties their minds, fills their stomachs, weakens their will, and strengthens their bodies; and by doing so he causes the people to be always stupid and without desires, so he can, as a wise [ruler, rule] without effort" (*Laozi yizhu* 7-8). In other words, stupid and well-fed people are easy pawns in the art of skillful governance; this is a strong and persistent message in the ancient Daoist classic. This is not the Dao underscored in the writings of Wu and Merton, but is a very pragmatic Dao expressed in the *Daodejing*. One who carefully reads the text wonders if, in the end, the entire work is foremost a political strategy for keeping subjects dumb and manageable, that the Daoism of the *Daodejing* is actually less the "mystical" philosophy admired by Christian intellectuals such as Wu and Merton than a guide for how to retain political supremacy. But what of Merton's and Wu's Christian engagement with the writings of Zhuangzi?

### Beyond the Dusty World: Zhuangzi, Laozi and the Departure from the World

In one of Thomas Merton's letters to Wu he praises Zhuangzi as "one of the *great* wise men," and adds the provocative assertion that "The wisdom of Chuang Tzu demands the resurrection, for the resurrection goes beyond all moralities and moral theories, it is a totally new life in the Spirit" (*Merton & Tao* 185 [4/1/1961]). Again, is this idea actually near to what Zhuangzi intended in his essays on how to live according to the Dao? Sadly, John Wu's response to this letter drifts away from this point, and their future letters increasingly touch upon Buddhism and the more mundane matters of securing publishers for their works and arranging for meetings with like-minded intellectuals. Merton's translations of selections from the *Zhuangzi*'s Inner Chapters are among the most elegant renderings of the text available in English today. In his introduction to his book, *The Way of Chuang Tzu*, he acknowledges John Wu as the "chief abettor and accomplice" in the project and asserts, "I have enjoyed writing this book more than any other I can remember."[48]

---

46. See Robert G. Henricks, *Lao Tzu's Tao Te Ching: A Translation of the Startling New Documents Found at Guodian* (New York: Columbia University Press, 2000) 4-5.

47. 是以聖人之治，虛其心，實其腹，弱其志，強其骨；常使民無知無欲，是夫智者不敢為也.

48. Thomas Merton, *The Way of Chuang Tzu* (New York: New Directions, 1965) 9-10; subsequent references will be cited as "*WCT*" parenthetically in the text.

Throughout the correspondence between Wu and Merton one actually sees little evidence of Wu's assistance in the important technical realm of translation, and as Bede Bidlack has suggested, "Merton faced several liabilities in this work," not the least of which was the impossible task of rendering a deeply challenging classical Chinese text into English without any training in Chinese.[49] Merton's renderings of Zhuangzi's concise and often esoteric sayings were based on four Western-language translations: one German, one French and two English.

The strength of Merton's version of the Daoist Zhuangzi is largely in its highly readable English and its wide reach to non-Daoist Western readers. Bidlack also points out that Thomas Merton "reveals himself as an inheritor of a particular kind of Chinese interpretation of Daoism – that of Christian missionaries" (*Merton & Tao* 87). His elegant prose and somewhat Christian coloring of the text is perhaps why Merton's Zhuangzi remains so popular today, but one is left longing for a more substantive Christian dialogue with ancient Daoism than one finds in Merton's *The Way of Chuang Tzu*. That Merton's interpretation of Zhuangzi's ideas is represented through the lens of his own Christian worldview is helpful inasmuch as he discusses Daoism in ways that are better understood by other Christians, but arguably, his presentation of Zhuangzi's message sometimes obscures what the ancient Chinese philosopher was getting at. One example might illustrate this point – Merton includes one of my favorite passages from the *Zhuangzi*, the so-called "Joy of Fishes" dialogue between Zhuangzi and his interlocutor, Huizi (*WCT* 97-98). Merton renders the encounter in fine free verse: "Chuang Tzu and Hui Tzu / Were crossing the Hao river / By the dam. / Chuang said: / 'See how free / The fishes leap and dart: / That is their happiness.'"[50] Huizi challenges Zhuangzi's assertion that the fish they see below them are happy; after all, Huizi wonders, "Since you are not a fish / How do you know / What makes fishes happy?"[51] Zhuangzi's ready retort enters the dialogue into more philosophical depth: "Since you are not I / How can you possibly know / That I do not know / What makes fishes happy?"[52]

By leaving this passage unexamined the Christian or Daoist reader is left to infer what Merton's intended implication is. What, then, is Zhuangzi's point here, and how does that point compare with Christian ontology? One could, I suppose, suggest that Zhuangzi's dialogue with

---

49. Bede Bidlack, "Merton's *Way of Zhuangzi*: A Critique" (*Merton & Tao* 84).

50.莊子與惠子遊於濠梁之上。莊子曰：「儵魚出遊從容，是魚樂也。」. The original Chinese passage can be found in *Zhuangzi* 443-44.

51. 子非魚，安知魚之樂？

52.子非我，安知我不知魚之樂？

Huizi is simply intended to underscore how some things cannot be known objectively. Perhaps Merton wishes the passage to express how the ineffability of God is unknowingly expressed in the writings of this ancient Chinese Daoist. Such a reading superimposes a modern Judeao-Christian reading on a text that would resist such a reading. In fact, Zhuangzi's message was more likely intended to dispute the reliability of language and objective claims altogether. Merton's renderings were published before the "linguistic turn" in modern academic discourse had blossomed in Jacques Derrida's (1930-2004) 1967 publication, *De la Grammatologie*, in which Derrida sets out to discover the underlying "condition of all linguistic systems," to identify the fundamental components that make communication by language at all possible.[53]

Derrida, like Zhuangzi, questions how effective language can be at conveying reality, and Merton's depiction of Zhuangzi dwells more in his own sense of mysticism than in the linguistic playfulness that colors all of Zhuangzi's original Chinese text. Non-Christian scholars, such as the French sinologist Henri Maspero (1883-1945), were perhaps the first Westerners to truly engage Daoism based upon a preliminary mastery of the language and context of China's early thinkers, and reading such works in tandem with the translations of Thomas Merton enriches one's understanding of the *Zhuangzi*, while also providing more information upon which to base one's comparison between Christianity and ancient Chinese thought.[54] In the end, the musings on the Way found in the epistolary exchange between John Wu and Thomas Merton leave us with more questions than answers, which is perhaps precisely the kind of mysticism that both men would have hoped future readers of their writings would dwell upon.

There are several areas of especially John Wu's writing that do, however, demonstrate how the dialogue between Christianity and Daoism can "help us find our way" toward a better "Way" of understanding the perennial teachings of Christianity. Arguably the most insightful of Wu's books comparing Chinese thought to Christianity is a collection of essays published together as *Chinese Humanism and Christian Spirituality*. In one of his essays, "St. Thérèse and Lao Tzu," John Wu compares the Christian views of St. Thérèse of Lisieux to the Daoist teachings of the *Daodejing*. He begins by conjuring an account in the Gospel of John, wherein John the Baptist identifies himself as the forerunner to the Christ.

53. Jacques Derrida, *Of Grammatology*, trans. Gayatri Chakravorty Spivak (Baltimore: Johns Hopkins University Press, 1974) 60.

54. See Henri Maspero, *Taoism and Chinese Religion*, trans. Frank A. Kierman, Jr. (Amherst: University of Massachusetts Press, 1981).

John the Baptist responds to his interlocutors: "The bride belongs to the bridegroom. The friend who attends the bridegroom waits and listens for him, and is full of joy when he hears the bridegroom's voice. That joy is mine, and it is now complete. He must become greater; I must become less" (Jn. 3:29-30). Wu compares the last sentence in this passage to St. Thérèse's so-called "little way," which follows the advice that "He must become greater; I must become less." He describes this "little way" as analogous to the Daoist notion that "It is through complete self-loss that her self is fully realized."[55]

The notion that loss equals gain is one of the most basic beliefs of Daoism. Toward the end of the *Daodejing* we are told that: "There is nothing as weak and submissive than water, yet for overcoming that which is hard and powerful nothing can surpass it. . . . Weakness overcomes strength and submissiveness conquers the powerful."[56] The Daoist qualities of leadership are precisely the qualities exalted by Christianity: humility, meekness, self-sacrifice and placing others before oneself. As John Wu puts it, "To be poor is to be truly rich. Suffering is a blessing. To come down is to rise. To be little is to be great. Weakness is strength" and "To die is to live" (Wu, *Chinese* 96). In a way, this ideal expressed in both Christianity and Daoism reflects the words of Christ, who said, "Truly I tell you, unless you change and become like little children, you will never enter the kingdom of heaven" (Mt. 18:3).

Another area of convergence between Christianity and Chinese Daoism is the use of gendered terms to illustrate apparent paradox. In chapter sixty-one of the *Daodejing*, we read that: "A great country is like a low-land into which all streams flow, and it is the exchange place of all under heaven. It is the world's feminine aspect, which conquers the masculine by its stillness."[57] In other words, the lowliest place, the hidden place, is the place where greatness is to be found. In a letter to her sister Céline, St. Thérèse wrote: "Jesus is a hidden treasure, a good beyond price that few souls can find, for it is hidden and the world loves things that glitter. . . . To find a hidden thing, we must ourselves be hidden. . . . We must be like Jesus, like Jesus whose look was hidden."[58] Daoism and Christianity,

---

55. John C. H. Wu, *Chinese Humanism and Christian Spirituality: Essays of John C. H. Wu* edited by Paul K. T. Sih (Jamaica, NY: St. John's University Press, 1965) 95-96; subsequent references will be cited as "Wu, *Chinese*" parenthetically in the text.

56.天下莫柔弱於水，而攻堅強者莫之能勝…弱之勝強，柔之勝剛(*Laozi yizhu* 170-71).

57.大國者下流，天下之交，天下之牝。牝常以靜勝牡，以靜為下(*Laozi yizhu* 139).

58. *The Collected Letters of St. Thérèse of Lisieux*, trans. Frank J. Sheed (New York: Sheed & Ward, 1949) 197.

as Merton and Wu understood well, delight in paradox; as the *Daodejing* asserts, "Bow down to become whole, be curved to become straight, be empty to become full, and be worn out to become new."[59] This is one of the many Daoist passages that echoes the implication of John the Baptist when he affirmed that our smallness is what makes us genuinely great.

Finally, another convergence between Daoism and Christianity can be seen in the impulse to retreat from the harmful influences that can be found in society. Christian hermits and Daoist hermits share much of the same desire to avoid what the early Chinese called the "dusty world." They compared the temptations of the world, such as career success, wealth, social power and pride, to be like a pesky dust that covers one's person and is difficult to remove. Indeed, the desert fathers largely held that to be away from the world was more edifying than living within the mix of humanity. An abbot named Moses in Scete once told one of the brothers: "Go, sit in your cell, and your cell will teach you everything" (*WD* 30). This same impulse is expressed in a beautiful passage located in the *Zhuangzi* (see *WCT* 93-94). One day while Zhuangzi was fishing in the Pu River he was approached by two high-ranking officials sent by the King of Chu to offer him an exalted job. Without even turning to see the two men, Zhuangzi asked the officials if it was true that in Chu, "there is a sacred tortoise stored in the king's ancestral temple wrapped with [fine] cloth, that has been dead for three thousand years?" (*Zhuangzi* 441).[60] He then asked, "Do you think that this tortoise would rather be dead and have its bones worshipped, or would it rather be alive and drag its tail through the mud? Go away! I, too, would rather drag my tail in the mud!" (*Zhuangzi* 441).[61] Both the Christian and Daoist hermits suggest that our true nature is best discovered and lived outside of the false allurements of the dusty world.

These passages, of both the Daoist masters and the desert fathers, were favorites of Thomas Merton and John Wu, and they underscore how a Christian dialogue with early China's intellectual and religious traditions can serve to both obfuscate and illuminate similarities and differences. I have confronted how, and perhaps even why, Professor John Wu and Father Thomas Merton have fastened upon the Daoist idea of "the Way," but I do so only because these two Christian men have bequeathed to us a legacy of rigorous and spiritually discerning interrogations into the graspings of the mind toward better understanding the meaning of

---

59. 曲則全，枉則直，窪則盈，弊則新 (*Laozi yizhu* 52).
60. 吾聞楚有神龜，死已三千歲矣，王巾笥而藏之廟堂之上?
61. 寧其死為留骨而貴乎？寧其生而曳尾於塗中乎？ … 往矣！吾將曳尾於塗中!

human existence. Scholars today can wander freely through the room of East-West comparison and dialogue only because the likes of Wu and Merton have opened the door for us. In the conclusion of Wu's memoir, *Beyond East and West*, he quotes from the collected poetry of the Daoist scholar, Lu Yun[62] (262-303), who wrote:

> Beyond the dusty world,
> I enjoy solitude and peace.
> I shut my door,
> I close my window.
> Harmony is my Spring,
> Purity my Autumn.
> Thus I embody the rhythms of life,
> And my cottage becomes a Universe. (Wu, *Beyond* 355)

In Chinese traditional writings, especially Daoist and Buddhist, "dust" is a euphemism for the polluting and harmful trap of the world. Perhaps more than anything else, John Wu and Thomas Merton turned toward the Dao as a possible Way to move "beyond the dusty world," and find an alternative place, one better equipped to provide the "solitude and peace" of the God of Christianity.

---

62.陸雲.

# Young Adult Spiritual Lives:
# Merton, Moran and Monastic Resources

*Padraic O'Hare*

According to Thomas Merton:

> the spiritual life is the life of man's real self, the life of that interior self whose flame is so often allowed to be smothered under the ashes of anxiety and futile concern.[1]

> The spiritual life is, then, first of all a matter of keeping awake. We must not lose our sensitivity to spiritual inspirations.[2]

> If you want to have a spiritual life you must unify your life. A life is either all spiritual or not spiritual at all. No man can serve two masters. Your life is shaped by the end you live for. You are made in the image of what you desire. (*TS* 56)

What we want for young adults (what we want for all) are lives that are real, awake, unified, sensitive to inspiration, purposeful, happy, transcending self-absorption and the trivial – lives made possible by cultivating ready access to our interior selves, our real selves.

Assisting one another to grow in this fashion, to excel at the human vocation, is called education. My teacher, Gabriel Moran, writes: "The most comprehensive form of education is community. . . . [And] the word presence and community [are] synonymous."[3] The great "schools," as St. Benedict called them, for nurturing communities of presence are monasteries. Education in presence ("to other persons, to oneself and to the world of non-persons," Moran continues) hinges on cultivating the capacity for stillness or silence; it is a work of contemplation education, of which monastics are principal exemplars.

What follows assesses universal human values enshrined in healthy monastic life, guided by Raimundo Panikkar, Michael Casey, Joan Chittister, Rowan Williams and, always, Thomas Merton. An exemplary monastic community, the Benedictine community in Weston, Vermont is

---

1. Thomas Merton, *No Man Is an Island* (New York: Harcourt, Brace, 1955) ix.

2. Thomas Merton, *Thoughts in Solitude* (New York: Farrar, Straus and Cudahy, 1958) 47; subsequent references will be cited as "*TS*" parenthetically in the text.

3. Gabriel Moran, *Living Non-Violently: Language for Resisting Violence* (Lanham, MD: Lexington Books, 2011) 168; subsequent references will be cited as " Moran, *Living*" parenthetically in the text.

described. And young adults, moved by that community, give testimony. The essay concludes by returning to Moran and to the educational question. What nurtures communities of persons who are present, who strive to reshape their lives and grow in "patient attentiveness and non-violent receptiveness to what is real"? What nurtures contemplative practice, what nurtures contemplative young adults? What is contemplation education? The intent of the essay is to inform and encourage religious and theological educators to expose young adults to monastic values embodied in monastic persons and in doing so to cultivate with them, where they are, communities of real contemplation and compassion.

## Universal Monastic Values

In *Blessed Simplicity: The Monk as Universal Archetype*, Raimundo Panikkar speaks of the "symptomatic polarity" of what he calls "monkhood" (an odd usage we won't adopt): "On the one hand [monastic life] is something special, something difficult even – with tinges of social and cultural non-conformity; on the other hand, it is something so very much human that it is ultimately claimed to be the vocation of every human being."[4] Panikkar speaks of monastics' "urge" to "break something in themselves for the sake of the 'thing' which encompasses or transcends everything." Some kind of challenging and vital human work! Panikkar says that this work is cultivating simplicity. "The monk down the ages . . . sails against the wind . . . in search of the simplicity of the source. . . . God is simple. Brahman is utter simplicity. The monk believes the Absolute is simple and that the goal of life is to attain that very simplicity" (Pannikar 11).

Michael Casey leads us further into monasticism's universal values in *An Unexciting Life: Reflections on Benedictine Spirituality*. Casey emphasizes the importance of living *calm* lives! "For us who live in a sensate society dominated by an appetite for excitement, no matter how vacuous its courses, the preferential option for a quiet life may seem a little peculiar." But "a life faithful to the spirit of Saint Benedict cannot be entertaining. It seeks to activate deeper levels of the human psyche. For this a high level of sensory calm is necessary."[5] (The point is made eloquently in Merton's essay "Rain and the Rhinoceros," written from

---

4. Raimundo Panikkar, *Blessed Simplicity: The Monk as Universal Archetype* (New York: Seabury Press, 1982) 9; subsequent references will be cited as "Panikkar" parenthetically in the text.

5. Michael Casey, OCSO, *An Unexciting Life: Reflections on Benedictine Spirituality* (Petersham, MA: St. Bede Publications, 2005) 14; subsequent references will be cited as "Casey" parenthetically in the text.

the hermitage, in the woods, at night, in the rain. Merton says that in that setting he is not having "fun," not having or doing anything, except living and breathing and wearing pants. His definition of the fun he is not having is "a state of diffuse excitation that can be measured by the clock and 'stretched' by an appliance."[6] In *Disputed Questions* he writes: "the function of diversion is simply to anesthetize the individual as individual, and to plunge him in the warm, apathetic stupor of a collectivity which, like himself, wishes to remain amused."[7])

Casey identifies the "five challenges of Benedictine life": 1) living a "settled life"; 2) "avoidance of extremes"; 3) "embracing opposites"; 4) cultivating "invisibility"; and 5) framing a "vision of community." Here we focus on Casey's second, third and fourth Benedictine challenges. Casey writes of avoiding extremes: "Benedict is . . . boring because he does not make the mistake of identifying what is good with what is dramatic." Casey links avoiding dramatic extremes to "accepting an authority outside ourselves" (Casey 17). Here something very subtle and rich begins to unfold, something which also ties in monastic embrace of opposites and striving for invisibility. The monastic acceptance of authority is neither the end of equality nor the dissolution of personality.

Monastics avoid extremes brought on by dramas of the will (the term is Rowan Williams'), the unchecked ego, by consenting to the authority of the community. They try to nurture and cultivate communities which embrace opposites in which persons become more and more free to be who they are. The monks and nuns practice to be invisible, a metaphor Casey links to cultivating humility and poverty of spirit. Merton spoke time and time again of this as forgetting oneself on purpose, getting over wanting to be noticed and ceasing to measure one's life, opting instead to live life, not watch oneself live it. For example, "man has lost the courage and the faith without which he cannot be content to be 'unseen.' He is pitifully dependent on self-observation and self-assertion. That is to say, he utterly is exiled from God and from his own true self, for neither in God nor in our inmost self can there be any aggressive self-assertion: there is only the plain presence of love and truth."[8] Avoiding extremes, practicing to be invisible, embracing opposites, calming the ego by practicing humility,

---

6. Thomas Merton, *Raids on the Unspeakable* (New York: New Directions, 1966) 14; subsequent references will be cited as "*RU*" parenthetically in the text.

7. Thomas Merton, *Disputed Questions* (New York: Farrar, Straus and Cudahy, 1960) 178.

8. Thomas Merton, *The Inner Experience: Notes on Contemplation*, ed. William H. Shannon (San Francisco: HarperCollins, 2003) 36; subsequent references will be cited as "*IE*" parenthetically in the text.

we can all give each other space to be who we are!

Casey means something very specific by embrace of opposites, something palpable if one spends much time around healthy monks and nuns. Monasteries which succeed in embracing opposites, "provide habitat for an astonishing array of personalities, all unique characters, albeit unselfconsciously so." This is the really subtle and rich counter-intuitive feature of monastic life: a healthy monastic community, by definition, "shuns institutionalization." "The largeness of heart that is able to encompass differences" in such a monastery entails no "artificial consensus," no "rigid control" (Casey 19-20). Everyone rises at the same hour, works during the same time periods, eats together mostly the same food and ostensibly retires at the same hour. During the *Opus Dei*, the work of God praying the hours and the Eucharist, everyone dresses alike! Yet no healthy monastery is – Merton's oft used word – a "collectivity"! The real and healthy monastery is the model of community, the repudiation of collectivity. Here men and woman are free. Freedom is the monastic function.

Merton speaks of the "anonymous authority of the collectivity" (*IE* 4) and indicts it most powerfully in the essay mentioned above, "Rain and the Rhinoceros," the rhinoceros, as in Ionesco's eponymous play, being one who literally runs with the crowd: "We suffer all the needs that society demands we suffer, because if we do not have these needs we lose our 'usefulness' in society – the usefulness of suckers" (*RU* 22). Merton also makes the connection between collective consciousness and hateful behavior: "If we push our analysis of collective thinking a little further we will find that the dialectic of power and need, of submission and satisfaction, ends by being a dialectic of hate . . . . [It] destroy[s] whoever cannot be absorbed. Paradoxically, one of the needs of collectivity is to reject certain classes, or races, or groups, in order to strengthen its own self-awareness" (*RU* 21-22).

We turn to Joan Chittister, a witness to the universality of monastic values of such passion, intelligence, prophecy and humor that one can imagine her rivaling Merton himself, the two being merry together, but also deadly serious! In our time, Chittister, perhaps more than any other, reveals the *Rule* of St. Benedict as an unfathomable resource for the "average person who intends to live life beyond the superficial or the uncaring, to live calmly in the midst of chaos, productively in an arena of waste, lovingly in a maelstrom of individualism, gently in a world full of violence"[9] – and in this way, "living the ordinary life extraordinarily

9. Joan Chittister, OSB, *Wisdom Distilled from the Daily: Living the Rule of Saint Benedict Today* (New York: HarperCollins, 1991) 4; subsequent references will be cited

well" (Chittister 4). Here we look especially at her discussion of listening, spiritual life as practice of listening, monastic life as modeling advanced and sustained listening.

The first words of the *Rule* of St. Benedict call us to listen to the "Master's counsel," "with the ear of your heart." Everything in the personal and social lives of monks and nuns is designed to enhance the capacity to really listen. We grow in the capacity to listen to the Gospel, to the *Rule*, to one another and the world, as well as to "my own underlying life messages," for example "what makes me afraid." In chapter seven of the *Rule* on the twelve steps of humility (on which Chittister has written a fine short text, *Twelve Steps to Inner Freedom: Humility Revisited*[10]) four of the twelve entail listening to others. We know, as Chittister writes, that "listening and love are clearly a piece," and that "if we really listened to the Gospels, we would question a lifestyle that endlessly consumes and hoards and is blind to the homeless" (Chittister, *Wisdom* 21). Merton notes "the simple fact that by being attentive, by learning to listen (or recovering the natural capacity to listen which cannot be learned any more than breathing), we can find ourself engulfed in such happiness that it cannot be explained: the happiness of being at one with everything in that hidden ground of Love for which there can be no explanations."[11]

Rowan Williams, formerly Archbishop of Canterbury, is our final source of guidance. In April 2003, Williams delivered a presentation to the Trinity Conference, at Trinity Church, Wall Street, in New York City. The theme of the event was "Shaping Holy Lives: A Conference on Benedictine Spirituality." Williams' address, the text from which I draw, is entitled "God's Workshop."[12] (Williams teasingly noted his trepidation at following the previous speaker, Sister Joan Chittister!) For Williams the heart of Benedictine (monastic) spirituality is "the habitual acceptance of the otherness of others" (149); "The holiness envisaged by the *Rule* is entirely inseparable from the common life" (148). To the extent a monastic community successfully nourishes acceptance of others as others (Casey's "embracing opposites"), it also serves as a model for fidelity in families and for life within the larger Church.

---

as "Chittister, *Wisdom*" parenthetically in the text.

10. Joan Chittister, OSB, *Twelve Steps to Inner Freedom: Humility Revisited* (Erie, PA: Benetvision, 2003).

11. Thomas Merton, *The Hidden Ground of Love: Letters on Religious Experience and Social Concerns*, ed. William H. Shannon (New York: Farrar, Straus, Giroux, 1985) 115.

12. Rowan Williams, "Shaping Holy Lives: God's Workshop," in *The Oblate Life*, ed. Gervase Holdaway, OSB (Collegeville, MN: Liturgical Press, 2008) 148-58; Archbishop Williams' presentation is also available at: http://rowanwilliams.archbishopofcanterbury.org/articles.php/654/shaping-holy-lives-a-conference-on-benedictine-spirituality.

The "long-term sameness" of life in a family, a church, a community, a monastery is likely to "breed bitterness, cynicism, fear of openness . . . habitual response which belongs at the surface level" (149-50) and admits of no genuine human vulnerability. Monks and nuns promote "the habitual acceptance of others as others" by practicing to be transparent, peacemaking and accountable. Transparency is the practice of honesty; Williams underlines the twenty-fourth of the list of "tools of good works" in chapter four of the *Rule*, in which the brothers are enjoined "not to entertain deceit in their hearts" (150). Williams understands the *Rule* as emphasizing "honesty about yourself," which requires that the "chains of fantasy" (150) which feed dishonesty be broken. The technique here, noted several times in the *Rule*, is encouragement to speak to "an experienced elder" (150) about these illusions, a practice linked to the desert fathers, Evagrius and Cassian especially.

The monk as peacemaker, practicing "this daily discipline of mending" (151), is aided by the *Rule*'s awareness "of temptations of drama, the staging of emotional turbulence in which the unexamined ego is allowed to rampage unchecked" (152) – referred to earlier as "dramas of the will" (152) – and accountability. Monastic men and women practice to grow in the ability to live the maxim: "I promise I will not hide from you, and that I will also at times help you not to hide from me or from yourself" (152). Finally, "the product of the [Benedictine] workshop is people who are really there," with "skills to diagnose all inside them that prompts them to escape themselves" (154-55). Benedict, Williams tells us, "regards monastic life as a discipline for being where you are" (155).

## Weston Priory

Consider, next, an actual monastic community, known to this author and to many score of young adults who have journeyed there with me over a generation, a community embodying many of these values. Weston (Benedictine) Priory was founded in 1953 as a dependency of the Dormition Abbey on Mount Zion in Jerusalem by that monastery's abbot, Leo von Rudloff. Abbot Rudloff remained responsible for the priory until 1968, when Brother John Hammond, who had served as Abbot Leo's prior since 1964, assumed leadership for the community. In that year, Rudloff resigned his abbatial status, assumed the place of "Brother Leo," and lived as a brother among brothers until his death in 1982. Abbot Leo was a German monk who possessed a genius for the renewal of monastic life. It is captured in this comment on his intent in founding Weston Priory: "At Weston, the monk's work was to be *within* the monastery and whether ordained or non-ordained they would relate to one another on the basis of *equality.*"[13] Modeling a community of equals and attending "meticulously" to their common life itself has been the brothers' work over the ensuing seven decades.

The word "meticulous" best captures the quality the monks of Weston Priory bring to cultivating their "within" life together. It is borrowed from Paul Ricoeur's characterization of the monks of Taizé, the renowned ecumenical monastic community in France. Ricoeur, one of the greatest philosophers of our times, in his widowerhood spent the last years of his life living among the monks of Taizé. He writes of them: "At times I have the impression that, in the kind of patience and meticulousness that characterizes all the members of the community, everyone obeys without anyone giving any orders. This creates the impression of joyful service. . . . And we the participants [guests] . . . benefit from it . . . the example that is given . . . a shared peacefulness."[14]

Despite elements in the 1500-year-old *Rule* of Benedict which are remarkably, if implicitly, egalitarian, like its injunction that young monks should be listened to, or its preference for seniority over social status, Western Christian monasticism nevertheless developed along hierarchical lines, initially influenced by social status and then by canonical distinctions between ordained and non-ordained. The brothers at Weston Priory appear to many of us who spend a good deal of time with them to have dismissed hierarchy from their midst entirely. The brothers have often employed a phrase for table welcome to Eucharist: "This is a table at which there are no superiors or inferiors." It genuinely characterizes the brothers' lives together. (In *With the Gospel as Our Guide*, they write of the acceleration of the evolution of their community of equals with Brother John Hammond's election as prior, monastic leadership becoming more a "non-hierarchal service for unity" rather than "a fatherly solicitude for sons").

In their work forming a community of equals, the brothers of Weston Priory are a model, certainly for me and those to whom I am most intimately linked, of family as a community of friendship. One of the young adults cited below at length says, "Weston Priory sets a new standard for community life."

The brothers speak of themselves as a monastic family, and the

---

13. Monks of Weston Priory, *With the Gospel as Our Guide* (available at: http://www.westonpriory.org/gospel/guide2.html).

14. Quoted by Brother John of Taizé, "A Spiritual Crossroads of Europe: The Taizé Community's Adventures with the Young," in James L. Heft, SM, ed., *Passing on the Faith: Transforming Traditions for the Next Generations of Jews, Christians and Muslims* (New York: Fordham University Press, 2006) 160.

concrete witness of their family life fares well in the light of family studies. The authors W. Robert Beavers and Robert B. Hampson say of "borderline dysfunctional families" that they "are characterized by chaotic and overt power struggles, with persistent (but ineffective) efforts to build and maintain stable patterns of domination and subordination. . . . Individual family members have little ability to attend to and accept emotional needs in themselves and others."[15] And of "optimal families" they write: "intimacy is sought and usually found, a high level of respect for individuality and the individual perspective is the norm, and capable negotiation and communicational clarity are the results. . . . Conflict and ambivalence . . . are handled directly, overtly, and (usually) negotiated efficiently" (Beavers & Hampson 48).

Alongside working for a community of equality, and therefore of genuine friendship, Abbot Leo's original vision was that at "Weston the monks' work was to be *within* the monastery" (*With the Gospel as Our Guide*). This decision set the monastery apart. Bruno Barnhart, OSBCam writes: "solitude, silence and contemplative prayer have seldom remained the central concerns of Roman Catholic monasticism which has become engaged very largely in pastoral, cultural and educational activities."[16] The decision, fine-tuned over many faithful years, has helped create a masterpiece of prayerfulness. At Weston, the Liturgy of the Hours is prayed with great richness, simplicity and diversity, sometimes weaving Native American elements with classic psalmody and a contemporary sound of haunting beauty. And the community's Eucharist "challenges the brothers [and guests] to respond to the presence of the God of Jesus by loving, gifting and committing themselves to others" (*With the Gospel as Our Guide*). (The brothers' distinctive and thoroughgoing embrace of interfaith sensibilities turns Good Friday prayer into a celebration of a Jew, Jesus.)

The prayerfulness generated by the brothers' decision to remain *within* is multivalent. Rabbi Abraham Heschel, a friend of Abbot Leo, captures its levels: prayer and the inner life, prayer and situating the ego properly, prayer and social justice (alternately – psychological, theological and ethical levels). Heschel writes: (1) "Prayer saves the inner life from oblivion."[17] (2) "The self is not the hub, but the spoke of the revolving

15. W. Robert Beavers and Robert B. Hampson, *Successful Families* (New York: Norton, 1990) 51; subsequent references will be cited as "Beavers & Hampson" parenthetically in the text.

16. Bruno Barnhart & Joseph Wong, *Purity of Heart and Contemplation: A Monastic Dialogue between Christian and Asian Traditions* (New York: Continuum. 2001) 292-93.

17. *Moral Grandeur and Spiritual Audacity: Essays of Abraham Joshua Heschel*, ed. Susannah Heschel (New York: Farrar, Straus and Giroux, 1996) 258.

wheel. In prayer we shift the center of living from self-consciousness to self-surrender. God is the center toward which all forces tend."[18] (3) "Prayer is meaningless unless it is subversive, unless it seeks to overthrow and ruin pyramids of callousness, hatred, opportunism."[19]

The quality of prayerfulness is expressed well in this exhortation by Brother John Hammond:

> the wise tell us that God abides in silence, that God abides in the silence of the heart. Let us not speak of silence, rather let silence speak to us of God. Together let us enter through the door of serenity the silence of our hearts. The chatter of our fears, our angers, our anxieties, the chatter of our desire and curiosity, of our projected plans and unfinished work fall away in serenity and makes space, an open space for a new heart, created in the silence of prayer, created in the prayer of silence. A heart that is free, peaceful, quiet and calm, a heart that is one, a heart so large and wide that it embraces the God of all and the all of God. The God who in silence speaks in all creatures, the God who in silence speaks in all languages, the God who in silence speaks one word, the God who speaks of love.[20]

Remaining *within* and offering hospitality has resulted, over many faithful years of "encouraging growth here and discouraging it there,"[21] in a beautiful place in the country. As a Weston monk, Brother Elias, has said, the priory is a place whose beauty evokes a sense of gift, the gift a sense of gratefulness, the gratefulness an urge to share. Merton might have been describing Weston Priory:

> A life that is quiet, lived in the country, in touch with the rhythm of nature and the seasons. A life in which there is manual labor, the exercise of arts and skills, not in a spirit of dilettantism, but with genuine reference to the needs of one's existence. The cultivation of the land, the care of farm animals, gardening. A broad and serious literary culture, music, art: again not in the spirit of *Time* or *Life* [glossy magazines of Merton's era] . . . but a genuine and creative appreciation of the way poems, pictures, etc., are *made*. A life in which there is such a thing as serious conversation, and little or no

---

18. Abraham Joshua Heschel, *I Asked for Wonder: A Spiritual Anthology*, ed. Samuel H. Dresner (New York: Crossroad, 1997) 20.

19. Abraham Joshua Heschel, "On Prayer," *Conservative Judaism* 25.1 (Fall 1970) 7-8.

20. Untitled prayer contained on the CD *Hear the Song of Your People* (Benedictine Foundation of the State of Vermont, 1998).

21. Brother John Hammond, voiceover on the brothers' fiftieth anniversary DVD *With One Heart* (2003).

TV. These things are mentioned not with the insistence that *only* life in the country can prepare a man for contemplation, but to show the type of exercise that is needed. (*IE* 131)

But the brothers have wrestled with "the tension between monastic observance and active engagement [which] was built into the origins of the Weston Priory community – a basic tenet of Brother Leo [was] that the monastery was not to be isolated from the contemporary world and society."[22] The struggle itself sheds light on another universal value, balancing contemplation and compassion. Over many years, the brothers worked to find the best balance between monastic silence and solidarity in a struggle for justice and peace in the realms of war and peace, racial justice and economic life. (Notice, the year Brother John Hammond assumed leadership was 1968!) Their many trips to Latin America and the witness they proclaim when they return, together with their decades-old covenantal relations with Mexican Benedictine Sisters, the Misioneras Guadalupanas de Christo Rey, are concrete expressions of their effort to live and teach a seamless interplay of contemplative practice and compassionate action. It is no exaggeration to say Merton captures the work of Weston Priory in these words: "The monastic life today stands over against the world with a mission to affirm . . . those most basic human values which the world most desperately needs to regain: personal integrity, inner peace, authenticity, identity, inner depth, spiritual joy, the capacity to love, the capacity to enjoy God's creation and give thanks."[23]

### Young Adult Witness to Monastic Values

Here is the testimony of five young adults, each of whom accompanied me on multiple occasions to Weston Priory, about the values they encountered there. The first respondent declares:

> I believe my experiences at Weston Priory helped me to recognize the simplicity of life and the need to slow down, listen, and just live as God wants us to live. Witnessing the brothers . . . carry out their daily tasks in such manner as they do (slowly, simply, happily, peacefully) helped me put my own busy-ness in perspective. Retreating quietly to the mountains of Vermont and living by the cycles of nature – truly listening to God as revealed in creation – is an experience that can be extraordinarily powerful. The fast-paced, goal-driven, material-

---

22. Brother John Hammond, *A Benedictine Legacy of Peace: The Life of Abbot Leo A. Rudloff* (Weston, VT: Weston Priory, 2005) 127.

23. Thomas Merton, *Contemplation in a World of Action* (Garden City, NY: Doubleday, 1971) 81.

possessing world in which we live can often cloud our ability to truly listen to God as God is revealed within the self. I found the Priory to be a refuge towards the end of my college years and during my time in graduate school. The balance of work and relaxation was extraordinarily conducive to prayer and allowed me time to participate in the rhythmic lifestyle that seemed to flow through the moments spent at Weston. I especially enjoyed the time of prayer throughout the course of the day, in particular evening prayer. I believe that led me to my current practice of engaging in prayer in the evening – more intently than at other points during the day. Finding the best time for personal prayer can be difficult, but I believe the brothers helped me to learn my own method based on their prayerful model. I . . . believe I have a better sense of listening to myself and knowing when I need time to simply be quiet.

According to the second respondent:

The Priory trip was a chance for reflection and breath. Being in such a different environ[ment] not only encourages, but forces mindful reflection. Witnessing the lives of the brothers, walking through the Priory, and even breathing the air all had a profound calming effect. In such a mindset I was able to reflect on my current path. I was aware that I was unhappy with the way things were going, but I failed to truly examine why. . . . I was aware my personal life was almost manic – trying to compensate for an unsatisfactory and high-stress professional one – but hadn't given it much thought. Going to the Priory gave me a chance to inspect my life and subsequently change it. Not too long after the retreat I left my job and focused on finding a path that would sustain a better life. Since the last Weston Priory retreat, I have been much more mindful of certain things. I took a sabbatical from the professional world and used the time to focus on myself and the life I want to lead. I would say that even now my job searches, the lessons I learned and decisions I made at the Priory affect choices I make. I take more time now to evaluate and reflect upon things that are important to me. If you ever watch masterful musicians playing together, you will often notice them making occasional eye-contact with each other. They play their own respective instrument, notes and melodies, but they remember to realize that it takes all respective instruments to make the composition sound the way it was intended. So it is with Weston Priory. As they take the time to exchange eye-contact in an initial greeting or as they pass food at meals, they too recognize every member's contributions, and remember that making masterful community come to life, like music, requires masterful contributions from each member. As we meet new friends, and encounter people who love us more perfectly and who hold us to higher standards, we develop a new understanding of the depth of friendship, and we acquire new standards for what kind of people constitute our best friends. So, too, the experience of meeting and growing to know the Weston Priory community sets a new standard for community life. . . . I have had numerous wonderful experiences on retreat at the Weston Priory. . . . One in particular, however, sticks out in my mind. On the first trip I participated in (Spring 2001) a fellow retreatant and I ventured outdoors for an evening snowshoe stroll. We trekked through fairly large drifts to the center of a field and sat down. . . . We decided to lie back and take a look at the unadulterated view of stars the clear sky and lack of light pollution afforded us. As we lay there, I realized that for the first time in my life I couldn't hear anything. I strained for any hint of noise and could hear nothing but the occasional snowflake hitting my ears. Experiencing profound silence in such an incredible setting has remained one of my most treasured memories.

Respondent three:

It was two years out of Merrimack College that I first encountered the Brothers of Weston Priory, while I was serving in the US Peace Corps in Tanzania. I had received a letter from O'Hare in which he had shared with me their short history. . . . I remember my excitement at the prospect of meeting these men who were supposedly living deliberate and compassionate lives in communion. I participated . . . in the Weston retreat in 2002. My expectations of the kindness and compassion of the brothers were exceeded. I have grown in my friendship with the brothers, and often, in the midst of the craziness of my life and work, place myself there in silent contemplation, my imagination and quietness being sufficient to help me bring the calm that I experience when I am physically present with my friends the brothers.

Respondent four:

Peace. The word that most stands out in my mind when I think about the Weston Priory is peace. From the moment we pull onto the narrow dirt road marked by the small wooden sign reading "Weston Priory" I feel a deep, abiding peace. . . . The peace grows through praying, working and living with the brothers in a contemplative atmosphere.

Praying with the brothers is unlike any other prayer in which I have ever participated. My favorite prayer with the brothers is morning prayer at 5:00 AM . . . . They pray and sing in the candle-light as the sun rises outside. Unique to the brothers are their gestures, which I feel joins me with the community and unlocks and releases the hard things in my heart in order to bring in light and peace. [The brothers] are so full of life and love. I feel such joy and holiness radiating from each one of them whenever I converse with them, joy and holiness that I cannot help but to absorb into myself in the process. Their holiness is not one of self-righteousness but one of real and deep connection to God and to self. This shows itself not only in their commitment to contemplation and prayer, but also in their commitment towards real work for peace and justice. My generation is a highly connected generation – never far from a cell phone, iPad or computer to contact friends or update the world about our whereabouts. The Priory is out of reach of cell-phone and internet service. It is a weekend apart from that connectivity, and the peace that this brings – the peace to only be connected to yourself, the brothers, the community you're with, nature and God – is a peace rarely found in the fast-paced culture of today's society. Not only does that peace arise from being unplugged from technology, but it is replaced with the peace that arises from silent contemplation in prayer, from not having a hectic schedule of work and people to keep track of, from enjoying the company of the brothers and of one's community, and from the time to just be by oneself in peace and silence. Though I am always too soon brought down from the mountain and brought back to the busy-ness of life, this peace and absolute centeredness is something I strive to hold on to as I go about my activities. I feel it as joy in my heart and a lightness that I radiate after time spent with the brothers.

Respondent five:

The alarm goes off. The buzz of reality drags me from the unconsciousness of a dream. Opening my eyes for just long enough to slap the snooze button, I roll back to sleep. Again the alarm sounds and I muffle the sound of the day's obligations with another slap at the snooze button. . . . Weston Priory is an unforgettable place. The priory provided for an environment that sparked a new understanding of myself and freed me from the shackles of the snooze-button mentality. I was in need of an awakening, and my time at Weston woke me up. At Weston Priory the world is at balance, at peace. I clearly recall the refreshing feeling of the mountain air and my lungs on arriving and the cool air cradling my attention. Even my mornings at the Priory were different than they had been. When I awoke it was not because I was compelled by responsibility. I awoke freely without the need for an alarm. My eyes snapped open and directly into consciousness and mental sharpness followed throughout the day. If someone can consciously control their choices, then they can build upon themselves and become the person they want to be. They can find their authentic self, their unique identity that exists in us all prior to being bombarded by determining social forces. In the quiet of Weston, one is capable of quiet communion with their soul. Everything at Weston felt more honest. Whether it was the gracious greens of the trees or simply breathing, things seemed more truthful. Late at night, equipped with my notebook, I began peeling back the layers of self. At the time of my [first] trip there I was a vegetarian. It was the clarity of my final night in Weston that allowed me to evaluate my choice further and ultimately led me to my current vegan lifestyle. . . . One must turn their beliefs into action for them to matter; one must attempt to live their virtue in order to be truly satisfied with their living. Each day at Weston is special, but one night in particular was truly incredible. As I approached our cabin with my notebook, planning to end the night with a few entries, I noticed people gathered outside the cabin. Four of my fellow visitors were staring up at something in amazement. At first I did not understand why, but as I began to summit the steep hill that leads to the cabin I saw it. The clouds had cleared and revealed a shockingly beautiful mosaic of nature. The stars seemed bigger and brighter than I had ever seen them before, and there were thousands of them that I was sure I had never seen before. We stood there in awed silence for hours. . . . No one was looking forward to sleeping or escaping into their dreams; we were all enthralled. Eventually conversations began about our common appreciation for the event and we all went to sleep realizing that our experience highlighted something that was missing in our everyday lives. During an ordinary day, we regularly chose not to pay attention to the beauty around us. The beauty of stars, however, could not be ignored. In the wake of this experience, I began thinking of nature less as an equation of divinity and more as an expression of an artist. I began wondering, who is this artist and what is this artist trying to say? When I personify God this way, I see the universe more clearly and more completely. The closest connection I have felt with the Creator, with the Being we call God, arises from the moments when I followed this spiritual strand. It comes from those moments when I leave my soul exposed to myself and then proceed to interact with the expression of God. At Weston, I learned God is not a moral politician, but rather an artist of advanced perspective. [But] after all, nature was not the only nurturer at Weston. The brothers completed the experience. Each wore the countenance of a friend and was remembered by all for their eloquence and warmth. . . . By watching them during Mass, at work in the field, at work in the barn . . . I was able to gain insight into their lifestyle. I learned that a lifestyle should not be based solely in control. A lifestyle choice is about living a life of action that is rooted in beliefs. It was the brothers' model of living that captivated me . . . their calmness, confidence and patience. . . . At times I find myself contemplating the model of the brothers and consequently I begin thinking of my life as well. Upon returning home, I found myself energized and clarified my experience at Weston Priory. Outside the shadow of the snooze button, life was brought into focus. I emerged from my experience with greater self-awareness and a deeper, clearer spiritual vision. People tend to think of these awakenings as moments of clarity, but at Weston Priory I encountered something different. There was not a single *moment* [respondent's emphasis] that defined my time at the Priory. There was a constant absorbing of insight from a seemingly endless stream of epiphany. At Weston Priory I began my spiritual – whittling and revealed the authenticity of identity that lies in the core of every individual. Once we can see this soul, we can become it. I spent a lot of time whittling while I was at Weston, and I continue to work to shape my identity, to carve a life that is true to my soul.

These five young men and women were chosen from about 150 who journeyed to Weston Priory over more than fifteen years. They are certainly spiritually attuned, but many young adults are. And while the monks of Weston Priory are unique, they are not singular. Indeed, what is called "the New Monasticism" is among the most prominent and hopeful movements of young adults in the churches. In an essay in *Christianity Today* Rob Moll characterized it as "a wave of Evangelicals and some Catholics, who see in community life an answer to societal materialism and the church's complacency toward it . . . turning to an ancient tradition to provide spiritual sustenance for their ministries."[24]

---

24. Rob Moll, "The New Monasticism: A Fresh Crop of Christian Communities Is Blossoming All Over America," *Christianity Today* (September, 2003) 40.

### Contemplative Education, Community, Non-Violence & Silence

So, Panikkar, Casey, Chittister, Williams, the monks of Weston Priory, and always Merton, evoking monastic resources; young adults expressing their experience of monastic qualities; aspiring to a heroic life of simplicity and calm, beyond self-indulgence, possessions and power; transcending isolation, meaninglessness, alienation and violence with love, prayer, hospitality and non-violence; embracing community, embracing simplicity; infusing the sameness of long-term commitment with energy and imagination; refusing to be turned into a rhinoceros as the price of getting along; accepting the otherness of others through transparency and peacemaking; attending to beauty, to depths of friendship, doing things slowly and well; practicing being there! – and listening! – this is the monastic witness!

And the educational practice to get us there? Here Gabriel Moran's words bear repeating: "The most comprehensive form of education is community." "The words presence and community [are] synonymous: to be in a community is to be present. Presence is a mode of relationship which a person has to other persons, to oneself and to the world of non-persons." "Community . . . refers to a human unity [so] at the least the human is not destroyed but affirmed . . . [refers to] the first and continuing experience of humanness . . . to be confronted with otherness . . . [refers to] the specifically human activity of forming mutual or reciprocal relations" (Moran, *Living* 167-68).

The moral implications of this practice stand out prominently. Morally "adult" people "let the choice(s) flow from the center of our receptivity to being . . . in resonance with fellow travelers on earth; . . . our actions will have a gentleness that lessens the violence in the world."[25] And, of young adults specifically, "the special test in our era for this age of life is a growing understanding of non-violence. . . . The realization of a life of non-violence depends on being tolerant of others' views and being willing to learn from enemies."[26]

There is no doubt Moran privileges contemplation education. He writes: "religious silence is . . . in the deep life of the community: speech arises constantly from the well of silence and when one is finally speechless in ecstasy or sorrow, a silence that is full is at the center of things."[27] This silence, the work of contemplation practice, stills the distorting in-

---

25. Gabriel Moran, *No Ladder to the Sky: Education and Morality* (San Francisco: Harper and Row, 1987) 61ff.

26. Gabriel Moran, *Religious Education Development: Images for the Future* (Minneapolis: Winston Press, 1983) 89.

27. Gabriel Moran, *Education toward Adulthood* (New York: Paulist Press, 1979) 73.

ner voice of self-absorbed ego, and the traits of true community become manifest: human unity, affirmation and mutuality, encountering others in their otherness, practicing presence and non-violence. For those of us who work especially to nurture religious communities, the inspiration, in Meister Eckhart's words, is that in all creation "there is nothing so like God as silence."[28] But the importance of meditative silence across the curriculum of schools is becoming better appreciated more broadly. Writing in *The Chronicle of Higher Education* about meditative practice, Natalie Houston says: "The rigor of these disciplined practices prepares the mind to process information in new and perhaps unexpected ways. Contemplative practice unlocks the power of deep inward observation, enabling the learner to tap into a wellspring of knowledge about the nature of mind, self and other."[29] Houston echoes Maria Harris, years earlier: "The first moment in teaching is contemplation . . . to begin the teaching activity by seeing what is there. Thus we do not begin by preparing our material, we begin by being still. In this moment we are asked to see teaching as a Thou, so that we might bring to it an attitude of silence, reverence and respect."[30]

## Conclusion

Monastic communities, new monastic communities and inspiring traditional communities such as Weston Priory, are places where what Gabriel Moran calls "peaceful education" goes on all the time. At the end of *Living Nonviolently: Language for Resisting Violence*, he writes:

A peaceful education would be one that leads toward peace by traveling on a path that resists violence at every step of the way. Peace is both a personal quality and a condition for political life. The individual person can get discouraged because the world is a violent place. The temptation is to try to withdraw into a private sphere where peace seems possible. However, the violence of the world intrudes on every life unless one develops a language of non-violence, skills at conflict

---

28. Meister Eckhart, "Fragment 29," in *Meister Eckhart: A Modern Translation*, trans. Raymond Blakney (New York: Harper & Brothers, 1941) 243, which reads: "Nothing in all creation is so like God as stillness" ("silence" is frequently substituted for "stillness," as in Matthew Fox, *A Way to God: Thomas Merton's Creation Spirituality Journey* [Novato, CA: New World Library, 2016] 65).

29. Natalie Houston, "Breathing and Pedagogy," *The Chronicle of Higher Education* (17 August 2010); available online at http://www.chronicle.com/blogs/profhacker/breathingpedagogy/26230.

30. Maria Harris, *Teaching and Religious Imagination* (San Francisco: Harper and Row, 1987) 24.

resolution and an interior life of quiet moments in the midst of passionate activity. (Moran, *Living* 185)

A language of nonviolence, interior lives of "quiet moments," passionate
activity and peace. The monastic school! On the last day of his life Merton
said of monasticism: "It is imperishable. It represents an instinct of the
human heart, and it represents a charism given by God to man. It cannot
be rooted out, because it does not depend on man. It does not depend on
cultural factors, and it does not depend on sociological or psychological
factors. It is something much deeper."[31] And Dostoevsky's Father Zossima
in T*he Brothers Karamazov* says to his monks: "monks are not a different
sort of man, but only such as all men on earth ought to be. Only then will
our hearts be moved to a love that is infinite, universal and that knows
no satiety. Then each of us will be able to gain the whole world by love
and wash away the world's sins with his tears."[32] Monastic resources for
young adults' spiritual lives.

---

31. Thomas Merton, *The Asian Journal*, ed. Naomi Burton Stone, Brother Patrick
Hart and James Laughlin (New York: New Directions, 1973) 342.

32. Fyodor Dostoevsky, *The Brothers Karamazov*, trans. Richard Pevear and Larissa
Volokhonsky (New York: Farrar, Straus and Giroux, 1990) 164.

# Relevance and Ambivalence: A Bibliographic Review of Thomas Merton's Centenary (2015)

*Joseph Quinn Raab*

## Introduction

The centenary of Thomas Merton's birth generated a slew of publications about him.[1] As early as January they started coming in force and they did not seem to let up in any month. Indeed, since Pope Francis addressed the U.S. Congress in September of 2015 and lifted Merton up as one of the four Americans we ought to follow into the twenty-first century, the waning months of the year saw no corresponding fall in publications. Rather the autumn of 2015 was more like a second spring. Full-length books, book chapters, scholarly articles and short personal homages sprouted throughout the entire year.[2] The bibliography for 2015 compiled by Dr. Paul M. Pearson at the Thomas Merton Center at Bellarmine University in Louisville numbers close to two hundred items; this alone testifies to Merton's relevance. This essay will selectively discuss publications that came out about or by Merton in 2015 and will treat them according to a loose typology.[3] For example, introductory books and articles will be set apart from more substantive or investigative books and articles, and pieces about Thomas Merton treated apart from pieces by him.

Merton remains relevant because he expresses and nourishes a basic and timeless human hunger for what is true and good and beautiful. However, he is also relevant because with stinging conviction he exposes stubborn injustices, our flight from understanding, our collective

---

1. For a helpful guide to some of the more important book-length publications leading up to and initiating the centenary see Patrick F. O'Connell's "Wisdom and Discontent: Diverse Books Mark the 100th Birthday of the Great Mystic and Writer Thomas Merton," *Sojourners* (January 2015) 40-44.

2. Book chapters are not covered in this essay due to spatial constraints, but I want to mention as especially noteworthy Belden C. Lane's "Holy Folly: Aravaipa Canyon and Thomas Merton" in *Backpacking with the Saints: Wilderness Hiking as Spiritual Practice* (New York: Oxford University Press, 2015) 193-206, and Patrick F. O'Connell's "Continuing the Dialogue: Thomas Merton and Albert Camus" in *Creating Albert Camus: Foundations and Explorations of His Philosophy of Communication*, edited by Brent C. Sleasman (Madison, NJ: Fairleigh Dickinson University Press, 2016) 139-60.

3. I wish to express my gratitude to Professor Melissa Sissen, reference librarian at Siena Heights University, for helping me track down many of the pieces reviewed in this essay.

fear, pettiness and cruelty. In this way Merton is a classic.[4] David Tracy explains that a "classic," be it a text, song, symbol or even a person, is a kind of concrete universal that confronts us with an excess or surplus of meaning and that challenges and transforms our personal horizons.[5] It is the surplus of meaning and the enduring capacity to challenge and transform that merits the designation "classic." Being transformed by a classic is appealing, even alluring, but being challenged by one annoys and afflicts. Getting very close to this idea, Dorothy Day said that the prophet is one who "comforts the afflicted and afflicts the comfortable."[6] Since Merton was doubtless a prophet our response to him and to his legacy will be marked by profound ambivalence. This ambivalence frames my brief concluding reflection.

## (Re)Introductions and Commemorations

The vast majority of the publications related to Thomas Merton in 2015 were simple introductions or reintroductions to the writer, monk and poet that explored why, a century after his birth, Merton still matters. This parade of "meet Thomas Merton" type publications appeared in a wide variety of venues and in an impressive array of languages.[7] On the whole these were reliable and responsible testimonies to Merton's continuing and growing importance that challenge those of older generations to look afresh on a familiar face, and inspire younger generations to seek Merton out for the first time. For example, Fr. Dan Horan's piece "Merton (Still) Matters" succinctly and convincingly elucidates Merton's perennial appeal and relevance in an accurate and responsible way.[8] Likewise, Michael W. Higgins' piece, "Enduring Voice of the World's Monk" is an insightfully solid introduction.[9]

---

4. Philip Sheldrake presents Thomas Merton as a "classic" in chapter seven of his *Explorations in Spirituality: History, Theology, and Social Practice* (Mahwah, NJ: Paulist Press, 2010).

5. See David Tracy, *The Analogical Imagination: Christian Theology and the Culture of Pluralism* (New York: Crossroad, 1981) 100-107.

6. This quotation is regularly attributed to Dorothy Day – sometimes in reference to the gospel, sometimes to saints and prophets; see for example, Sr. Helen Prejean's *Dead Man Walking* (New York: Vintage Books, 1993) 5.

7. See for example (1) Fernando Beltrán Llavador, "El Legado de Thomas Merton para el Siglo XXI," *El Notre de Castilla* 212 (Septiembre 26, 2015) 4-5; (2) Aleksandra Klich, "Uwaga, Niebezpieczny Tomasz Merton," *Gazeta Wyborcza* (31 stycznia-1 lutego, 2015) 34-36; and (3) Andreas Ebert, "Was Kann Man Huete von Thomas Merton Lernen?" *Publik-Forum* 3 (2015) 42-43.

8. Daniel P. Horan, OFM, "Merton (Still) Matters: How the Trappist Monk and Author Speaks to Millennials," *America* (19-26 January 2015) 20-23.

9. Michael W. Higgins, "Enduring Voice of the World's Monk," *The Tablet* (31

A rare exception to this reliability, however, is a piece by John Cooney that appeared in *The Irish Times*.[10] Cooney's version of Merton's story is fraught with problems. For example, Cooney says that Merton met with D. T. Suzuki in 1968, but Suzuki had actually passed away in 1966, two years after his meeting with Merton in New York. He claims that M. was nineteen, while Merton reports that she was twenty-five.[11] He suggests that Merton was so distraught over the liturgical reforms of the Second Vatican Council that he might have joined Archbishop Lefebvre in schism.[12] But the most troubling piece of Cooney's article is his strongly asserted but wholly unsupported "conclusion" that Merton had committed suicide because of his remorse over losing M. Merton scholars will easily spot the falsities and ungrounded speculations in this article but it is difficult to find comfort in that. Reading Cooney's piece I was reminded of Steven Colbert's facetious fondness for "truthiness" over truth and of Ira Glass, who recently said we are living in "a post-truth age . . . when it has never been easier to establish the facts yet facts have never seemed less important."[13]

In addition to the numerous introductory and commemorative pieces that appeared singly in periodicals and journals, a commemorative anthology deserves special mention. *Mertonianum 100: Comemoraçá do Centenário de Thomas Merton* is the first major publication of the Brazilian Society of Friends of Thomas Merton and aims to offer readers of Portuguese something similar to what Gray Henry and Jonathan Montaldo offered a bit earlier in English.[14] This is a delightful collection of essays of varying degrees of formality that movingly convey how Merton continues to challenge, guide, inspire and entertain so many.

---

January 2015) 8-9.

10. John Cooney, "Thomas Merton: The Hermit Who Never Was, His Young Lover and Mysterious Death," *The Irish Times* (10 November 2015).

11. See Thomas Merton, *Learning to Love: Exploring Solitude and Freedom. Journals, vol. 6: 1966-1967*, ed. Christine M. Bochen (San Francisco: HarperCollins, 1997) 130.

12. Archbishop Lefebvre was excommunicated for ordaining four bishops of his Society of Pius X without papal approval. The archbishop rejected "the Spirit of Vatican II" which he identified with a "false ecumenism" that he believed was behind all of the conciliar developments. His letters to Pope John Paul II can be found online at: http://www.sspxasia.com/Documents/Archbishop-Lefebvre/Apologia/Vol_three/Chapter_26.htm.

13. Ira Glass, "Episode 599: Seriously?" *This American Life*, aired October 21, 2016 on National Public Radio.

14. *We Are Already One: Thomas Merton's Message of Hope – Reflections in Honor of His Centenary (1915-2015)*, ed. Gray Henry and Jonathan Montaldo (Louisville, KY: Fons Vitae, 2014).

## Books

Book-length introductions to Thomas Merton's life and thought also appeared, such as Michael W. Higgins' excellent and engaging introduction *The Unquiet Monk: Thomas Merton's Questing Faith* which receives individual attention in the following section of this volume.[15] Following last year's publication of his *Thomas Merton: Faithful Visionary*,[16] which was a more general introductory piece, Higgins offers here a still brief but slightly more in-depth introduction to Merton's thought and intellectual contributions. True to form, Higgins displays his detailed knowledge of his subject as well as his own gifts for highlighting and explaining how Merton continues to be ahead of our time in so many ways.

A second effective example of an introduction is Linus Mundy's *Simply Merton: Wisdom from His Journals*.[17] Anyone familiar with Mundy's Elf-help series and CareNotes booklets knows that he has a gift for making spiritual concerns and insights broadly accessible and finding ways to express wisdom in simple ways. In *Simply Merton* Mundy applies that skill to breaking open and sharing from Merton's voluminous journals. In fifteen chapters dealing with themes drawn from Merton's spiritual life, Mundy offers his own reflections and guides readers to do the same. Mundy succeeds in rendering a fine little book that serves as an effective introduction to Merton's life and work and as a practical touchstone for prayer and meditation.

As an important aside, 2015 was also the centenary of the birth of Merton's dearest friend Robert Lax, and the fifteenth anniversary of Lax's death. Two noteworthy books mark this occasion: Michael McGregor's *Pure Act: The Uncommon Life of Robert Lax*, which is reviewed in the following section of this volume,[18] and S. T. Georgiou's *In The Beginning Was Love: Contemplative Words of Robert Lax*.[19] McGregor's book blends first-person memoir with some solid biographical research, a combination that is both engaging and informative and gives the reader a sense

15. Michael W. Higgins, *The Unquiet Monk: Thomas Merton's Questing Faith* (Maryknoll, NY: Orbis Books, 2015).

16. Michael W. Higgins, *Thomas Merton: Faithful Visionary* (Collegeville, MN: Liturgical Press: 2014).

17. Linus Mundy, *Simply Merton: Wisdom from His Journals* (Cincinnati, OH: Franciscan Media, 2014).

18. Michael N. McGregor, *Pure Act: The Uncommon Life of Robert Lax* (New York: Fordham University Press, 2015).

19. *In The Beginning Was Love: Contemplative Words of Robert Lax*, edited with an Introduction by S. T. Georgiou with a Foreword by Jonathan Montaldo (Springfield, IL: Templegate, 2015).

of intimacy with a poet who manages to remain mysteriously private. Georgiou's work, on the other hand, is a kind of extended found poem, lifted from Lax's own corpus that is introduced, arranged and edited by Georgiou. The result is stunningly beautiful. The eighty-one sections that comprise the book can be read as a single extended poem, or individually as mantra-like meditations leading to silent wonder and awe. Either way, Lax's contemplative words read like a prayer, revealing not only Lax's stark and austere attention to created things but also a bit of the Creator, the One with whom Lax is utterly and ultimately preoccupied.

Beyond the broad-ranging introductory books, some tightly focused and detailed studies of particular aspects of Merton's life appeared as well, three of which I will just mention here since they also receive individual attention in the review section of this volume. First, Donald Grayston's *Thomas Merton and The Noonday Demon: The Camoldoli Correspondence* is a brilliant examination of Merton's perpetual restlessness.[20] Grayston uses his discovery of a previously largely unknown correspondence to unpack the depths of Merton's vulnerabilities to the siren song of eremitic life and in his spiritual battle against the sickness of acedia. Next, Roger Lipsey's *Make Peace Before the Sun Goes Down* is a revealing and penetrating examination of the richly complex relationship between Thomas Merton and his Abbot James Fox that adds depth and balance to the record.[21] Finally, Fiona Gardner's *The Only Mind Worth Having: Thomas Merton and the Child Mind* is a fascinating exploration of Merton's spiritual journey as a response to Christ's call to become like children.[22] Gardner, utilizing her psychoanalytic expertise and her tools as an accomplished Merton scholar, helps the reader appreciate the only mind worth having while being on guard against the pathological substitutes that are merely masks for narcissism, regression or childish petulance.

## Scholarly Articles

In addition to the books, many scholarly articles appeared that contributed to our developing understanding of Merton's life and legacy. Here I can mention only a few. "Los Puentes Culturales y Literarios de la Traducion Poetica: Thomas Merton y Ernesto Cardenal" by Marcela Raggio uses Thomas Merton's engagements with Latin American poetry and a

---

20. Donald Grayston, *Thomas Merton and the Noonday Demon: The Camaldoli Correspondence* (Eugene, OR: Cascade Books, 2015).

21. Roger Lipsey, *Make Peace Before the Sun Goes Down: The Long Encounter of Thomas Merton and His Abbot, James Fox* (Boston: Shambhala, 2015).

22. Fiona Gardner, *The Only Mind Worth Having: Thomas Merton and the Child Mind* (Eugene, OR: Cascade Books, 2015).

theoretical framework provided by Antoine Berman to think about how translation requires and facilitates transcultural bridge-building and cultural interpenetration.[23] By looking at Merton's translations of Cardenal's work, Raggio unveils how each influenced and enriched the other.

Ron Dart renders a rather compelling comparison of two of the twentieth century's greatest spiritual writers in his piece "C. S. Lewis and Thomas Merton: Soul Friends," where he examines "both the thematic affinities between Lewis and Merton and, equally important, the explicit references both men make, in an appreciative manner, about one another."[24] Dart comments that for whatever reason the scholars and admirers of these two great figures self-segregate. Let's hope that elucidating their complementarity as Dart does here will provide some impetus for bridge building.

Jack Downey's "The Great Compassion: Thomas Merton in Asia" explores the religious interpenetration of Catholicism and Buddhism within Thomas Merton.[25] Downey, well versed in what the Vatican calls "the dialogue of theology," portrays Merton as an unexpected embodiment of the phenomenon known as "multi-religious belonging."[26] By carefully examining Merton's appropriation of Buddhism, with all its promises and potential problems, Downey also highlights how Buddhism, especially in America, has appropriated Thomas Merton. This piece opens up exciting avenues of inquiry for those who share Merton's interest in and recognize the importance of the interreligious dialogue.

Paul M. Pearson's "The Whale and the Ivy – Journey and Stability in the Life and Writings of Thomas Merton"[27] is a thorough fleshing-out of Merton's profound understanding of his monastic vow of stability, which effectively functioned as a protection against Merton's innate restlessness. Pearson suggests that Merton's capacity to notice, his attentiveness to and even empathy with his natural and artificial surroundings, is in no small part due to his living stability. Throughout this insightful essay Pearson illustrates how the vow of stability "encourages the inner journey" which Merton says is "far more crucial and infinitely more important than any

---

23. Marcela Raggio, "Los Puentes Culturales y Literarios de la Traducion Poetica: Thomas Merton y Ernesto Cardenal" *e-latina* 13.51 [Buenos Aires] (Abril-Junio 2015).

24. Ron Dart, "C. S. Lewis and Thomas Merton: Soul Friends," *Crux* 50.2 (Summer 2014) 23-31.

25. Jack Downey, "The Great Compassion: Thomas Merton in Asia," *American Catholic Studies* 126.2 (2015) 107-25.

26. See *Many Mansions?: Multiple Religious Belonging and Christian Identity* edited by Catherine Cornille (Eugene, OR: Wipf and Stock, 2010).

27. Paul M. Pearson, "The Whale and the Ivy – Journey and Stability in the Life and Writings of Thomas Merton," *Cithara* 54.2 (May 2015) 18-32.

journey to the moon."[28]

In the same journal issue as Pearson's piece, F. Douglas Scutchfield has explored Merton's relationship with his "godfather" in his article "Thomas Izod Bennett, MD and Thomas Merton: A History and Examination of their Interaction."[29] While the essay does not shed a lot of new light on Merton, it certainly does so on Bennett. Scutchfield provides nearly two full pages of dossier that present Dr. Bennett as a celebrated physician and respected researcher who published in premier medical journals. By filling out a broader picture of Bennett, Scutchfield helps us appreciate the extent to which Bennett played a role in Tom's formation and education, and how Bennett influenced Merton's sensibilities and tastes.

## Works by Merton

The centenary was also a year for publications *by* Merton, some appearing for the first time and some reappearing from the past. Merton's *Early Essays, 1947-1952*[30] and the seventh volume of Merton's novitiate conferences, *Charter, Customs, and Constitutions of the Cistercians*,[31] are especially significant and receive individual attention in the review section of this volume. Patrick F. O'Connell's masterful editing and introducing of these works, the detailed precision and erudition loaded into each of his textual notations, guarantees the solid scholarly contribution these two books make.

In addition to these, *Cistercian Studies Quarterly* published a short piece by Merton on "*Lectio Divina*," the art and science of sacred reading that had been preserved in the Bellarmine archives as a mimeograph manuscript.[32] Sections of this thoughtful explication are maturely realized such as Merton's explanation of liturgy as the Church's hermeneutical key to the Scriptures, while other parts remain cursory and slip into mere jottings, such as when he writes: "To jump over . . . steps . . . may end in self-deception and waste of time. Practical hint: a) Pre-reading – looking at contents, preface, dipping into chapters; get a general idea of the plan" (13). The combination of formally developed prose and notational frag-

---

28. Thomas Merton, *The Wisdom of the Desert: Sayings from the Desert Fathers of the Fourth Century* (New York: New Directions, 1960) 23.

29. F. Douglas Scutchfield, MD, "Thomas Izod Bennett, MD and Thomas Merton: A History and Examination of Their Interaction," *Cithara* 54.2 (May 2015) 5-17.

30. Thomas Merton, *Early Essays, 1947-1952* edited by Patrick F. O'Connell with a foreword by Jonathan Montaldo (Collegeville, MN: Cistercian Publications, 2015).

31. Thomas Merton, *Charter, Customs, and Constitutions of the Cistercians: Initiation into the Monastic Tradition 7* edited by Patrick F. O'Connell, Preface by John Eudes Bamberger, OCSO (Collegeville, MN: Cistercian Publications, 2015).

32. Thomas Merton, "*Lectio Divina*," *Cistercian Studies Quarterly* 50.1 (2015) 5-37.

ments gives the piece a kind of unfinished freshness and warmth. It should be noted that in addition to this original Merton piece *Cistercian Studies Quarterly* dedicated many pages to Merton-related works in 2015.[33]

Paulist Press used the occasion of Merton's one-hundredth birthday to reissue some books that had fallen out of print. Two of them were Merton's biographies of the Cistercians Mother M. Berchmans[34] and Saint Lutgarde of Aywières.[35] *Exile Ends in Glory*, originally published in 1947, is the tale of Mary Piguet, who was born in 1877 and at the age of three and a half was dropped off at the Convent of the Redemption in Lyon, France to be raised by the sisters. She grew up to become a Cistercian nun, taking the name Mary Berchmans, and later became a missionary member of a small cottage convent in Japan. Merton's account of Mother Berchmans' story illuminates her struggle to discern what within her was essentially Christian and Benedictine from what within her was French or European. The question for her was pressing since being in Japan presented a challenge for her to accept and encourage the cultural values of her Japanese charges while mentoring their Christian faith and spiritual development. Unfortunately, Paulist Press misidentified the subject of Merton's biography in its blurb on the book's back jacket, declaring that the book was about the Irish-born Sister of Charity, Anne Daly (who also became a Mother Berchmans) instead of the French-born Cistercian, Mary Piguet, the actual subject of Merton's biography.

The second biography, *What Are These Wounds?* originally appeared in 1948, the same year as *The Seven Storey Mountain*, and tells the story of St. Lutgarde, a medieval mystic and contemporary of St. Francis of Assisi whose communion with Christ is manifest in her body's bearing the wounds of Jesus and in her devotion to His Sacred Heart. While both of

---

33. For example Bonnie Thurston's piece "Waking from a Dream of Separateness: Thomas Merton's Principles of Interreligious Dialogue," *Cistercian Studies Quarterly* 50.1 (2015) 83-97; Bernardo Bonowitz, OCSO, "Reaping What Merton Has Sown: A Retreat for the Merton Centenary," *Cistercian Studies Quarterly* 50.1 (2015) 39-64; Monica Weis, SSJ, "Finding Oneself in the Cosmic Dance: Nature's Grace for Thomas Merton," *Cistercian Studies Quarterly* 50.1 (2015) 65-81. Also, *Cistercian Studies Quarterly* published for the first time in English translation a fine study of Merton as a diarist: Ramón Cao Martínez, "The Readings of a Diarist: Thomas Merton as a Reader of Journals and Related Works," *Cistercian Studies Quarterly* 50.2 (2015) 195-241; 50.3 (2015) 319-69. The original article, "Las Lecturas de un Diarista: Thomas Merton como Lector de Diarios Obras Afines," appeared in *Cistercium* 65.261 (2013).

34. Thomas Merton, *Exile Ends in Glory: The Life of Trappistine Mother M. Berchmans, O.C.S.O.* (Mahwah, NJ: Paulist Press, 2015).

35. Thomas Merton, *What Are These Wounds? The Life of Cistercian Mystic Saint Lutgarde of Aywières* (Mahwah, NJ: Paulist Press, 2015).

these biographies can strike the twenty-first-century reader as belonging to a more sentimental and pietistic age, the protagonists are compelling figures and Merton's storytelling skill and his disarming humor keep both books readable and enjoyable.

*Ishi Means Man*, however, also rereleased by Paulist Press, strikes me as much more timely.[36] Originally posthumously published by Unicorn Press in 1976, *Ishi Means Man* is comprised of five essays about indigenous peoples of the Americas and their struggles for survival in the modern age, and includes a short introduction by Dorothy Day. While Merton's word choice of "Indians" to refer to Native Americans or First Nations people dates the book a bit from an academic if not a popular point of view, his interest "in the ways in which an oppressed and humiliated 'primitive' civilization seeks to recover its identity . . . against the overwhelming threat of a society which can rely on unlimited backing from the great powers, precisely because it is white" (39) ensures that his insights remain poignant. It was nothing short of chilling to be reading *Ishi* as the World Series was played and some students were heading west to Standing Rock. This is when Merton's relevance angers and upsets.

## Conclusion

As the Cleveland Indians played in the World Series against the Chicago Cubs, and fans sported caps adorned with the ridiculous mug of Chief Wahoo, actual Native Americans were engaged in a much more serious struggle. Cleveland's Tribe got more attention than the tribes in the path of the Dakota Access Pipeline (DAPL) who stood in solidarity at Standing Rock, North Dakota to protect their sacred lands and water. These tribes stood against a for-profit corporation that tried to exercise the "right" of eminent domain and to employ the lever of local sheriffs and state police forces to push a gas pipeline through. While the land and water protectors exercised non-violent and unarmed civil disobedience, armed police used stun grenades and rubber bullets to disperse them. Activist Winona LaDuke framed the whole crisis in terms of colonialism and racism and hoped that the standoff at Standing Rock would illuminate the dark shadow of the powerful's disregard and disdain for the land and the powerless poor. In an interview with Democracy Now journalist Amy Goodman, LaDuke stated:

> This is not just about one pipeline but about the new direction we need in moving away from fossil fuels for a sustainable future for the planet. Indians here don't benefit from this pipeline, it serves

---

36. Thomas Merton, *Ishi Means Man* (Mahwah, NJ: Paulist Press, 2015).

only the interest of the owners at the expense of these people and the planet. Indian reservations here need infrastructure, health care and education, not a pipeline. [37]

Police action at Standing Rock against unarmed resisters sharply contrasted with the government's non-interventionist approach to the armed occupiers in Oregon a year before. Ammon and Ryan Bundy and their supporters staged a forty-one-day armed occupation of federal property in protest over land access issues with the Bureau of Land Management. [38] The Bundys and their supporters were surprisingly acquitted in late October 2016 of charges of unlawfully carrying firearms in a federal facility and conspiring to prevent federal employees from doing their jobs through intimidation. One can't help but wonder how federal agents would have responded had they been dealing with armed occupiers who were Native Americans, or how a jury would have decided had the defendants been a group of Black Lives Matter activists or young Muslims. Were the Bundys treated differently simply because they were white and wore cowboy hats? Again, what would Merton be saying about all of this? If he were in the woods today with his silent Tsus and Fus I can't help but think that he would have with him some Winona LaDuke and some Russell Means. If he were planning a retreat today, I imagine it would be a penitential one on the theme of biocide or white privilege. Whatever the case may be, one hundred years after Merton's birth his relevance strikes with a profound ambivalence; we are consoled by the gospel he lived and revealed but afflicted by our addictions and moral illnesses that cause us to shrink before its light. While 2015 was a banner year for Merton-related publications, whatever is coming next will surely be addressing our most troubling times.

---

37. See Amy Goodman's September 12, 2016 interview with Winona LaDuke (available online at http://www.democracynow.org/search?utf8=%E2%9C%93&query=Winona+LaDuke).

38. See Julie Turkewitz, "Bundy Brothers Defend Armed Occupation of Oregon Refuge," *The New York Times* (29 September 2016) (available online at http://www.nytimes.com/2016/09/30/us/ryan-ammon-bundy-oregon.html?_r=0).

# Reviews

MERTON, Thomas, *Charter, Customs, and Constitutions of the Cistercians: Initiation into the Monastic Tradition 7*, edited by Patrick F. O'Connell, Foreword by John Eudes Bamberger, OCSO (Collegeville, MN: Cistercian Publications, 2015), pp. lxii ı 263. ISBN 978-0-87707-041-0 (paper) $29.95.

*Charter, Customs, and Constitutions of the Cistercians* is the seventh installment in Cistercian Publications' *Initiation into the Monastic Tradition* series, ably edited by Patrick F. O'Connell. This series has made available in book format the formation conferences offered by Thomas Merton during his years (1955-1965) as novice master for the Trappist community at the Abbey of Gethsemani in Kentucky. As the title suggests, the book contains Merton's notes for the conferences he delivered to Gethsemani's novices on the original Cistercian *Carta Caritatis* and *Consuetudines*, both dating from the twelfth century, and on the 1925 *Constitutions of the Order of Cistercians of the Strict Observance*, under which Merton and his students were living at the time these conferences were delivered.

Other books in the series (e.g. *Pre-Benedictine Monasticism*, *Introduction to Christian Mysticism* and *The Life of the Vows*) frankly make for more exciting history and/or provide richer, more accessible spiritual doctrine. The series editors were wise to publish those other texts first as they will serve as better entry points for most readers to the teaching Merton offered during his years as a monastic formator. This book should probably be considered supplementary rather than essential for all but those who are specialists in Merton or Cistercian studies. Nonetheless, this book contributes to our appreciation of Merton and Cistercianism in important ways.

Thomas Merton is best known for being a popularizer of monasticism and a prophetic Christian voice during the dramatic social and ecclesial changes of the mid-twentieth century. As Merton's former student Abbot John Eudes Bamberger indicates in the preface to the present volume, Merton should probably be better appreciated as an American pioneer of the *ressourcement* (return to the sources) movement which was so important for the Second Vatican Council in general and for the reform of religious life in particular (cf. viii-ix). Merton was an excellent historical theologian who possessed wide and deep knowledge of the Catholic spiritual tradition and especially of Cistercian sources. He was able to use his vast knowledge of monastic and ecclesiastical history and texts to identify with clarity the contours of his charism and so recall his fellow monks to what Vatican II called the "primitive inspiration" of their founders (*Perfectae caritatis* 2).

Since the novice master's task was largely to introduce new members of the community to the textual monuments and history of the order, Merton's gifts as a historical theologian and accomplishments in *ressourcement* are obviously well-showcased in his formation conferences. To offer just a couple examples of Merton's encyclopedic historical knowledge from this volume, he deftly contrasts the treatment of the monastic calefactory (warming room) in the twelfth century with the descriptions of the calefactory in documents from the fifteenth and nineteenth centuries (cf. 21-22), and provides a highly detailed commentary on the history of personal grooming in the order (cf. 37-39). Merton's maturing as a thinker is demonstrated in the way he was no longer explaining Cistercian life by way of polemical contrast with the Black Benedictines and Cluniac tradition, as he did in the recently published but early-authored *In the Valley of Wormwood*, but rather was articulating an internally coherent vision of Cistercian life, grounded in the sources, that stood well on its own terms. Not surprisingly Merton provided in this collection a sketch of the Cistercian charism that highlighted silence, contemplation, prayer, penance and cloister. This book also underlines some aspects of early Cistercian identity which have become so commonplace in religious life at large that it is easy to forget they were not always normative in monastic life but were only introduced by the great Cistercians of the twelfth century – namely the prohibition of child oblation and the international organization of religious orders.

Abbot James Fox would have been hard-pressed to find anyone in the Gethsemani community more intellectually equipped than Merton to pass on knowledge of the Cistercian tradition to novices. However, the novice master needed to be more than a purveyor of historical detail. He was not simply a teacher; he was a superior. According to Merton himself, the novice master "represents the abbot" in the matter of the whole "formation of the novices" (168). Given the now familiar narrative that Merton had a contentious relationship with his abbot, it is intriguing that Fox would have appointed Merton to the office of representing him and his will to the junior-most element of the monastic community and thus forming the future of the monastery. Merton was clearly intellectually qualified for the work, but would he form the men as the abbot would have them formed?

If this text is any indication, the answer to that question was yes. Merton took his position as novice master very seriously and carried it out dutifully. As O'Connell explains in his excellent introduction, while Merton may have been personally attracted to controversies and might have preferred to devote all his formation conferences to "the spiritual teachings of the desert fathers, or the Christian mystical tradition, or the rich texts and rituals of the liturgical cycle, or the lives and writings of the great contemplative Cistercians of the first generation," he knew that he had to also communicate to his novices the "much more mundane details of schedules and governance, of meals and dormitory arrangements, of monastic jobs and monastic sanctions," etc. (xv). Merton accomplished his task of communicating the expectations for living at Gethsemani to novices by extrapolating upon the ancient charter, customs and constitutions, and illuminating for his charges how those older guidelines were now expected to be carried out, which was often still quite strictly.

Merton's obedience and fidelity to his duties as novice master comes into especially high relief at those moments when he had to communicate values and expectations that he obviously struggled with himself. For example, in discussing the "hidden life" to which Trappists should aspire, Merton told his novices: "monks should not get involved in matters savoring of controversy" (98), and "the desire of *publicity* of *any kind* is extremely dangerous and can easily ruin the monastic spirit" (135). It is always difficult to preach against one's own weaknesses and one wonders how many of Merton's novices realized how much Merton may have felt implicated by his own words. Yet Merton communicated these values, because it was his duty to do so. There are also the rules that Merton may have privately questioned but which he nonetheless delivered soberly to his charges. For instance, he communicated the expectation of total abstention from alcohol in American Trappist houses even though this was not a practice in Europe (127-28), and the rather clerical and conspicuously non-Benedictine pre-conciliar practice of having novice priests placed in seniority above non-ordained novices (163). One suspects that Merton would not have agreed with either of these policies, but there is nothing to suggest that Merton encouraged insubordination or even doubt among his charges. This is to his great credit.

This book contributes to our appreciation of Merton as a historical theologian and to our understanding of the Cistercian charism, the integrity and beauty of which Merton, as always, illuminates in an attractive way. What perhaps makes the book most special, however, is the way it

displays Merton's love for his living community and his dutiful coopera-
tion with his abbot in his role as novice master.

Christian Raab, OSB

MERTON, Thomas, *Early Essays, 1947-1952*, edited by Patrick F.
O'Connell, Foreword by Jonathan Montaldo (Collegeville, MN: Cistercian Publications, 2015), pp. vii + 168. ISBN 978-0-87907-266-7 (paper)
$19.95.

I would like to focus this review of Thomas Merton's *Early Essays,
1947-1952* on the *simple experience* of appreciating this particular set
of writings within the general context of Merton's work. Not to be too
cryptic or provocative at the outset, I will thus proceed in a fairly mundane
manner only to give way to joyful celebration in signaling how this book
enables us to better appreciate Merton's overall expressive life that helps
crack open our lives so that our living life dawns on us.

Simply put, this is a collection of twelve essays, mainly written by
Merton between 1947 and 1950, with one lone article from 1952. The
timeframe is important because the original edition of *The Seven Storey
Mountain* was published in 1948, followed by a mass-market edition
in 1952. Remember how his remarkable autobiography concludes with
an Epilogue, penned in 1947, in which Merton claims that "America is
discovering the contemplative life."[1] It is from this rooster-like announcement that these "early essays" begin to rise and spread the vital news of
such a discovery.

As usual, Patrick O'Connell continues his dependable, impeccable
scholarship in handling Merton's writings with archival brilliance; in this
case, he has elected to neatly organize the essays into two groups: the first
six essays in the collection were published in *The Commonweal* (as it was
then called), while the second set of six were published in five different
publications (two in the magazine *Integrity*). O'Connell's Introduction
and insightful summaries of each article supply the publishing history
and any other background information the reader might suddenly wonder about, making the entire book a complete study in and of itself. The
Foreword is gracefully written by Jonathan Montaldo, a wayfarer-scholar
always helping readers appreciate the deep struggle in Merton's voice,
journey and soul as he expresses the life within him and brings hope to
our own struggles. Montaldo recognizes, here, that though Merton's voice
may seem young in these first public essays, it is unmistakably Merton's
spirited voice we are listening to. And there is much to hear.

---

1. Thomas Merton, *The Seven Storey Mountain* (New York: Harcourt, Brace, 1948) 414.

The topics of the essays are familiar themes and questions pursued throughout Merton's writing career, but here we are privileged to behold the initial trajectory of his contemplative vision before it fully enters the hot crucible of argument, correction, objection, dismissal, suspicion, doubt and fires of criticism where he will be often misunderstood, even rejected. In these early essays, then, are the first workings of Merton's articulate style. His voice is fresh, eager, positive, enthusiastic and naturally unaware of all the costs that authentic communion must eventually entail.

Merton is writing these essays some six years after becoming a monk, and although he is just beginning to find his pedagogical voice, it is especially clear that he is still using his notes from studying Thomas Aquinas and working from a sense of how contemplation seems to open the system of life. And yet, we see too his reliance on John of the Cross for correcting any easy logics regarding contemplation's flight above systems, structures, concepts, words and deeper into the mystery of transcendent life.

Merton's central theme in these early essays is contemplation, the merits and rigors of the contemplative life. He delves into related reflections on Trappist identity, the normalcy of mysticism, the discipline of devotion and asceticism, but the overarching concern is centered on the meaning, primacy and necessity of contemplation in human life. He is clear and adamant that true contemplation is available to all and yet he realizes that few will uncover the signs of access to this narrow road that begins within their own heart. Merton speaks because he wants us to hear the deep voice within us. His words are echoes of that Voice. He will learn soon enough just how much of a cacophony results when voices begin to battle one another in destroying the silence one needs for listening within. Hence one of the substantial values of this collection is the inclusion of three interrelated articles with battle scars: one is Merton's essay on "Active and Contemplative Orders" (28-38), which another writer heavily criticized as "perplexing" in an article included in the Appendix (146-60) – followed by Merton's veiled but broadened response to that criticism in his journal, defending the "primacy of contemplation" (161-66). The entire exchange provides a glimpse of the pounding and hounding that would shadow Merton's struggles between lucidity and misunderstanding.

The most remarkable essay in this collection, in my opinion, is "Contemplation in a Rocking Chair" (91-102), originally published in *Integrity* in August 1948. He opens the essay with a critique of the "genius for evasions" (92) generated by middle-class culture's most popular ways of avoiding thinking and becoming so easily deadened by accepting substitute activities for living action. The essay is a creative, updated critique of quietism as false contemplation, and reveals Merton's burgeoning penchant for contemplative critique wherever "activity" becomes "a refuge" for laziness and evading the darkness of God seems too close for comfort. He argues for one duty: "the evasion of all these evasions and the discovery of reality" (101).

Perhaps a temptation facing a long-time reader of Merton might be to over-qualify these early essays as not quite ready for prime time. Everything Merton ever wrote, however, came out of genuine experience. We can no more separate these early essays from his mature work than we can dismiss his later essays because he died at the young age of 53. Seeds of contemplation were swirling around Merton when he was born. His expressive life has consistently helped us see and gather seeds swirling around our own lives. Between 1947 and 1952, therefore, we see Merton harvesting the bounty from earlier seeds while new seeds are being planted and cultivated. Seeds are flying everywhere in these early essays!

What surprises me the most about this book is how much it illuminates the sweep of all of Merton's oeuvre, the way in which these "early essays" reflect Merton's consistent, living voice. Using 1948 for anchoring these essays in relation to his autobiography, imagine Merton just ten years before – 1938 – writing his master's thesis on William Blake, concluding that Blake cannot be understood using the analytical tools of his era (rationalism, materialism) because he worked in an intellectual climate akin to the saints.[2] Merton, like Blake, could also see a world in a grain of sand. In 1958, Merton had his Fourth & Walnut experience,[3] but he had been enlightened one week prior, tapped open by Gabriel Marcel's helpful distinction between obedience (to external authority) and fidelity (to internal authority, the one inside a grain of sand) (*SS* 179-81). When his world opened, the world responded by opening in Louisville. Then, in 1968, a few months before he left this grainy world, he wrote in his Alaskan journal that what he had been working on all of his life – the contemplative nature of life itself – was "really simple openness to God at every moment." And then he added: "It just means a deep realization in the very depths of our being that God has chosen and loved us from all eternity, that we really are His children and we really are loved by Him, that there really is a personal bond and He really is present. This is so

---

2. See Thomas Merton, *The Literary Essays of Thomas Merton*, ed. Patrick Hart, OCSO (New York: New Directions, 1981), Appendix I: "Nature and Art in William Blake" (385-453).

3. See Thomas Merton, *A Search for Solitude: Pursuing the Monk's True Life. Journals, vol. 3: 1952-1960*, ed. Lawrence S. Cunningham (San Francisco: HarperCollins, 1996) 181-82 [3/19/1958]; subsequent references will be cited as "*SS*" parenthetically in the text.

simple that there is no need to make a commotion about it."[4]

Merton's early essays are *really just that simple*. And best read without commotion.

Gray Matthews

*The Letters of Robert Giroux and Thomas Merton*, edited by Patrick Samway, SJ, with a Foreword by Jonathan Montaldo (Notre Dame, IN: University of Notre Dame Press, 2015), pp. x + 397. ISBN 978-0-268-01786-6 (paper) $29.

As with most epistolary adventures between famous individuals, readers get a greater glimpse of the tone and tenor of an ongoing relationship than mere biography can provide. The friendship between Thomas Merton and his editor and publisher Robert Giroux is a case in point. These two men, central to the American Catholic literary renaissance of the twentieth century, provide a fascinating history of the challenges both of them faced in their respective roles as celebrated Trappist writer and renowned publisher. In their correspondence one not only sees the ups and downs of their deep friendship for one another, but also finds a portal into the many important social, political and religious moments of the last century, especially during the exciting early years of the Second Vatican Council. The editor, Patrick Samway, does a fine job of carefully editing their correspondence so that one gets the measure of each of them, whether it be Merton's struggle with the censors of his Trappist Order or Giroux's struggle to maintain his personal and professional equilibrium with his famous friend. Through it all, though, we see the affectionate regard that both men had for each other.

Samway begins with a helpful introductory discussion summarizing the history of this friendship and their parallel journeys as writer and publisher: Merton and Giroux as college classmates at Columbia University and the influence upon them of a small cadre of friends and professors, including their English professor, Mark Van Doren; Merton's decision to enter religious life as Brother Louis at the Trappist monastery of Gethsemani, Kentucky; Giroux's rise as a publisher first with Harcourt, Brace and eventually at Farrar, Straus & Cudahy (later Farrar, Straus & Giroux); the play-by-play of getting *The Seven Storey Mountain* published, and the autobiography's incredible sensation with the general public; Giroux's growing fame as publisher to some of the great names of American arts and letters – T. S. Eliot, Robert Lowell, John Berryman and Flannery

---

4. Thomas Merton, *Thomas Merton in Alaska: The Alaskan Conferences, Journals, and Letters*, ed. Robert E. Daggy (New York: New Directions, 1989) 143-44.

O'Connor, to name but a few; and, finally, Merton's own deepening spiritual development as he moved into a hermitage and explored dialogue with Asian religious traditions. Merton scholars and aficionados know much of this information already, but the letters give a more complete dimension to the difficulty Merton faced in getting the necessary permissions from his religious order to get *The Seven Storey Mountain* published and Giroux's patient negotiations to ease that approval along. One also learns that Merton had the same difficulty with his Trappist censors almost two decades later when he tried to publish his other important work over the crisis of nuclear war, *Seeds of Destruction*. What is fascinating as one reads their epistolary exchange is the wide-ranging interests that gripped Merton, both religious and political – from monastic renewal and inter-religious dialogue to the political crises of the cold war and racial injustice in America. This volume gives us a nuanced understanding of the struggle that Merton faced between his monastic vocation and his desire to be a prophetic voice in the public square amidst the rapid changes that were taking place in both church and society. Through it all Merton continually grapples with his priorities: to be a monk first and a writer second. And yet in his letters to Giroux, at different points in Merton's life, we get a glimpse at how much of a sacrifice this vow of obedience to his religious order often was for him.

Much of their correspondence centers on Merton's literary affairs as his fame made more demands upon him and the concomitant misunderstandings that accrued between writer and publisher over the best way to nurture and protect Merton's status as an important writer of his day. Ironically, this misunderstanding is partially due to the fact that almost all communication at the Trappist monastery during this time was via postal letters and had to be approved – opened and read by the abbot of the monastery – before being handed over to Merton. We learn through their correspondence that sometimes Giroux's letters either didn't get to Merton in a timely manner or never made it into his hands at all. One such missing letter caused great consternation between the two of them. Merton, anxious to get as many things published as possible, and privately concerned that Giroux was holding up things on his end, made agreements with other publishers. From the beginning of their professional relationship Giroux had worked out a deal with Merton that the publisher New Directions could continue to issue Merton's works of poetry and contemplative essays. With this in mind, Merton naively entered into a contract in 1962 with the paperback giant Macmillan in order to garner a larger audience, all the while under contract with Giroux. Their exchanges suggest that an important letter from Giroux never made it to Merton. It specified the legal ramifications of breaking their contract. As Samway puts it in his introduction, "Had Merton received Giroux's important letter of March 28, 1962, which for some unexplained reason never arrived in his mailbox, [Merton] would never have continued his relationship with Macmillan" (17). The letters suggest that this episode put a deepening strain on their professional relationship.

Beyond the correspondence on publication contracts, deadlines and page proofs, the letters often reveal their thoughts about their contemporary situation, and the men and women – writers, artists, politicians – that they both admired. One comes across some wonderful exchanges when Merton is alive to what is going on around him outside his monastery. Merton tells Giroux about his epistolary interchange with the Russian writer Boris Pasternak (222), and the monk's personal sadness at his death (247, 249). We read later about the Second Vatican Council as he and Giroux discuss their fascination with the pseudonymous writer, Xavier Rynne, and his "Letter from Vatican City," the ongoing insider's commentary serially published in *The New Yorker* magazine about the debates happening at the Council (291). And most of all, at least for this reviewer, we learn of Merton's admiration for his fellow Catholic writer Flannery O'Connor (332, 341, 360), who was, of course, also published by Giroux. Merton claimed that "Judgment Day," her greatest – and final – story before her death was "the best thing she ever wrote and one of the best stories anybody ever wrote" (342). The volume, as a whole, is an important contribution to Merton studies, and sheds light on the significance that publishers such as Giroux had on nurturing some of the great lights of twentieth-century Catholic intellectual life in America. Fr. Samway is to be commended for making this history available to us.

Mark Bosco, SJ


GRAYSTON, Donald, *Thomas Merton and the Noonday Demon: The Camaldoli Correspondence*, Foreword by Douglas E. Christie (Eugene, OR: Cascade Books, 2015), pp. xxi + 297. ISBN: 978-1498209373 (paper) $37.00.

To say that Thomas Merton corresponded with a lot of people is to understate the fact. The Thomas Merton Center at Bellarmine University in Louisville, KY, the largest and most important repository of Merton's work, holds in its collection more than fifteen thousand pieces of his correspondence to over two thousand people. A fair amount of the best-known letters, at least from Merton's side of the discussion, was published under the editorial direction of William Shannon, Robert Daggy, Patrick Hart and Christine Bochen in the 1980s – a project that resulted in five large volumes of essential primary-source material. And yet, as the staggering count of extent letters in the Thomas Merton Center alone attests, there exist more unpublished letters than those currently accessible to the general public. With this in mind, Donald Grayston's book offers a notable contribution from the outset: at least a few more of the many thousands of unpublished letters have now been made available to a wider audience.

However, that Grayston has contributed to the accessibility of Merton's correspondence is not the only accomplishment of *Thomas Merton and the Noonday Demon*. In his Foreword to this volume, Douglas Christie offers a sometimes hyperbolic description of the events conveyed in this correspondence as so intriguing that they might merit descriptors like "potboiler" or "caper" (xi). While even Christie admits that this may be an overstatement, what he is nevertheless gesturing toward is the truth that this period of Merton's life (the mid-1950s) is one that often does not receive the attention it deserves and that it is far more interesting than most people realize. Although these letters fall short of the spy thriller bound for a Hollywood screenplay, they convey insight into an under-examined time of Merton's life between the initial fervor and zealousness of *The Seven Storey Mountain* and the "turn to the world" expressed in his later works on social justice, violence, civil rights and interreligious dialogue. And they merit a wide readership.

In a nutshell, Merton – like St. Augustine, to whom he is not infrequently compared – struggled at points in his life with a restless heart and uncertainty about which direction it was leading him. Merton came to some early awareness that he longed to be closer to God, in whom his heart might finally rest, but still wrestled with which way of life or vocation might best accomplish that goal. In the late 1930s it was with the Franciscan order; in the early 1940s it was between Catherine de Hueck's Friendship House or the Trappist Order; in the mid-1950s it was from among several cenobitic and eremitical options; and for a very short period of time in the mid-1960s, it was even between the married life and consecrated religious life. Grayston's book focuses on Merton's exploration of and discernment about which religious community God was calling him to in the 1950s.

With a metaphor that reads as part armchair psychology and part spiritual direction, Grayston posits that Merton was struggling with *acedia*, a kind of spiritual listlessness, boredom, dissatisfaction, or, we might say, *restlessness*. After an insightful and contextualizing introduction in which Grayston notes how he happened upon part of this previously unpublished correspondence while visiting the Italian community of Camaldoli in 2008, he shifts gears in chapter one to develop his operative metaphor of *acedia*, from which we get the patristic notion of the "noonday demon" that appears in the book's title. At first, the metaphor seems inapt, not the least because of its sometimes modern usage as an analogue for what we would otherwise call clinical depression. However, in the spirit of *ressourcement*, Grayston returns to the fourth-century spiritual writer and ascetic Evagrius Ponticus to provide helpful exegesis. In light of the patristic description of *acedia* as that temptation which, over time, occasions disdain for a particular place (e.g. a monastery such as Gethsemani) or community (e.g. the Order of Cistercians of the Strict Observance), Grayston's reliance on the concept to frame the correspondence more or less fits.

Unlike the perceptive introduction and first chapter, chapter two, Grayston's attempt at offering a summary of Merton's life and work, reads as idiosyncratic and incomplete. Granted, this reviewer acknowledges the difficulties that face any Merton scholar who embarks on condensing into a single chapter the life and times of such a complex person with such a complicated history. But the weaknesses of this biographical chapter range from what I might propose are odd emphases (e.g., spending so much time on Merton's encounter with Gregory Zilboorg) to simple errors in fact (e.g., Grayston's accounting of Merton's exploration of a Franciscan vocation, which reflects longstanding misassumptions I addressed at great length in chapter three of my 2014 book *The Franciscan Heart of Thomas Merton*[1]). Given the likely primary audience for this book – Merton scholars and students of contemporary monasticism – this chapter seems unnecessary. And for those who are interested in exploring the contours of Merton's life and times there are ample resources elsewhere.

The highlight of the book is undoubtedly the "Camaldoli Correspondence" itself. Nestled between chapters two and three, and weighing in at about one hundred pages, the annotated transcription of the correspondence offers readers precisely what they have come to expect from such a project: new glimpses into Merton's mind and heart. Grayston provides a helpful introduction to the key characters involved in the correspondence, which sets a firm foundation for the engrossing exchanges that follow. The correspondence delights the historical imagination, calling to mind the major figures – some widely known (Merton; Archbishop Montini, the future Pope Paul VI), others

---

1. Daniel P. Horan, OFM, *The Franciscan Heart of Thomas Merton: A New Look at the Spiritual Inspiration of His Life, Thought, and Writing* (Notre Dame, IN: Ave Maria Press, 2014) 55-77.

only giants in religious life (Abbot Fox; Dom Giabbani) – engaged in conversation about the current and future state of Merton's religious vocation, specifically whether he should transfer from Gethsemani to the more eremitical Camaldoli.

While Merton's letters are certainly fascinating, this reviewer was captivated especially by Abbot James Fox's May 16, 1955 letter to Archbishop Giovanni Battista Montini of Milan (122-26). It is an enlightening read, which offers a snapshot of the multivalent lens through which Fox saw Merton: part admiration, part concern, part exasperation, and all with affection hidden beneath an outwardly experienced "tough love." And still, one cannot help but read this letter as motivated in some significant part by the fear of "scandal" that might overcome the Abbey of Gethsemani and the American Church by Merton's departure to Camaldoli, a concern over which Fox spills much ink. Similarly engaging is Montini's August 20, 1955 letter to Merton (135-38). Whether arrived at independently or through the urgings of Fox, Montini's loving, gentle and inspiring recommendation to Merton to stay put is touching and worth the price of the book itself. He concludes his letter with: "it seems to me that your place of sanctification is the one where you now are. There you can have solitude, silence, peace and fervor, and from there you can give to so many souls that which God has given to you: the interior dwelling with him" (138).

The remaining chapters contain Grayston's close readings of the letters, reconstructions of the chronology surrounding the multilevel discussions, as well as interpretations of major themes present in the correspondence (in particular, *acedia* and "God's will") and how these vocational themes reappeared in later years with discernment about the possibility of a Trappist foundation in Latin America. Grayston's close reading of the letters is insightful and well researched, offering context when evidence allows and considered conjecture when speculation is more appropriate. This volume is required reading for the Merton scholar or committed admirer who wishes to delve deeper into this period of struggle and discernment, and a necessary addition for anyone seeking to fill their Merton library with key resources. But this book is also valuable for those interested in twentieth-century eremitical religious life more generally and the 1958 foundation of the New Camaldoli Hermitage in Big Sur, California more specifically, for the seeds of that religious community are seen being nourished in this same correspondence.

Daniel P. Horan, OFM

Roger Lipsey, *Make Peace Before the Sun Goes Down: The Long Encounter of Thomas Merton and His Abbot, James Fox* (Boston, Shambhala, 2015), pp. xiv + 323. ISBN 978-1-61180-225-2 (paper) $18.95.

This biography of two monks by Roger Lipsey is based on a thorough familiarity with the writings of the protagonists of this engagingly written work. Contact with certain monks who lived with Abbot Fox and with Merton add observations concerning them which give further color to the account of their manner of living and relating in a growing community. Lipsey came to visit the abbey and interviewed some monks who had known in varying degrees the two of them in the Gethsemani community. His theme is well stated in the subtitle of this book: the relations between the abbot and the monk who had suddenly become widely known through his autobiography *The Seven Storey Mountain*.

It is not possible to summarize this dual biography in a brief phrase, for the author provides extensive detail as he recounts the exchanges between these two monks who, after all, lived together in the same community or exchanged letters from the first day Merton entered the abbey until his death in 1968. Merton spent almost exactly half his life as a Gethsemani monk, entering at the age of twenty-six. Lipsey covers in concrete and extensive detail the whole period of their relationship. Their mutual dealings with one another increased with time, especially after Merton was named master of junior monks. I myself was a member of that group for the three years of simple vows and so profited from his lectures and spiritual guidance. He further provides a detailed and nuanced knowledge of those developments in the Order that were significant in their lives.

Lipsey contributes important insights that are subtle and essential to grasp the most personal factors in the relations of Merton and his abbot. Both were convinced they were required by their vocation to deal constructively with one another. In a lengthy citation from Merton's journal in which he expresses his frustrations in relation to the abbot, he adds as a final observation that it is Providence that the two are bound together (128). Lipsey notes that Merton and Dom James were united by a mutual personal affection that was providential.

One of the engaging features of the account of the two protagonists of this drama is the honest objectivity with which the foibles of each are portrayed in detail. Those of Merton are brought out prominently in the account of his party with two unexpected visitors (136-37). Against all monastic rules, Merton went swimming in the lake with his visitors. They also had a picnic lunch. Merton had no qualms over such behavior that was contrary to the life he had professed. Lipsey rather seems to accept this behavior on Merton's part, uncritically, though he recognizes it as unacceptable for young monks who would be sent away for such behavior.

A topic that occupies extensive attention in these pages is the effort repeatedly made by Merton to obtain permission from authorities to transfer to an order that included hermits, the Camaldolese. Since this desire for a more solitary life persisted over the years, the many details of the initiatives he took are treated at length. In the course of learning the specifics of these numerous efforts the reader is provided with considerable light on the relations Merton had with his abbot and with Rome. This issue became especially significant in the late 1950s. The vicissitudes accompanying these attempts to get permission to enter the Camaldolese provide insights into the complex dealings between Merton, his abbot and Rome. Well set out by Lipsey, the various exchanges allow the reader to gain an understanding of the struggles involved, especially for Dom James and then for the would-be hermit. Merton was very persuasive and managed to convince some of us as well as the Roman officials of his views. But Dom James proved up to the occasion and making a visit to Rome, supported by the Abbot General he was given the authority to decide the matter. Merton graciously accepted the refusal in a calm spirit of faith and asked Abbot James to continue to assign him to the position of novice master. The abbot readily acceded to his request. He faithfully carried on in this position for some years with dedication. How earnestly he sought to instill in novices the Cistercian way of life is evidenced by the recent publication of the conferences he gave to them regularly.[1]

A major reason why Lipsey shows appreciable insight into Merton's complex character is his obvious sympathy for the man. He consistently describes in detail the interactions and activities of both men, often citing their words and writings. However, it is well to keep in mind that while Thomas Merton was a poet and gifted wielder of the pen, the abbot had chosen to renounce the intellectual life in large measure when he entered the monastery. Since both are presented here in good part by their writings and, to a lesser extent, by persons who knew them, inevitably the abbot is at a disadvantage as concerns his personal life.

This appears most significantly in the discussion of Merton's relationship with the young student nurse, identified only as M, who had been assigned to care for him when in the hospital in Louisville. After this initial contact they developed a mutual affection that grew into a

---

1. See Thomas Merton's *Initiation into the Monastic Tradition* series of monastic conferences (volumes 1-8), edited by Patrick F. O'Connell (Kalamazoo, MI & Collegeville, MN: Cistercian Publications, 2005-2016). These volumes are part of the larger Monastic Wisdom Series, a joint project of Cistercian Publications and Liturgical Press.

strong, passionate attraction. This resulted in their clandestine meetings and phone calls for some time after his return to the monastery. Their contacts were forbidden when the abbot became aware of them. Merton for a time continued to call in spite of the abbot's prohibition. After a while he came to see that he had acted foolishly. In his journals he noted that he felt nothing as he burned her letters.[2]

The account that Lipsey provides of the subsequent and unforeseen developments that eventuated in the major changes in the lives of both Merton and Dom James moves along rapidly. When the abbot tells Merton he intends to resign and live as a hermit, a new situation is created for both. Merton encourages his abbot to carry out his desire to resign and live in a hermitage. What is not mentioned as this work comes to an end is that, in a strange and unforeseen way, Providence seems to indicate that Dom James was more intuitively correct than he is given credit for. The abbot's position that Merton could have more influence by remaining in the monastery than he could by traveling gains plausibility in light of Merton's tragic death.

Roger Lipsey presents both Dom James and Thomas Merton with extensive and reliable detail. He describes them with accuracy and insight. Merton had an uncommon gift of charm that was spontaneous. He communicated in a highly effective manner through writing but also through personal encounter. I was able to observe how certain of the younger monks would unconsciously imitate some of Fr. Merton's manner, so warmly did they respond to him. There was no trace of sentimentality involved on either side, however. Dom James, though definitely capable of effective writing when occasion called for it, usually gave little attention to style in his talks to the community. Lipsey is consciously sensitive to the role of this marked difference in causing the tension between the two. The reader does well to remember that Lipsey, while sharing with Merton the interests and gifts of a writer, never was a member of the community, never lived with or knew personally either protagonist of this work. His account is all the more commendable for that. Yet it is possible to appreciate the fuller significance of certain human relations only by personal participation in the various exchanges, made more significant in a cloistered, enclosed community.

That Merton himself may well have chosen to return to his Gethsemani hermitage after his travels seems to me a reasonable possibility. Two days before his accidental death he wrote to Brother Patrick Hart, his secretary, that on this Feast of the Immaculate Conception he felt homesick for the

---

2. See Thomas Merton, *The Other Side of the Mountain: The End of the Journey. Journals, vol. 7: 1967-1968*, ed. Patrick Hart (San Francisco: HarperCollins, 1998) 157.

abbey and sends warm greeting to his friends in the community.[3] His words are a sad and affectionate farewell to those of us who will always be indebted to our greatly appreciated brother and dedicated teacher.

John Eudes Bamberger, OCSO

GARDNER, Fiona, *The Only Mind Worth Having: Thomas Merton and the Child Mind*, Foreword by Rowan Williams (Eugene, OR: Cascade Books, 2015), pp. xiv + 228. ISBN 978-1-4982-3022-3 (paper) $27.00.

Early in her new book, Fiona Gardner notes that there is only a single reference to child/children in the indices to the seven volumes of Thomas Merton's complete journals (4), a statistic that might seem to indicate that this topic is rather peripheral to Merton's thought. But as she convincingly demonstrates in this perceptive and wide-ranging exploration of the theme of the "child mind" in Merton's writing, it is on the contrary a key image intrinsically linked with much of what is most significant in Merton's spiritual teaching. It has perhaps been too easily overlooked or taken for granted by readers and commentators, but that should change due to Gardner's thorough and thoroughly engaging presentation here.

The fundamental context for the entire discussion is the message of Jesus that "unless you change and become like children, you will never enter the kingdom of heaven" (Mt. 18:3; cf. Mk. 10:15, Lk. 18:17) (1). Merton is considered principally as a guide to understanding and putting into practice this gospel admonition, which is echoed in various ways by the poets, psychologists and spiritual writers whose insights are drawn on throughout the book. As an experienced psychoanalytic therapist and spiritual director, the author has both a wide and deep acquaintance with relevant theoretical sources and an extensive engagement in clinical and pastoral practice that guards against an overly cerebral or abstract treatment of the topic. Her approach is empathetic and (to use a favorite Merton term) sapiential, a participatory way of knowing marked, as Archbishop Rowan Williams points out in his preface, by her "sensitivity, warmth and candour" (x) that encourage the reader to place trust in her wisdom and spiritual maturity.

In her opening chapter (1-11) Gardner provides a concise articulation of her central thesis that for Thomas Merton the "child mind" is a synthesis of the openness and wonder of childhood responsiveness to the mystery of existence and the reawakening and recovery of this simplicity, this

---

3. Thomas Merton, *The School of Charity: Letters on Religious Renewal and Spiritual Direction*, ed. Patrick Hart (New York: Farrar, Straus, Giroux, 1990) 416-17.

purity of heart, in the midst of the complexities of adult experience. It is a rediscovery of authentic identity, of the true self called into being by the Creator, through a "letting go of the self or the disguise that we present to the world" (4). It is neither simplistic nor sentimental, neither reductive nor escapist, but a lived recognition of and response to the inner unity of all reality that is accessible through the self-surrender and immediate awareness of the divine presence in contemplation. It is not conformity to a static essence but (as Merton writes in the one passage on childhood referenced in the journal indices) an acceptance of one's essential status as a "child of God," which is an acceptance of "living growth, becoming, possibility, risk, and joy in the negotiation of risk," the dynamic growth of the child "in wisdom and grace" that is pleasing to God (4).[1]

The succeeding chapters of the book (helpfully outlined in the remainder of chapter 1) are grouped in three coherently organized but not rigid or constrictive sections: "Understanding" (chapters 2-6), which provides an overview of the multiple lenses through which the "child mind" can be considered; "Re finding" (chapters 7-10), an examination of "practical ways of orienting the adult mind to re-enter the mind of the child" (8); and "Becoming" (chapters 11-15), focused on the various dimensions of the actual experience of encountering the world through the reawakened "child mind."

Part I begins with a chapter on "Infancy and Rebirth" (15-27) that draws on poets such as Rilke, Wordsworth and Henry Vaughan, who recall childhood consciousness as having an intuitive awareness of the infinite, then moves on to theorists including D. W. Winnicott, Jacques Lacan and C. G. Jung, who recognize both the developing sense of selfhood and the fragility of this process, both the innocence of the child and its inevitable death, both the powerlessness and the freedom of the young. At the center of this discussion is the figure of Jesus, whose command to his disciples to become like a child is recognized "as equivalent to a koan" (26), a paradoxical self-realization that cannot be achieved by logical analysis, nor by a regression to an immature fantasy of a world, and a self, unmarked by evil, but only by a breakthrough that transcends the split between innocence and experience in the gift of purity of heart. Chapter 3 (28-42) presents what Gardner refers to as the "psychodynamics" of relating to God both as parent and as child, with particular emphasis on maternal images of God as found in Eckhart, the Curé of Ars, the early Cistercians and Julian of Norwich, and with Jesus as the supreme model both of total dependency on his Father and of a non-dualistic identification

---

1. Thomas Merton, *Dancing in the Water of Life: Seeking Peace in the Hermitage. Journals, vol. 5: 1963-1965*, ed. Robert E. Daggy (San Francisco: HarperCollins, 1997) 334.

with the Father. At the same time there is a parallel tradition of the child Christ, the indwelling Word, being continually reborn within oneself, a participation in the unending process of the Word becoming flesh, a sharing both in the role of Mary and in that of Christ himself, who is present in the depths of the person in order that each person may incarnate him in his or her own place and time.

While pertinent quotations from Merton are included and discussed in these preliminary chapters, the particular influences from the Christian spiritual and theological tradition on his developing understanding of the "child mind" are the central focus of chapter 4 (43-56): the Cistercians Bernard and Guerric, the Franciscans Bonaventure and Scotus as well as the Poverello himself, St. Thérèse of Lisieux and her "little way of spiritual childhood" (49), and the contemporary theologian Karl Barth, about whom Merton wrote memorably that his love for Mozart, "always a child 'in the higher meaning of that word'" though he was deprived by his musical genius of a "normal" childhood, would be his salvation: "Fear not, Karl Barth! Trust in the divine mercy. Though you have grown up to become a theologian, Christ remains a child in you" (55-56).[2] This survey of the Christian resources for Merton's awareness of the importance of the "child mind" is complemented in the following chapter (57-70) by a look to the East, where the Confucian master Mencius, the "beginner's mind" of Zen, and the necessity of becoming, or recognizing oneself as, the "child of Tao"[3] in the teaching of Chuang Tzu reinforce the insights gleaned from the New Testament and Christian tradition. Here Gardner cites the source for her book's title, Merton's prayer for his friend and guide to Oriental thought, John Wu, asking "the Lord to give you every blessing and joy and to keep ever fresh and young your 'child's mind' which is the only one worth having" (62).[4] (While it is quoted in part as an epigraph [vi] this passage appears in the text for the first time only at this point; it would perhaps be more effectively included in the opening chapter. Likewise Merton's other explicit use of the phrase "child mind," in a journal passage[5]

2. Thomas Merton, *Conjectures of a Guilty Bystander* (Garden City, NY: Doubleday, 1966) 3-4.

3. See Thomas Merton, *The Way of Chuang Tzu* (New York: New Directions, 1965) 133.

4. Thomas Merton, *The Hidden Ground of Love: Letters on Religious Experience and Social Concerns*, ed. William H. Shannon (New York: Farrar, Straus, Giroux, 1985) 614 [4/1/1961].

5. Thomas Merton, *The Other Side of the Mountain: The End of the Journey. Journals, vol. 7: 1967-1968*, ed. Patrick Hart (San Francisco: HarperCollins, 1998) 240 [11/2/1968]; subsequent references will be cited as "*OSM*" parenthetically in the text.

from Asia where he is discussing the great Tibetan master Milarepa as exemplifying "the 'child mind,' which is recovered *after* experience. Innocence – to experience – to innocence" is quoted only near the very end of the book [204] whereas it would also provide a valuable perspective on the significance of the phrase for Merton if it had been part of the introductory discussion.) For Zen and Eastern thought generally, Gardner points out, true childlikeness "does not mean a regression or a retreat to the naiveté of a child. It is not about being simplistic, stupid or ignorant; rather it is about approaching awake and alive with curiosity and enthusiasm" (70). To complete this first section Gardner in chapter 6 (71-82) draws on Merton's famous reference to moving "beyond the shadow and the disguise" (*OSM* 323) during his encounter with the Buddha statues at Polonnaruwa the week before his death, finding a parallel in Jung's concepts of the shadow – "the parts that we keep hidden or would rather not know about" – and the persona, or mask "that we present to the world about who we are" (72) – what Merton refers to as the false self. Here she considers the "life of care" that makes it so difficult for people to experience the fresh vision of the child mind, a difficulty increased by the materialism and technologism that results too often in the eclipse of mystery in the contemporary world. (While the social and cultural context of the contemporary world is recognized as contributing to the problem of estrangement from the true self or child mind, there is no discussion of whether or how the healing of the alienated self can lead to the healing of the alienated society. It would be interesting to consider the rediscovery of the child mind as having a prophetic as well as a sapiential dimension, as leading to a commitment to nonviolence and to liberation for the oppressed and excluded, as well as a sense of environmental responsibility. Perhaps Gandhi's practice of karma yoga, with its complete detachment from the fruits of one's actions and childlike trust that at the proper time God will make use of whatever work one has been given to do, might be a starting point for such reflection.)

Gardner's recognition of the burdens of "a life of care" prepares the reader for the second section of the book, "Re-finding." Here the author first examines (85-97) the pattern of enchantment and disenchantment that leads from innocence to experience of a fallen world and a fallen self, with the possibility of a re-enchantment through an awareness of a transcendent Center beyond the self. Merton's own early experience of loss and loneliness, of psychic and spiritual wounds, related in chapter 8 (98-110), links him with those who have endured similar and even more traumatic childhood crises, and his subsequent conversion and growth are presented by Gardner as a sign of hope for recovery of authentic freedom and healing. In chapter 9 (111-25), she considers three sources of this spiritual and psychological healing: first grace, the unexpected, unmerited transformative encounter with divine love and acceptance in the midst of the struggles and pain of everyday existence; then spiritual direction, the mediated insight into reality and the real self through the agency of a spiritual guide who enables someone to recognize difficult truths about oneself through a combination of honesty and acceptance on the part of both director and directee; and finally psychotherapy, a path to self-knowledge that can complement but not replace spiritual awareness. This attentiveness to both the outer and inner world, considered in chapter 10 (126-38), is what Merton often called paradise consciousness, insight into reality as intended by the Creator, often hidden but still present despite the deformation and degradation caused by human selfishness and human cruelty.

In her third and final section Gardner draws on Merton for images and resources to aid in the recovery of this transformed awareness. In chapter 11 (141-54) she focuses on Merton's evocation of the cosmic dance as a participation in the sacramentality of the created world, the "huge chorus of living beings" (153)[6] that testifies to the creative power, wisdom and goodness of God. In the following chapter (155-69) she turns to poetry as "the language of the child mind" (155), citing Merton's declaration that "All really valid poetry . . . is a kind of recovery of paradise" (156),[7] as illustrated by Louis Zukofsky, by Thoreau and Raïssa Maritain and Alice Meynell, by Peguy and Wordsworth and Blake, and by "Grace's House," Merton's own superb verse meditation on "paradise, O child's world! / Where all the grass lives / And all the animals are aware!" (158).[8] This consideration of poetic creativity leads to a more general reflection on the freedom of play, above all "The Divine Play of God" (170-82) in creation and the power of imagination to transcend pragmatic and utilitarian motivation and participate in this "pointless" celebration of the joy of being, beyond rational calculation and achievement. As Gardner notes in her penultimate chapter (183-

---

6. Thomas Merton, *The Sign of Jonas* (New York: Harcourt, Brace, 1953) 360.

7. Thomas Merton, *The Literary Essays of Thomas Merton*, ed. Patrick Hart, OCSO (New York: New Directions, 1981) 128.

8. Thomas Merton, *The Collected Poems of Thomas Merton* (New York: New Directions, 1977) 331; while "Grace's House" is arguably the best of Merton's poems on the child mind, it is far from the only one: see for example, "Aubade: Lake Erie," "The Winter's Night," "Evening," "St. Agnes: A Responsory" and "The Holy Child's Song," all from Merton's first published book of verse, *Thirty Poems* (*Collected Poems* 35, 38, 41-42, 54-55, 55-56).

95), this is the realm of "final integration" of which Merton speaks in his celebrated essay of that title,[9] reflecting on the psychotherapist Reza Arasteh's Sufi-inspired articulation of genuine human maturity not as successful adaptation to social norms but as the full realization of one's potential for self-transcendence (see 190-92). To conclude her presentation Gardner points out three "Epiphanies of the Child Mind," as she entitles her final chapter (196-208): first his profound experience of "the innocence of childhood" in celebrating Mass shortly after his ordination, when he discovers himself as one who is "agelessly reborn" in his identification with the Eucharistic Christ: "every day I am a day old, and at the altar I am the Child Who is God" (201);[10] second the better known "epiphany" at Fourth and Walnut Streets in downtown Louisville (see 202-204),[11] when he recognizes in all the passersby the presence of Proverb, the figure of Wisdom from Proverbs, chapter 8 who is the child playing before the presence of God in creation and who is perceived "shining like the sun" in "le point vierge," the virginal point, the "point of nothingness," the poverty, the indigence, the total depen dence of every human being on the graciousness of God the Creator and of Christ the divine and human brother and savior; and finally the recognition that "everything is emptiness and everything is compassion" that penetrates "beyond the shadow and the disguise" (*OSM* 323) at the shrine of Polonnaruwa (207), a clarity and simplicity in which Gardner recognizes the spiritual maturity of the authentic "child mind" that has recovered an experiential vision of wholeness from which nothing and no one is excluded. This, she implies in bringing this wise and luminous book to its conclusion, is Merton's ultimate legacy, the gift not of the child mind itself, but of his testimonies to its ineffaceable presence and power at the very center of the self, the self born and reborn through and in the One who called his followers to become as little children and so to share fully in the reign of God.

Patrick F. O'Connell

---

9. Thomas Merton, *Contemplation in a World of Action* (Garden City, NY: Doubleday, 1971) 205-17.

10. Thomas Merton, *Entering the Silence: Becoming a Monk and Writer. Journals, vol. 2: 1941-1952*, ed. Jonathan Montaldo (San Francisco: HarperCollins, 1996) 327 [6/19/1949]; occasionally, as here, the explicit connection of material to the theme of the child mind is left to the latter part of a discussion when it might be more effectively highlighted by using it at the beginning.

11. See the original journal entry for March 19, 1958 in Thomas Merton, *A Search for Solitude: Pursuing the Monk's True Life. Journals, vol. 3: 1952-1960*, ed. Lawrence S. Cunningham (San Francisco: HarperCollins, 1996) 181-82 and the revised version of the passage in *Conjectures* (140-42).

Ephrem Arcement, OSB, *In the School of Prophets: The Formation of Thomas Merton's Prophetic Spirituality* (Collegeville, MN: Cistercian Publications, 2015), pp. xxv + 218. ISBN 978-0-87907-265-0 (paper) $24.95.

In this book, Ephrem Arcement, OSB sets about the task of identifying the texts and thinkers that helped Thomas Merton give expression to his uniquely prophetic understanding of monasticism and spirituality in general after his experience on the street corner in Louisville. For the most part, I believe that Arcement succeeds in this endeavor, but at times this book elaborates upon occasions when Merton recognizes his newly found appreciation of prophetic spirituality in the work of others rather than examining how these thinkers helped him to develop his own thoughts on the matter.

To my mind, Arcement's best chapters cover Merton's reading of Blake, existentialism, especially Kierkegaard, and the fiction of Pasternak, Camus and Faulkner. Merton's affection for Blake has been well documented elsewhere, and Arcement avoids the temptation to provide his reader with a comprehensive treatment of the matter that would derail his overall project. Rather, Arcement focuses on Merton's identification of Blake as a seer, a person capable of seeing what is hidden from others (see 6). When coupled with creative imagination, the seer is able not only to recognize the shortcomings of the present, but also to envision a transformed reality that is more consonant with the gospel's proclamation of a redeemed world (see 11-13). The monk, then, is called to be an imaginative seer, one who sees a world in desperate need of redemption and creatively works to embody Christ in the world.

In this spirit, according to Arcement, Merton read the works of Pasternak, Camus and Faulkner. For Merton, these authors embodied what it meant to be an imaginative seer. In Pasternak, Merton saw someone who testified to the dehumanizing effects of Marxism in Russia despite the physical dangers in which doing so would place him (see 77). Camus called out the absurdity of living in such a way that denies the human demand to find meaning and coherence (see 86-87). For instance, how can people at the same time affirm such ideas as the value of authentic human existence and the importance of acting in accord with cultural norms that seem arbitrary at best? How can people claim that human persons are worthy of love, but tolerate the mass destruction of human life of World Wars I and II? Camus, according to Merton, did not promote such absurdity, but instead identified it to his readers and encouraged them to actively resist it through the examples of his characters. In Faulkner, finally, Merton sees a myth writer who symbolically conveys truths and wisdom that point to a more life-affirming way of living (see 105). All three writers meet the description of imaginative seers – individuals who not only recognize where human societies are lacking, but also imagine the rectification of these shortcomings.

The third area of strength for Arcement's book is his treatment of Merton's encounter with existentialism. Merton's understanding of existentialism, Arcement claims, consists of recognizing that a human life determined by external claims regarding happiness and meaning is lacking because people lose themselves in a "public mind" rather than discerning values that arise from within (116). If people lose themselves in such a way, they are faced with a terrifying void that leads to despair and a sense of futility regarding one's life. For Merton, freedom is the way out of this existential angst. By willingly recognizing and entering the void, human persons become able to affirm truths and values not on the authority of others or social norms, but by a personal encounter with God. Thus, the Christian is liberated from the public mind and emerges into a life marked by the willingness to allow God to act through the individual to make a difference in the world.

With the identification of these three influences on Merton, Arcement is able to provide a description of Merton's prophetic spirituality. The prophet is one whose life testifies to the presence of Christ in a world that stands so desperately in need of the Kingdom of God (see xvii-xx). By learning to see (Blake), the prophet recognizes where the world falls short of the Kingdom. By using their imagination (Pasternak, Camus and Faulkner), prophets envision a world transformed by the love of God. By affirming their freedom (existentialists), they choose to make a difference.

The identification of this pattern, which I shorten in my mind to recognition, imagination and action, is the strength of Arcement's work. I personally found it a valuable contribution to my attempts at understanding Merton's notion of prophetic spirituality, and I recommend it for anyone interested in how Merton's thoughts developed after the Louisville experience. Beyond this contribution, Arcement also includes a couple of chapters on Merton's reading of other authors in whose writings Merton found confirmation of his thoughts on prophets and spirituality, such as Latin American poets and the nature of poetry in general. These sections, however, are less geared towards explaining how certain authors influenced Merton and more towards indicating how poetry can serve a prophetic function and both arise out of and contribute to spiritual experiences. Arcement's work here is interesting insofar as it clarifies what Merton thought about poetry, but it doesn't quite seem to be on the same page as the rest of the book which focuses on texts that affected Merton's thinking rather than texts that agreed with Merton's developing thought. This dissonance, however, does not diminish Arcement's work. Instead, it adds another layer that people interested in Merton might find appealing.

Ian Bell

DEAR, John, *Thomas Merton, Peacemaker: Meditations on Merton, Peacemaking, and the Spiritual Life* (Maryknoll, NY: Orbis Books, 2015), pp. xv + 191. ISBN 978-1-62698-107-2 (paper) $20.00.

Thomas Merton's assertion that "The God of peace is never glorified by human violence," penned over sixty years ago in *No Man Is an Island*,[1] expresses a core assumption woven throughout this collection of twenty-seven meditations. The author, peace activist Fr. John Dear, also offers a corollary that equally anchors his reflections: "The God of peace is always glorified by human nonviolence" (xi). Indeed, Dear's meditations repeatedly name God as "the God of peace" and nonviolence as humanity's calling.

Dear includes Merton among a host of prophetic advocates who formed his own peacemaking vocation, one whose "writings and example have been a steady, daily source of strength, hope, and light, right up to today" (x). In tribute to this influence, Dear composed these "musings and meditations based on Merton's life and writings . . . [as] simple, free-flowing commentaries" (xiv) on a life of peace advocacy. They illuminate, therefore, how Merton's work has helped motivate and inspire one of today's most passionate and vocal spokespersons for ending war and the militarization of our world.

Since Dear presumes readers are already familiar with Merton (xiii), this is not primarily a resource to explore specifics about Merton, although he does summarize aspects of Merton's life and abundantly quotes Merton throughout. Rather, Dear mainly intends this volume to inspire and edify the reader's pilgrimage of "active nonviolence" and discovery of "the underlying communion that already exists among us" (xii). He focuses his meditations around such questions as, "What is the connection between the spiritual life of peace and nonviolence, and the social, economic, and political realities of war and violence?" and "How can we move out of the culture of war and violence and step deeper into the spiritual life of nonviolence?" For one thing, Dear responds, "We try to cultivate peace within us, that we might radiate peace around us" (xii), and his meditations explore how Thomas Merton can help us accomplish that.

Dear wrote these reflections in two blocks, about half penned during

---

1. Thomas Merton, *No Man Is an Island* (New York: Harcourt, Brace, 1955) 197.

a winter at his New Mexico hermitage and the other half while in rural southern France, a region where Merton spent several childhood years. In Dear's own words, these musings "are not presented systematically" (xiv); they do not follow a particular chronology of Merton's writings, nor are they thematically grouped. The reader encounters each as a unique and mostly self-contained reflection with minimal cross-reference to others. Given Dear's activist history, it does not surprise that many chapters focus heavily on implications for war, weaponry and human military aggression. But throughout, he also gives significant nods to how "nonviolence" challenges "injustice," "poverty," "racial prejudice," "climate catastrophe," etc. And – unavoidable when drawing upon Merton – Dear speaks as well to our need for interior cleansing of violent thought and intent when following the path of peacemaking.

The volume's open structure means that responses to a particular meditation will likely vary depending on the posture, needs and frame of mind each reader brings to them. I experienced this personally, as some meditations spoke to me differently during my second reading than during the first. A couple meditations struck me for their illumination of Merton's talent for bringing concepts often relegated to "otherworldly" realms down to Earth here and now. "Blessed Are the Nonviolent" (40-49), for example, accomplishes this regarding eschatology, the study of "end times." Here Dear reflects on Merton's 1966 essay, "Blessed Are the Meek: The Christian Roots of Non-Violence,"[2] adding passages from Merton's journals and a couple other published writings. To confront a "bad theology" that relegates Christ's teachings to a future epoch, Dear invokes Merton's comment that nonviolence has an "eschatological quality" which unites "the power of human poverty" with "the invisible strength of Christ." For Merton, this power is active now; it expresses "a profound existential understanding" that "the Kingdom has been established" (44). A Merton journal entry on "realized eschatology" asserts "the transformation of life and human relations by Christ *now* (rather than an eschatology focused on future cosmic and religious events)" (45). The Holy Spirit, repentance, seeing Christ in humanity, and the sacraments all gain immanent relevance, Merton suggests, through "a Christian peacemaking mission . . . the preaching of the gospel of unity, nonviolence, and mercy" (45). For Dear, Merton's "biblical insights into an eschatological understanding of the times we live in . . . [help] us to carry on the work of peace and the way of nonviolence, knowing that we are fulfilling God's work in . . . salvation history" (47).

---

2. Thomas Merton, *Faith and Violence: Christian Teaching and Christian Practice* (Notre Dame, IN: University of Notre Dame Press, 1968) 14-29.

Dear's meditation "Alleluia, Christ is Risen" (166-73) similarly expands the concept of "resurrection," drawing from Merton's 1967 sermon, *He Is Risen*.[3] Here Merton suggests we are risen with Christ now in this life, not simply into some future life:

> The Christian who is risen in Christ must dare to be like Christ . . . . to follow conscience even in unpopular causes . . . . to disagree with the majority . . . even when others do not understand why he is acting this way. . . . [This is] not because he is arrogant, but because he has humility to stand alone and pay attention to the purpose and the grace of God, which are often quite contrary to the purposes and the plans of an established human power structure. . . . [W]e must dare to stand by [Christ] . . . when the entire establishment both religious and civil turned against him as a modern state would turn against a dangerous radical. (171)

These words encourage Dear to "go forward in our work for peace and justice, first of all, because Jesus is risen and alive. . . . We have risen with Christ, therefore we carry on Christ's work and speak out against war and injustice with him, come what may" (171).

Dear's meditations also engage many other facets of Merton's thought: contemplation, silence, solitude, communion and unity with all, spiritual conversation/friendship with fellow travelers. "Not Survival, but Prophecy" (93-99) expands Merton's description of the monk's modern, prophetic vocation to include the individual Christian and the Church as a whole. For Dear, "We are not only a pastoral people, we are a prophetic people" (95). Dear's final few reflections crescendo in strength, offering insight into the feminine Sophia, our identity as "part of the universe" (147), unity and communion with humanity, and resurrection. They include my personal favorite: "The Universe Is My Home" (138-48), which highlights Merton's prescient awareness of humanity's desperate need to reconfigure our identity into one "purely and simply *part of nature*" (143) and in "unity with all living things" (147) – i.e., to transcend our species' arrogant drive to dominate over rather than integrate with the universe into which we are created.

Dear also helps expose the perpetual contemplation/action, faith/ practice tension with which many of us grapple. Some would prioritize contemplation, believing it inevitably leads one, as Dear puts it, "to commune with the living God of peace and live in nonviolent communion with all humanity and all creation" (6). Yet he also acknowledges a potential for "contemplative violence" (11), sharing an anecdote of nuns who shouted

---

3. Thomas Merton, *He Is Risen* (Niles, IL: Argus, 1975).

down Daniel Berrigan's criticism of the Vietnam War (11), and his own encounter with monks who declined to vow nonviolence as the first war on Iraq approached (12). Contemplative experience and nonviolence, it seems, invite simultaneous embrace in a dance of mutual reinforcement, rather than one leading directly to the other.

A strength of this book lies in bringing together diverse and extended Merton quotations – particularly those hidden in letters and journal entries – that illuminate the depth and breadth of his commitments to nonviolence. It also serves as a fine example of how sitting with Merton can elicit diverse and inspiring meditations if one has the patience and commitment to listen and learn from him, as Dear has. The author's injection of personal experiences and anecdotes of those who knew Merton add color and insight, as well.

As a series of reflections and commentary on Merton, though, distinctions between what primarily reflects Merton's thought, what reflects Dear's thought, and what reflects both sometimes blur. Specialists might quibble over certain historical or theological details noted about Merton and his spiritual pilgrimage. As Dear himself comments, his persistent and passionate mantra to cease war and violence may feel repetitive at times (see 79). But such distractions aside, *Thomas Merton, Peacemaker* offers a helpful collection of meditations that encourages and inspires us both to learn from Thomas Merton and to live out Christ's mission of reconciliation.

Gordon Oyer

COADY, Mary Frances, *Merton & Waugh: A Monk, A Crusty Old Man & The Seven Storey Mountain* (Brewster, MA: Paraclete Press, 2015), pp. 155. ISBN: 978-1-61261-628-5 (cloth) $22.

This is an engaging and attractive little book which is beautifully produced by Paraclete Press. Its focus is the surviving correspondence between Thomas Merton and Evelyn Waugh that took place between August 1948 and February 1952. This consists of 20 letters: thirteen from Merton and seven from Waugh. Unfortunately, as author/editor Mary Frances Coady explains, the Waugh Estate allowed no more than two-thirds of each letter from Waugh to Merton to be printed, although she advises how some of these letters can be read in their entirety on the relevant website.

The useful introduction explains how Waugh, an eminent English Catholic writer, received the manuscript of Merton's *The Seven Storey Mountain* with a request for an endorsement in the summer of 1948. By that time Waugh was famous in America for his novel *Brideshead Revis-*

*ited* and he gave positive affirmation of Merton's work – although he was also critical and thought that the book could do with some heavy editing. In the introduction Coady also covers Merton's history in a concise and helpful way including his early career as a published writer.

The book then comprises seven chapters, each of which explores a particular aspect of the relationship between the two men with the relevant correspondence. Coady frames the letters within a commentary that is both informative and lively, giving the reader an insightful sense of the characters of both men. Waugh emerges as a complex, somewhat curmudgeonly, complaining and often ill-humoured man – at times highly critical of all that is American. However he felt some excitement from reading Merton's autobiography and offered to edit an edition of *The Seven Storey Mountain* for publication in Britain; this seemed to mirror his optimism about American Catholics for the future of worldwide Catholicism and so he also agreed to write an article on the American Catholic Church for *Life* magazine. His interest in all this involved various trips to the US and the start of his correspondence with Merton.

Coady writes with a light and perceptive style and the account of the developing relationship is most entertaining. From the initial correspondence it is clear that Merton admires Waugh and encourages him to offer commentary on his writing. He states: "I am in a difficult spot here as a writer. . . . Therefore I need criticism the way a man dying of thirst needs water." Merton explains how his writing is out of his control – he is being told to write by Father Abbot but his work is often changed by censors and publishers and "half the time I haven't the faintest idea whether the thing is good or bad or what it is" (31). Merton's relationship at this point is, as Coady points out, as if to a father confessor and Waugh responds with gusto with a number of blunt criticisms. He admonishes Merton on his view of Cambridge and the Franciscans and asks for clarity about Merton's love affairs – were they "carnal and how far purely sentimental" (36) and then launches into an attack on Merton's style which he sees as typically American and therefore "long-winded." Waugh contrasts this with his own preference for "the laconic. . . . I fiddle away rewriting any sentence six times mostly out of vanity. I don't want anything to appear with my name that is not the best I am capable of. You have clearly adopted the opposite opinion . . . banging away at your typewriter on whatever turns up" (36-37). He warns Merton against what he calls mass-production (a situation explored in further detail later in the book) and sends Merton a book from which Merton copies a line: "Faults of style are largely faults of character" (39).

The roles seem reversed a couple of letters later when it seems that

Merton becomes Waugh's spiritual director and is seen as someone in whom he could confide some of his troubles. The descriptions of Waugh's trips to the United States to write an article for *Life* magazine are highly entertaining. Coady comments how he crossed the Atlantic "seeking religious enlightenment and spiritual renewal in the country he had, a year earlier, disparaged" (52). He demanded a huge amount for travel expenses, staying in the best hotels and being entertained at high-class clubs, cocktail parties and fashionable luncheons. He was a serious drinker, later an alcoholic. The account of his visit to Dorothy Day places him on the far end of a continuum of sensitivity: "The bread line was forming for the noon meal as Waugh's car, a Cadillac, pulled up at the Catholic Worker's House of Hospitality. He immediately earned Day's disapproval by suggesting he take her and her staff to lunch at Le Chambord, one of the most expensive restaurants in the city" (53-54).

It was on this US visit that Waugh and Merton met at the Abbey of Gethsemani where both were mildly surprised at how the other looked. In his journal Merton writes: "I expected him [Waugh] to be taller and more dashing, but he was very nice and friendly" (56). As Coady notes, this latter phrase is bland and perhaps includes an added irony as from all accounts of Waugh the phrase "very nice and friendly" is not one that remotely springs to mind. She allows herself some speculation in this section, wondering whether the famous English writer "dressed in his tailor-made three-piece suit, fresh from the worldly elegance of high-society parties featuring caviar and fine wines" (57) became aware as a serious Christian of his personal shortcomings in the light of the stark abbey church and the young monks embracing a life of contemplation and sacrifice.

An interesting aspect of the book for this reviewer were the details given of the editing that was made by Waugh both for *The Seven Storey Mountain*, which became *Elected Silence* for a British readership, and his later editing of *The Waters of Siloe*, with the changed title of *The Waters of Silence*. His editing technique was usually to cut rather than to rewrite – Merton's phrases "in other words" and "this means" presaged a Waugh edit. He also took out sentences involving Merton's excessive self-castigation and what followed the word "because" – signaling over-explanation. Whole swathes of "unnecessary piety" were cut and paragraphs describing Merton's bitterness towards Cambridge were taken out because, as Waugh had written to Merton, he thought the problem lay with the student and his recklessness rather than with the university itself (see 65-68). The task of editing *The Waters of Siloe/Silence* appears in the end to have defeated him; he rearranged part of the book and cut the whole prologue but nearly half received little editing, with Waugh commenting: "I find I have bitten off more than my failing teeth can chew" (111).

As the relationship tapers off Coady offers an interesting Epilogue. She sees how Merton's confidence in his writing grew in the 1950s although he continued to "ponder ambivalently on his life as a writer" (139) and how writing competed and contrasted with his desire for greater solitude and silence. Waugh struggled with ill health and associated depression and felt bitter about the changes the Catholic Church was making. Merton notes in his journal for August 1964 a letter from "a crusty old man called Evelyn Waugh" (142) to the magazine *Commonweal* supporting conservatism; Merton continued "I understand conservatism – he is one of the genuine conservatives: he wishes to conserve not what might be lost but what is not even threatened because it vanished long ago" (142). As Coady insightfully notes, the bohemian Merton would always have clashed at some point with the established order that was essential to Waugh's world. Yet both men reflect through their writings their search for the absolute and in this they were united.

Fiona Gardner

MOSES, John, *Divine Discontent: The Prophetic Voice of Thomas Merton*, Foreword by Rowan Williams (New York: Bloomsbury, 2014), pp. xxiii + 242. ISBN 978-1-4411-8062-9 (cloth) $32.95.

Certain authors possess a magnetism. Their mirroring of our own discontent, our own experience of the human predicament, enthralls us. Thomas Merton is one of these authors. John Moses' *Divine Discontent: The Prophetic Voice of Thomas Merton* is a notable addition to the list of volumes prepared for the centennial of his birth. Moses seeks to understand the fascination we have with Merton, to comprehend his paradoxes, and to perceive his prophetic voice in eight chapters, preceded by a Foreword by Rowan Williams. Moses argues that the all-too-human contradictions and tensions of Merton's various vocations are forged into a prophetic voice replete with divine discontents.

The opening chapter explores the reasons for our enduring intrigue with Merton. His "compromised but compelling" (20) discipleship entices, drawing the reader to become invested in Merton's own questions and contradictions. Moses uses this opening chapter to set up the following five, each of which examines one of Merton's vocations: the call to monasticism, the urge to write, the necessity of contemplation, the responsibility to social criticism and the longing for ecumenical dialogue. While Moses understands these to compete in Merton for time and energy, they simultaneously fructify each other. Moses insists that Merton's primary calling was to life as a Trappist monk, which serves as the context, the desert soil, for his other vocations. At the same time, Gethsemani provides the stability and silence necessary for Merton's pursuit of the mystery of God and in doing so gives him the panoramic perspective from which he would offer wisdom to the world.

Moses masterfully weaves together the contradictions and discontents of the many sides of Merton to highlight the manner in which each deepened and enabled the others. For example, Moses argues that Merton's perception of his responsibility to engage the world sits in tension with his chosen life as a Trappist. Thus, while Merton feels compelled to write and is best known for it, contemplation is the real "heartbeat" (89) of his life. The austerity and *kenosis* of the contemplative life, which led Merton to encounter God, also provided him with the perspective and credibility to gain a hearing as a Christian social critic. For Moses, Merton's social criticism is unique precisely as a contribution offered by a *contemplative*. Again, the contradictions are fruitful. Merton's contemplative encounters with Christ functioned as the theological foundations of his criticism and directed him to highlight love as "the key to the meaning of the entire creation" (116) and to insist upon the dignity and freedom of human persons. These thoroughly Christian insights Merton brought to bear on the issues of his time: abuses of power, oppression and discrimination, war and peace, interreligious dialogue. *Divine Discontent* depicts monastic vocation and contemplative life as the impetus for Merton's dialogical quest for the divine. While renouncing all vapid and syncretistic forms of dialogue, Merton's Christological contemplation expanded the horizons of his ecumenism to include non-Christian religions. Ultimately, the shared experience of seeking after the divine led Merton to the East and to his untimely death.

After the comprehensive overview of Merton's many callings, *Divine Discontent* contends that his contradictions cannot adequately account either for the depths of his discontents or the profundity of our enduring intrigue. Thus Moses asks, "Is it the nature of the human condition that he is exposing, or is it something of the truth about himself? Is it a mirror that he is holding up before the reader, or is it a light that he is shining into the depth of his own psyche?" (166). Moses prudently avoids any eisegesis of Merton's writing or psychoanalysis of his mind, allowing Merton and his correspondents to lead the reader to infer that Merton's contradictions do not represent neurosis, but natural human reactions to the problems of life. Yet Moses pushes further, asking whether Merton might be "a study in *divine* discontent" (171) and arguing that Merton's "long desert of difficulties" experienced in the Abbey of Gethsemani led to "the element of transfiguration that makes it possible to speak of *divine* discontent" (174). Moses leads the reader to ask whether she hears in Merton the voice of one whose encounter with God compels him to give voice to the divine displeasure with the way things are.

The concluding chapter, "A Prophetic Voice" (183-211), asks whether Merton's desert transfiguration validates the perception of a truly prophetic expression of *divine* discontent in the American monk. Merton, Moses maintains, not only addressed a number of relevant issues, but through them, prophetically identified the dominant crisis of his day: alienation – "men and women's estrangement from God and from their deepest selves as human beings" (189). Moses concludes that Merton indeed speaks with a prophetic voice, offering evocative images of the theological humanism needed to address alienation. The many faces of Merton, replete with their contradictions and his discontents, may ultimately serve as his credentials "to a world that struggles to come to terms with its persistent and enduring experience of alienation" (211). For those of us who, like John Moses, remain fascinated by Thomas Merton, the credentials remain valid. "The voice continues to be heard" (211).

Throughout, Moses successfully narrates the tensions and mutually supporting accents of Merton's vocations with Merton's own words. The image which emerges is not a vapid two-dimensional copy of Merton twisted to fit the author's pet interests, but the voice of Merton speaking from within his discontents to the world, compelling and challenging as always. *Divine Discontent* is an enjoyable read. One need not be a Merton aficionado to understand the book. Yet, even the most avid Merton reader can benefit from what Rowan Williams describes as a "coherent and comprehensive" (xi) reminder of why Merton still matters.

Although the book is not a difficult read and despite the fact that I agree with Moses that Merton's voice still matters and might be called prophetic, I am not sure the argument convinced me. Moses does not adequately deal with the problems of Merton's failures as a monk, most notably the affair with "M.," which might detract from the claim that he prophetically gives voice to divine discontent. I think the problems could be addressed, but Moses does not do so sufficiently. If Moses did not convince me, Merton did. Since Moses does succeed in letting Merton speak for himself, the prophetic quality of his voice shines through. The world has undergone tremendous change in the nearly five decades since Merton's death, yet his concerns remain relevant. People remain alienated from God, from each other, and from themselves. War remains a global problem. Ecumenical and interreligious dialogue could go a long way to easing strife and building peace. *Divine Discontent* is a welcome reminder of the wisdom and challenge of Merton's voice, a voice whose discontents we'd be wise to heed.

Joshua Brumfield

PRAMUK, Christopher, *At Play in Creation: Merton's Awakening to the Feminine Divine* (Collegeville, MN: Liturgical Press, 2015), pp. xii + 138. ISBN 978-0-8146-4816-2 (paper) $17.95.

Christopher Pramuk describes *At Play in Creation* as a "crystallization" (x) of his widely acclaimed volume, *Sophia: The Hidden Christ of Thomas Merton* – an illuminating and ground-breaking study of Merton's sapiential Christological vision.[1] In 2011, The International Thomas Merton Society recognized the publication of *Sophia* by awarding Christopher Pramuk a "Louie" for "bringing provocative insight and fresh direction to Merton Studies." Pramuk characterizes *At Play in Creation* as a collection of "retreat conferences" (x). As such, each chapter, although integral to the book as a whole, is nevertheless complete in itself. Reading the chapters and ruminating on each – one by one – would be very much in sync with Pramuk's conception of the essays as conferences. The somewhat conversational tone of the book, which grew out of presentations in a host of settings – retreats, workshops and the like, is engaging and invites reflection and dialogue with the text. The sense that one is hearing Pramuk speak is enhanced by his interjection of personally revelatory anecdotes about his family as well as his sharing of the story of his own encounters and engagement with Merton's writings. Built on a foundation of a deep and meticulous scholarship, the book is guaranteed to delight readers across the spectrum – those new to Merton and those deeply immersed in his writings.

*At Play in Creation* is as appealing in appearance as it is profound in content. The cover, printed on textured card stock enhanced by French flaps, features an ink drawing by Thomas Merton entitled "Christ Unveils the Meaning of the Old Testament" that visually illustrates the subtitle, *Merton's Awakening to the Feminine Divine*. The cover image appears again in the book, along with three additional Merton ink drawings, a photo of the young Tom Merton peeking out from behind a door and a haunting photo of Etty Hillesum. These images alternate with carefully chosen epigraphs to draw the reader into the book's chapters. The back

1. Christopher Pramuk, *Sophia: The Hidden Christ of Thomas Merton* (Collegeville, MN: Liturgical Press, 2009).

cover features a photograph of Merton, taken during the 1960s by Merton's friend Gene Meatyard.

In addition to an Introduction, there are nine chapters. The title of each is a carefully chosen phrase that not only highlights the theme of the chapter but also serves as a focal point for meditation: I. "Rivers of Night"; II. "Liminal Spaces"; III. "Dawn of Wisdom"; IV. "From End to End Mightily"; V. "The Night Face of Sophia"; VI. "Bearer of Hope"; VII. "She Cannot Be a Prisoner"; VIII. "Breathe in the Air"; and IX. "To Say Something Worthy of God." Pramuk's endnotes (119-38) deserve special mention; in addition to providing the customary citations, many notes suggest related readings and fresh lines of inquiry.

Throughout the book, Pramuk is drawing on Merton's *Hagia Sophia*,[2] written in the spring of 1961, a prose poem Pramuk sees as a quintessential expression of the fruit of contemplative spirituality and a catalyst for his witness to peace and justice. In the first chapter of the book, "Rivers of Night" (1-11), Pramuk tells us how he "was hooked" (1) by Merton at the age of fifteen and in subsequent years discovered how Merton calls us back to our deepest selves to "hear again the music of our faith" (2). Then, reading Merton after 9/11, Pramuk was "haunted" (5) by *Hagia Sophia*, the poem Merton wrote during "a season of fury" (6) in the sixties. Ending with a reprise of Merton's biography, Pramuk emphasizes Merton's stirrings and awakenings. In the second chapter, "Liminal Spaces" (13-19), Pramuk highlights "Merton's 'sapiential,' 'sophianic,' or Wisdom-haunted way of seeing" (13). As a "poet of the liminal spaces of our lives" (15), who recognized the Incarnation as an ongoing event, Merton invites us to awaken "in mystery to our essential kinship with the whole cosmos" (21) and to join in the "general dance" (25) about which he writes so movingly in the concluding chapter of *New Seeds of Contemplation*.[3]

Chapters III and IV, "Dawn of Wisdom" (27-38) and "From End to End Mightily" (41-48), focus on *Hagia Sophia*. Pramuk identifies the "constellation of events" (38) in the late fifties that led to the breakthrough of Sophia in Merton's own life and culminated in the writing of the prose poem: his reading of Russian theologians; his dream of Proverb; his epiphany at Fourth and Walnut; his viewing of artist friend Victor Hammer's triptych, "Hagia Sophia Crowning the Young Christ." The writing of *Hagia Sophia*, Pramuk observes, coincided with the writing of the "Prayer to God the Father on the Vigil of Pentecost," which Merton recorded in

2. Thomas Merton, *Emblems of a Season of Fury* (New York: New Directions, 1963) 61-69; subsequent references will be cited as "*ESF*" parenthetically in the text.

3. Thomas Merton, *New Seeds of Contemplation* (New York: New Directions, 1961) 290-97.

his journal[4] and later included in *Conjectures of a Guilty Bystander*.[5] In the prayer, Merton asks for the "the courage to 'be a man of peace and to help bring peace to the world,' to learn the way 'of truth and nonviolence,' and for the grace to accept whatever difficult consequences might follow" (33). Reflecting on the third and fourth sections of *Hagia Sophia*, Pramuk highlights two important themes: "the wonder of Sophia's reception in the world of creatures" by creatures who give "glory to God simply 'by being themselves'" (44); and Sophia as the "'mercy of God in us'" (45). Pramuk also discusses the "mysterious ink drawing" (46) reproduced on the book's cover and on page 40, "Christ Unveils the Meaning of the Old Testament." The drawing "celebrates, if obscurely, the *wholeness* of God, the integral fullness of the *imago Dei*, male and female, realized (made real) wherever human beings seek to be and become Love in the rough and beautiful tumble of their ordinary lives" (47). In Merton's words (*ESF* 62-63): "Gentleness comes to him when he is most helpless and awakens him, refreshed, beginning to be made whole. Love takes him by the hand, and opens to him the door to another life, another day" (47). The final scene of *Hagia Sophia* (*ESF* 69) is of a "homeless God" (48) – a testament to the "piercing loneliness" of God (47).

In Chapter V, entitled "The Night Face of Sophia" (51-58), Pramuk draws attention to a passage Thomas Merton wrote in January, 1965 in which Merton reflects on "living together with wisdom" (52) and records a thought that came to him during meditation. Pramuk quotes the somewhat lengthy passage, recorded in Merton's journal *Dancing in the Water of Life*.[6] It merits a place in this review as well because it illustrates so powerfully what all who seek to live together with wisdom today need to recognize and confront:

> The error of racism is the logical consequence of an essentialist style of thought. Finding out what a man is and then nailing him to a definition so that there can be no change. A White Man is a White Man, and that is it. A Negro, even though he is three parts white is "A Negro" with all that our rigid definition predicates of a Negro. And so the logical machine can devour him because of his essence. Do you think that in an era of existentialism this will get better?

4. Thomas Merton, *Turning Toward the World: The Pivotal Years. Journals, vol. 4: 1960-1963*, ed. Victor A. Kramer (San Francisco: HarperCollins, 1996) 120-21.

5. Thomas Merton, *Conjectures of a Guilty Bystander* (Garden City, NY: Doubleday, 1966) 159-61.

6. Thomas Merton, *Dancing in the Water of Life: Seeking Peace in the Hermitage. Journals, vol. 5: 1963-1965*, ed. Robert E. Daggy (San Francisco: HarperCollins, 1997) 200-201.

On the contrary: definitions, more and more schematic, are fed into computers. The machines are meditating on the most arbitrary and rudimentary of essences, punched into IBM cards, and defining you and me forever without appeal. "A priest," "A Negro," "A Jew," "A Socialist," etc. (52)

In his dreams and waking hours, Merton confronted the "'the dark face, the "night face" of Sophia,' the Child bound and disfigured by 'the world of rapacious men,'" and in her, Christ still crucified (54). Turning to Merton's relationship with M., the student nurse with whom Merton fell in love in 1966, Pramuk quotes a revealing passage from Merton's journal *Learning to Love*:[7] "Strange connection in my deepest heart – between M. and the 'Wisdom' figure – and Mary – and the Feminine in the Bible – Eve, etc. – Paradise – Most Mysterious, haunting, deep, lovely, moving, transforming!" (56). Merton's love for M. enabled him to "believe – that is, to experience and trust – that at the base of all reality is the wisdom of Love, Sophia, a wisdom which deepens whenever we truly love another person" (57). Reading Merton's relationship with M. in the context of Merton's encounters with Sophia opens the door to viewing Merton's falling in love with M. as one of a number of epiphanies of Merton's life.

In Chapter VI, "Bearer of Hope" (61-69), Pramuk strikes a chord that is particularly germane for our times: "the breakthrough of Sophia corresponds with the crisis of hope in the human community" (61). Mindful of the times in which Merton was writing *Hagia Sophia* and of the times in which we are living, I find myself resonating with Pramuk's thesis: "Hope in the key of Wisdom awakens 'that freedom which we have often looked for,' drawing us into the future, the future of God's own imagining" (63). Sophia is "the great stabilizer" (61) in the face of evil and suffering. As Merton expressed it in *Hagia Sophia* (*ESF* 61-62), "It is like the One Christ awakening in all the separate selves that ever were separate and isolated and alone in all the lands of the earth. It is like all minds coming back together into awareness from all distractions, cross-purposes and confusions, into unity of love" (63).

As in Chapter VI he remembers the words of hope written by Fr. Alfred Delp, a Jesuit priest executed by the Nazis,[8] in Chapter VII, "She Cannot Be a Prisoner" (71-85), Pramuk honors the memory of Etty

---

7. Thomas Merton, *Learning to Love: Exploring Solitude and Freedom. Journals, vol. 6: 1966-1967*, ed. Christine M. Bochen (San Francisco: HarperCollins, 1997) 131.

8. See Thomas Merton, "The Prison Meditations of Father Delp," in *Faith and Violence: Christian Teaching and Christian Practice* (Notre Dame, IN: University of Notre Dame Press, 1968) 47-68.

Hillesum, a twenty-nine-year-old Dutch Jew executed at Auschwitz. The title of the chapter captures the freedom of Hillesum's spirit – a freedom that could not be extinguished by "cruelty and arbitrary violence" (81). In her diary, published under the title of *An Interrupted Life*,[9] Hillesum wrote: "at unguarded moments, when left to myself, I suddenly lie against the naked breast of life, and her arms round me are so gentle and so protective" (72). In another passage, she records a prayer in which she identifies what really matters: "that we safeguard that little piece of You, God, in ourselves" (74). In women consenting to the divine presence – in Mary the Mother of Jesus, in Hillesum, in women demanding justice such as Sr. Dorothy Stang, the "Mothers of the Disappeared," Somaly Mam and other Cambodian women; in women of the Bible such as Hagar and Mary Magdalen; in literary characters and artists – in all these women and the multitude of others, women and men who go unnamed, "divine Wisdom cries out from the crossroads in protest, identifying herself especially with the little, the hidden, and the forgotten ones and with suffering earth, the Mother of all God's children" (82-83). In Merton's words (*ESF* 64), Wisdom-Sophia "cannot be a prisoner" (83). "Hope in the key of Wisdom," Pramuk concludes, "refuses to accommodate itself to the lock-tight logic of The Way Things Are as preached by the powers and principalities in society or church" (84).

The title of Chapter VIII, "Breathe in the Air" (87-95), is inspired by African-American theologian Howard Thurman, who recalled walking a Florida beach at night:[10] "I had the sense that all things, the sand, the sea, the stars, the night, and I were one lung through which all of life breathed. Not only was I aware of a vast rhythm enveloping all, but I was a part of it and it was a part of me" (89). Thurman's unitive vision is not merely descriptive; it is prescriptive – as is Merton's. Breathing in the air is breathing *in* Sophia-Wisdom – breathing *Her in* and breathing *in Her*. So doing, we come "to see with eyes of mercy and love" (93).

Noting that the whole book "has circled around the question of God, and thus, the struggle for faith, hope, and love, in unsettling times," Pramuk begins the last chapter, "To Say Something Worthy of God" (97-109), with this simple, but nonetheless profound, observation: "So much depends on our image of God! So much depends

---

9. Etty Hillesum, *An Interrupted Life and Letters from Westerbork* (New York: Henry Holt, 1996).

10. Howard Thurman, *With Head and Heart: The Autobiography of Howard Thurman* (New York: Harcourt Brace, 1979).

on our idea of humanity" (97). Merton guides us as we seek to see God as God is and to see humanity as it is – knowing the discovery of God and self-discovery are two aspects of a single movement. As prophet and poet, Merton "unveil[s]" Sophia as "the power of God's mercy" (99), thus showing us who God is and who we are. Drawing from Walter Brueggemann's book *The Prophetic Imagination*,[11] Pramuk notes that the prophet and the poet "must speak for a silent God" (103). Prophets draw us into "the breach," and poets, Merton wrote,[12] "help us to get back to ourselves before it is too late" (103). Inspired by Merton's Sophia-God, we can, as Pramuk does, see God not only as a person in Jesus Christ but as Woman, Mother, Child, Lover, Sister, Companion, Friend (104). In closing, Pramuk returns full circle to his pre-eminent theme: "*Sophia, the feminine child, is playing in the world, obvious and unseen, playing at all times before the Creator*" (107; *ESF* 66).

This book is a must-read. In it, Merton's life, theology and spirituality come alive in a way that can make a difference in how we see God and ourselves as well as how we read and understand Merton. This is not just another book about Merton. Rather, Pramuk challenges the reader to take Merton seriously as a spiritual and moral guide and thus to go "beyond Merton." While he contextualizes Merton's experience and vision in his own times, Pramuk urges the readers to respond to our times as Merton did to his. Just as Merton interjected "the gentle voice of Sophia" into what he termed "a season of fury," so too must we awaken to Sophia in our own time of fury. In his Introduction to *At Play in Creation*, Pramuk expresses an aim in the form of "an author's humble prayer: that these pages might stir in others what awakens in me as I engage Merton's dance with Sophia – a renewed sense of God's nearness and friendship, and above all a fierce hope, rising not from any formal 'theology' as such but divined from the hidden matrices of life itself, Life made from Love. For Wisdom 'cries out to all who will hear, and she cries out particularly to the little, to the ignorant and the helpless'" (xi). It is not enough to be content with learning what Merton had to say about Sophia-Wisdom; we need to awaken to the life-giving presence of Sophia-Wisdom as Merton did and then to live joyfully and justly with one another in Her presence on this earth that is our common home.

Christine M. Bochen

---

11. Walter Brueggemann, *The Prophetic Imagination* (Minneapolis: Fortress, 2001).

12. See Thomas Merton, *The Literary Essays of Thomas Merton*, ed. Patrick Hart, OCSO (New York: New Directions, 1981) 340.

HIGGINS, Michael W., *The Unquiet Monk: Thomas Merton's Questing Faith* (Maryknoll, NY: Orbis Books, 2015), pp. 126. ISBN 978-1-62698-112-6 (paper) $15.00.

Michael W. Higgins is no stranger to those in the world of Merton studies. He is the current president of the International Thomas Merton Society and has published widely on Merton. In addition to numerous academic and popular articles, Higgins is the author of several books on Merton, including *Heretic Blood: The Spiritual Geography of Thomas Merton* (1998) and *Thomas Merton: Faithful Visionary* (2014), as well as co-editing *Thomas Merton: Pilgrim in Process* (1983).

The genesis of Higgins' most recent book, *The Unquiet Monk: Thomas Merton's Questing Faith*, can be found in two events that occurred in 1978 – a symposium on the life and thought of Merton at the Vancouver School of Theology and the creation of a radio documentary entitled *Thomas Merton: Extraordinary Man* which aired on CBC Radio to coincide with the tenth anniversary of Merton's death in Bangkok. Higgins was heavily involved in both the symposium and the radio documentary, with the documentary relying in large part on the scholarship that emerged from the symposium. As Higgins notes in the acknowledgements, *The Unquiet Monk* is structured along the lines of the documentary and draws upon previously unpublished interviews and proceedings from the program itself. At the same time, Higgins also draws upon his own subsequent research as well as upon the waves of Merton scholarship since 1978.

The book contains six chapters, although the sixth is essentially a brief conclusion of two pages (123-24). The first (11-38) is a concise but thorough biography of Merton that incorporates extensive quotations from Merton's books and recordings from his talks to the novices. The narrative is also punctuated by the insights of prominent scholars such as Donald Grayston and Christine Bochen, as well as by friends of Merton such as John Howard Griffin and Br. Paul Quenon. In each of the following chapters, Higgins follows this pattern of supplementing his account with extended quotations from scholars and friends. The second chapter, entitled "Window, Tower and Circle: The Poetic Merton" (39-66), introduces the reader to Merton's autobiographical works and poetry. Given the breadth of Merton's autobiographical writings, and given that Higgins has extensively studied his poetry, it comes as no surprise that this is the longest chapter of the book. The third chapter, "Solitary Critic" (67-86), examines Merton's engagement with the issues of war and racial injustice, paying close attention to the interchange between contemplation and engagement with the world. In the fourth chapter, "Merton's

Religious Imagination" (87-103), Higgins looks at Merton's spirituality, examining both his understanding of contemplation and how this understanding translated into ecumenical and interreligious dialogue. A more thorough examination of Merton's interreligious study and dialogue follows in the fifth chapter, "Pilgrim to the East" (104-22). Here the focus is primarily on Merton's engagement with Eastern religions, specifically Zen Buddhism, and the chapter ends with an account of the significance of Merton's Asian journey.

Higgins writes beautifully and with the characteristic enthusiasm that he brings to his projects. He also writes accessibly. *The Unquiet Monk* serves as an excellent introduction to the life and thought of Thomas Merton both because it concisely covers the main parameters of his biography and writings, and because it immerses readers in the voices of prominent Merton scholars and friends. As someone who is frequently asked for recommendations for where to start with Merton, I would heartily recommend this book as a jumping-off point towards reading Merton himself. Moreover, for those who teach courses on Merton, each of the book's chapters provides worthwhile introductions to various facets of Merton's thought that could be used as a guide prior to engaging the writings themselves. Higgins' chapter on Merton's autobiographical writings and his poetry is particularly valuable in this regard, not least because of its clear and concise introduction to Merton's poetry, arguably the least accessible facet of his corpus. But Higgins' book is not just for Mertonian beginners. For those already familiar with Merton, *The Unquiet Monk* has the potential to rekindle enthusiasm for a man whose writings continue to inspire and convict.

Gregory K. Hillis

MCGREGOR, Michael N., *Pure Act: The Uncommon Life of Robert Lax* (New York: Fordham University Press, 2015), pp. 472. ISBN 978-0-82326-801-6 (cloth) $34.95.

In 1985 Michael McGregor journeyed to Europe with questions. He had spent the previous three years traveling the world, writing about the systematic oppression that characterizes the existence of so many on this planet, keeping them impoverished. McGregor had reached a point where he felt he had to respond to such suffering concretely, that he couldn't just write about it but wanted to devote himself more fully to finding a grand solution that he was young enough to believe possible to find. So he quit his job, sold his car and flew to Europe in search of answers. After six months he made it to Greece, and by this time, having decided to write a novel about his experiences, he looked for a removed place to think and write. A Greek island, any Greek island, seemed to fit the bill, so he boarded the next ferry out, whose first stop was Patmos. However, before departing, he stopped in an English-language bookstore and happened upon an inexpensive copy of Thomas Merton's *The Seven Storey Mountain*, a book he had heard about but never read. McGregor read the book in the evenings he spent in the chilly apartment he rented. He loved the book, but what most appealed to him was the famous interaction between Merton and Robert Lax, in which Lax asked Merton what he wanted to be and, dissatisfied with Merton's answer, told him that he should want to be a saint, and that all he needed to do to become one was to desire it. McGregor was taken by this idea, and resolved to look up Lax in other books when he returned home. It was only on the boat ride away from Patmos – the days had become too cold for him to stay – that McGregor learned that Lax actually lived on the island he had just left. On his subsequent return to Patmos, McGregor decided to find Lax, leaving a note for him at the post office to ask if he would meet at a nearby pub. Lax came to the pub, and the two struck up a friendship that lasted until Lax's death in 2000.

Because of his personal connection to Lax, *Pure Act: The Uncommon Life of Robert Lax* is more than just a biography of the late poet based on research in archives, though McGregor has done plenty of that. It is also in part a beautiful account of a friendship between an established writer and a man searching for a vocation and meaning. Interspersed throughout the book, therefore, are invaluable personal vignettes that give us glimpses into Lax as friend and spiritual director. In this way we learn that conversation with Lax involved both long silences and laughter so exuberant that Lax would fall to the floor. And we learn that Lax "didn't force his views or wisdom on you but stated them plainly in the course of conversation, enthusiastic enough to want to offer a thought but patient and polite enough to wait his turn" (15). Most chapters begin with a brief personal story either about McGregor's interaction with Lax or about something McGregor encountered in the course of his research related to the chapter itself. To place himself so fully in the narrative was a risky move for McGregor, for to do so chances obscuring the subject matter and/or disrupting the flow of the narrative. Neither is the case in this book, for the personal vignettes end up illuminating Lax as a person in addition to demonstrating the clear effect one person can have on another – in this case, the role played in shaping and directing McGregor as a writer and seeker.

Lax's journey wove its way through an education at Columbia –

where he met those who would become his closest friends, especially Merton – through short stints working for magazines such as *The New Yorker* and *Jubilee*, through brief tenures as a teacher or visiting professor at various colleges, through finally finding his identity and home in Europe, particularly on the Greek islands of Mytilene and Patmos, where he would spend most of the last half of his life. The principle that McGregor says governed Lax's life was his pursuit of what Lax came to call "pure act." A student of Thomas Aquinas, Lax adapted Aquinas' understanding of God as "pure act" and "pure love" in contrast to a universe that is always in *potentia*, and Lax understood that we can become "pure act" ourselves when we act consciously and yet spontaneously. When we do this we become like God, provided we act in love. Lax witnessed what he understood to be pure act in perhaps unexpected places. In an interview late in his life, Lax talked about his love of jazz and particularly his love for jam sessions when all the customers have left and the musicians are simply playing for each other and with each other. Each musician is fully conscious of the present moment, of himself, and also of the other musicians, such that they are able to improvise and yet still remain in harmony with one another. Lax understood this ability to be consciously in the moment in a way that led both oneself and others to flourish, to be "pure act" in the flesh. Lax saw other examples of this elsewhere in circus performers. From an early age Lax was fascinated with the circus, and in 1949 he had the opportunity to travel with the Cristianis, a circus family who were the most famous bareback riders in the world. Here again Lax saw what he viewed as pure act, the ability to exist and be so fully present and in the moment as to create something of profound beauty. While with the Cristianis, Lax even performed as a clown, but more importantly, he learned from them how to live moment by moment, fully present. And when Lax went to the Greek island of Kalymnos, where he ended up living for years before moving to Patmos, McGregor argues that Lax witnessed an entire community living out what he saw as pure act. He saw there a place where people truly lived, a striving without striving, a way of existing in the world without conforming to the illusory notions of success tied to financial gain.

McGregor compellingly suggests that this understanding of pure act came to govern Lax's own life. He was most miserable when he conformed his identity to the measures of economic success and the success of being known as a writer. He found peace when he abandoned such measures and instead chose to imitate those who lived in pure act, and to devote himself to a life lived in the moment, consciously but spontaneously. And it is for this reason that Lax ended up living a minimalist life on

Patmos. Moreover, this approach to life profoundly affected his poetry, which become more spare, "reducing whatever he saw and valued to its essentials – its 'purity' – and conveying his 'reverence' for what he saw, a reverence akin to the mystic's ecstatic vision" (289).

Robert Lax emerges from the pages of McGregor's biography as an immensely compelling person and writer, and someone who merits far more attention than he currently receives. McGregor's book travels a great distance in filling the gaps, but it also points toward further research that could and should be done. McGregor does a wonderful job of giving us a window into Lax's personality, and his analysis of Lax's poetry in the context of his life is helpful. What is not examined thoroughly enough is an understanding of Lax as a contemplative thinker. While McGregor devotes extensive attention to the friendship between Merton and Lax, I would have liked him also to devote attention to an examination of Lax's conversion to Roman Catholicism and the way in which his Catholicism influenced his understanding of contemplation and the spiritual life. We get hints at this in *Pure Act*, but more work needs to be done on Lax the contemplative.

Overall, *Pure Act* is a beautifully written and captivating work that will no doubt spur on further research into a man whose way of existing and approaching the world continues to have something to say to us today.

Gregory K. Hillis

# Contributors

*Kathleen M. Baker* is associate professor of geography and director of the W. E. Upjohn Center for the Study of Geographical Change at Western Michigan University. While most of her writing is for scientific journals, her poetry has been published in *The Wayfarer*, *Penwood Review*, *The Merton Journal* and *The Merton Seasonal*.

*John Eudes Bamberger, OCSO* was born in 1926 and received an MD from the University of Cincinnati in 1949. After interning at Georgetown University Hospital, he entered the Abbey of Gethsemani in 1950, took his final vows in 1955, and was ordained a priest in 1956. He returned to Georgetown as a resident in psychiatry for two years. He studied theology in Rome from 1969-1970. At Gethsemani, he served as Master of Students and Novice Master, and was Secretary General of the Cistercian Praesidium. He was Abbot of the Genesee from 1971 until his retirement in 2001, after which he lived as a hermit, briefly interrupted to serve as Superior of Guimaras in the Philippines. He is the author of *Thomas Merton, Prophet of Renewal* (2005).

*Ian Bell* is Professor of Religious Studies at Siena Heights University, Adrian, Michigan, where he teaches courses in systematic and biblical theology and also serves as chair of the humanities division. His research interests focus on mystical-political theology, especially in the context of the thought of Bernard Lonergan.

*Christine M. Bochen*, Professor of Religious Studies and holder of the William H. Shannon Chair of Catholic Studies at Nazareth College, Rochester, New York, is a founding member and former president of the International Thomas Merton Society. She has edited numerous works by Thomas Merton, including *The Courage for Truth*, the fourth volume of Merton's collected letters, and *Learning to Love*, the sixth volume of his complete journals; she co-edited, with William H. Shannon, *Thomas Merton: A Life in Letters* and *Cold War Letters*, and is co-author with William H. Shannon and Patrick F. O'Connell of *The Thomas Merton Encyclopedia*.

*Mark Bosco, SJ* is Associate Professor of English and Theology at Loyola University Chicago, and the director of Loyola's Joan and Bill

Hanks Center for the Catholic Intellectual Heritage. His main research focuses on the intersection of religion and art. He is the author of *Graham Greene's Catholic Imagination* (2005), and editor of *Finding God in All Things: Celebrating Bernard Lonergan, John Courtney Murray, and Karl Rahner* (2007). A collection of essays on Flannery O'Connor published by Catholic University of America Press is forthcoming in 2017. His current research includes a full-length documentary on the life of Flannery O'Connor, *Mystery and Manners*, now in postproduction, for the PBS series *American Masters*.

*Jason M. Brown* grew up in Southern California and studied anthropology at Brigham Young University as an undergraduate. His master's work was in Forestry and Theology at Yale, where he received joint master's degrees. He is currently a Ph.D. candidate at the University of British Columbia in Vancouver. His research specialty focuses on Religion and Ecology, Spiritual Ecology and Phenomenology of Sacred Landscapes.

*Joshua Brumfield* is Assistant Professor of Theology at the University of Holy Cross in New Orleans, where he also serves as Coordinator for Undergraduate Theology.

*David Chang* is an educator with teaching experience in Japan, Mexico and Canada. He taught secondary English for a decade before working as a teacher-educator at Simon Fraser University, in Vancouver, British Columbia. He completed his master's degree at the University of British Columbia; his thesis explored the intersection between neuroscience, meditation and ecology. He is currently a Ph.D. candidate in the Faculty of Education at SFU, where he studies ecological ethics and contemplative inquiry. As a philosopher, Zen meditator, musician and ecologist, he aims to integrate intellectual investigation with contemplative practice, music with conceptual exploration, human relationships with ecological ethics.

*Anthony E. Clark* is Edward B. Lindaman Endowed Chair and Associate Professor of Chinese History at Whitworth University, Spokane, Washington. He is author of *Heaven in Conflict: Franciscans and the Boxer Uprising in Shanxi* (2015) and *China's Saints: Catholic Martyrdom during the Qing* (2011). His research focuses on the intellectual exchange between Asia and the West.

*Fiona Gardner* is a psychoanalytic psychotherapist, spiritual director and writer living in the United Kingdom. She is the author of *Journeying Home* (2004), *The Four Steps of Love* (2007), *Precious Thoughts* (2011) and *The Only Mind Worth Having: Thomas Merton and the Child Mind*

(2015) as well as psychoanalytic books and articles. Former chair of the Thomas Merton Society of Great Britain and Ireland (2004-2008) and former coeditor of *The Merton Journal* (2008-14), she is currently a member of the Board of Directors of the International Thomas Merton Society and was awarded a "Louie" in 2015 at the ITMS Centenary Conference.

*Donald Grayston* is a retired priest of the Anglican diocese of New Westminster, British Columbia. For fifteen years he taught Religious Studies at Simon Fraser University, during the last three of which he was also the director of the Institute for the Humanities. A past president of the Thomas Merton Society of Canada (2003-05) and the International Thomas Merton Society (2007-09), his most recent book is *Thomas Merton and the Noonday Demon: The Camaldoli Correspondence* (2015). He has also edited Thomas Merton's *Solitude and Resistance: Thomas Merton's "Day of a Stranger"* (forthcoming). Between 1988 and 2011, he was director of the Pacific Jubilee Program in Spiritual Formation and Spiritual Direction, and the initiator of Jubilee Associates, a Canadian network of spiritual direction programs. Since retirement from SFU in 2004, he has been actively involved in promoting public response to the Israeli-Palestinian conflict.

*Gregory K. Hillis*, a native of Alberta, Canada, joined the faculty of Bellarmine University in the Department of Theology in August 2008. He is an historical theologian with particular expertise in the patristic period (2nd-8th centuries) of Christian history and theology. His research and teaching interests also include Christian spirituality, ecclesiology, sacramental theology, nineteenth- and twentieth-century Roman Catholic theology, Thomas Merton and Eastern Christian history and theology. He regularly writes brief reflections on theology and spirituality on his blog *My Unquiet Heart*.

*Daniel P. Horan, OFM* is a Franciscan friar who teaches systematic theology and spirituality at the Catholic Theological Union in Chicago. A columnist for *America* Magazine, he is the author of numerous articles and several books including the award-winning *The Franciscan Heart of Thomas Merton: A New Look at His Life, Thought, and Writing* (2014). He currently serves on the Board of Directors of the ITMS and is a former William H. Shannon Fellow and ITMS Daggy Scholar. His current projects include editing the correspondence between Thomas Merton and Naomi Burton Stone.

*Gray Matthews*, Assistant Professor of Communication at the University of Memphis, is a former co-editor of *The Merton Annual*. He has served on the International Thomas Merton Society (ITMS) Board of Directors and on various committees and was site coordinator of the 2007 ITMS General Meeting in Memphis. He has been a regular presenter at ITMS conferences and has published articles and reviews in *The Merton Annual* and *The Merton Seasonal*.

*Michael N. McGregor* is a professor of Creative Writing and English at Portland State University. His book *Pure Act: The Uncommon Life of Robert Lax* received awards for literary excellence from the Association of Catholic Publishers and the Catholic Press Association and was a finalist for a Washington State Book Award and the Religion News Association's Excellence in Nonfiction Religion Book Award.

*Patrick F. O'Connell*, Professor of English and Theology at Gannon University, Erie, Pennsylvania, is a founding member and former president of the International Thomas Merton Society and editor of *The Merton Seasonal*. He is co-author (with William H. Shannon and Christine M. Bochen) of *The Thomas Merton Encyclopedia* (2002) and has edited eight volumes of Thomas Merton's monastic conferences, most recently *The Cistercian Fathers and Their Monastic Theology* (2016), as well as Merton's *Selected Essays* (2013) and *Early Essays: 1947-1952* (2015).

*Padraic O'Hare* is Professor of Religious and Theological Studies at Merrimack College in North Andover, Massachusetts, where he regularly conducts courses on Dorothy Day and Thomas Merton; he was the founder (1993) and for 18 years the director of the school's Center for the Study of Jewish–Christian–Muslim Relations. He is the author and/or editor of eight books on contemplation education, interfaith relations and religious education.

*Gordon Oyer* holds an M.A. in history from the University of Illinois at Urbana-Champaign and recently retired from an administrative position with the University of Illinois system. His book *Pursuing the Spiritual Roots of Protest* received a 2015 Louie award. He currently serves as co-chair of the International Thomas Merton Society Nominations Committee.

*Paul M. Pearson*, Director of the Thomas Merton Center at Bellarmine University, Louisville, Kentucky and Chief of Research for the Thomas Merton Legacy Trust, is Resident Secretary of the International Thomas Merton Society, which he served as tenth president. He has edited *Seeking Paradise: Merton and the Shakers* (2003), *A Meeting of Angels: The Correspondence of Thomas Merton with Edward Deming & Faith Andrews* (2008) and *Thomas Merton on Christian Contemplation* (2012).

*Michael Plekon* is a professor in the department of Sociology/Anthropology and the Program in Religion and Culture of Baruch College of the City University of New York, where he has taught for almost forty years. He is a priest in the Orthodox Church in America, attached to St. Gregory the Theologian Church, Wappingers Falls, New York. He is the author of numerous books, most recently *Uncommon Prayer* (2016).

*Christian Raab, OSB* is a Benedictine monk of Saint Meinrad Archabbey, St. Meinrad, Indiana, where he has held positions as Associate Vocation Director and Coordinator of the One Bread One Cup College Ministry Internship Program. In 2015 he successfully completed doctoral studies at the Catholic University of America in Washington, DC, where he also served in association with campus ministry. His dissertation investigated the theology of religious priesthood. He is Assistant Professor of Systematic Theology at Saint Meinrad Seminary and School of Theology.

*Joseph Q. Raab* is professor of Religious Studies and Theology at Siena Heights University in Adrian, Michigan, where he also directs the Liberal Arts Studies Core Seminar Program. He did his graduate studies at the Toronto School of Theology, where he earned an S.T.L. (Regis) and a Ph.D. (St. Michael's), with a dissertation on Thomas Merton and D. T. Suzuki. He has served as co-editor of *The Merton Annual* since 2012.

*Angus Stuart*, an Anglican priest currently living in Vancouver, British Columbia, is former Chair of the Thomas Merton Society of Great Britain and Ireland (2002-2004) and has been a board member of the Thomas Merton Society of Canada since 2005. He was editor of two volumes of conference papers from the British Merton Society: *With the World in My Bloodstream* (2002) and *Across the Rim of Chaos* (2005) and co-edited with Ross Labrie the volume *Thomas Merton: Monk on the Edge* (2012). He has written and spoken widely on Thomas Merton, with a particular interest in Merton and the American counterculture.

*Monica Weis, SSJ*, Professor Emerita of English at Nazareth College, Rochester, New York, has long been active in the International Thomas Merton Society and has presented extensively on Merton and nature. She is the author of *Thomas Merton's Gethsemani: Landscapes of Paradise* (2005), *The Environmental Vision of Thomas Merton* (2011) and *Thomas Merton and the Celts: A New World Opening Up* (2016).

# Index

# The International Thomas Merton Society

The ITMS came into being in 1987 to promote a greater knowledge of the life and writings of Thomas Merton, one of the most influential religious figures of our time. The Society sponsors a biennial conference devoted to Merton and his work and supports the writing of general-interest and scholarly books and articles about Merton. In addition, the ITMS regularly awards grants to researchers and scholarships to young people. It encourages a variety of activities such as Merton retreats. Local Chapters of the ITMS throughout the world reflect a wide range of personal interest and approaches to Thomas Merton.

*Finding the ITMS has been among the most enriching experiences of my life as a student and teacher of Thomas Merton. None who have been fed by Merton should deny themselves the banquet of the ITMS. None should refuse the Society the fruits of their Merton insights.*

*Walt Chura*
*Albany, NY*

## ITMS Members Benefits

Members of the ITMS receive information on a regular basis about events connected with Thomas Merton at international, national, regional, and local levels. Members receive *The Merton Seasonal* quarterly (which includes the ITMS *Newsletter* twice a year).

An enhanced membership package also includes *The Merton Annual* at a reduced rate. Both publications contain articles and updated bibliographies giving members access to the most recent thinking about Merton. Members are entitled to reduced rates for General Meetings and have access to the rich collection of Merton manuscripts, photographs, drawings, and memorabilia at the Thomas Merton Center at Bellarmine University in Louisville, Kentucky.

## ITMS Conferences

The ITMS holds a General Meeting every other year. These forums produce lively exchanges, spiritual renewal and new scholarly Merton research on an international scale.

# ITMS Fellowships and Scholaships

*Shannon Fellowships*

. . . Are awarded annually to enable qualified researchers to visit the Thomas Merton Center archives at Bellarmine University in Louisville, Kentucky, or other repositories of Merton materials, such as Columbia University, Harvard University and St. Bonaventure University. The awards are named in honor of William H. Shannon, founding President of the International Thomas Merton Society.

*The ITMS has played an essential role in my studies of Thomas Merton's works, beginning with the Shannon Fellowship which launched my research at the archives in Louisville. Since then, I have met a host of fascinating colleagues who work together to further Merton studies and many friends who share in the causes of peace and spiritual hospitality promoted by the ITMS.*

> *Lynn Szabo*
> *Langley, British Columbia*
> *Shannon Fellow*

*Daggy Youth/Student Scholarships*

. . . Enable young people (ages 14-29) to participate in an ITMS General Meeting, thereby inspiring the next generation of Merton readers and scholars. These scholarships honor the late Robert E. Daggy, founding member and second president of the ITMS.

*A fascinating experience to be surrounded by such deep minds and wise souls. Merton is serving as a marvelous vehicle for bringing people of intellect and spirit together to share knowledge, stories, and life. Not least among these were the Daggy scholars, who simply astounded me with their abilities and their concern for our world. No more intriguing and inspiring group of young people have I been a part of.*

> *David W. Golemboski*
> *Louisville, Kentucky*
> *Daggy Scholar*

*It was a great spiritual blessing for me to have shared this faith affirming experience with such a diverse crowd, people also interested in what Merton was so successful at doing in his own life: transforming the deep silence of faith into real, audible, and tangible action.*

> *Rob Peach*
> *Philadelphia, Pennsylvania*
> *Daggy Scholar*

3576228